AF531280

DISCRETE MATHEMATICS

By
S.C. Sharma

DISCOVERY PUBLISHING HOUSE
NEW DELHI-110002

First Published – 2007

Reprinted – 2026

ISBN: 978-81-8356-220-1

Discrete Mathematics

Published by:

DISCOVERY PUBLISHING HOUSE
4383/4B, Ansari Road, Darya Ganj
New Delhi-110 002 (India)
Phone: +91-11-23279245; 23253475; 43596065
Mobile: +91 9811179893 / +91 9871656464
E-mail: discoverybooksindia@gmail.com
orderdphbooks@gmail.com
namitwasan9@gmail.com
web: www.discoverypublishinggroup.com

Printed at:
Infinity Imaging Systems
Delhi

Preface

This book 'Discrete Mathematics' has been written for the students who are preparing for an advance degree programme. With the background necessary for further study in theoretical computer science, it can be use either a one or a two semester course. A major future of this text is its versatility. Sufficient topic have been included to accommodate students with varied background.

The subject matter has been discussed in such a way that students will find no difficulty to understand it. Suggestions for the improvement of the book will be gratefully received.

Author

CONTENTS

1

PRELIMINARY NOTATION

INTRODUCTION

In twentieth-century mathematics has been its recognition of the power of the abstract approach. This has given rise to a large body of new results and problems and has infact led us to open up whole new areas of mathematics whose very existence had not even been suspected.

The algebra which has evolved as an out growth of all this is not only a subject with an independent life and vigor, it is one of the important current research areas in mathematics, but it also series as the unifying thread which interlaces almost all of mathematics—geometry, number theory, analysis topology and even applied mathematics.

This book is intended as an introduction to that part of mathematics that today goes by the name of abstract algebra. The term "abstract" is a highly subjective one; what is abstract to one person is very often concrete and down to earth to another and *vice-versa*.

SET NOTATION AND DESCRIPTION

The term *set* is intuitively understood by most people to mean a collection of objects which are called *elements* (of the set). This concept is the starting point on which we will build more complex ideas, much as in geometry, where they concepts of point and the line are left undefined.

Because a set is such a simple notion, you may be surprised to learn that it is one of the most difficult concept for mathematicians to defined to their own liking. For example, the description above is not a proper definition because it requires the definition of a collection. (How would you define "collection"?) Even deeper problems arise when you consider the possibility that a set could contain itself. Although, these problems are of real concern to some mathematicians, they will not be of any concern to us.

Our first concern will be how to describe a set; that is, how do we most conveniently describe a set and the elements that are in it? If we are going to discuss a set for any length of time, we usually give it a name in the form of a capital letter (or occasionally some other symbol). In discussing set A, if x is an element of A, then we will write $x \in A$. On the other hand, if x is not an element of A, we write $x \notin A$. The most convenient way of describing the elements of a set will vary depending on the specific set.

Method 1: Enumeration

When the elements of a set are enumerated (or listed) it is traditional to enclose them in braces. For example the set of binary digits is {0, 1} and the set of decimal digits is {0, 1, 2, 3, 4, 5, 6, 7, 8, 9}. The choice of a name for these sets would be arbitrary; but it would be "logical" to call them B and D, respectively. The choice of a set name is much like the choice of an identifier name in programming. Some large sets can be enumerated without actually listing all the elements. For example,, the letters of the alphabet and the integers from 1 to 100 could be described as

A = {a, b, c, ..., x, y, z} and

G = {1, 2, ..., 99, 100}.

The three consecutive dots are called an ellipsis. We use them when it is clear what elements are included but not listed. An ellipsis is used in two other situations. To enumerate the positive integers, we would write {1, 2, 3, ...}, indicating that the list goes on infinitely. If we want to list a more general set, such as the integers between 1 and n, where n is some undertermined positive integer, we might write {1, ..., n}.

Method 2: Standard Symbols

Frequently used sets are usually given symbols that are reserved for them along. For example, since we will be referring to the positive integers throughout this book, we will use the symbol P instead of writing {1, 2, 3, ...}. A few of the other sets of numbers that we will use frequently are:

N = natural numbers = {0, 1, 2, 3, ...}

Z = the integers = {..., –3, –2, –1, 0, 1, 2, 3,...}

Q = the rational numbers

R = the real numbers

C = the complex numbers

Method 3: Set-Builder Notation

Another way of describing sets is to use *set-builder notation*. For example, we could define the rational numbers as

$$Q = \{a/b : a, b \in Z, b \neq 0\}.$$

Note that in the set-builder description for the rational numbers:

(1) a/b indicates that a *typical* element of the set is a "fraction."

(2) The colon is read "such that" or "where" and is used interchangeably with a vertical line,.

(3) a, b $\in$ Z is an abbreviated way of saying a $\in$ Z and b $\in$ Z.

(4) All commas in mathematics are read as "and".

The important fact to keep in mind in set notation, or in any mathematical notation, is that it is mean to be a help, not a hindrance. We hope that notation will assist us in a more complete understanding of the collection of objects under consideration and will enable us to describe it in concise manner. However, brevity of notation is not the aim of sets. If you prefer to write a $\in$ Z and b $\in$ Z, you should do so. Also, there are frequently m any different, and equally good, ways of describing sets. For example, $\{x \in R: x^2 - 5x + 6 = 0\}$ and $\{x : x \in \mathbf{R}, x^2 - 5x + 6 = 0\}$ both describe the solution set $\{2, 3\}$.

A proper definition of the real numbers is beyond the scope of its text. It is sufficient to think of the real numbers as the set of points on a number line. The complex numbers can be defined using set-builder notation as C = $\{a + bi;\ a, b \in \mathbf{R}\}$, where i is the square root of -1.

Definition: Finite Set. *A set is finite if it has a finite number of elements. Any set that is not finite is an infinite set.*

Definition: Cardinality. *Let A be a finite set. The number of different elements in A is called its cardinality and is denoted by #A.*

As we will see later, there are different infinite cardinalities. We can't make this distinction now, so will restrict cardinality to finite sets until later.

SUBSETS

Definition: Subset. *Let A and B be set. We say that A is a subset of B *(notation $A \subseteq B$) if and only if every element of A is an element of B.*

Example 1.1:

(a) If $A = \{3, 5, 8\}$ and $B = \{5, 8, 3, 2, 6\}$, then $A \subseteq B$.

(b) $N \subseteq Z \subseteq R \subseteq C$.

(c) If $A = \{3, 5, 8\}$ and $B = \{5, 3, 8\}$, then $A \subseteq B$ and $B \subseteq A$.

Definition: Equality. *Let A and B be sets. We say that A is equal to B (notation $A = B$) if and only if every element of A is an element of B and conversely every elements of B is an element of A; that is , $A \subseteq B$ and $B \subseteq A$.*

Example 1.2:

(a) In Example 1.1c, $A = B$. Note that the ordering of the elements is unimportant.

(b) The number of times that an element appears in an enumeration doesn't affect a set. For example, if $A = \{1, 5, 3, 5\}$ and $B = \{1. 5, 3\}$, then $A = B$.

A few comments are in order about the expression *if and only if* as used in our definitions.

This expression means "is equivalent to saying" or, more exactly, that the word (or concept) being defined can at any time be replaced by the defining expression. Conversely, the expression which defines the word (or concept) can be replaced by the word.

Occasionally there is need to discuss the set which contains no elements namely the *empty set,* which is denoted by the Norwegian letter ϕ. This set is also called the *null set.*

It is clear, we hope, from the definition of a subset that given any set A we have $A \subseteq A$ and $f \subseteq A$. Because of this, given any set A, both ϕ and A are called *improper subsets* of A. If $B \subseteq A$, $B \neq \phi$, and $B \neq A$, then B is called *a proper subset* of A.

BASIC SET OPERATIONS

Definition: Intersection. *Let A and B be sets. The intersection of A and B (denoted by $A \cap B$) is the set of all elements which are in both A and B. That is, $A \cap B = \{x : x \in A \text{ and } x \in B\}$.*

Example 1.3:

(a) Let $A = \{1, 3, 8\}$ and $B = \{-9, 22, 3\}$. Then $A \cap B = \{3\}$.

(b) Let $A = \{(x, y): x + y = 7, x, y \in R\}$

(c) $\mathbf{Z} \cap \mathbf{Q} = \mathbf{Z}$.

(d) Let $A = \{3, 5, 9\}$ and $B = \{-5, 8\}$. Then $A \cap B = \phi$.

Definition: Disjoint Sets. *Two sets are disjoint they have no elements in common (as in Example 1.3d); i.e., $A \cap B = \phi$.*

Definition: Union. *Let A and B be sets. The union of A and B (denoted by $A \cup B$) is the set of all elements which are in A or in B or in both A and B. That is,* $A \cup B = \{x : x \in A \text{ or } x \in B\}$

It is important to note in the set-builder notation for $A \cup B$, the word or is used in the *inclusive* sense; it includes the case where x is in both A and B.

Example 1.4:

(a) If $A = \{2, 5, 8\}$ *and* $B = \{7, 5, 22\}$, *then* $A \cup B = \{2, 5, 8, 7, 22\}$.

(b) $\mathbf{Z} \cup \mathbf{Q} = \mathbf{Q}$

(c) $A \cup \phi = A$ *for any set A.*

Frequently, when doing mathematics, we need to establish a ***universe***, or set of elements under discussion. For example, the set $A = \{x : 81x^4 - 16 = 0\}$ contains different elements depending on what kinds of numbers we allow ourselves to use in solving the equation $81x^4 - 16 = 0$. This set of numbers would be our universe. For example, if the universe is the integers, then A is ϕ. If our universe is the rational numbers, then A is $\{2/3, -2/3\}$, and if the universe is the complex numbers, then A is $\{2/3, -2/3, 2i/3, -2i/3\}$.

Definition: Universe. *The universe, or universal set, is the set of all elements under discussion for possible membership in a set.*

We reserve the letter U for a universe in general discussion.

If an element a belongs to a set A, then we express it by writing :

$$a \in A.$$

Which can also be read as "a is an element of the set A" or "A contains a as one of its elements." If on the contrary, an element a is not a member of a set A, then we write

$$a \notin A.$$

A set can be specified in following two ways. We can make use of any of the two notations according our convenience.

(a) Roster Method (Tabular Form) : In this method, a set is represented by listing all its elements within braces {}. For example, the set of vowels in the English alphabets would be written as {a, e, i, o, u}.

(b) Rule Method (Set-builder Form) : In this method, a set is represented by describing its elements in terms of one or several characteristic properties which enable us to decide whether a given object is an element of the set under consideration or not. For example, the set of all natural numbers can be denoted as follows :

N = {x : x is a natural number} or

{x | x is a natural number} which is read as the set of all x such that x belongs to N.

The symbol : or/stands for 'such that' and $\in$ for 'belongs to' as explained earlier. A few examples of set notations by Roster and Rule Methods are given below :

(i) Set of all odd numbers.

(a) O = {1, 3, 5, . . .) (Roster method)

(b) O = {x : x is an odd number} (Rule method)

(ii) Set of all odd numbers between 2 and 10.

(a) B = {3, 5, 7, 9, . . .) (Roster method)

(b) B = {x : x < 0, 2 < x < 10} (Rule method)

Remark: It is worth mentioning that a set is not just any collection. For a collection to be a set it is essential that given any element, one should be able to decide whether it does or does not belong to the set. The assumption that every collection is a set leads to a paradox known as :

Russel Paradox : The following example will illustrate the basic idea underlying this Paradox.

A barber in a certain town shaved all those and only those, who did not shave themselves. If A be the collection of all those whom the barber shaved, is the barber a member of A or not?

The two answer are possible :

(i) The barber is a member of A.

(ii) The barber is not a member of A.

But these two are contradictory statements for if the barber is a member of A, then the barber has shaved himself and since he has shaved himself, he can not be a member of A.

STATEMENTS

We communicate our ideas to others through sentences. In our mathematical language, *the sentences which can be judged to be true or false are known as statements.* For Example 2 + 3 = 5 is a true statement while, (3 + 4) < 6 is a false statement. Also, Ram is a handsome boy, is a sentence, not a statement. We use connectives *'and'* and *'or'* to combine two statements to form a compound statement.

We know that for any three numbers a, b, c we always have a (a + b) = a.b + a.c.

We say that in numbers, multiplication distributes addition.

But a + (bc) ≠ (a + b), (a + c) *i.e.,* addition does not distribute multiplication is numbers. However, is statements 'and' *distributes* 'or' and 'or' *distributes* 'and'.

Thus for any statements p, q and r we have,

p and (q or r) = (p & q) or (p & r)

and p or (q & r) = (p or q) and (P or r).

We shall be using the symbols '∀' and '∃' for *'for all values of'* and *'there exists'* respectively. Also,

(i) If (p ⇒ q and q ⇒ p), the we write, '**p ⇒ q**' *i.e.,* p *implies and is implied by q.*

(ii) we write, '**p ⇒ q**', if whenever p is true, the q is true and we say that, *p implies q.*

Tautologies

A statement which is always true is called tautology. Thus, for a statement to be a tautology its truth value should be T for all its entries in the truth value.

TYPES OF SETS

Singleton Set : *A set consisting of a single element is called a Singleton Set.*

Examples:

(i) A set of positive integers between 4 and 6 will be a singleton set, consisting of one element 5, *i.e.,* {5}.

(ii) {ϕ} is a set whose only element is a null set, therefore {ϕ} is singleton.

Finite Set : *A set is finite if it consists of a finite number of different elements, i.e., if in counting the different members of the set the counting process can come to an end.*

For example, if A is the set of the week days, it is finite as its elements are seven in number.

Empty Set : *A set is said to be empty or null or void set if it has no element and it is denoted by ϕ.*

In Roster method, ϕ is denoted by {}.

Obviously, a set A is an empty set if the statement x ∈ A is not true for any x. For example following are the null sets :

(i) A set of even number greater than 8 and less than 10.

(ii) Let A = {x : x^2 = 4, x is odd}. Then B is the empty set because $x^2 = 4$ $\Rightarrow x = \pm 2$ and 2 is not odd.

Infinite Set : *A set is infinite if it contains infinite number of elements, i.e., it is not possible to count all members of the set. For example, if B = {2, 4, 6, 8, . . .), then B is infinite.*

Cardinal Numbers of a Finite Set : *The number of elements in a finite set A is called cardinal number* or order of the set A and is denoted by n(A).

Equal Sets : *Two sets A and B are said to be equal if every element of A is a member of B, and every element of B is a member of A.*

If sets A and B are equal, we write A = B and A ≠ B when A and B are not equal.

If A = {2, 4, 5, 7} and B = {5, 7, 2, 4}. Then A = B, because each element of A is an element of B and *vice-versa.* Note that the elements of a set may be listed in any order.

Note: It follows from the above definition of equivalent sets that equal sets are equivalent but equivalent sets need not be equal.

Equivalent Sets : *Two finite sets A and B are equivalent if their cardinal numbers are same, i.e.,*

$$n(A) = n(B).$$

SUBSETS

If every element in a set A is also a member of a set B, then A is called a subset of B. More specifically, A is a subset of B if $x \in A \Rightarrow x \in B$.

The symbol ⇒ stands for "implies". We denote this relationship by writing

$$A \subset B.$$

Which can also be read as "A is contained is B". Also B is called the *Super Set* of A and can be written as $B \supset A$. Thus if $x \in A \Rightarrow x \in B$, then $A \subset B$.

Examples:

(i) Let A = {x : x is even}, *i.e.*, A = {2, 4, 6, . . .) and let B = {x : x is a positive power of 2}, *i.e.*, B = {2, 4, 8, 16}. Then $A \subset B$, *i.e.*, A is contained in B.

(ii) If P be the set of all parallelograms and S is the set of all squares in a plane, *i.e.*,

P = {all parallelograms in the plane}

and S = {all squares in the plane}

Then S is a subset of P, *i.e.*,

$$S \subset P.$$

Note: Some authors use symbol ⊆ to express a subset. If A is not a subset of B, we write it as $A \not\subset B$ or $A \not\subseteq B$.

Remarks: (1) If we have to prove $A \subset B$, then we should prove that

$$x \in A \Rightarrow x \in B.$$

Symbolically, $A \subset B$ iff $(x \in A \Rightarrow x \in B)$.

(2) If we have to prove that $A \not\subset B$ then we should show that there exists atleast one element x such that

$$x \in A \text{ but } x \notin B.$$

Symbolically, $A \not\subset B$ iff $\{\exists\, x \in A$ s.t. $x \notin B)$.

The symbol $\exists$ stands for 'there exists' and s.t. for 'such that'.

Example: *Write the subset of the following set :*

$$A = \{1, 2, 3\}$$

Solution: The required subsets are :

$$\phi, \{1\}, \{2\}, \{3\}, \{1, 2\},$$
$$\{1, 3\}, \{2, 3\}, \{1, 2, 3\}.$$

Equality of Sets : Set A is said to be equal to set B if both of them have the same members, *i.e.*, every element which belongs to A also belongs to B ($A \subset B$) and every element which belongs to B also belongs to A ($B \subset A$). We denote the equality of sets A and B by

$$\Rightarrow A = B.$$

Proper Subsets : Let A and B be two sets. If $B \subset A$ and $B \neq A$, then B is said to be a proper subset of A.

For example, if A {1, 2, 3} and B = { 2, 3} then B is proper subset of A because all the elements of B are in A but one element 1 of A is not in B.

Theorem 1:

The total number of subsets of a finite set containing n elements is 2^n.

Proof:

Let A be a finite set containing n elements. Let $O \leq r \leq n$. Consider those subsets of A that have r elements each.

We know that the number of ways in which r elements can be chosen out of n elements is ${}^nC_r$. Therefore, the number of subsets of A having r elements each is ${}^nC_r$.

Hence, the total number of subsets of A.

$$= {}^nC_0 + {}^nC_1 + {}^nC_2 + \ldots + {}^nC_r + \ldots + {}^nC_n$$
$$= (1 + 1)^n = 2^n.$$

Theorem 2:

Null set ϕ is a subset of every set.

Proof:

Let A be any given set. We shall prove that $\phi \subset A$. Let us suppose, on contrary, that $\phi \not\subset A$.

$\phi \not\subset A \Rightarrow$ there is atleast one element x such that $x \in \phi$

and $x \notin A$ ...(1)

But since ϕ is a null set,

therefore $x \notin \phi$ ...(2)

Therefore, (1) and (2) $\Rightarrow x \in \phi$ and $x \notin \phi$, which is absurd and therefore, our assumption is wrong. Consequently $\phi \subset A$.

Since A is an arbitrary set ϕ is a subset of every set.

Theorem 3:

Every set is a subset of itself.

Proof:

Let A be any set. Then each element of A is clearly in A itself. Hence $A \subset A$.

Theorem 4:

If $A \subset B$ and $B \subset C$ then $A \subset C$.

Proof:

We must show that every element in A is also an element is C. Let x be an element of A, *i.e.*,

$$x \in A.$$

But it is given that $A \subset B$.

$\therefore \quad x \in A \Rightarrow x \in B$ ...(1)

Also $\quad B \subset C$

$\therefore \quad x \in B \Rightarrow x \in C$ ...(2)

Hence from (1) and (2)

$$x \in A \Rightarrow x \in C$$

$\therefore \quad A \subset C.$

Number of Subsets of a Finite Set : Consider a set {a}. It has two possible subsets {a} and ϕ. Again for the set {a, b}, the possible subsets are ϕ, {a}, {b}, {a, b} which are 4 subsets in number. A set {a, b, c} has as many as the following subsets.

ϕ, {a}, {b}, {c}, {a, b}, {b, c}, {a, c}, {a, b, c}.

which are eight in numbers.

Thus we can generalize the result as follows :

A set with 1 element has 2^1 subsets.

A set with 2 element has 2^2 subsets.

A set with 3 element has 2^3 subsets.

POWER SET

The set of all subsets of a given set A is called the power set of A and is denoted by the symbol P(A).

i.e., $P(A) = \{T : T \subset A\}$

ϕ and A are both members of P(A).

Example: Let $A = \{a, b\}$

then $P(A) = \{\phi, \{a\}, \{b\}, \{a, b\}\}$.

BASIC SET OPERATIONS

Union of Sets : Let A and B be two given sets. *The set which contains every element contained in A or B or both A and B is called the union (or join) of A and B.* In fact union is an 'either' 'or' idea. The symbol $\cup$ is used to denote the union of sets. Thus, $A \cup B$ is read as 'A union B' or 'A join B' or 'A Cup B'. Symbolically, $A \cup B = \{x : x \in A \text{ or } x \in B\}$.

The shaded part represent $A \cup B$ in the following Venn diagram :

Examples:

(i) Let $A = \{1, 2, 3\}$

and $B = \{2, 4, 6\}$,

then $A \cup B = (1, 2, 3, 4, 6\}$.

(ii) If $A = \{x : x = 2n + 1, n \in Z\}$

and $B = \{x : x = 2n, n \in Z\}$.

then $A \cup B = \{x : x \text{ is an odd integer}\}$

$\cup\{x : x \text{ is an even integer}\}$

$= \{x : x \text{ is an integer}\} = Z$.

Notes:

(1) Each element in a set is listed once only because the repetition of elements is meaningless in a set. If A is a set of cricket players, B is a set of tennis players and some players are common to both the teams, then

$A \cup B$ = Set of all players in the two teams.

(2) From the definition it is clear that A and B are the subsets of $A \cup B$.

Symbolically, $A \subset (A \cup B)$ and $B \subset (A \cup B)$.

(3) The union of a finite number of sets $A_1, A_2, \ldots, A_n$ is denoted by

$$A_1 \cup A_2 \cup A_3, \ldots \cup A_n$$

or by $\bigcup_{i=1}^{n} A_1$.

Intersection of Sets : Let A and B be two given sets. *The set containing all the elements which are contained in A as well as in B is called the intersection of A and B.* This is why it is said that intersection is an 'and' idea. The symbol $\cap$ is used to denote the intersection of sets.

Thus, $A \cap B$ is read as the intersection of A and B.

Symbolically, $A \cap B = \{x : x \in A \text{ and } x \in B\}$.

In the following Venn diagram the shaded part represents $A \cap B$.

Examples:

(i) If $A = \{a, b, i, z\}$

$B = \{b, c, i, u, v\}$

Then $A \cap B = \{b, i\}$.

(ii) If $A = \{x : x = 2n, n \in Z\}$ and

$B = \{x : x = 3n, n \in Z\}$,

Then $A \cap B = \{x : x = 2n, n \in Z\} \cap \{x : x = 3n, n \in Z\}$

$= \{\ldots, -4, -2, 0, 2, 4, 6, \ldots\} \cap \{\ldots, -9, -6, -3, 0, 3, 6, 9, \ldots\}$

$= \{\ldots, -6, 0, 6, 12, \ldots\} = \{x : x = 6n, n \in Z\}$.

Notes:

(1) If A and B are any two sets, then

$A \cap B \subset A$ and $A \cap B \subset B$.

(2) The intersection of finite number of sets

$A_1, A_2, \ldots, A_n$ is denoted by

$$A_1 \cap A_2 \cap \ldots \cap A_n$$

or by $\bigcap_{i=1}^{n} A_1$

Disjoint Sets : *Two sets A and B are said to be disjoint sets if they have no element in common, i.e., if their intersection is a null set, i.e.,*

$$A \cap B = \phi.$$

Thus, $A \cap B = \phi \Rightarrow$ A and B are disjoint. For example, if

$$A = \{a, b, c\} \text{ and } B = \{p, q, r\}$$

then A and B are disjoint sets as there is no element common to both of them.

Difference of Two Sets : Let A and B be two sets. The difference of A and B, written as A – B, is the set of all those elements of A which do not belong to B.

Thus, $\quad A - B = \{ x : x \in A \text{ and } x \notin B\}$

or $\quad A - B = \{ x \in A : \text{and } x \notin B\}.$

In Fig. 1.1 (i) the shaded part represents A – B.

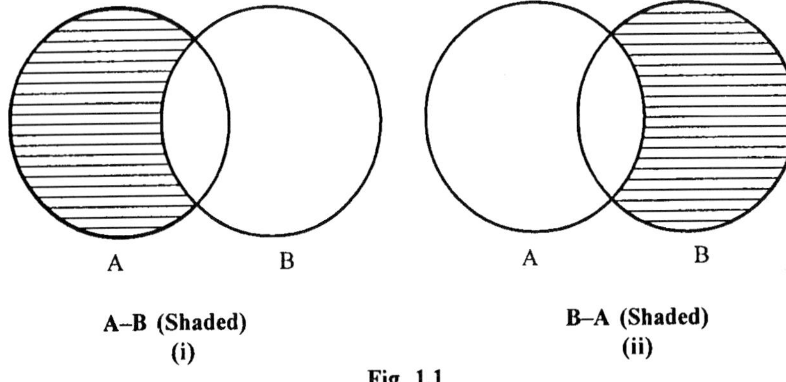

A–B (Shaded)
(i)

B–A (Shaded)
(ii)

Fig. 1.1

Similarly the difference B – A is the set of all those elements of B that do not belong to A, *i.e.*,

$$B - A = \{x \in B : x \notin A\}$$

In Fig. 1.4 (ii) the shaded part represents B – A

Example: If $\quad A = \{2, 3, 4, 5, 6, 7\}$

and $\quad B = \{ 3, 5, 7, 9, 11, 13\},$

then $\quad A - B = \{2, 4, 6\}$

and $\quad B - A = \{9, 11, 13\}.$

VENN-EULER DIAGRAMS

A clerke known as Venn -Eular diagram is very often used to assist thinking on the relation which ma[illegible] between some subset of the universal set. Swiss mathematician Euler, [illegible] of all gave an idea to represent a set by the points in a closed curve (usually a circle but not necessarily circle). Later on British Mathematician Venn brought this idea to practice. That is why the diagrams drawn for this purpose are called Venn-Euler diagrams or simply Venn-diagrams. In Venn diagrams the universal set U is represented by points within a rectangle and its subsets are represented by the points in closed curves (usual circles) within the rectangle. These diagrams are very useful for the beginners to understood the set theoric ideas, though they are not of much importance as the records advances.

The idea of $A \subset B$ and $A \neq B$ can be represented by the following diagram.

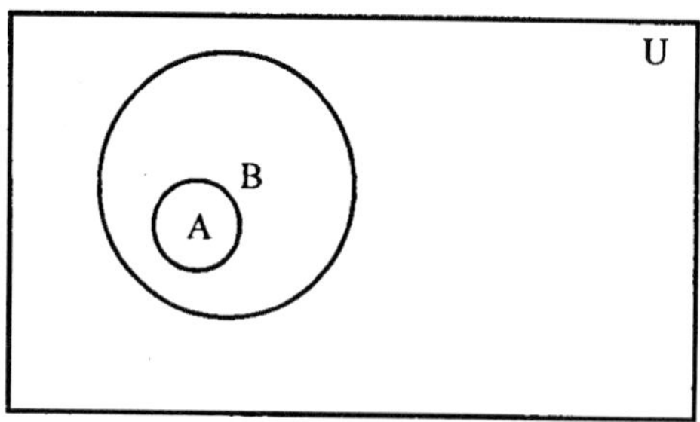

Fig. 1.2

Symmetric Difference of Two Sets : Let A and B be two sets. The symmetric difference of sets A and B is the set $(A - B) \cup (B - A)$ and is denoted by $A \Delta B$.

Thus, $A \Delta B = (A - B) \cup (B - A)$

$= \{x : x\ A \cap B\}$

In following figure shaded part represents $A \Delta B$.

For example, If $A = \{1, 2, 3\}$

$B = \{3, 4, 5)$

then $A - B = \{1, 2\}$

$B - A = \{4, 5\}$

$\therefore\ A \Delta B = \{1, 2, 4, 5\}$.

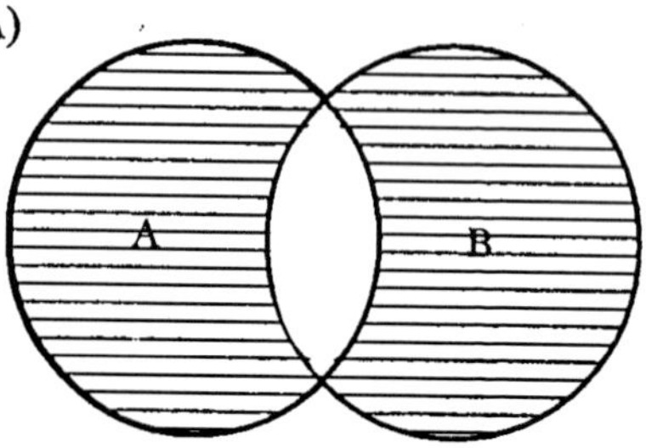

Fig. 1.3 : A Δ B (Shaded).

Complement of a Set : The complement of a given set A is defined as the set consisting of those elements of the universal set which are not contained in the given set A. It is denoted by the symbol A' or $\overline{A}$.

Symbolically, $A' = \{x : x \in U, x \notin A\}$.

In the following Venn-diagram shaded portion represents A'.

Example: Le N, the set of all natural numbers be taken as the universa set and let

$$A = \{x : x \text{ is an even number and } x \in N\},$$

then $$A' = \{x : x \text{ is an odd number, } x \in N\}.$$

Notes :

(1) The set A and its complement A' are disjoint sets.

(2) Let A and B be two sets. The set $X = \{x : x \in A, x \notin B)$ is called the complement of the set B with respect to A (*i.e.*, A – B).

COUNTING PRINCIPLE

If A, B and C are finite sets, and U be the finite universal set, then

(i) $n(A \cup B) = n(A) + n(B) - n(A \cap B)$

(ii) $n(A \cup B) = n(A) + n(B) \Leftrightarrow$ A, B are disjoint non-void sets

(iii) $n(A - B) = n(A) - n(A \cap B)$, *i.e.*,

$n(A - B) + n(A \cap B) = n(A)$.

(iv) $n(A \Delta B)$ = No. of elements which belong to exactly one of A or B

$= n((A - B) \cup (B - A)$

$= n(A - B) + n(B - A)$ ($\because$ (A–B) and (B–A) and disjoint)

$= n(A) - n(A \cap B) + n(B) - n(A \cap B)$

$= n(A) + n(B) - 2n(A \cap B)$

(v) $n(A \cup B \cup C) = n(A) + n(B) + n(C) - n(A \cap B) - n(B \cap C) - n(A \cap C) + n(A \cap B \cap C)$

(vi) No. of elements in exactly two of the sets A, B, C

$= n(A \cap B) + n(B \cap C) + n(C \cap A) - 3n(A \cap B \cap C)$

(vii) No. of elements in exactly one of the sets A, B, C.

$= n(A) + n(B) + n(C) - 2n(A \cap B) - 2n(B \cap C) - 2n(A \cap C) + 3n(A \cap B \cap C)$

(viii) $n(A' \cup B') = n((A \cap B)')$

$= n(U) - n(A \cap B)$

(ix) $n(A' \cap B') = n((A \cup B)')$

$= n(U) - n(A \cup B)$.

LAWS OF ALGEBRA OF SETS

I. Idempotent Laws : *For any set A, we have*

(i) $A \cup A = A$,

(ii) $A \cap A = A$

Proof:

(i) $A \cup A = \{x : x \in A \text{ or } x \in A\}$

$= \{x : x \in A\} = A$

(ii) $A \cap A = \{x : x \in A \text{ and } x \in A\}$

$= \{x : x \in A\} = A.$

II. Identity Laws : *For any set A, we have,*

(i) $A \cup \phi = A$

(ii) $A \cap U = A$

i.e., ϕ and U are identity elements for union and intersection respectively.

Proof:

(i) $A \cup \phi = \{x : x \in A \text{ or } x \in \phi\}$

$= \{x : x \in A\} = A$

(ii) $A \cap U = \{x : x \in A \text{ and } x \in U\}$

$= \{x : x \in A\} = A.$

III. Commulative Laws : *For any sets A and B, union and intersection are commulative, i.e.,*

(i) $A \cup B = B \cup A$, *(ii)* $A \cap B = B \cap A$.

Proof:

(i) Let x be an arbitrary element of $A \cup B$. Then

$x \in A \cup B \Rightarrow x \in A \text{ or } x \in B$

$\Rightarrow x \in B \text{ or } x \in A$

$\Rightarrow x \in B \cup A$

$\therefore A \cup B \subset B \cup A$

Similarly, $B \cup A \subset A \cup B$

$\therefore A \cup B = B \cup A.$

(ii) Let y be an arbitrary element of $A \cap B$. Then

$x \in A \cap B \Rightarrow y \in A \text{ and } y \in B$

$\Rightarrow y \in B \text{ and } y \in A$

$\Rightarrow y \in B \cap A$

$\therefore A \cap B \subset B \cap A$

Similarly, $B \cap A \subset A \cap B$

$\therefore A \cap B = B \cap A.$

IV. Associative Laws : *If A, B and C are any three sets, then*

(i) $(A \cup B) \cup C = A \cup (B \cup C)$

(ii) $A \cap (B \cap C) = (A \cap B) \cap C$

i.e. union and intersection are associative.

Proof:

(i) Let x be an arbitrary element of $(A \cup B) \cup C$. Then

$x \in (A \cup B) \cup C$

$\Rightarrow$ $x \in (A \cup B)$ or $x \in C$

$\Rightarrow$ $(x \in A$ or $x \in B)$ or $x \in C$

$\Rightarrow$ $x \in A$ or $(x \in B$ or $x \in C)$

$\Rightarrow$ $x \in A$ or $(x \in B \cup C)$

$\Rightarrow$ $x \in A \cup (B \cup C)$

$\therefore$ $(A \cup B) \cup C \subset A \cup (B \cup C)$

Similarly, $A \cup (B \cup C) \subset (A \cup B) \cup C$

$\therefore$ $(A \cup B) \cup C = A \cup (B \cup C)$

(ii) Let y be an arbitrary element of $A \cap (B \cap C)$. Then

$y \in A \cap (B \cap C)$

$\Rightarrow$ $y \in A$ and $y \in (B \cap C)$

$\Rightarrow$ $y \in A$ and $(y \in B$ and $y \in C)$

$\Rightarrow$ $(y \in A$ and $y \in B)$ and $y \in C$

$\Rightarrow$ $y \in (A \cap B)$ and $y \in C$

$\Rightarrow$ $y \in (A \cap B) \cap C$

$\therefore$ $A \cap (B \cap C) \subset (A \cap B) \cap C$

Similarly, $(A \cap B) \cap C) \subset A \cap (B \cap C)$

Hence, $A \cap (B \cap C) = (A \cap B) \cap C.$

V. Distributive Laws : *If A, B and C are any three sets, then*

(i) $A \cup (B \cup C) = (A \cup B) \cap (A \cup C)$

(ii) $A \cap (B \cap C) = (A \cap B) \cup (A \cap C)$

i.e. union and intersection are distributive over intersection and intersection respectively.

Proof:

(i) Let x be an arbitrary element of $A \cup (B \cap C)$. Then

$$x \in A \cup (B \cap C)$$
$$\Rightarrow \quad x \in A \text{ or } x \in (B \cap C)$$
$$\Rightarrow \quad (x \in A) \text{ or } (x \in B \text{ and } x \in C)$$
$$\Rightarrow \quad (x \in A \text{ or } x \in B) \text{ and } (x \in A \text{ or } x \in C)$$

[$\because$ 'or' is distributive over 'and']

$$\Rightarrow \quad x \in (A \cup B) \text{ and } x \in (A \cup C)$$
$$\Rightarrow \quad x \in (A \cup B) \cap (A \cup C)$$
$$\therefore \quad A \cup (B \cap C) \subset (A \cup B) \cap (A \cup C)$$

Similarly, $(A \cup B) \cap (A \cup C) \subset A \cup (B \cap C)$

Hence, $A \cup (B \cap C) = (A \cup B) \cap (A \cup C)$

(ii) Let y be an arbitrary element of $A \cap (B \cup C)$. Then

$$x \in A \cap (B \cup C)$$
$$\Rightarrow \quad x \in A \text{ and } x \in (B \cup C)$$
$$\Rightarrow \quad x \in A \text{ and } (x \in B \text{ or } x \in C)$$
$$\Rightarrow \quad (x \in A \text{ and } x \in B) \text{ or } (x \in A \text{ and } x \in C)$$
$$\Rightarrow \quad x \in (A \cap B) \text{ or } x \in (A \cap C)$$
$$\Rightarrow \quad x \in (A \cap B) \cup (A \cap C)$$
$$\therefore \quad A \cap (B \cap C) \subset (A \cap B) \cup (A \cap C)$$

Similarly, $(A \cap B) \cup (A \cap C) \subset A \cap (B \cup C)$

$$\therefore \quad A \cap (B \cup C) = (A \cap B) \cup (A \cap C).$$

VI. De-Morgan's Laws : *If A, B are any two sets, then*

(i) $(A \cup B)' = A' \cap B'$

(ii) $(A \cap B)' = A' \cup B'$

Proof:

(i) Let x be an arbitrary element of $(A \cup B)'$. Then

$$x \in (A \cup B)'$$
$$\Rightarrow \quad x \notin (A \cup B)$$
$$\Rightarrow \quad x \notin A \text{ and } x \notin B$$
$$\Rightarrow \quad x \in A' \text{ and } x \in B'$$

$\Rightarrow \quad x \in A' \cap B'$

$\therefore \quad (A \cup B)' \subset A' \cap B'$

Again, let y be an arbitrary element of $A' \cap B'$. Then

$y \in A' \cap B'$

$\Rightarrow \quad y \in A'$ and $y \in B'$

$\Rightarrow \quad y \notin A$ and $y \notin B$

$\Rightarrow \quad y \notin A \cup B$

$\Rightarrow \quad y \notin (A \cup B)'$

$\therefore \quad A' \cap B' \subset (A \cup B)'$

Hence, $\quad (A \cup B)' = A' \cap B'$.

(ii) Let x be an arbitrary element of $(A \cap B)'$. Then

$x \in (A \cap B)'$

$\Rightarrow \quad x \notin (A \cap B)$

$\Rightarrow \quad x \notin A$ or $x \notin B$

$\Rightarrow \quad x \in A'$ or $x \in B'$

$\Rightarrow \quad x \in A' \cup B'$

$\Rightarrow \quad (A \cap B)' \subset A' \cup B'$

Again, let y be an arbitrary element of $A' \cup B'$. Then

$y \in (A' \cup B')$

$\Rightarrow \quad y \in A'$ or $y \in B'$

$\Rightarrow \quad y \notin A$ and $y \notin B$

$\Rightarrow \quad y \notin (A \cap B)$

$\Rightarrow \quad y \in (A \cap B)'$

$\therefore \quad A' \cup B' \subset (A \cap B)'$

$\therefore \quad (A \cap B)' = A' \cup B'$.

Theorem 1:

If A and B are any two sets, then

(i) $A - B = A \cap B'$

(ii) $B - A = B \cap A'$

(iii) $A - B = A \Leftrightarrow A \cap B = \phi$

(iv) $(A - B) \cup B = A \cup B$

(v) $(A - B) \cap B = \phi$

(vi) $A \subset B \Leftrightarrow B' \subset A'$

(vii) $(A - B) \cup (B - A) = (A \cup B) - (A \cap B)$.

Proof:

(i) Let x be an arbitrary element of A – B. Then

$$\begin{aligned} & x \in A - B \\ \Rightarrow\quad & x \in A \text{ and } y \notin B \\ \Rightarrow\quad & x \in A \text{ and } x \in B' \\ \Rightarrow\quad & x \in A \cap B' \\ \therefore\quad & (A - B) \subset A \cap B' \qquad \text{...(i)} \end{aligned}$$

Again, let y be an arbitrary element of $A \cap B'$. Then

$$\begin{aligned} & y \in A \cap B' \\ \Rightarrow\quad & y \in A \text{ and } y \in B' \\ \Rightarrow\quad & y \in A \text{ and } y \notin B \\ \Rightarrow\quad & y \in (A - B) \\ \therefore\quad & A \cap B' \subset A - B \qquad \text{...(ii)} \end{aligned}$$

Hence, from (i) and (ii), we have

$$(A - B) = A \cap B'.$$

(ii) Proceed as in (i).

(iii) In order to prove that $A - B \Leftrightarrow A \cap B = \phi$, we shall prove that.

(i) $A - B = A \Rightarrow A \cap B = \phi$ and

(ii) $A \cap B = \phi \Rightarrow A - B = A$.

First, let $A - B = A$. Then we have to prove that $A \cap B = \phi$. If possible, let $A \cap B \neq \phi$. Then

$$\begin{aligned} A \cap B \neq \phi \Rightarrow\ & \text{there exists } x \in A \cap B \\ & \Rightarrow x \in A \text{ and } x \in B \\ & \Rightarrow x \in A - B \text{ and } x \in B \qquad [\because A - B = A] \\ & \Rightarrow (x \in A \text{ and } x \notin B) \text{ and } x \in B \\ & \Rightarrow x \in A \text{ and } (x \notin B \text{ and } x \in B) \end{aligned}$$

But $x \notin B$ and $x \in B$ both can never be possible simultaneously. Thus, we arrive at a contradiction. So, our supposition is wrong.

$$\begin{aligned} \therefore\quad & A \cap B = \phi. \\ \text{Hence,}\quad & A - B = A \\ \Rightarrow\quad & A \cap B = \phi. \qquad \text{...(i)} \end{aligned}$$

Conversely, let $A \cap B = \phi$. Then we have to prove that $A - B = A$.

For this we shall show that $A - B \subset A$ and $A \subset A - B$.

Let x be an arbitrary element of $A - B$. Then

$x \in A - B$

$\Rightarrow$ $x \in A$ and $x \notin B$

$\Rightarrow$ $x \in A$

$\therefore$ $A - B \subset A$

Again, let y be an arbitrary element of A. Then

$y \in A$

$\Rightarrow$ $y \in A$ and $y \notin B$ $[\because A \cap B = \phi]$

$\Rightarrow$ $y \in A - B$ [By definition of $A - B$]

$\therefore$ $A \subset A - B$.

So, $A - B = A$.

$\therefore$ $A \cap B = \phi \Rightarrow A - B = A$ ...(ii)

Hence, from (i) and (ii), we have

$A - B = A \Leftrightarrow A \cap B = \phi$.

(iv) Let x be an arbitrary element of $(A - B) \cup B$. Then

$x \in (A - B) \cup B$

$\Rightarrow$ $x \in A - B$ or $x \in B$

$\Rightarrow$ $(x \in A$ and $x \notin B)$ or $x \in B$

$\Rightarrow$ $(x \in A$ or $x \in B)$ or $(x \notin B$ or $x \in B)$

$\Rightarrow$ $x \in A \cup B$

$\therefore$ $(A - B) \cup B \subset A \cup B$

Let y be an arbitrary element of $A \cup B$. Then

$y \in A \cup B$

$\Rightarrow$ $y \in A$ or $y \in B$

$\Rightarrow$ $(y \in A$ or $y \in B)$ and $(y \notin B$ or $y \in B)$

$\Rightarrow$ $(y \in A$ and $y \notin B)$ or $y \in B$

$\Rightarrow$ $y \in (A - B) \cup B$

$\therefore$ $A \cup B \subset (A - B) \cup B$

Hence, $(A - B) \cup B = A \cup B$.

(v) If possible, let $(A - B) \cap B \neq \phi$. Then there exists atleast one element x, say in $(A - B) \cap B$.

Now, $x \in (A - B) \cap B$

$\Rightarrow \quad x \in (A - B)$ and $x \in B$

$\Rightarrow \quad (x \in A$ and $x \notin B)$ and $x \in B$

$\Rightarrow \quad x \in A$ and $(x \notin B$ and $x \in B)$

Both $x \notin B$ and $x \in B$ both can never be possible simultaneously. Thus, we arrive at a contradiction. So, our supposition is wrong. Hence, $(A - B) \cap B = \phi$.

(vi) First, let $A \subset B$. Then we have to prove that $B' \subset A'$. Let x be an arbitrary element of B'. Then

$x \in B'$

$\Rightarrow \quad x \notin B$

$\Rightarrow \quad x \notin A \qquad [\because A \subset B]$

$\Rightarrow \quad x \in A'$

$\therefore \quad B' \subset A'$ ...(i)

Thus, $\quad A \subset B \Rightarrow B' \subset A'$

Conversely, let $B' \subset A'$. Then we have to prove that $A \subset B$. Let y be an arbitrary element of A. Then

$y \in A \Rightarrow y \notin A'$

$\Rightarrow \quad y \notin B' \qquad [\because B' \subset A']$

$\Rightarrow \quad y \in B$

$\therefore \quad A \subset B$

Thus, $\quad B' \subset A \Rightarrow A \subset B$ ...(ii)

From (i) and (ii), we have

$A \subset B \Leftrightarrow B' \subset A'$.

(vii) Let x be an arbitrary element of $(A - B) \cup (B - A)$. Then

$x \in (A - B) \cup (B - A) \Rightarrow x \in (A - B)$ or $x \in (B - A)$

$\Rightarrow \quad (x \in A$ and $x \notin B)$ or $(x \in B$ and $x \notin A)$

$\Rightarrow \quad (x \in A$ or $x \in B)$ and $(x \notin B$ and $x \notin A)$

$\Rightarrow \quad x \in (A \cup B)$ and $x \notin (A \cap B)$

$\Rightarrow \quad x \in (A \cup B) - (A \cap B)$

$\therefore \quad (A - B) \cup (B - A) \subset (A \cup B) - (A \cup B)$ ...(i)

Again, let y be an arbitrary element of $(A \cup B) - (A \cap B)$.

Then $\quad y \in (A \cup B) - (A \cap B)$

$\Rightarrow \quad y \in A \cup B$ and $y \notin A \cap B$

$\Rightarrow \quad (y \in A$ or $y \in B)$ and $(y \notin A$ and $y \notin B)$

$\Rightarrow$ (y $\in$ A and y $\notin$ B) or (y $\in$ B and y $\notin$ A)

$\Rightarrow$ y $\in$ (A – B) or y $\in$ (B – A)

$\Rightarrow$ y $\in$ (A – B) $\cup$ (B – A)

$\therefore$ (A $\cup$ B) – (A $\cap$ B) $\subset$ (A – B) $\cup$ (B – A) ...(ii)

Hence, from (i) and (ii), we have

$$(A - B) \cup (B - A) = (A \cup B) (A \cup B).$$

Theorem 2:

If A, B and C are any three sets, then

(i) $A - (B \cap C) = (A - B) \cup (A - C)$

(ii) $A - (B \cup C) = (A - B) \cap (A - C)$

(iii) $A \cap (B - C) = (A \cap B) - (A \cap C)$

(iv) $A \cap (B \Delta C) = (A \cap B) \Delta (A \cap C)$

Proof:

(i) Let x be any element of A – (B $\cap$ C).

Then x $\in$ A – (B $\cap$ C) $\Rightarrow$ x $\in$ A and x $\notin$ (B $\cap$ C)

$\Rightarrow$ x $\in$ A and (x $\notin$ B or x $\notin$ C)

$\Rightarrow$ (x $\in$ A and x $\notin$ B) or (x $\in$ A and x $\notin$ C)

$\Rightarrow$ x $\in$ (A – B) or x $\in$ (A – C)

$\Rightarrow$ x $\in$ (A – B) $\cup$ (A – C)

$\therefore$ A – (B $\cap$ C) $\subset$ (A – B) $\cup$ (A – C)

Similarly, (A – B) $\cup$ (A – C) $\subset$ A – (B $\cap$ C)

Hence, A – (B $\cap$ C) = (A – B) $\cup$ (A – C)

(ii) Let x be arbitrary element of A – (B $\cup$ C). Then

x $\in$ A – (B $\cup$ C) $\Rightarrow$ x $\in$ A and x $\notin$ (B $\cup$ C)

$\Rightarrow$ x $\in$ A and (x $\notin$ B and x $\notin$ C)

$\Rightarrow$ (x $\in$ A and x $\notin$ B) and (x $\in$ A and x $\notin$ C)

$\Rightarrow$ x $\in$ (A – B) and x $\notin$ (A – C)

$\Rightarrow$ x $\subset$ (A – B) $\cap$ (A – C)

$\therefore$ A – (B $\cup$ C) $\subset$ (A – B) $\cap$ (A – C)

Similarly, (A – B) $\cap$ (A – C) $\subset$ A – (B $\cup$ C)

Hence, A – (B $\cup$ C) = (A – B) $\cap$ (A – C)

(iii) Let x be any arbitrary element of $A \cap (B - C)$. Then

$$x \in A \cap (B - C)$$
$$\Rightarrow \quad x \in A \text{ and } x \in (B - C)$$
$$\Rightarrow \quad x \in A \text{ and } (x \in B \text{ and } x \notin C)$$
$$\Rightarrow \quad (x \in A \text{ and } x \in B) \text{ and } (x \in A \text{ and } x \notin C)$$
$$\Rightarrow \quad (x \in A \cap B) \text{ and } x \notin (A \cap C)$$
$$\Rightarrow \quad x \in (A \cap B) - (A \cap C)$$
$$\therefore \quad A \cap (B - C) \subset (A \cap B) - (A \cap C)$$

Similarly, $(A \cap B) - (A \cap C) \subset A \cap (B - C)$

$$\therefore \quad A \cap (B - C) = (A \cap B) - (A \cap C)$$

(iv) $A \cap (B \Delta C) = A \cap [(B - C) \cup (C - B)]$

$= [A \cap (B - C)] \cup [A \cap (C - B)]$ (By distributive law)

$= [(A \cap B)-(A \cap C)]\cup[(A \cap C)-(A \cap B)]$ (From (iii))

$= (A \cap B) \Delta (A \cap C)$.

DUALITY PRINCIPLE

It may be noticed that if any law of the algebra of sets, universal set U is replaced by ϕ, ϕ by U, $\cup$ by $\cap$ and $\cap$ by $\cup$ wherever these occur, the new statement thus obtained is also a law of the algebra of sets. This fact is known as the *Duality Principle,* and any law obtained as a result of its application is called the dual of the original law. It is sometimes called primal law. For example, the dual of the law.

$$A \cup (B \cap C) = (A \cup B) \cap (A \cup C)$$

is

$$A \cap (B \cup C) = (A \cap B) \cup (A \cap C)$$

It will be observed that this principle is always true.

ORDERED PAIRS

If x and y be any two elements, then (x, y) is called their ordered pair. The element x is said to be the first member or the first coordinate of (x, y) and the element y is called the second member or coordinate of the ordered pair (x, y). It is clear from here that

$$(a, b) = (c, d) \Leftrightarrow a = c, b = d$$

Example: If ordered pairs $(2x - 1; -5)$ and $(x, y + 1)$ are equal, then

$$2x - 1 = x \Rightarrow x = 1$$

and

$$-5 = y + 1 \Rightarrow y = -6.$$

PRINCIPLE OF MATHEMATICAL INDUCTION

Let P(n), $n \in N$ be a statement such that (i) P(1) is true, and (ii) truth of P(r) implied the truth of P(r + 1). Then, by the principle of mathematical induction, the statement P(n) is true for all $n \in N$. Obviously, the principle of mathematical induction involves the following steps :

(i) First, we prove that the result is true for n = 1,

(ii) Then, we assume that the result is true for n = r.

(iii) Finally, we prove that the result is true for n = r + 1.

Then, we conclude by the principle of mathematical induction that the statement is true for all $n \in N$.

Some Other Results on Operations on Sets

Theorem 1:

For any sets A and B, prove that:

(i) $A - B = A \cap B'$

(ii) $(A - B) \cup B = A \cup B$.

(iii) $(A - B) \cap B = \phi$.

Proof:

(i) Let x be an arbitrary element of (A – B).

Then, $x \in (A - B)$

$\Rightarrow$ $x \in A$ and $x \notin B$

$\Rightarrow$ $x \in A$ and $x \in B'$

$\Rightarrow$ $x \in (A \cap B')$.

$\therefore$ $(A - B) \subseteq (A \cap B')$

Similarly, $(A \cap B') \subseteq (A - B)$

Hence $(A - B) = (A \cap B')$.

(ii) Let x be an arbitrary element of $(A - B) \cup B$

Then $x \in (A - B) \cup B$

$\Rightarrow$ $x \in (A - B)$ $\Rightarrow$ $x \in B$

$\Rightarrow$ $(x \in A \ \& \ x \notin B)$ $\Rightarrow$ $(x \in B)$

$\Rightarrow$ $(x \in A \Rightarrow x \in B)$ and $(x \notin B \Rightarrow :: \in B)$ [$\because$ 'or' distributes '&']

$\Rightarrow$ $x \in (A \cup B)$

$\therefore$ $(A - B) \cup B \subseteq (A \cup B)$ ...(i)

Again, let y be an arbitrarily element of $(A \cup B)$. Then

$y \in (A \cup B)$

$\Rightarrow (y \in A \Rightarrow y \in B)$

$\Rightarrow (y \in A \Rightarrow y \in B)$ and $(y \notin B \Rightarrow y \in B)$

$\Rightarrow (y \in A \;\&\; y \notin B) \Rightarrow (y \in B)$ ['or' distributes '&']

$\Rightarrow y \in (A - B) \Rightarrow (y \in B)$

$\Rightarrow y \in (A - B) \cup B$ ...(ii)

Hence from (i) and (ii), we have $(A - B) \cup B = (A \cup B)$.

(iii) If possible, let $(A - B) \cap B \neq \phi$

and let $x \in (A - B) \cap B$.

Then, $x \in (A - B) \cap B$

$\Rightarrow x \in (A - B)$ and $x \in B$

$\Rightarrow (x \in A \;\&\; x \notin B)$ and $(x \in B)$

$\Rightarrow x \in A$ and $(x \notin A \;\&\; x \in B)$

But, $x \notin B$ and $x \in B$ both can never hold simultaneously.

Thus, we arrive at a contradiction.

Since the contradiction arises by assuming that $(A - B) \cap B \neq \phi$, hence $(A - B) \cap B \neq \phi$.

Theorem 2:

Using various laws on operations on sets, prove the following:

(i) $A \cap (B \Delta C) = (A \cap B) \Delta (A \cap C)$

(ii) $A - (A - B) = A \cap B$

(iii) $(A \cup B) - (A \cap B) = (A - B) \cap (B - A)$.

Proof:

(i) We have $A \cap (B \Delta C)$

$= A \cap [(B - C) \cup (C - B)]$

$= [A \cap (B - C)] \cup [A \cap (C - B)]$ (Distributive law)

$= [(A \cap B) - (A \cap C)] \cap (A \cap C) - (A \cap B)]$

$= (A \cap B) \Delta (A \cap C)$.

(ii) We have

$A - (A - B) = A - (A \cap B')$ $[\because A - B = A \cap B']$

$= A \cap (A \cap B')'$

$= A \cap (A' \cup B')$ [by De-Morgan's law]

$= (A \cap A') \cup (A \cap B)$

$= \phi \cup (A \cap B) = A \cap B.$

(iii) $(A \cup B) - (A \cap B)$

$= (A \cup B) \cap (A \cap B)'$

$= (A \cap B)\ (A' \cup B')$ [De-Morgan's law]

$= [A \cap (A' \cup B')' \cup [\ B \cap (A' \cup B')]$ (Distributive law)

$= [(A \cap A) \cup (A \cap B')] \cup [(B \cap A') \cup (B \cap B')]$ (Distributive law)

$= [\phi \cup (A \cap B')] \cup [(B \cup A') \cup \phi]$

$= (A \cap B') \cup (B \cap A')$

$= (A - B) \cup (B - A).$

Example: *Let* $A = N$ *and for each* $\lambda \in A$.

Let $A_\lambda = \{1,\ 1/2,\ 1/3\}$

Let $U = \{x \in R,\ 0 \leq x \leq 1\}$

Find $U\{A_\lambda:\ \lambda \in A.$

Solution: Here $\lambda = 1, 2, 3, 4, \ldots$, so that we have

$A_1 = \{1\}$, $A_2 = \{1, 1/2\}$. $A_3 = \{1, 1/2, 1/3\}$ etc.

it is clear that

$U\{A_\lambda:\ \lambda \in A\} = \{1, 1/2, 1/3, \ldots 1/\lambda, 1/\lambda+1\}$

PRODUCTS OF SETS

We shall often have occasion to weld together the sets of a given class into a single new set called their *product* (or their *Cartesian product*). The ancestor of this concept is the coordinate plane of analytic geometry, that is, a plane equipped with the usual rectangular coordinate system. We give a brief description of this fundamental idea with a view to paving the way for our discussion of products of sets in general.

First, a few preliminary comments about the *real line*. We have already used this term several times without any explanation, and of course what we mean by it is an ordinary geometric straight line whose points have been identified with—or coordinatized by—the set R of all real numbers. We use the letter R to denote the real line as well as the set of all real numbers, and we often speak of real numbers as if they were points on the real line, and of points on the real line as if they were real numbers. Let no one be deceived into thinking that the real line is a simple thing, for its structure is exceedingly intricate. Our present view of it, however, is as naive and uncomplicated. Generally speaking, we assume that the reader is familiar with the simpler properties of the real line—those relating to inequalities and the basic algebraic operations of addition, subtraction, multiplication, and division. One of the most significant facts about the real number system is perhaps less well known. This is the so-called *least upper bound property*, which asserts that every non-empty set of real numbers which has an upper bound has a least upper bound. It is an easy consequence of this that every non-empty set of real numbers which has a lower bound has a greatest lower bound. All these matters can be developed rigorously on the basis of a small number of axioms, and detailed treatments can often be found in books on elementary abstract algebra.

To construct the coordinate plane, we now proceed as follows. We take two identical replicas of the real line, which we call the x axis and the y axis, and paste them on a plane at right angles to one another in such a way that they cross at the zero point on each. The usual picture is given in Fig. 1.7. Now, let P be a point in the plane. We project P perpendicularly onto points P_x and P_y on the axes. If x and y are the coordinates of P_z and P_y on their respective axes, this process leads us from the point P to the uniquely determined ordered pair (x, y) of real numbers, where x and y are called the *x coordinate* and *y coordinate* of P. We can reverse the process, and, starting with the ordered pair of real numbers, we can recapture the point. This is the manner in which we establish the familiar one-to-one correspondence between points P in the plane and ordered pairs (x, y) of real numbers. In fact, we think of a point in the plane (which is a geometric object) and its corresponding ordered pair of real numbers (which is an algebraic object) as being—to all intents and purposes—identical with one another. The essence of analytic geometry lies in the possibility of exploiting this identification by using algebraic tools in geometric arguments and giving geometric interpre-tations to algebraic calculations.

It is perhaps necessary to comment on one possible source of mis-understanding. When we speak of R^2 as a plane, we do so only to establish an intuitive bond with the reader's previous experience in analytic geometry. Our present attitude is that R^2 is a pure set and has no structure whatever, because no structure has yet been assigned to it. We remarked earlier (with deliberate vagueness) that a space is a set to which has been added some kind of algebraic or geometric structure. We shall convert the set R^2 into the space of analytic geometry by defining the distance between any two points (x_1, y_1) and (x_2, y_2) to be

$$\sqrt{(x_1 - x_2)^2 + (y_1 - y_2)^2}\,.$$

This notion of distance endows the set R^2 with a certain "spatial" character, which we shall recognize by calling the resulting space the *Euclidean plane* instead of the coordinate plane.

We assume that the reader is fully acquainted with the way in which the set C of all complex numbers can be identified (as a set) with the coordinate plane R^2. If 2 is a complex number, and if 2 has the standard form x + y where x and y are real numbers, then we identify z with the ordered pair (x, y), and thus with an element of R^2. The complex numbers, however, are much more than merely a set. They constitute a number system, with operations of addition, multiplication, conjugation, etc. When the coordinate plane R^2 is thought of as consisting of complex numbers and is enriched by the algebraic structure it acquires in this way, it is called the *complex plane.* The letter C is used to denote either the set of all complex numbers or the complex plane.

This definition of the product of two sets extends easily to the case of n sets for any positive integer n. If $X_1, X_2, \ldots, X_n$ are non-empty sets, then their product $X_1 \times X_2 \times \ldots \times X X_n$ is the set of all ordered n-tuples $(x_1, x_2, \ldots, x_n)$, where x_i is in X_i for each subscript i. If the X_i's are all replicas of a single set X, that is, if

$$X_1 = X_2 = \ldots. = X_n = X,$$

then their product is usually denoted by the symbol X^n.

These ideas specialize directly to yield the important sets R^n and C^n. R^1 is just R, the real line, and R^2 is the coordinate plane, R^3 — the set of all ordered triples of real numbers—is the set which underlies solid analytic geometry, and we assume that the reader is familiar with the manner in which this set arises, through the introduction of a rectangular coordinate system into ordinary three-dimensional space. We can draw pictures here just as in the case of the coordinate plane, and we can use geometric language as much as we please, but it must be understood that the mathematics of this set is the mathematics of ordered triples of real numbers and that the pictures are merely an aid to the intuition. Once we fully grasp this point of view, there is no difficulty whatever in advancing at once to the study of the set R^n of all ordered n-tuples $(x_1, x_2, \ldots, x_n)$ of real numbers for any positive integer n. It is quite true that when n is greater than 3 it is no longer possible to draw the same kinds of intuitively rich pictures, but at worst this is merely an inconvenience. We can (and do) continue to use suggestive geometric language, so all is not lost. The set C^n is defined similarly: it is the set of all ordered n-tuples $(z_1, z_2, \ldots, z_n)$ of complex numbers. Each of the sets R^n and C^n plays a prominent part in our later work.

We emphasized above that for the present the coordinate plane is to be considered as merely a set, and not a space. Similar remarks apply to R^n and C^n. In due course] we shall impart form and content to each of these sets by suitable definitions. We shall convert them into the *Euclidean and*

Unitary n-spaces which underlie and motivate so many developments in modern pure mathematics. But as of now—and this is the point we insist on—neither one of these sets has any structure *at all.*

As the reader doubtless suspects, it is not enough that we consider only products of finite classes of sets. The needs of topology compel us to extend these ideas to arbitrary classes of sets.

We defined the product $X_1 \times X_2 \times .... \times X_n$ to be the set of all ordered n-tuples $(x_1, x_2, ..., x_n)$ such that x_1 is in X_i for each subscript i. To see how to extend this definition, we reformulate it as follows. We have an index set 7, consisting of the integers from 1 to n, and corresponding to each index (or subscript) i we have a non-empty set X_i. The n-tuple $(x_1, x_2, ... , x_n)$ is simply a function (call it x) defined on the index set I, with the restriction that its value $x(i) = x_i$ is an element of the set X_i for each i in I. Our point of view here is that the function x is completely determined by, and is essentially equivalent to, the array $(x_i, x_2, ... , X_n)$ of its values.

The way is now open for the definition of products in their full generality. Let $\{X_1\}$ be a non-empty class of non-empty sets, indexed by the elements i of an index set I. The sets X_i need not be different from one another; indeed, it may happen that they are all identical replicas of a single set, distinguished only by different indices.

The *product* of the sets X_i, written $P_{ieI} X_i$, is defined to be the set of all functions x defined on I such that x(i) is an element of the set X_i for each index i. We call X, the *ith coordinate set.* When there can be no misunderstanding about the index set, the symbol P_{ieI} X, is often abbreviated to P_iX_i. The definition we have just given requires that each coordinate set be non-empty before the product can be formed. It will be useful if we extend this definition slightly by agreeing that if any of the X_i's are empty, then P,X, is also empty.

This approach to the idea of the product of a class of sets, by means of functions defined on the index set, is useful mainly in giving the definition. In practice, it is much more convenient to use the subscript notation x_i instead of the function notation (x_i). We then interpret the product P_iX_i as made up of elements x, each of which is specified by the exhibited array $\{x_i\}$ of its values in the respective coordinate sets X_i. We call x_i the *ith coordinate* of the element $x = \{x_1\}$.

The mapping p_i of the product P_iX_i onto its tth coordinate set X_i which is defined by $p_i(x) = x_i$—that is, the mapping whose value at an arbitrary element of the product is the ith coordinate of that element—is called the projection onto the tth coordinate set. The projection p_i selects the zth coordinate of each element in its domain. There is clearly one projection for each element of the index set I, and the set of all projections plays an important role in the general theory of topological spaces.

If A and B are any two sets, then set of all distinct ordered pairs whose first coordinate is an element of A and whose second coordinate is an element of B is called the *Cartesian product.* A and B and is denoted by A × B.

Symbolically, $A \times B = \{a, b) : a \in A \text{ and } b \in B\}$

For example, if $A = \{a, b, c\}$ and

$B = \{x, y, z)$ then

$$A \times B = \{(a, x), (a, y), (a, z), (b, x)\ (b, y), (b, z), (c, x), (c, y), (c, z)\}$$

and $$B \times A = \{(x, a), (x, b), (x, c), (y, a)\ (y, b), (y, c), (z, a), (z, b), (z, c)\}.$$

Notes:

(1) $A \times B \neq B \times A$, *i.e.*, cartesian product is not commutative.

(2) If the set A and B have m and n elements respectively, then the set A × B has *mn* elements.

(3) *If either A or B is a null set then the set A × B is also a null set.*

(4) *If either A or B is an infinite set and other is a non-empty set, then (A × B) is also an infinite set.*

(5) $A \times B = B \times A \Rightarrow A = B.$

DEDUCTION AND INDUCTION

Deduction : The process of deducing particular results from a general result is called *deduction.* For example, we know that the sum of the first n natural numbers is $\frac{n(n+1)}{2}$. From this result, we deduce that the sum of the first 50 natural numbers is 1275.

Induction : The process of establishing a valid general result from particular results is called *induction.* The principle of mathematical indiction is used to establish the validity of a general result involving natural numbers.

Consider the following statement :

$$P(n) = \text{“}n(n+1) \text{ is even”}.$$

When $n = 2$, we have $P(2) = 2(3) = 6$ is even.

We cannot continue like this by testing for all natural numbers $n \in N$. We can prove that the result is true by using the following argument. Let n be even. Then n (n + 1) is even. Let n be odd. Then (n + 1) is even. Therefore n(n +1) is even. The result is proved. However, all the statements as given above may not be as simple to prove.

SOLVED EXAMPLES

Example 1: *If A, B and C are any three sets, then prove that:*

(a) $A \times (B \cap C) = (A \times B) \cap (A \times C)$,

(b) $A \times (B \cup C) = (A \times B) \cup (A \times C)$.

Solution:

(a) We shall show that

$A \times (B \cap C) \subset (A \times B) \cap (A \times C)$

and $(A \times B) \cap (A \times C) \subset A \times (B \cap C)$

Firstly, let $(x, y) \in A \times (B \cap C)$, then

$(x, y) \in A \times (B \cap C)$

$\Rightarrow$ $x \in A$ and $y \in (B \cap C)$

$\Rightarrow$ $x \in A$ and $[y \in B$ and $y \in C]$

$\Rightarrow$ $[x \in A$ and $y \in B]$ and $[x \in A$ and $y \in C]$

$\Rightarrow$ $(x, y) \in (A \times B)$ and $(x, y) \in (A \times C)$

$\Rightarrow$ $(x, y) \in (A \times B) \cap (A \times C)$

Thus, $A \times (B \cap C) \subset (A \times B) \cap (A \times C)$ ...(1)

Again, let $(x, y) \in (A \times B) \cap (A \times C)$, then

$(x, y) \in (A \times B) \cap (A \times C)$

$\Rightarrow$ $(x, y) \in A \times B$ and $(x, y) \in (A \times C)$

$\Rightarrow$ $(x \in A, y \in B)$ and $(y \in A, y \in C)$

$\Rightarrow$ $x \in A, y \in B \cap C$

$\Rightarrow$ $(x, y) \in A \times B \cap C$

$\therefore$ $(A \times B) \cap (A \times C) \subset A (B \cap C)$ ...(2)

From (1) and (2)

$A \times (B \cap C) = (A \times B) \cap (A \times C)$

(b) Firstly, let $(x, y) \in A \times (B \cup C)$, then

$(x, y) \in A \times (B \cup C)$

$\Rightarrow$ $x \in A, y \in (B \cup C)$

$\Rightarrow$ $x \in A, [y \in B$ or $y \in C]$

$\Rightarrow$ $[x \in A, y \in B]$ or $[x \in A, y \in C]$

$\Rightarrow$ $(x, y) \in A \times B$ or $(x, y) \in A \times C$

$\Rightarrow$ $(x, y) \in (A \times B) \cup (A \times C)$.

Since, $(x, y) \in A \times (B \cup C)$

$\Rightarrow \quad (x, y) \in (A \times B) \cup (A \times C)$

$\therefore \quad A \times (B \cup C) \subset (A \times B) \cup (A \times C)$ ...(1)

Similarly, it can be proved that

$(x, y) \in (A \times B) \cup (A \times C)$

$\Rightarrow \quad (x, y) \in A \times (B \cup C),$

$\therefore \quad (A \times B) \cup (A \times C) \subset A \times (B \cup C)$ ...(2)

From (1) and (2).

$A \times (B \cup C) = (A \times B) \cup (A \times C)$

Example 2: *If $A \subset B$ show that $A \times A \subset (A \times B) \cap (B \times A)$.*

Solution: Let $(x, y) \in A \times A$, then

$(x, y) \in A \times A,$

$\Rightarrow \quad x \in A, y \in A$

Since $A \subset B$ is given,

$x \in A \Rightarrow y \in B.$

$\therefore \quad (x, y) \in A \times A$

$\Rightarrow \quad x \in A, y \in B$

$\Rightarrow \quad (x, y) \in (A \times B)$ ...(1)

Also, $(x, y) \in A \times A$

$\Rightarrow \quad x \in A, y \in A$

$\therefore \quad x \in B, y \in A$ $[\because A \subset B]$

$\Rightarrow \quad (x, y) \in B \times A$ ...(2)

Hence, from (1) and (2),

$(x, y) \in A \times A$

$\Rightarrow \quad (x, y) \in (A \times B)$ and $(x, y) \in B \times A$

$\Rightarrow \quad (x, y) \in (A \times B) \cap (B \times A)$

$\therefore \quad A \times A \subset (A \times B) \cap (B \times A).$

Example 3: *If $A \subset B$, prove that $A \times C \subset B \times C$ for any set C.*

Solution: Let (x, y) be any arbitrary element of $A \times C$. Then,

$(x, y) \in A \times C$

$\Rightarrow \quad x \in A$ and $y \in C$

$\Rightarrow \quad x \in B$ and $y \in C$ $[\because A \subset B]$

$$\Rightarrow \quad (x, y) \in B \times C$$

$$\therefore \quad A \times C \subset B \times C.$$

Example 4: Prove, using mathematical induction that $10^{2n-1} + 1$ is divisible by 11 for all $n \in N$.

Solution:

Let P(n) be the statement.

$$P(n): \text{"}10^{2n-1} + 1 \text{ is divisible by 11."}$$

When $n = 1$, we get $10^{2n-1} + 1 = 10 + 1 = 11$,

Which is divisible by 11. Hence, P(1) is true.

Let the result be true for P(r), *i.e.*, $10^{2r-1} + 1$ is divisible by 11. Therefore,

$$10^{2r-1} + 1 = 11k, \; k \in N.$$

or $$10^{2r-1} = 11k - 1.$$

We are now to prove that P(r + 1) is true.

Now, $$= P(r + 1): 10^{(2r+1)-1} - 1 = 10^{2r+1} + 1$$

$$= 10^{2r-1}.10^2 + 1 + (11k-1)\,100 + 1 = 11(100k - 9)$$

$$= \text{multiple of } 11.$$

Hence, 10^{2r+1} is divisible by 11. That is, P(r + 1) is true. By the principle of mathematical induction P(n) is true for all $n \in N$.

Example 5:

Using mathematical induction prove that $(1 + x)^n > 1 + nx$, for $n \geq 2$ and $x > -1$, $(\neq 0)$.

Solution:

Let the given result be denoted by P(n).

When n = 1, we get

$$(1 + x) > 1 + x$$

Which is not true (this is given in the problem).

When n = 2, we get

$$(1 + x)^2 > 1 + 2x + x^2 > 1 + 2x$$

Which is true. Therefore, P(2) is true.

Let the result P(r) be true, *i.e.*,

$$(1 + x)^r > 1 + rx \qquad ...(1)$$

We are to prove that P (r + 1) is true,

i.e., $(1 + x)^{r+1} > 1 + (r + 1)x$

Now $(1 + x)^{r+1} = (1 + x)^r (1 + x)$

$> (1 + rx)(1 + x)$ (using (1))

$= 1 + rx + x + rx^2$

$= 1 + (r + 1)x + rx^2$

$> 1 + (r + 1)x$

Therefore P (r + 1) is also true. Hence, P (n) is true for all $n \geq 2$, $n \in N$.

Examples 5(a): *Prove that $(A')' = A$.*

Solution: We have to prove $(A')' \subset A$ and $A \subset (A')'$.

Let $x \in (A')'$ then

$x \in (A')' \Leftrightarrow x \notin A'$

$\Leftrightarrow x \in A$

Thus $x \in (A')' \Leftrightarrow x \in A$

$\Rightarrow (A')' \subset A$ and $(A')' \supset A$

$\Rightarrow (A')' = A.$

Example 5(b): *Using mathematical induction prove that for every integer $n \geq 1$,* $\left(3^{2^n} - 1\right)$ is divisible by 2^{n+2} but not by 2^{n+3}.

Solution: Let P(n) be the statement P(n): $3^{2^n} - 1$ is divisible by 2^{n+2} but not by 2^{n+3}. For n = 1, we have $P(1) = 3^2 - 1 = 8 = 2^3$, which is divisible by 2^3 but not by 2^4.

Hence P(1) is true. Let the statement P(r) be true. That is

P (r): $3^{2^r} - 1$ is divisible by 2^{r+2} but not by 2^{r+3}

Therefore, we can write

P (r): $3^{2^r} - 1 = k \cdot 2^{r+2}$

where k is odd (if k is even, then $k.2^{r+2}$ is divisible by 2^{r+3}).

Hence $3^{2^r} = 1 + k\, 2^{r+2}$, k odd.

Now, P (r + 1): $3^{2^{r+1}} - 1 = 3^{(2^r . 2)} - 1$

$= \left(3^{2^r}\right)^2 - 1 = (1 + k \cdot 2^{r+2})^2 - 1$

$$= k^2 . 2^{2(r+2)} + 2k . 2\ 2^{r+2} + 1 - 1$$

$$= k^2 . 2^{2r+4} + k . 2^{r+3} = k^2 . 2^{r+3} . 2^{r+1} + k . 2^{r+3}$$

$$= k . 2^{2r+3} [1 + k . 2^{r+1}]$$

Which is divisible by 2^{r+3}, but not by 2^{r+4} as k is odd. Hence P(r + 1) is true. By mathematical induction, P(n) is true fro all $n \in N$.

Example 5(c): *Let $p \geq 3$ be an integer and α, β be the roots of $x^2 - (p + 1) x + 1 = 0.]$*

Solution: Since α, β are the roots of the equation $x^2 - (p + 1) x + 1 = 0$, we have

$$\alpha + \beta = p + 1, \text{ and } \alpha \beta = 1 \qquad ...(1)$$

Let $P(n) = \alpha^n + \beta^n$. We are to prove that P(n) is an integer.

For n = 1, we get

$P(1) = \alpha + \beta = p + 1.$

Which is an integer since p is an integer.

Hence, P(1) is true. Let P(r) be true.

That is, $P(r) = \alpha^r + \beta^r$ is an integer.

Now, $$P(r + 1) = \alpha^{r+1} + \beta^{r+1}$$

$$= \alpha (\alpha^r) + \beta(\beta^r)$$

$$= \alpha (\alpha^r + \beta^r) - \alpha\beta^r + \beta (\alpha^r + \beta^r) - \beta \alpha^r$$

$$= (\alpha + \beta) (\alpha^r + \beta^r) - \alpha\beta(\alpha^{r-1} + \beta^{r-1}$$

$$= (p + 1) (\alpha^r + \beta^r) - (\alpha^{r-1} + \beta^{r-1}). \qquad ...(2)$$

Since p is an integer, p + 1 is an integer and $\alpha^r + \beta^r$ is an integer. Therefore P (r + 1) is an integer, if $\alpha^{r-1} + \beta^{r-1}$ is an integer putting r = r – 1 in (2), we get

$$P (r) = \alpha^r + \beta^r = (p + 1) (\alpha^{r-1} + \beta^{r-1}) - (\alpha^{r-2} + \beta^{r-2}) \qquad ...(3)$$

Again, since (p + 1) and $(\alpha^r + \beta^r)$ are integers, $\alpha^{r-1} + \beta^{r-1}$ is an integer, if $\alpha^{r-2} + \beta^{r-2}$ is an integer. Setting r = r–1 in (3), we find $\alpha^{r-2} + \beta^{r-2}$ is an integer this way, we get that $\alpha^2 + \beta^2$ is an integer if $\alpha + \beta$ is an integer. But $\alpha + \beta = p + 1$ is an integer.

Hence, $\alpha^2 + \beta^2$ is an integer, $\alpha^3 + \beta^3$ is an integer . . . . . $\alpha^{r-1} + \beta^{r-1}$ is an integer.

Hence, by mathematical induction, $\alpha^n + \beta^n$ is an integer.

Examples 6: *Prove the following*

(a) $A \Delta \phi = A$,

(b) $A \Delta A = \phi$,

(b) $A \Delta B = \phi \Leftrightarrow A = B$.

Solution:

(a) $A \Delta \phi = (A - \phi) \cup (\phi - A)$

$= A \cup \phi \qquad (\because A - \phi = A, \phi - A = \phi)$

$= A.$

(b) $A \Delta A = (A - A) \cup (A - A)$

$= \phi \cup \phi = \phi$

(c) $A \Delta B = \phi \quad \Rightarrow (A - B) \cup (B - A) = \phi$

$\Rightarrow A - B = \phi$ and $B - A = \phi$

$\Rightarrow A = B$

and $\qquad A = B \Rightarrow A - B = \phi$ and $B - A = \phi$

$\Rightarrow (A - B) \cup (B - A) = \phi$

$\Rightarrow A \Delta B = \phi$

Hence, $\qquad A \Delta B = \phi \Rightarrow A = B.$

Examples 7: *If* $\quad$ *A = set of all students,*

B = set of all students offering mathematics,

C = set of all women,

D = set of industrious person,

E = set of all first class students.

Write the following statement symbolically. Some industrious women students are the students of mathematics but they are not first class".

Solution: Set of women students = $A \cap C$. Set of industrious women students

$= A \cap C \cap D$

Set of industrious women students offering mathematics

$= A \cap C \cap D \cap B.$

Set of all those industrious women students offering mathematics who are not first class = $A \cap C \cap D \cap B - E$. According to the statement there are some students of this type. Hence,

$$A \cap C \cap D \cap B - E \neq \phi.$$

Example 8(a): *By mathematical induction, prove that* $7^{2n} + (2^{3n-3})3^{n-1}$ *is divisible by 25,* $n \in N$.

Solution: Let the statement P(n) be defined as

$$P(n) = \text{"}7^{2n} + (2^{3n-3})\, 3^{n-1} \text{ is divisible by 25"}$$

When $n = 1$, we get

$$P(1) = 7^2 + 1\,(1) = 50$$

Which is divisible by 25,

Let the result P(r) be true.

That is $7^{2r} + (2^{3r-3})\, 3^{r-1}$ is divisible by 25

Let $7^{2r} + (2^{3r-3})\, 3^{r-1} = 25\,k,\ k \in N$ ....(1)

Now

$$\begin{aligned} P(r+1) &= 7^{2r+2} + (2^{3r})\, 3^{r} \\ &= 7^{2r}\,(49) + (2^{3r-3} \,.\, 2^3)\, 3^{r-1} \,.\, 3 \\ &= 49\,(7^{2r}) + 24\,(2^{3r-3})\, 3^{r-1} \\ &= (50-1)\,(7^{2r}) + (25-1)\,(2^{3r-3})3^{r-1} \\ &= 50\,(7^{2r}) + 25\,(2^{3r-3})\, 3^{r-1} - [7^{2r} + (2^{3r-3})\, 3^{r-1}] \\ &= 25\,[2\,(7^{2r}) + (2^{3r-3})\, 3^{r-1}] - 25\,k \quad \text{(from (1))} \\ &= 25\,[2\,(7^{2r}) + (2^{3r-3})\, 3^{r-4} - k] \\ &= \text{divisible by 25.} \end{aligned}$$

Therefore, P (r + 1) is also true. By mathematical induction, P(n) is true for all $n \in N$.

Example 8(b): *If A, B and C are any three sets, then prove that :*

(a) $A \times (B \cap C) = (A \times B) \cap (A \times C)$,

(b) $A \times (B \cup C) = (A \times B) \cup (A \times C)$,

Solution:

(a) We shall show that

$$A \times (B \cap C) \subset (A \times B) \cap (A \times C)$$

and

$$(A \times B) \cap (A \times C) \subset A \times (B \cap C)$$

Firstly, let $(x, y) \in A \times (B \cap C)$, then

$$\begin{aligned} & (x, y) \in A \times (B \cap C) \\ \Rightarrow\ & x \in A \text{ and } y \in (B \cap C) \\ \Rightarrow\ & x \in A \text{ and } [y \in B \text{ and } y \in C] \\ \Rightarrow\ & [x \in A \text{ and } y \in B] \text{ and } [x \in A \text{ and } y \in C] \end{aligned}$$

$\Rightarrow \quad (x, y) \in (A \times B)$ and $(x, y) \in (A \times C)$

$\Rightarrow \quad (x, y) \in (A \times B) \cap (A \times C)$

Thus, $A \times (B \cap C) \subset (A \times B) \cap (A \times C)$ ...(1)

Again, let $(x, y) \in (A \times B) \cap (A \times C)$, then

$(x, y) \in (A \times B) \cap (A \times C)$

$\Rightarrow \quad (x, y) \in A \times B$ and $(x, y) \in (A \times C)$

$\Rightarrow \quad (x \in A, y \in B)$ and $(y \in A, y \in C)$

$\Rightarrow \quad x \in A, y \in B \cap C$

$\Rightarrow \quad (x, y) \in A \times B \cap C$

$\therefore \quad (A \times B) \cap (A \times C) \subset A\ (B \cap C)$ ...(2)

From (1) and (2)

$$A \times (B \cap C) = (A \times B) \cap (A \times C)$$

(b) Firstly, let $(x, y) \in A \times (B \cup C)$, then

$(x, y) \in A \times (B \cup C)$

$\Rightarrow \quad x \in A, y \in (B \cup C)$

$\Rightarrow \quad x \in A, [y \in B$ or $y \in C]$

$\Rightarrow \quad [x \in A, y \in B]$ or $[x \in A, y \in C]$

$\Rightarrow \quad (x, y) \in A \times B$ or $(x, y) \in A \times C$

$\Rightarrow \quad (x, y) \in (A \times B) \cup (A \times C)$.

Since, $(x, y) \in A \times (B \cup C)$

$\Rightarrow \quad (x, y) \in (A \times B) \cup (A \times C)$

$\therefore \quad A \times (B \cup C) \subset (A \times B) \cup (A \times C)$ ...(1)

Similarly, it can be proved that

$(x, y) \in (A \times B) \cup (A \times C)$

$\Rightarrow \quad (x, y) \in A \times (B \cup C)$,

$\therefore \quad (A \times B) \cup (A \times C) \subset A \times (B \cup C)$ ...(2)

From (1) and (2)

$$A \times (B \cup C) = (A \times B) \cup (A \times C)$$

Example 9(a): *If $A \subset B$ show that $A \times A \subset (A \times B) \cap (B \times A)$.*

Solution: Let $(x, y) \in A \times A$, then

$(x, y) \in A \times A$,

$\Rightarrow \quad x \in A, y \in A$

Since $A \subset B$ is given,

$$x \in A \Rightarrow y \in B.$$

$\therefore$ $(x, y) \in A \times A$

$\Rightarrow$ $x \in A, y \in B$

$\Rightarrow$ $(x, y) \in (A \times B)$ ...(1)

Also, $(x, y) \in A \times A$

$\Rightarrow$ $x \in A, y \in A$

$\therefore$ $x \in B, y \in A$ $[\because A \subset B]$

$\Rightarrow$ $(x, y) \in B \times A$ ...(2)

Hence, from (1) and (2),

$(x, y) \in A \times A$

$\Rightarrow$ $(x, y) \in (A \times B)$ and $(x, y) \in B \times A$

$\Rightarrow$ $(x, y) \in (A \times B) \cap (B \times A)$

$\therefore$ $A \times A \subset (A \times B) \cap (B \times A)$.

Example 9(b): *If $A \subset B$, prove that $A \times C \subset B \times C$ for any set C.*

Solution: Let (x, y) be any arbitrary element of $A \times C$. Then,

$(x, y) \in A \times C$

$\Rightarrow$ $x \in A$ and $y \in C$

$\Rightarrow$ $x \in B$ and $y \in C$ $[\because A \subset B]$

$\Rightarrow$ $(x, y) \in B \times C$

$\therefore$ $A \times C \subset B \times C$.

Example 9(c): *Prove, using mathematical induction that $10^{2n-1} + 1$ is divisible by 11 for all $n \in N$.*

Solution: Let P(n) be the statement.

P(n) : "$10^{2n-1} + 1$ is divisible by 11."

When $n = 1$, we get $10^{2n-1} + 1 = 10 + 1 = 11$,

Which is divisible by 11. Hence, P(1) is true.

Let the result be true for P(r), *i.e.*, $10^{2r-1} + 1$ is divisible by 11. Therefore,

$$10^{2r-1} + 1 = 11k, k \in N.$$

or $10^{2r-1} = 11k - 1$.

We are now to prove that P(r + 1) is true.

Now, $= P(r + 1) : 10^{(2r+1)-1} - 1 = 10^{2r+1} + 1$

$= 10^{2r-1}.10^2 + 1 + (11k-1)\,100 + 1 = 11(100k-9)$

= multiple of 11.

Hence, 10^{2r+1} is divisible by 11. That is, P(r + 1) is true. By the principle of mathematical induction P(n) is true for all $n \in N$.

Example 10: *Using mathematical induction prove that* $(1 + x)^n > 1 + nx$, *for* $n \geq 2$ *and* $x > -1$, $(\neq 0)$.

Solution: Let the given result be denoted by P(n).

When n = 1, we get

$$(1 + x) > 1 + x$$

Which is not true (this is given in the problem).

When n = 2, we get

$$(1 + x)^2 > 1 + 2x + x^2 > 1 + 2x$$

Which is true. Therefore, P(2) is true.

Let the result P(r) be true, *i.e.*,

$$(1 + x)^r > 1 + rx \qquad ...(1)$$

We are to prove that P (r + 1) is true,

i.e., $(1 + x)^{r+1} > 1 + (r + 1)\,x$

Now $(1 + x)^{r+1} = (1 + x)^r (1 + x)$

$> (1 + rx)(1 + x)$ (using (1))

$= 1 + rx + x + rx^2$

$= 1 + (r + 1)\,x + rx^2$

$> 1 + (r + 1)\,x$

Therefore P (r + 1) is also true. Hence, P (n) is true for all $n \geq 2$, $n \in N$.

Example 11: *Show that* $n\{P[P.(P(\phi))]\} = 4$

Solution: We have $P(\phi) = \{\phi\}$

$\therefore$ $P(P(\phi)) = \{\phi, \{\phi\}\}$

$\Rightarrow$ $P[P(P(\phi))] = \{\phi, \{\phi\}\}, [\{\phi\}]\ \{\phi, \{\phi\}\}\}$

$\therefore$ $n\{P[P.(P(\phi))]\} = 4.$

Example 12: *If* $A = \{a, \{b\}\}$, *find* $P(A)$.

Solution: Let B = {b}. Then A = {a, B}

$$\therefore \quad P(A) = \{\phi, \{a\}, \{B\}, \{a, B\}\}$$
$$= \{\phi, \{a\}, \{\{b\}\}, \{\{a\}, \{b\}\}\}$$

Example 13: *Set A has three elements and set B has six elements. What can be the minimum number of elements in the set A ∪ B? Find also the maximum number of elements in A ∪ B.*

Solution: We have n(A) = 3, and n(B) = 6. Therefore, the maximum number of elements in A ∩ B is 3, since

$$n(A \cup B) = n(A) + n(B) - n(A \cap B)$$

the minimum number of elements in A ∪ B is given by

$$\text{minimum } [n(A \cup B)] = n(A) + n(B) - \text{max. } [n(A \cap B)]$$
$$= 3 + 6 - 3 = 6$$

Therefore, the minimum number of elements in A ∪ B = 6.

The number of elements in A ∪ B is maximum when A and B are disjoint. In this case

$$n(A \cup B) = n(A) + n(B) = 3 + 6 = 9$$

The maximum number of elements in A ∪ B is 9.

Examples 14(a): *The necessary and sufficient condition for a set Y to be a subset of X is that X ∪ Y = X.*

Solution: Let $Y \subset X$, then

$$x \in Y \Rightarrow x \in X \quad \text{...(i)}$$

Now, $x \in X \cup Y \Rightarrow x \in X \text{ or } x \in Y$

$$\Rightarrow x \in X$$

$$\therefore \quad X \cup Y \subset X \quad \text{...(ii)}$$

Also, we know that

$$X \subset X \cup Y \quad \text{...(iii)}$$

(ii) and (iii) $\Rightarrow X \cup Y = X$.

Conversely,

if $X \cup Y = X$, we have to prove that $Y \subset X$.

Now, $X \cup Y = X \Rightarrow X \cup Y \subset X$

and $X \subset X \cup Y$

$\Rightarrow$ $X \cup Y \subset X$

$$\Rightarrow \quad X \subset X \text{ and } Y \subset X$$

$$\Rightarrow \quad Y \subset X.$$

Examples 14(b): *Prove that $(A')' = A$.*

Solution: We have to prove $(A')' \subset A$ and $A \subset (A')'$.

Let $x \in (A')'$ then

$$x \in (A')' \Leftrightarrow x \notin A'$$

$$\Leftrightarrow x \in A$$

Thus $x \in (A')' \Leftrightarrow x \in A$

$$\Rightarrow (A')' \subset A \text{ and } (A')' \supset A$$

$$\Rightarrow (A')' = A.$$

Examples 15: *Let A, B, C be three sets then*

$$(A - B) \cap (A - C) = A - (B \cup C)$$

Solution: Let $x \in (A - B) \cap (A - C)$ then

$$x \in (A - B) \cap (A - C) \Leftrightarrow x \in (A - B) \text{ and } x \in (A - C)$$

$$\Leftrightarrow x \in A,\ x \notin B \text{ and } x \in A,\ x \notin C$$

$$\Leftrightarrow x \in A,\ x \notin B \text{ and } x \notin C$$

$$\Leftrightarrow x \in A,\ x \notin B \cup C$$

$$\Leftrightarrow x \in A - (B \cup C)$$

Which implies that $(A - B) \cap (A - C) = A - (B \cup C)$

Examples 16: *Prove the following*

(a) $A \Delta \phi = A$,

(b) $A \Delta A = \phi$,

(b) $A \Delta B = \phi \Leftrightarrow A = B$.

Solution: (a) $A \Delta \phi = (A - \phi) \cup (\phi - A)$

$$= A \cup \phi \qquad (\because A - \phi = A,\ \phi - A = \phi)$$

$$= A.$$

(b) $A \Delta A = (A - A) \cup (A - A)$

$$= \phi \cup \phi = \phi$$

(c) $A \Delta B = \phi \quad \Rightarrow (A - B) \cup (B - A) = \phi$

$$\Rightarrow A - B = \phi \text{ and } B - A = \phi$$

$$\Rightarrow A = B$$

and $$A = B \Rightarrow A - B = \phi \text{ and } B - A = \phi$$

$$\Rightarrow (A - B) \cup (B - A) = \phi$$

$$\Rightarrow A \Delta B = \phi$$

Hence, $A \Delta B = \phi \Rightarrow A = B$.

Examples 17: *If* A = *set of all students,*

B = *set of all students offering mathematics,*

C = *set of all women,*

D = *set of industrious person,*

E = *set of all first class students.*

Write the following statement symbolically. Some industrious women students are the students of mathematics but they are not first class".

Solution: Set of women students = $A \cap C$. Set of industrious women students

$$= A \cap C \cap D$$

Set of industrious women students offering mathematics

$$= A \cap C \cap D \cap B.$$

Set of all those industrious women students offering mathematics who are not first class = $A \cap C \cap D \cap B - E$. According to the statement there are some students of this type. Hence,

$$A \cap C \cap D \cap B - E \neq \phi.$$

Example 18: *Set A has three elements and set B has six elements. What can be the minimum number of elements in the set $A \cup B$? Find also the maximum number of elements in $A \cup B$.*

Solution: We have n(A) = 3, and n(B) = 6. Therefore, the maximum number of elements in $A \cap B$ is 3, since

$$n(A \cup B) = n(A) + n(B) - n(A \cap B)$$

the minimum number of elements in $A \cup B$ is given by

minimum $[n(A \cup B)] = n(A) + n(B) - \max. [n(A \cap B)]$

$$= 3 + 6 - 3 = 6$$

Therefore, the minimum number of elements in $A \cup B = 6$.

The number of elements in $A \cup B$ is maximum when A and B are disjoint. In this case

$$n(A \cup B) = n(A) + n(B) = 3 + 6 = 9$$

The maximum number of elements in $A \cup B$ is 9.

Examples 19: *In a certain examination, the candidates can offer papers in English or Hindi or both the subjects. The number of candidates who appeared in the examination is 1000 of whom 650 appeared in English and 200 appeared in both English and Hindi. Find,*

(i) the number of candidates who offered paper in Hindi.

(ii) the number of candidates who offered paper in English only.

(iii) the number of candidates who offered paper in Hindi only.

Solution: Let A = The set of candidates who offered paper in English

B = The set of candidates who offered paper in Hindi.

Therefore, $n(A \cup B) = 1000$, $n(A) = 650$, $n(A \cap B) = 200$.

(i) We have $n(A \cup B) = n(A) + n(B) - n(A \cap B)$

$\Rightarrow \quad 1000 = 650 + n(B) - 200$

$\Rightarrow \quad n(B) = 550$

$\therefore$ Number of candidates who offered paper in Hindi = 550.

(ii) Now, the set of candidates who offered paper in English only is

$A - B = \{\text{candidate} : \text{candidate} \in A \text{ and candidate} \notin B\}$

Now, $n(A - B) = n(A) - n(A \cap B)$

$= 650 - 200 = 450.$

Number of candidates who offered paper in English only = 450.

(iii) Similarly, the set of candidates who offered paper in Hindi only is B – A.

Now, $n(B - A) = n(B) - n(A \cap B)$

$= 550 - 200 = 350.$

Example 20: *If $a \in N$ such that $aN = \{ax : x \in N\}$. Describe the set $3N \cap 7N$.*

Solution: We have $aN = \{ax ; x \in N\}$

$\therefore \quad 3N = [3x : x \in N\} = \{3, 6, 9, 12, \ldots,\}$

and $\quad 7N = [7x : x \in N\} = \{7, 14, 21, 28, \ldots,\}$

Hence $\quad 3N \cap 7N = \{21, 42, \ldots\}$

$= \{21x : x \in N\} = 21N.$

Example 21: *For any natural number a, we define* $aN = \{ax : x \in N\}$. *If* $b, c, d \in N$ *such that* $bN \cap cN = dN$, *then prove that d is the l.c.m. of b and c.*

Solution: We have

$bN = \{bx : x \in N\}$ = The set of positive integral multiples of b.

$cN = \{cx : x \in N\}$ = The set of positive integral multiples of c.

$\therefore$ $bN \cap cN$ = The set of positive integral multiples of b and c both.

$\Rightarrow$ $bN \cap cN = \{kx : x \in N\}$, where k is the *l*.c.m. of b and c.

Hence, $d = l$.c.m of b and c.

Example 22: *Two finite sets have m and n elements. The total number of subsets of the first set is 56 more than the total number of subsets of the second set. Find the values of m and n.*

Solution: Let A and B be two sets having m and n elements respectively. Then,

Number of subsets of A = 2^m,

Number of subsets of B = 2^n,

It is given that $2^m - 2^n = 56$

$\Rightarrow$ $2^n(2^{m-n} - 1) = 2^3(2^3 - 1)$

$\Rightarrow$ $n = 3$ and $m - n = 3$

$\Rightarrow$ $n = 3$ and $m = 6$.

Example 23: *If* $X = \{4^n - 3n - 1 : n \in N\}$ *and* $Y = \{9(n - 1) : n \in N\}$, *prove that* $X \subset Y$.

Solution: Let $x_n = 4^n - 3n : n \in N$. Then $x_1 = 4 - 3 - 1 = 0$.

And for $n \geq 2$, we have $x_n = 4^n - 3n - 1$

$= (1 + 3)^n - 3n - 1$

$= {}^nc_0 + {}^nc_1.3 + {}^nc_2 + 3^2 + \ldots + {}^nc_n.3^n - 3n - 1$

[Using Binomial Theorem]

$= 1 + 3n + {}^nc_2.3^2 + {}^nc_3.3^3 + \ldots + {}^nc_n.3^n - 3n - 1$

$[\because {}^nc_n = 1, {}^nc_1 = n]$

$= 3^2 \{{}^nc_2 + {}^nc_3.3 + {}^nc_4.3^2 + \ldots + {}^nc_n.3^{n-2}\}$

$= 9 \{{}^nc_2 + {}^nc_3.3 + {}^nc_4.3^2 + \ldots + {}^nc_n.3^{n-2}\}$

Thus, x_n is some positive integral multiple of 9 for $n \geq 2$.

Hence, X consists of all positive integral multiples of 9 of the form

$$9\,[{}^nc_2 + 3.{}^nc_3 + 3^2\,.{}^nc_4 + \ldots + 3^{n-2}.{}^nc_n]$$

together with zero.

Now, $Y = \{9(n-1) : n \in N\}$. This shows that Y consists of all integral multiples of 9 together with 0.

In fact, we have $X = \{0, 9, 54, 243, \ldots\}$

and $Y = \{0, 9, 18, 27, 36, 54, \ldots\}$

Thus $X \subset Y$.

***Example 24:** Suppose $A_1, A_2, \ldots, A_{30}$ are thirty sets each with five elements and $B_1, B_2, \ldots, B_n$ are n sets each with three element.*

Let $\bigcup_{i=1}^{30} A_i = \bigcup_{j=1}^{n} B_j = S.$

Assume that each element of S belongs to exactly ten of the A_i's and exactly 9 of B_j's. Find n.

Solution: Since each A_i has 5 elements and each element of S belongs to exactly 10 of A_i's.

$$\therefore \quad S = \bigcup_{i=1}^{30} B_j \Rightarrow n(S) = \frac{1}{10}\sum_{i=1}^{30} n(A_i)$$

$$= \frac{1}{10}(5 \times 30) = 15 \qquad \ldots(1)$$

Again each B_j has 3 elements and each element of S belongs to exactly 9 of B_j's.

$$\therefore \quad S = \bigcup_{j=1}^{n} B_j \Rightarrow n(S) = \frac{1}{9}\sum_{i=1}^{30} n(B_j)$$

$$= \frac{1}{9}(3n) = \frac{n}{3} \qquad \ldots(2)$$

From (i) and (2), we get

$$15 = \frac{n}{3} \Rightarrow n = 45.$$

***Example 25:** In town of 10,000 families it was found that 40% families buy newspaper A, 20% families newspaper B and 10% families buy newspaper C. 5% families buy A and B, 3% buy B and C and 4% buy A and C. If 2% families buy all the three newspapers, find the number of families which buy (i) A only (ii) B only (iii) None of A, B and C.*

Solution: Let P, Q and R be the set of families buying newspaper A, B and C respectively.

Let U be the universal set.

$n(P) = 40\%$ of $10{,}000 = 4000$,

$n(Q) = 20\%$ of $10{,}000 = 2000$,

$n(R) = 10\%$ of $10{,}000 = 1000$,

$n(P \cap Q) = 5\%$ of $10{,}000 = 500$,

$n(Q \cap R) = 3\%$ of $10{,}000 = 300$,

$n(R \cap P) = 4\%$ of $10{,}000 = 400$,

$n(P \cap Q \cap R) = 2\%$ of $10{,}000 = 200$,

and $n(U) = 10{,}000$.

(i) Required number $= n(P \cap Q' \cap R')$

$= n(P \cap (Q' \cap R)')$

$= n(P) - n[(P \cap (Q \cup R)]$ $[\because n(A \cap B)' = n(A - n(A \cap B)]$

$= n(P) - n[(P \cap Q) \cup (P \cap R)]$

$= n(P) - [n(P \cap Q) + n(P \cap R) - n\{(P \cap Q) \cap (P \cap R)\}]$

$= n(P) - [n(P \cap Q) + n(P \cap R) - n\{(P \cap Q \cap R)]$

$= 4000 - [500 + 400 - 200]$

$= 3300.$

(ii) Required number $= n(P' \cap Q \cap R')$

$= n(Q \cap (P' \cap R')$

$= n(Q \cap (P \cup R)')$

$= n(Q) - n[(Q \cap (P \cup R)]$ $[\because n(A \cap B)' = n(A) - n(A \cap B)]$

$= n(Q) - n[(Q \cap P) \cup (Q \cap R)]$

$= n(Q) - [n(Q \cap P) + n(Q \cap R) - n\{(Q \cap P) \cap (Q \cap R)\}]$

$= n(Q) - [n(P \cap Q) + n(Q \cap R) - n\{(P \cap Q \cap R)]$

$= 2000 - [500 + 300 - 200]$

$= 1400.$

(iii) Required number $= n(P' \cap Q' \cap R')$

$= n[(P \cup Q \cup R)']$

$= n(U) - n(P \cup Q \cup R)$

$= n(U) - n[n(P) + n(Q) + n(R) - n(P \cap Q) - n(Q \cap R)$
$- n(R \cap P) + n(P \cap Q \cap R)$

$= 10000 - [4000 + 2000 + 1000 - 500 - 300 - 400 + 200]$

$= 4000.$

Example 26(a): *Prove that if* $A \subset B$ *and* $C \subset D$*, then* $A \times C \subset B \times D$.

Solution: Let $(x, y) \in A \times C$, then

$(x, y) \in A \times C$

$\Rightarrow$ $x \in B$ and $y \in D$ $[\because A \subset B, C \subset D]$

$\Rightarrow$ $(x, y) \in B \times D$

$\therefore$ $A \times C \subset B \times D.$

Example 26(b): *By mathematical induction, prove that*

$$7^{2n} + (2^{3n-3})\, 3^{n-1} \text{ is divisible by } 25,\ n \in N.$$

Solution: Let the statement P(n) be defined as

$P(n) =$ "$7^{2n} + (2^{3n-3})\, 3^{n-1}$ is divisible by 25"

When $n = 1$, we get

$P(1) = 7^2 + 1\,(1) = 50$

Which is divisible by 25,

Let the result P(r) be true.

That is $7^{2r} + (2^{3r-3})\, 3^{r-1}$ is divisible by 25

Let $7^{2r} + (2^{3r-3})\, 3^{r-1} = 25\,k,\ k \in N$ ....(1)

Now $P(r + 1) = 7^{2r+2} + (2^{3r})\, 3^r$

$= 7^{2r}\,(49) + (2^{3r-3} \,.\, 2^3)\, 3^{r-1} \,.\, 3$

$= 49\,(7^{2r}) + 24\,(2^{3r-3})\, 3^{r-1}$

$= (50 - 1)\,(7^{2r}) + (25 - 1)\,(2^{3r-3}) 3^{r-1}$

$= 50\,(7^{2r}) + 25\,(2^{3r-3})\, 3^{r-1} - [7^{2r} + (2^{3r-3})\, 3^{r-1}]$

$= 25\,[2\,(7^{2r}) + (2^{3r-3})\, 3^{r-1}] - 25\,k$ (from (1))

$= 25\,[2\,(7^{2r}) + (2^{3r-3})\, 3^{r-4} - k]$

$=$ divisible by 25.

Therefore, P (r + 1) is also true. By mathematical induction, P(n) is true for all $n \in N$.

Example 27: *Using mathematical induction prove that for every integer* $n \geq 1$, $\left(3^{2^n} - 1\right)$ is divisible by 2^{n+2} but not by 2^{n+3}.

Solution: Let P(n) be the statement P(n) : $3^{2^n} - 1$ is divisible by 2^{n+2} but not by 2^{n+3}.

For n = 1, we have $P(1) = 3^2 - 1 = 8 = 2^3$, which is divisible by 2^3 but not by 2^4.

Hence P(1) is true. Let the statement P(r) be true. That is

$$P(r) : 3^{2^r} - 1 \text{ is divisible by } 2^{r+2} \text{ but not by } 2^{r+3}$$

Therefore, we can write

$$P(r) : 3^{2^r} - 1 = k \,.\, 2^{r+2}$$

where k is odd (if k is even, then $k.2^{r+2}$ is divisible by 2^{r+3}).

Hence $3^{2^r} = 1 + k\, 2^{r+2}$, k odd.

Now, $P(r+1) : 3^{2^{r+1}} - 1 = 3^{(2^r \cdot 2)} - 1$

$$= \left(3^{2^r}\right)^2 - 1 = (1 + k \,.\, 2^{r+2})^2 - 1$$

$$= k^2 \,.\, 2^{2(r+2)} + 2k \,.\, 2\, 2^{r+2} + 1 - 1$$

$$= k^2 \,.\, 2^{2r+4} + k \,.\, 2^{r+3} = k^2 \,.\, 2^{r+3} \,.\, 2^{r+1} + k \,.\, 2^{r+3}$$

$$= k \,.\, 2^{2r+3}\, [1 + k \,.\, 2^{r+1}]$$

Which is divisible by 2^{r+3}, but not by 2^{r+4} as k is odd. Hence P(r + 1) is true. By mathematical induction, P(n) is true fro all $n \in N$.

Example 28: *Let* $p \geq 3$ *be an integer and* α, β *be the roots of* $x^2 - (p + 1)x + 1 = 0$. *Using mathematical induction show that* $\alpha^n + \beta^n$ *is an integer.*

Solution: Since α, β are the roots of the equation

$x^2 - (p + 1)x + 1 = 0$, we have

$\alpha + \beta = p + 1$, and $\alpha\beta = 1$ ...(1)

Let $P(n) = \alpha^n + \beta^n$. We are to prove that P(n) is an integer.

For n = 1, we get

$P(1) = \alpha + \beta = p + 1$.

Which is an integer since p is an integer.

Hence, P(1) is true. Let P(r) be true.

That is, $P(r) = \alpha^r + \beta^r$ is an integer.

Now, $P(r + 1) = \alpha^{r+1} + \beta^{r+1}$

$$= \alpha(\alpha^r) + \beta(\beta^r)$$

$$= \alpha(\alpha^r + \beta^r) - \alpha\beta^r + \beta(\alpha^r + \beta^r) - \beta\alpha^r$$

$$= (\alpha + \beta)(\alpha^r + \beta^r) - \alpha\beta(\alpha^{r-1} + \beta^{r-1})$$

$$= (p + 1)(\alpha^r + \beta^r) - (\alpha^{r-1} + \beta^{r-1}) \quad ...(2)$$

Since p is an integer, p + 1 is an integer and $\alpha^r + \beta^r$ is an integer. Therefore P (r + 1) is an integer, if $\alpha^{r-1} + \beta^{r-1}$ is an integer putting r = r – 1 in (2), we get

$$P(r) = \alpha^r + \beta^r = (p + 1)(\alpha^{r-1} + \beta^{r-1}) - (\alpha^{r-2} + \beta^{r-2}) \quad ...(3)$$

Again, since (p + 1) and $(\alpha^r + \beta^r)$ are integers, $\alpha^{r-1} + \beta^{r-1}$ is an integer, if $\alpha^{r-2} + \beta^{r-2}$ is an integer. Setting r = r–1 in (3), we find $\alpha^{r-2} + \beta^{r-2}$ is an integer this way, we get that $\alpha^2 + \beta^2$ is an integer if $\alpha + \beta$ is an integer. But $\alpha + \beta = p + 1$ is an integer.

Hence, $\alpha^2 + \beta^2$ is an integer, $\alpha^3 + \beta^3$ is an integer . . . . . $\alpha^{r-1} + \beta^{r-1}$ is an integer.

Hence, by mathematical induction, $\alpha^n + \beta^n$ is an integer.

Example 29: *Two finite sets have m and n elements. The total number of subsets of the first set is 56 more than the total number of subsets of the second set. Find the values of m and n.*

Solution: Let A and B be two sets having m and n elements respectively. Then,

Number of subsets of A = 2^m,

Number of subsets of B = 2^n,

It is given that $2^m - 2^n = 56$

$\Rightarrow$ $2^n(2^{m-n} - 1) = 2^3(2^3 - 1)$

$\Rightarrow$ n = 3 and m – n = 3

$\Rightarrow$ n = 3 and m = 6.

Examples 30: *The necessary and sufficient condition for a set Y to be a subset of X is that $X \cup Y = X$.*

Solution:

Let $Y \subset X$, then

$$x \in Y \Rightarrow x \in X \quad ...(i)$$

Now, $x \in X \cup Y \Rightarrow x \in X \text{ or } x \in Y$

$$\Rightarrow x \in X$$

$\therefore \quad X \cup Y \subset X$ ...(ii)

Also, we know that

$X \subset X \cup Y$ ...(iii)

(ii) and (iii) $\Rightarrow X \cup Y = X$.

Conversely,

if $\quad X \cup Y = X$, we have to prove that $Y \subset X$.

Now, $\quad X \cup Y = X \Rightarrow X \cup Y \subset X$

and $\quad X \subset X \cup Y$

$\Rightarrow \quad X \cup Y \subset X$

$\Rightarrow \quad X \subset X$ and $Y \subset X$

$\Rightarrow \quad Y \subset X$.

Example 31: *Prove that the operation* $*$ *on the set Z of all integers defined by* $a * b = a + b + 1 \ \forall a, b \in Z$ *satisfies the closure property the associativity and the commutativity. Find the identity element. What is the inverse of an integer a?*

Solution: For all integers a and b, $a \in b \in I \Rightarrow a + b + 1 \in I$ and therefore $a * b$ is clearly an integer. So, closure property is satisfied.

Also, $(a * b) * c = (a + b) * c \Rightarrow (a + b + 1)* c$

$\Rightarrow (a + b + 1) + c + 1 \Rightarrow a + b + c + 2$

and $\quad a * (b * c) = a * (b + c + 1)$

$= a + (b + c + 1) + 1 = (a + b + c) + 2$

$\therefore \quad (a * b) * c = a * (b * c)$ " a, b, c $\in Z$.

Thus, the associative law is satisfied.

Similarly, commutative law can be established.

Now, if e is the identity element in Z for $*$, then

$$a * e = a \Rightarrow a + e + 1 = a \Rightarrow e = -1.$$

So, -1 is the identity for $*$ in Z.

Also, $\quad a * b = -1 \Rightarrow a + b + 1 = -1$

$\Rightarrow b - (2 + a)$.

So, the inverse of a is $-(2 + a)$.

Examples 32: *In a certain examination, the candidates can offer papers in English or Hindi or both the subjects. The number of candidates* *who appeared in the examination is 1000 of whom 650 appeared in English and 200 appeared in both English and Hindi. Find :*

(i) The number of candidates who offered paper in Hindi.

(ii) The number of candidates who offered paper in English only.

(iii) The number of candidates who offered paper in Hindi only.

Solution: Let A = The set of candidates who offered paper in English

B = The set of candidates who offered paper in Hindi.

Therefore, $n(A \cup B) = 1000$, $n(A) = 650$, $n(A \cap B) = 200$.

(i) We have

$$n(A \cup B) = n(A) + n(B) - n(A \cap B)$$

$$\Rightarrow \quad 1000 = 650 + n(B) - 200$$

$$\Rightarrow \quad n(B) = 550.$$

$\therefore$ Number of candidates who offered paper in Hindi = 550.

(ii) Now, the set of candidates who offered paper in English only is

$$A - B = \{\text{candidate: candidate} \in A \text{ and candidate} \notin B\}$$

Now, $n(A - B) = n(A) - n(A \cap B)$

$= 650 - 200 = 450.$

Number of candidates who offered paper in English only = 450.

(iii) Similarly, the set of candidates who offered paper in Hindi only is $B - A$.

Now, $n(B - A) = n(B) - n(A \cap B)$

$= 550 - 200 = 350.$

Example 33: *If $a \in N$ such that $aN = \{ax: x \in N\}$. Describe the set $3N \cap 7N$.*

Solution: We have

$$aN = \{ax ; x \in N\}$$

$\therefore \quad 3N = [3x: x \in N\} = \{3, 6, 9, 12, \ldots,\}$

and $\quad 7N = [7x: x \in N\} = \{7, 14, 21, 28, \ldots,\}$

Hence $\quad 3N \cap 7N = \{21, 42, \ldots\}$

$= \{21x: x \in N\} = 21N.$

Example 34: *For any natural number a, we define $aN = \{ax: x \in N\}$. If $b, c, d \in N$ such that $bN \cap cN = dN$, then prove that d is the l.c.m. of b and c.*

Solution: We have

$bN = \{bx: x \in N\}$ = The set of positive integral multiples of b.
$cN = \{cx: x \in N\}$ = The set of positive integral multiples of c.
$\therefore$ $bN \cap cN$ = The set of positive integral multiples of b and c both.
$\Rightarrow$ $bN \cap cN = \{kx: x \in N\}$, where k is the *l*.c.m. of b and c.

Hence, d = *l*.c.m of b and c.

Examples 35: *Let A, B, C be three sets then*

$$(A - B) \cap (A - C) = A - (B \cup C)$$

Solution: Let $x \in (A - B) \cap (A - C)$ then

$$\begin{aligned} x \in (A - B) \cap (A - C) &\Leftrightarrow x \in (A - B) \text{ and } x \in (A - C) \\ &\Leftrightarrow x \in A, x \notin B \text{ and } x \in A, x \notin C \\ &\Leftrightarrow x \in A, x \notin B \text{ and } x \notin C \\ &\Leftrightarrow x \in A, x \notin B \cup C \\ &\Leftrightarrow x \in A - (B \cup C) \end{aligned}$$

Which implies that $(A - B) \cap (A - C) = A - (B \cup C)$.

RELATIONS

Basic Definitions

We introduced the concept of the Cartesian product of sets. Let's assume that a person owns three shirts and two pairs os slacks. More precisely, let A = {blue shirt, tan shirt, mint green shirt} and B = {grey slacks, tan slacks}. Then certainly $A \times B$ is the set of all possible combinations (six) of shirts and slacks that the individual can weal. However, the individual may wish to restrict himself or herself to combinations which are color coordinated, or "related". This may not be all possible pairs in $A \times B$ but will certainly be a subset of $A \times B$. For example, one such subset may be {(blue shirt, grey slacks), (blue shirt, tan slacks), (mint green shirt, tan slacks)}.

Definition: Relation. *Let A and B be set. A relation from A into B is any subset of* $A \times B$.

In other words, let A and B be two sets. A relation from A to B is a subset of $A \times B$. *Symbolically, R is a relation from A to B iff* $R \subset A \times B$.

If (x, y) be a member of a relation set R, we express it by writing x R y and say that 'x is in the relation R to y'. Thus

$$(x, y) \in R \Leftrightarrow x\, R\, y.$$

For example, if A = {2, 3, 5, 6} and R means 'divides' then

2R2, 2R6, 3R3, 3R6, 5R5, 6R6 and as such relation set R = {(2, 2), (2, 6), (3, 3) (3, 6), (5, 5), (6, 6)}.

Furthermore if I be the set of all integers, the statement "x is less than y where x, y ∈ I" determines a relation in I. If we denote this relation by R, then we may describe the set R in the set builder notation as given below.

$$R = \{(x, y) : x, y \in I, x < y\}$$

Example 1: *Let A = {1, 2, 3} and B = {4, 5}. Then {(1, 4), (2, 4), (3, 5)} is a relation from A into B. Of course, there are many others we could describe; 64, to be exact.*

Example 2: *Let A = {2, 3, 5, 6} and define a relation r from A into A by (a, b) Î r if and only if a divides evenly into b. So r = {(2, 2), (3, 3), (5, 5), (6, 6), (2, 6), (3, 6)}.*

The word relation is not unfamiliar even to a child. He is aware of his various relations with family members. As he grows up he comes across the other types of relations also, *e.g.* relation between money and its purchasing power, relation of education with school etc. The description of relation in above language is very vague. Here we shall try to define and describe relation in the precise language of mathematics.

First we shall restrict ourselves only to the relations between only two objects. The relations which associate only two objects are known as *'Binary relation'*. Below we give a mathematical definition of a relation.

GRAPHS OF RELATIONS

In this section we will give a brief explanation of procedures for graphing a relation. A graph is nothing more than an illustration that gives us, at a glance, a clearer idea of the situation under consideration. A road map indicates where we have been and how to proceed to reach our destination. A flow chart helps us to zero in on the procedures to be followed to code a problem. The graph of the function y = 2x + 3 in algebra helps us to understand how the function behaves. Indeed, it tells us that the graph of this function is a straight line. The pictures of relations in the previous section gave us an added insight into what a relation is. They indicated that there are several different ways of graphing relations. We will investigate two additional methods.

Example 1: *Let A = {0, 1, 2, 3}, and let r be the relation {(0, 0), (0, 3), (1, 2), (2, 1), (3, 2), (2, 0)}. The elements of A are called the vertices of the graph. Place the vertices, enclosed in a circle or denoted by a point. Connect vertex a to vertex b with an arrow, called an edge of the graph, going from vertex a to vertex b if and only if a r b. This type of graph of a relation r is called a directed graph or digraph.*

The actual locations of the vertices is immaterial. The main idea is to place the vertices in such a way that the graph is easy to read, a help to you.

Obviously, after a rough draft graph of a relation, we may decide to relocate and or order the vertices so that the final result will be neater Figure 6.2.1. could be presented as in Figure 6.2.2.

A vertex of a graph is also called a *node, a point, or a junction.* An edge of a graph is also referred to as an *are a line, or a branch.* Do not be concerned if two graphs of a even relation look different. It is nontrivial problem to determine if two graphs are graphs of the same relation.

Example 2: *Consider the relation s whose digraph is Figure 6.2.3. What information does this give us? Certainly we know that s is a relation of a set A, where A = {1, 2, 3} and s = {(1, 2), (2, 1), (1, 3), (3, 1), (2, 3), (3, 3)}.*

Example 3: *Let B = {a, b}, and let A = ϕ (B) = {ϕ, {a}, {b}, {a, b}}. Then $\subseteq$ is a relation on A.*

This digraph is helpful insofar as it reminds us that each set is a subset of itself (How?) and shows us at a glance the relationship between the various subsets in ϕ (B).

Some relations, such as this one, can also be conveniently depicted by what is called a *Hasse, or ordering diagram.* To read a Hasse diagram for a relation on a set A, remember:

(1) Each vertex of A must be related to itself, so the arrows from a vertex to itself are not necessary.

(2) If vertex b appears above vertex a and if vertex a is connected to vertex b by an edge, then a r b, so direction arrows are not necessary.

(3) If vertex c is above vertex a and if c is connected to a by a sequence of edges, then a r c.

(4) The vertices (or nodes) are denoted by *points* rather than by "circles".

Example 4: *Consider the relation s whose Hasse diagram is Figure 6.2.6. How do we read this diagram? What is A? What does the digraph of s look like? Certainly A = {a, b, c, d, e} and a s c, c s d, a s, d, a s e, etc. so*

$$s = \{(a, a), (b, b), (c, c), (d, d), (e, e), (a, c),$$
$$(a, d), (a, e), (a, b), (c, d), (c, e), (d, e), (b, e)\}$$

PROPERTIES OF RELATIONS

Consider the set B = {1, 2, 3, 4, 6, 12, 36, 48} and the relations "divides" and $\leq$ on B. We notice that these two relations on B have several properties in common. In fact:

(1) Every element in B divides itself and is less than or equal to itself. This is called the *reflexive property.*

(2) If we search for "two" element from B where the first divides the second and the second divides the first, then we are forced to choose the same first and second number. The reader can verify that a similar result is true for the relation $\leq$ on B. This is called the antisymmetric property.

(3) Next if we choose three numbers from B such that the first divides (or is $\leq$) the second and the second divides (or is $\leq$) the third, then this forces the first number to divide (or be $\leq$) the third. This is called the *transitive property.*

Sets on which relations are defined which satisfy the above properties are of special interest to us. More detailed definitions follow.

Example 1: *Let A be a set. Then ϕ (A) together with the relation $\subseteq$ is a poset. To prove this we show that the three properties hold:*

(1) Let $B \in \phi$ (A). We must show that $B \subseteq B$. This is true by definition of subset. Hence, the relation is reflexive.

(2) Let B_1, B_2, $\in \phi$ (A) and assume (Why?) that $B_1 \subseteq B_1$ and $B_1 \neq B_1$. Could it be that $B_2 \subseteq B_1$? No. Why? Hence, the relation is antisymmetric.

(3) Let B_1, B_2, $B_3 \in \phi$ (A) and assume that $B_1 \subseteq B_2$ and $B_2 \subseteq B_3$. Does it follow that $B_1 \subseteq B_3$? Yes. Hence, the relation is transitive.

Example 2: *Consider the relation s defined by the Hasse diagram in Figure 6.2.6. A relation defined by a Hasse diagram is always a partial ordering. Let's convince ourselves of this.*

(1) First, s is reflexive. If this is not clear draw the digraph of the above relation.

(2) Next, s is antisymmetric. From the diagram, can we find two different elements, say c_1 and c_2, such that c_2 s c_1 and c_1 s c_2? No. If this argument is not clear, try the following: From the diagram find "two" elements such that the first is related through s to the second and the second is related to the first. The only elements that work are pairs of identical elements.

(3) Finally, s is transitive. How do we show that? We must show that for any three elements chosen such that the first, is related to the second and the second is related to the third, ten the first must be related to the third. Consider, for example, the three elements c, d and e. From the diagram, c s d and d s e, so the hypothesis is satisfied. We

must show that c s e. This is true from the diagram. How? If this is not clear, the diagraph of s may be helpful. Does this one example show transitivity?

Another property that is frequently referred to is that of symmetry.

MATRICES OF RELATIONS

We have discussed two of the many possible ways of representing a relation, namely as a digraph or as a set of ordered pairs. In the exercise of Section 6.3. We mentioned a third, that is , as a linked list. In this section we will discuss the representation of relations by matrices and some of its applications.

Example:

If $$R = \begin{bmatrix} 0 & 1 & 0 & 0 \\ 1 & 0 & 1 & 0 \\ 0 & 1 & 0 & 1 \\ 0 & 0 & 1 & 0 \end{bmatrix} \text{ and } S = \begin{bmatrix} 0 & 1 & 1 & 1 \\ 0 & 0 & 1 & 1 \\ 0 & 0 & 0 & 1 \\ 0 & 0 & 0 & 0 \end{bmatrix},$$

then $$RS = \begin{bmatrix} 0 & 0 & 1 & 1 \\ 0 & 1 & 1 & 1 \\ 0 & 0 & 1 & 1 \\ 0 & 0 & 0 & 1 \end{bmatrix} \text{ and } SR = \begin{bmatrix} 1 & 1 & 1 & 1 \\ 0 & 1 & 1 & 1 \\ 0 & 0 & 1 & 0 \\ 0 & 0 & 0 & 0 \end{bmatrix},$$ *using Boolean arithmetic.*

DOMAIN AND RANGE OF A RELATION

Let R be a relation from A to B. Then the set of all first co-ordinates of the members of the relation set R is called the *domain* of R and the set of all second members of R is called the *range* of R. Thus

$$\text{Domain } R = \{x : (x, y) \in R\}$$

$$\text{Range } R = \{y : (x, y) \in R\}\ .$$

Fore example if A = {1, 2, 3, 4}, B = {3, 4, 5}, then

$$A \times B = \{(1, 3), (1, 4), (1, 5). (2, 3), (2, 4)$$
$$(2, 5), (3, 3), (3, 4). (3, 5), (4, 3)$$
$$(4, 4), (4, 5)\}.$$

Now, if R stands for 'less than', then relation set

$$R = \{(1, 3), (1, 4), (1, 5). (2, 3), (2, 4)$$
$$(2, 5), (3, 4). (3, 5), (4, 5).$$

Domain R = set of first co-ordinates of ordered pairs in the relation set = {1, 2, 3, 4}

Range R = set of second co-ordinates of ordered pairs in the relation set = {3, 4, 5}

COMPOSITION OF RELATIONS

Let A, B, and C be sets, and let R be a relation from A to B and let S be a relation from B to C. Obviously, R is a subset of A × B and S is a subset of B × C. Then R and S give rise to a relation from A to C denoted by RoS and defined by

a (RoS) c if for some b ∈ B we have a R b and b S c.

Symbolically :

$$RoS = \{(a, c) : \forall\ b \in B \text{ for which } (a, b) \in R \text{ and } (b, c) \in S\}$$

Relation RoS is called the *composition of* R and S. It is sometimes denoted as RS.

Let R is a relation on a set A. Then RoR, the composition of R with itself is always defined, and is sometimes denoted by R^2. Similarly, $R^3 = R^2oR$ = RoRoR and so on. Thus R^n is defined for all positive n.

Theorem:

Let A, B, C and D be sets. Suppose R is a relation from A to B, S is a relation from B to C and T is a relation from C to D. Then show that

$$(RoS)\ oT = Ro\ (SoT)$$

Proof:

Here, we need to show than each ordered pair in (RoS) oT belongs to Ro (SoT) and vice versa.

Let (a, d) belongs to (RoS) oT.

Then, there exists a c in C such than (a, c) ∈ RoS and (c, d) ∈ T.

Since (a, c) ∈ RoS, there exists a b in B such that (a, b) ∈ R and (b, c) ∈ S.

Since (b, c) ∈ S and (c, d) ∈ T,

we have (b, d) ∈ SoT.

Again, since (a, b) ∈ R and (b, d) ∈ SoT,

we have (a, d) ∈ Ro (SoT).

Therefore, (RoS) oT $\subset$ Ro (SoT) . . . (1)

Similarly, Ro (SoT) $\subset$ (RoS) oT . . . (2)

From (1) and (2), we get

Ro (SoT) = (RoS) oT.

TOTAL NUMBER OF RELATIONS

Let A and B be two non-empty finite sets consisting of m and n elements respectively. Then A × B consists of mn ordered pairs, So, total number of subsets of A × B is 2^{mn}.

Since each subset of A × B defines a relation from A to B, so total number of relations from A to B is 2^{mn}. Among these 2^{mn} relations the void relation ϕ and the universal relation A × B are trivial relations from A to B.

Relation on a Set : Let A be a non-void set. Then, a relation of A × A, is called relation on set A.

Inverse Relation : Let A, B be two sets and let R be a relation from a set A to a set B. Then the inverse of R, denoted by R^{-1}, is a relation from B to A and is defined by

$$R^{-1} = \{(b, a) : (a, b) \in R\}.$$

Clearly, $(a, b) \in R \Leftrightarrow (b, a) \in R^{-1}$

Also Dom (R) = Range (R^{-1}) and

Range (R) = Dom (R^{-1}).

TYPES OF RELATIONS

Void Relation : Let A be as set. Then $\phi \subset A \times A$ *and so it is a relation on A. This relation is called the void or empty relation on A.*

Universal Relation : Let A be a set. Then A × A $\subset$ A × A and so it is a relation on A. This relation is called the *universal relation* on A.

Note: Void and the universal relations on a set A are respectively the smallest and the largest relations on A.

Identity Relation : Let A be a set. Then the relation $I_A = \{(a, a) : a \in A\}$ on A is called the *identity relation* on A.

Obviously, the relation I_A on A is called the identity relation if every element of A is related to itself only.

Reflexive Relation : *A relation R on a set A is said to be reflexive if every element of A is related to itself.* Thus, R is reflexive $\Leftrightarrow (a, a) \in R$ for all $a \in A$.

A relation R on a set A is not reflexive if there exists an element a ∈ A such that (a, a) ∉ R.

Example:

(i) The universal relation on a non-void set A is reflexive.

(ii) The relation R on N defined by (x, y) ∈ R ⇔ x ≥ y is a reflexive relation on N, because every natural number is greater than or equal to itself.

Symmetric Relation : *A relation R on a set A is said to be a symmetric relation iff (a, b)* ∈ *R* ⇒ *(b, a)* ∈ R for all a, b ∈ A.

i.e. a R b ⇒ b R a for all a, b ⇒ A.

Example:

(i) The identity and the universal relation on a non-void set are symmetric relations.

(ii) Let L be the set of all lines in a plane and let R be a relation defined on L by the rule (x, y) ∈ R ⇔ x is perpendicular to y. Then R is a symmetric relation on L, because $L_1 \perp L_2 \Rightarrow L_2 \perp L_1$, *i.e.*, $(L_1, L_2) \in R \Rightarrow (L_2, L_1) \in R$.

Note: A relation R on set A is not a symmetric relation if there are at least two elements a, b ∈ A such that (a, b) ∈ R but (b, a) ∉ R.

Transitive Relation : *Let A be any set. A relation R on A is said to be a transitive relation iff (a, b)* ∈ *R and (b, c)* ∈ *R* ⇒ *(a ,c)* ∈ *R for all a, b, c* ∈ *R,*

i.e. a R b and b R c

⇒ *a R c for all a, b, c,* ∈ *A.*

Example:

(i) The relation R on the set N of all natural numbers defined by (x, y) ∈ R ⇔ x divides y, for all x, y ∈ N is transitive.

(ii) On the set N of natural numbers, the relation R defined by x R y ⇒ x is less than y is transitive, because for any x, y, z ∈ N

$x < y$ and $y < z \Rightarrow x < z \Rightarrow$

x R y and y R z ⇒ x R z.

Antisymmetric Relation : *Let A be any set. A relation R on set A is said to be an antisymmetric relation iff*

(a, b) ∈ *R and (b, a)* ∈ R

⇒ a = b for all a, b ∈ A.

Examples:

(i) The identity relation on a set A is an antisymmetric relation.

(ii) Let R be a relation on the set N of natural numbers defined by

$x \, R \, y \Leftrightarrow$ 'x divides y' for all $x, y \in N$.

This relation is an antisymmetric relation on N. Since for any two numbers $a, b \in N$

$$a \mid b \text{ and } b \mid a \Rightarrow a = b, \textit{ i.e.}, a \, R \, b$$

$$\text{and } b \, R \, a \Rightarrow a = b.$$

Note: If $(a, b) \in R$ and $(b, a) \notin R$, then also R is an antisymmetric relation.

Equivalence Relation : *A relation R on a set A is said to be an equivalence relation on A iff*

(i) it is reflexive, i.e. $(a, a) \in R$ for all $a \in A$.

(i) it is symmetric, i.e. $(a, b) \in R \Rightarrow (b, a) \in R$ for all $a, b \in A$.

(i) it is transitive, i.e. $(a, b) \in R$ and $(b, c) \in R \Rightarrow (a, c) \in R$ for all $a, b, c, \in A$.

PARTITIONS AND EQUIVALENCE RELATIONS

In the first part of this section we consider a non-empty set X, and we study decompositions of X into non-empty subsets which fill it out and have no elements in common with one another. We give special attention to the tools (equivalence relations) which are normally used to generate such decompositions.

A *partition* of X is a disjoint class $\{X_i\}$ of non-empty subsets of X whose union is the full set X itself. The X_i's are called the *partition sets.* Expressed somewhat differently, a partition of X is the result of splitting it, or subdividing it, into non-empty subsets in such a way that each element of X belongs to one and only one of the given subsets.

If X is the set {1, 2, 3, 4, 5}, then {1, 3, 5}, {2, 4} and {1, 2, 3}, {4, 5} are two different partitions of X. If X is the set R of all real numbers, then we can partition X into the set of all rationals and the set of all irrationals, or into the infinitely many closed-open intervals of the form [n, n + 1) where n is an integer. If X is the set of all points in the coordinate plane, then we can partition X in such a way that each partition set consists of all points with the same x coordinate (vertical lines), or so that each partition set consists of all points with the same y coordinate (horizontal lines).

Other partitions of each of these sets will readily occur to the reader. In general, there are many different ways in which any given set can be partitioned. These manufactured examples are admittedly rather uninspiring and serve only to make our ideas more concrete. Later in this section we consider some others which are more germane to our present purposes.

A *binary relation* in the set X is a mathematical symbol or verbal phrase, which we denote by R in this paragraph, such that for each ordered pair (x, y) of elements of X the statement x R y is meaningful, in the sense that it can be classified definitely as true or false. For such a binary relation, x R y symbolizes the assertion that x is related by R to y, and x R y the negation of this, namely, the assertion that x is *not* related by R to y. Many examples of binary relations can be given, some familiar and others less so, some mathematical and others not. For instance, if X is the set of all integers and R is interpreted to mean "is less than," which of course is usually denoted by the symbol $<$, then we clearly have $4 < 7$ and $5 \nless 2$. We have been speaking of binary relations, which are so named because they apply only to ordered pairs of elements, rather than to ordered triples, etc. In our work we drop the qualifying adjective and speak simply of a *relation* in X, since we shall have occasion to consider only relations of this kind.'

We now assume that a partition of our non-empty set X is given, and we associate with this partition a relation in X. This relation is defined in the following way: we say that x is *equivalent* to y and write this $x \sim y$ (the symbol $\sim$ is pronounced "wiggle"), if x and y belong to the same partition set. It is obvious that the relation $\sim$ has the following properties:

(1) $x \sim x$ for every x (reflexivity);

(2) $x \sim y \Rightarrow y \sim x$ (symmetry);

(3) $x \sim y$ and $y \sim z \Rightarrow x \sim z$ (transitivity).

This particular relation in X arose in a special way, in connection with a given partition of X, and its properties are immediate consequences of its definition. Any relation whatever in X which possesses these three properties is called an *equivalence relation* in X.

We have just seen that each partition of X has associated with it a natural equivalence relation in X. We now reverse the situation and show that a given equivalence relation in X determines a natural partition of X.

Let $\sim$ be an equivalence relation in X; that is, assume that it is reflexive, symmetric, and transitive in the sense described above. If x is an element of X, the subset of X defined by $[x] = \{y : y \sim x\}$ is called the *equivalence set* of x. The equivalence set of x is thus the set of all elements which are equivalent to x. We show that the class of all distinct equivalence sets forms a partition of X. By reflexivity, x ε [x] for each element x in X, so each equivalence set is non-empty and their union is X.

It remains to be shown that any two equivalence sets [x_1] and [x_2] are either disjoint or identical. We prove this by showing that if [x_1] and [x_2] are not disjoint, then they must be identical. Suppose that [x_1] and [x_2] are not disjoint; that is, suppose that they have a common element z. Since 2 belongs to both equivalence sets, z ~ x_1 and a ~ x_2, and by symmetry, x_1 ~ z. Let y be any element of [x_1], so that y ~ x_1. Since y ~ x_1 and x_i ~ z, transitivity shows that y ~ z. By another application of transitivity, y ~ z and z ~ x_2 imply that y ~ x_2, so that y is in [x_2]. Since y was chosen arbitrarily in [xi], we see by this that [x_1] ⊆ [x_2]. The same reasoning shows that [x_2] ⊆ [x_1], and from this we conclude (see the last paragraph of Sec. 1) that [x_1] = [x_2].

The above discussion demonstrates that there is no real distinction (other than a difference in language) between partitions of a set and equivalence relations in the set. If we start with a partition, we get an equivalence relation by regarding elements as equivalent if they belong to the same partition set, and if we start with an equivalence relation, we get a partition by grouping together into subsets all elements which are equivalent to one another. We have here a single mathematical idea, which we have been considering from two different points of view, and the approach we choose in any particular application depends entirely on our own convenience. In practice, it is almost invariably the case that we use equivalence relations (which are usually easy to define) to obtain partitions (which are sometimes difficult to describe fully).

We now turn to several of the more important simple examples of equivalence relations.

Let I be the set of all integers. If a and b are elements of this set, we write a = b (and say that a *equals* b) if a and 6 are the same integer. Thus, 2 + 3 = 5 means that the expressions on the left and right are simply different ways of writing the same integer. It is apparent that = used in this sense is an equivalence relation in the set I:

(1) a = a for every a;

(2) a = b ⇒ b = a;

(3) a = b and b = c ⇒ a = c.

Clearly, each equivalence set consists of precisely one integer.

Another familiar example is the relation of equality commonly used for fractions. We remind the reader that, strictly speaking, a fraction is merely a symbol of the form a/b , where a and b are integers and b is not zero. The fractions 2/3 and 4/6 are obviously not identical, but nevertheless we consider them to be equal. In general, we say that two fractions a/b and c/d are *equal*, written a/b = c/d, it ad and be are equal as integers in the usual sense (see the above paragraph). We leave it to the reader to show that this is an equivalence relation in the set of all fractions. An equivalence set of fractions is what we call a *rational number*. Everyday usage ignores the distinction between fractions and rational numbers, but it is important to recognize that from the strict point of view it is the rational numbers (and not the fractions) which form part of the real number system.

Our final example has a deeper significance, for it provides us with the basic tool for our work of the next two sections.

For the remainder of this section we consider a relation between pairs of non-empty sets, and each set mentioned (whether we say so explicitly or not) is assumed to be non-empty. If X and Y are two sets, we say that X is *numerically equivalent* to Y if there exists a one-to-one correspondence between X and Y, *i.e.*, if there exists a one-to-one mapping of X onto Y. This relation is reflexive, since the identity mapping $i_x : X \to X$ is one-to-one onto; it is symmetric, since it $f:X \to Y$ is one-to-one onto, then its inverse mapping $f^{-1}: Y \to X$ is also one-to-one onto; and it is transitive, since it $f:X \to Y$ and $g: Y \to Z$ are one-to-one onto, then $gf : X \to Z$ is also one-to-one onto. Numerical equivalence has all the properties of an equivalence relation, and if we consider it as an equivalence relation in the class of all non-empty subsets of some universal set U, it groups together into equivalence sets all those subsets of U ä which have the *same number of elements*. After we state and prove the following very useful but rather technical theorem.

The theorem we have in mind—the *Schroeder-Bernstein theorem*—is the following: if X and Y *are two sets each of which is numerically equivalent to a subset of the other, then all of X is numerically equivalent to all of Y.* There are several proofs of this classic theorem, some of which are quite difficult. The very elegant proof we give is essentially due to Birkhoff and MacLane.

Now for the proof. We assume that $f:X \to Y$ is a one-to-one mapping of X into Y, and that $g : Y \to X$ is a one-to-one mapping of Y into X. Our task is to produce a mapping $F:X \to Y$ which is one-to-one onto. We may assume that neither f nor g is onto, since if f is, we can define F to be f, and if g is, we can define F to be g^{-1}. Since both f and g are one-to-one, it is permissible to use the mappings f^{-1} and g^{-1} as long as we clearly understand that f^{-1} is defined only on f(X) and g^{-1} only on g(Y). We obtain the mapping F by splitting both X and Y into subsets which we characterize in terms of the ancestry of their elements. Let x be an element of X. We apply g^{-1} to it (if we can) to get the element $g^{-1}(x)$ in Y. If $g^{-1}(x)$ exists, we call it the first ancestor of x. The element x itself we call the zeroth ancestor of x. We now apply f^{-1} to $g^{-1}(x)$ if we can, and if $(f^{-1}g^{-1})(x)$ exists, we call it the second ancestor of x. We now apply g^{-1} to $(f^{-1}g^{-1})(x)$ it we can, and if $(g^{-1}f^{-1}g^{-1})(x)$ exists, we call it the third ancestor of x. As we continue this process of tracing back the ancestry of x, it becomes apparent that there are three possibilities.

(1) x has infinitely many ancestors. We denote by X_i the subset of X which consists of all elements with infinitely many ancestors.

(2) x has an even number of ancestors; this means that x has a last ancestor (that is, one which itself has no first ancestor) in X. We denote by X_e the subset of X consisting of all elements with an even number of ancestors.

(3) x has an odd number of ancestors; this means that x has a last ancestor in Y. We denote by X_o the subset of X which consists of all elements with an odd number of ancestors. The three sets X_i, X_e, X_o form a disjoint class whose union is X. We decompose Y in just the same way into three subsets Y_i, Y_e, Y_o. It is easy to see that f maps X_i onto Y_i and Xe onto Y_o, and that g^{-1} maps X_o onto Y_e; and we complete the proof by defining F in the following piecemeal manner:

$$F(x) = \begin{cases} f(x) & \text{if } x \in X_i \cup X_e, \\ g^{-1}(x) & \text{if } x \in X_o, \end{cases}$$

CLOSURE OPERATIONS ON RELATIONS

In Section 6.1., we studied relations and one important operation on relations, namely composition. This operation enabled us to generated new relations from previously known relations. In Section 6.3, we discussed some key properties of relations. We now wish to consider the situation of constructing a new relations r from a previously known relation r where, first r contains r and, second r satisfies the transitive property.

Consider a telephone network in which the main office a is connected to, and can communicate to, individuals b and c. Both b and c can communicate to another person, d; however, the main office cannot communicate with d. Assume communication is only one way, as indicated. This situation can be described by the relation r = {(a, b), (a, c), (b, d), (c, d)}. We would like to change the system so that the main office a can communicate with person d and still maintain the previous system. We, of course, want the most economical system.

This can be rephrased as follows: Find the smallest relation r^+ which contains r as a subset and which is transitive; $r^+ = \{(a, b), (a, c), (b, d), (c, d), (a,d)\}$.

Definition: Transitive Closure. *Let A be a set and r be a relation on A. The transitive closure of r, denoted by r^+, is the smallest relation which contains r as a subset and which is transitive.*

Example 1: *Let $A = \{1, 2, 3, 4\}$, and let $S = \{(1, 2), (2, 3), (3, 4)\}$ be a relation on A. This relation is called the successor relation on A since each element is related to its successor. How do we compute S^+?*

By inspection we note that (1, 3) must be in S^+. Let's analyze why. This is so since $(1, 2) \in S$ and $(2, 3) \in S$, and the transitive property forces (1, 3) to be in S^+. In general, it follows that if $(a, b) \in S$ and $(b, c) \in S$, then $(a, c) \in S^+$. This condition is exactly the membership requirement for the pair (a, c) to be in the composition $SS = S^2$. So every element in S^2 must be an element in S^+. So far S^+ contains at least $S \cup S^2$. In particular, for this example, since $S = \{(1, 2), (2, 3), (3, 4)\}$ and $S^2 = \{(1, 3), (2, 4)\}$, we have $S \cup S^2 = \{(1, 2), (2, 3), (3, 4), (1, 3), (2, 4)\}$.

Is the relation $S \cup S^2$ transitive? Again, by inspection (1, 4) is not an element of $S \cup S^2$, but it must be an element of S^+ since (1, 3) and (3, 4) are required to be in S^+. From above, $(1, 3) \in S^2$ and $(3, 4) \in S$, and the composite $S^2S = S^3$ produces (1, 4).

This shows that $S^3 \subseteq S^+$. This process must be continued until the resulting relation is transitive. If A is finite, as is true in this example, the transitive closure will be obtained in a finite number of steps. Here, $S^+ = S \cup S^2 \cup S^3$.

Theorem 1:

If S is a relation on a set A and if #A = n, then the transitive closure $S^+ = S \cup S^2 \cup S^2 \cup \ldots \cup S^n$.

Let's now consider the matrix analogue of the transitive closure.

Example 2: *Consider the relation $r = \{(1, 4), (2, 1), (2, 2), (2, 3), (3, 2), (4, 3), (4, 5), (5, 1)\}$ on the set $A = \{1, 2, 3, 4, 5\}$. The matrix R of r is*

$$\begin{bmatrix} 0 & 0 & 0 & 1 & 0 \\ 1 & 1 & 1 & 0 & 0 \\ 0 & 1 & 0 & 0 & 0 \\ 0 & 0 & 1 & 0 & 1 \\ 1 & 0 & 0 & 0 & 0 \end{bmatrix}.$$

Recall that $r^2, r^3, \ldots$ can be determined through computing the matrices $R^2, \ldots$ Here,

$$R^2 = \begin{bmatrix} 0 & 0 & 1 & 0 & 1 \\ 1 & 1 & 1 & 1 & 0 \\ 1 & 1 & 1 & 0 & 0 \\ 1 & 1 & 0 & 0 & 0 \\ 0 & 0 & 0 & 1 & 0 \end{bmatrix}, \; R^3 = \begin{bmatrix} 1 & 1 & 0 & 0 & 0 \\ 1 & 1 & 1 & 1 & 1 \\ 1 & 1 & 1 & 1 & 0 \\ 1 & 1 & 1 & 1 & 0 \\ 0 & 0 & 1 & 0 & 1 \end{bmatrix}$$

$$R^4 = \begin{bmatrix} 1 & 1 & 1 & 1 & 0 \\ 1 & 1 & 1 & 1 & 1 \\ 1 & 1 & 1 & 1 & 1 \\ 1 & 1 & 1 & 1 & 1 \\ 1 & 1 & 0 & 0 & 0 \end{bmatrix}, \text{ and } R^5 = \begin{bmatrix} 1 & 1 & 1 & 1 & 1 \\ 1 & 1 & 1 & 1 & 1 \\ 1 & 1 & 1 & 1 & 1 \\ 1 & 1 & 1 & 1 & 1 \\ 1 & 1 & 1 & 1 & 0 \end{bmatrix}$$

How do we related $\bigcup_{i=i}^{5} r^i$ to the powers of R?

Theorem 2:

Let R^+ be the matrix of r^+, the transitive closure of r, which is a relation on a set of n elements. Then $R^+ = R + R^2 + \ldots + R^r$, where addition is done using Boolean arithmetic.

Using this theorem, we find R^+ is the 5×5 matrix consisting of all 1's thus, r^+ is all of $A \times A$.

SOME THEOREMS ON EQUIVALENCE RELATIONS

Theorem 1:

The union of two equivalence relations on a set is not necessarily an equivalence relation on the set.

Proof:

Let A = {a, b, c} and let R and S be two relations on A, given by

R = {(a, a), (b, b), (c, c), (a, b), (b, a)}

and S = {(a, a), (b, b), (c, c), (b, c), (c, b)}

It can be easily seen that each one of R and S is an equivalence relation on A. But $R \cup S$ is not transitive, because $(a, b) \in R \cup S$ and $(b, c) \in R \cup S$ but $(a, c) \notin R \cup S$. Hence, $R \cup S$ is not an equivalence relation on A.

Theorem 2:

If R is an equivalence relation on a set A, then R^{-1} is also an equivalence relation on A.

Or

The inverse of an equivalence relation is an equivalence relation.

Proof:

Since R is a relation on A. So, $R \subset A \times A \Rightarrow R^{-1} \subset A \times A \Rightarrow R^{-1}$ is also a relation on A.

Now, we shall show that R^{-1} is an equivalence relation on A.

Reflexivity : Let a be an arbitrary element of A. Then.

$a \in A \Rightarrow (a, a) \in R$ $(\because$ R is reflexive)

$\Rightarrow (a, a) \in R^{-1}$

Thus, $(a, a) \in R^{-1}$ for all $a \in A$. So, R^{-1} is reflexive on A.

Symmetry : Let $(a, b) \in R^{-1}$, Then

$(a, b) \in R^{-1} \Rightarrow (b, a) \in R$ (By def. of R^{-1})

$\Rightarrow (a, b) \in R$ $(\because$ R is symmetric)

$\Rightarrow (b, a) \in R^{-1}$ (By def. of R^{-1})

Thus, $(a, b) \in R^{-1}$

$\Rightarrow (b, a) \in R^{-1}$ for all $a, b \in A$, So, R^{-1} is symmetric on A.

Transitivity : Let $(a, b) \in R^{-1}$

and $(b, c) \in R^{-1}$. Then

$(a, b) \in R^{-1}$ and $(b, c) \in R^{-1}$

$\Rightarrow (b, a) \in R$ and $(c, b) \in R$ (By def. of R^{-1})

$\Rightarrow (c, b) \in R$ and $(b, a) \in R$

$\Rightarrow (c, a) \in R$ $(\because$ R is transitive)

$\Rightarrow (a, c) \in R^{-1}$ (By def. of R^{-1})

Thus, $(a, b) \in R^{-1}$ and $(b, c) \in R^{-1}$

$\Rightarrow (a, c) \in R^{-1}$ for all a, b, c, $\in$ A. So R^{-1} is transitive on A.

Hence, R^{-1} is an equivalence relation on A.

Theorem 3:

If R and S are two equivalence relations on a set A then $R \cap S$ is also an equivalence relation on A.

Or

The intersection of two equivalence relations on a set is an equivalence relation on the set.

Proof:

It is given that R and S are relations on set A.

$\therefore \quad R \subset A \times A$ and $S \subset A \times A$

$\Rightarrow \quad R \cap S \subset A \times A$

$\Rightarrow \quad R \cap S$ is also a relation on A.

Now, we shall show that it is an equivalence relation on A.

We observe the following properties:

Reflexivity : Let a be an arbitrary element of A. Then.

$a \in A \Rightarrow (a, a) \in R$ and $(a, a) \in S$ [$\because$ R and S are reflexive]

$\Rightarrow (a, a) \in R \cap S$

Thus, $(a, a) \in R \cap S$ for all $a \in A$, so, $R \cap S$ is a reflexive relation on A.

Symmetry : Let a, b, $\in$ A such that $(a, b) \in R \cap S$. Then

$(a, b) \in R \cap S \Rightarrow (a, b) \in R$ and $(a, b) \in S$

$\Rightarrow (b, a) \in R$ and $(b, a) \in S$

($\because$ R and S are symmetric)

$\Rightarrow (b, a) \in R \cap S$.

Thus, $(a, b) \in R \cap S \Rightarrow (b, a) \in R \cap S$ for all $(a, b) \in R \cap S$. So, $R \cap S$ is symmetric an A.

Transitivity : Let a, b, c $\in$ A such that $(a, b) \in R \cap S$ and $(b, c) \in R \cap S$. Then, $(a, b) \in R \cap S$ and $(b, c) \in R \cap S$.

$\Rightarrow \{(a, b) \in R$ and $(a, b) \in S)\}$ and $\{(b, c) \in R$ and $(b, c) \in S)\}$

$\Rightarrow \{(a, b) \in R$ and $(b, c) \in R)\}$ and $\{(a, b) \in S$ and $(b, c) \in S)\}$

$\Rightarrow (a, c) \in R$ and $(a, c) \in S$

($\because$ R and S are transitive, so, $(a, b) \in R$ and $(b, c) \in R \Rightarrow (a, c) \in R$)

$\Rightarrow (a, c) \in R \cap S$

Thus, $\quad (a, b) \in R \cap S$ and $(b, c) \in R \cap S$

$\Rightarrow (a, c) \in R \cap S$. So, $R \cap S$ is transitive on A.

Hence, $R \cap S$ is an equivalence relation on A.

CLOSURE PROPERTIES

Let A is a set. Consider the collection of all relations on A. Let P be a property of such relations such as being symmetric or being transitive. A relation with property P will be called a P-relation.

P will be called *R-closable* if P satisfies the following two conditions.

(i) There is a P-relation S containing R.

(ii) The intersection of P-relations is a P-relation.

P-closure of an arbitrary relation R on A, written P (R), is a P-relation such that,

$$R \subseteq P(R) \subseteq S.$$

Reflexive, Symmetric and Transitive Closures : Let $\Delta_A = \{(a, a) : a \in A\}$ is the equality relation on A. Let R be a relation on set A, then.

(i) $R \cup R^{-1}$ is symmetric closure of R

(ii) $R \cup \Delta_A$ is reflexive closure of R.

(iii) $R^* = \bigcup_{i=1}^{\infty} R^i$ is the transitive closure of R.

EQUIVALENCE CLASSES

Let A be any non-empty set and let R be an equivalence relation in A. Further let a be an arbitrary element of A for which a R b, is known as equivalence class of a. We shall denote this equivalence class by [a] or $\bar{a}$. Evidently *an equivalence class is a subset of the given set, such that any two elements on it are equivalent to each other.*

Some authors denote the equivalence class of a determined by a relation R in A by the symbol a/R. The set of all equivalence classes will be denoted by A/R and read as *"A modulo R". This* is called the quotient set of A by R.

Thus the set of all disjoint equivalence classes defined by an equivalence relation R over a set A is called the Quotient set of A relative to R and also denoted by $\bar{A}$.

Example: Let A be the set of all triangles in a plane and let R be an equivalence relation in A defined by "x is congruent to y", x, y ∈ A. When x ∈ A we shall mean by the equivalence class [x] the set of all triangles of A congruent to the triangle x. Similarly, when y ∈ A we shall mean by the equivalence class [y] the set of all triangles of A congruent to the triangle y.

Properties of Equivalence Classes

Let A be non-empty set and let R be an equivalence relation in A. Let x and y be arbitrary element in A. Then

(i) $x \in [x]$,

(ii) If $y \in [x]$, then $[y] = [x]$

(iii) $[x] = [y] \Leftrightarrow (x, y) \in R$ *i.e.* iff x R y.

(iv) Either [x] = [y] or $[x] \cap [y] = \phi$,

i.e. two equivalence classes are either disjoint or identical.

PARTITIONS OF A SET

Let X be a non-empty set. A set P = {A, B, C} of non-empty subsets of X will be called a partition of X if

(i) $A \cup B \cup C \ldots = X$, *i.e.* the set X is the union of the sets in P and

(ii) The intersection of every pair of distinct subsets of $X \in P$ is the null set *i.e.* if A and $B \in P$ then either A = B or $A \cap B = \phi$.

Example: *Consider the set X = {1, 2, ...9, 10} and its subsets* $B_1 = \{1, 3\}$, $B_2 = \{7, 8, 10\}$, $B_3 = \{2, 5, 6\}$, $B_4 = \{4, 9\}$

The set $P = \{B_1, B_2, B_3, B_4\}$ is such that

(i) B_1, B_2, B_3, B_4 are all non-empty subsets of X.

(ii) $B_1 \cup B_2 \cup B_3 \cup B_4 = X$.

(iii) For any sets B_i, $B_i \cap B_j = \phi$.

Hence the set $\{B_1, B_2, B_3, B_4\}$ is a partition of X.

Theorem 1:

An equivalence relation defined in a set de composes the set into disjoint equivalence classes.

Proof:

Let an equivalence relation R be defined in a set S. Let $a \in S$ and T be a subset of S consisting of all those elements which are equivalent to a, *i.e.*

$$T = \{x : x \in S \text{ and } x\,R\,a\}$$

Then $a \in T$, for a R a (R is reflexive).

Any two elements of T are equivalent to each other, for if $x, y \in T$.

Then x R a and y R a.

Again x R a, y R a

$\Rightarrow$ x R a, a R y (R is symmetric)

$\Rightarrow$ x R y (R is transitive)

Thus T is an equivalence class.

Let T_1 be another equivalence class, *i.e.*

$$T_1 = \{x : x \in S \text{ and } x\,R\,b\},$$

where b is not equivalent to a.

Then the class T and T_1 must be disjoint. For if they have a common element s, s R a and s R b, so that b R a which is contrary to our hypothesis.

The set S can now be decomposed into equivalence classes T, T_1, T_2, ... such that every element of S belongs to one of these classes. Since these classes are mutually disjoint, we obtain the required partition of S.

***Theorem 2*:**

If R is an equivalence relation in a non-empty set X, Then the quotient set $X|R$ is a partition of x.

Proof:

Each $x \in X$ must belong to some equivalence class. Also, the equivalence classes are pairwise disjoint, for if $z \in x|R \cap y|R$ then x R z, y R z, Since y R z $\Rightarrow$ z R y, x R z and z R y $\Rightarrow$ x R y, it follows that $x|R$ and $y|R$ must be identical. Hence two equivalence classes are either disjoint or identical. The set of equivalence classes is therefore a *partition.* Further, if x, y be any two members of the some set of this partition, they stand in a relation R to each other, showing that the partition induces the relation R.

Converse : If C be a partition of X, then the induced relation is an equivalence relation whose set of equivalence classes is $X|C$.

PRODUCT OF EQUIVALENCE RELATIONS

Let A, B be two sets and R, S be equivalence relations in A and B respectively.

The relation $R \times S$ in $A \times B$, defined by $(x, y)\ R \times S\ (z, u) \Leftrightarrow x\ R\ z$ and y S u, is an equivalence relation in $A \times B$.

$R \times S$ is called the product of the relations R and S.

Every equivalence class of $A \times B$ is of the form $P \times Q$ where P is an equivalence class of $A \times B$ is of the form $P \times Q$ where P is an equivalence class of X and R and Q is an equivalence class of Y mod S.

TOTALLY ORDERED SET

The word 'partial-order' in the phrase 'partially ordered set' is inclined to emphasize that there may be some elements in a partially ordered set which are uncomparable.

If every two elements of a partially ordered set are comparable then the set A is called a *totally ordered set* or *linearly ordered set or chain, e.g.* the set N with usual order is totally ordered set.

SUBSET OF A PARTIALLY ORDERED SET

Let (A, R) be a partially ordered set and let $B \subset A$ be arbitrary. Then the partial order in A induces a partial order R, in B such that

$$aR'b : a, b \in B \Rightarrow aRb.$$

Then, we say that (B, R') is a subset of a partially ordered set (A, R). Generally the subset of a partially ordered set $(A, \leq)$ is denoted by $(B, \leq)$. *It is clear that any subset of a partially ordered set is a partially ordered set and similar is the case for a linearly ordered set.*

PARTIAL ORDER RELATIONS

A relation $\leq$ on a set A is called a *partial order relation iff* it is *reflexive, antisymmetric and transitive* and in this case the set A is called a *partial ordered set* and is denoted by the symbol $(A, \leq)$.

Remark: The relation in N defined by '$x < y$' is a partial order and is called *natural order or usual order in N.*

Comparable Elements : Two elements x, y in a partially ordered set $(A, \leq)$ are said to be *comparable* if either $x \leq y$ or $y \leq x$.

Uncomparable Elements : Two elements x, y in a partially ordered set $(A, \leq)$ are said to *uncomparable* if

$$x \leq y \text{ and } y \leq x \text{ both do not hold.}$$

Example: Let A = {1, 2, 3, 4, 5, 8, 16} Define a relation < is A by requiring $x < y$ iff $2x = y$.

The relation < in A is a partial order. Here the elements 1, 3 are not comparable. So, we write $1 \nless 3$.

Similarly, $1 \nless 5, 5 \nless 1, 3 \nless 8, 8 \nless 3$.

The elements 4, 8 are comparable and so write $4 < 8$.

Similarly, $8 < 16, 2 < 4$ etc.

UPPER AND LOWER BOUNDS

Let $(X, \leq)$ be a partially ordered set and let $(A, \leq)$ be a subset of $(X, \leq)$.

An element $a \in X$ is said to be an *upper bound of A if $x \leq a \ \forall \ x \in A$.*

An upper bound b of A is said to be a *least upper bound or supremum of A.* If $b \leq a$ for every upper bound a of A.

In brief, we write *l.u.b.* in place of 'least upper bound'. Similarly, we write *sup.* for the word supremum. The supremum of A is denoted by the symbol sup. (A).

An element $a \in X$ is called *lower bound of A* if

$$a \leq x \ \forall \ x \in A.$$

A lower bound b of A is called *greater lower bound or infimum of A,* if $a \leq b$ for every lower bound a of A.

In short, greatest lower bound is written as g.l.b.

Similarly, the infimum of A denoted by the symbol inf. (A).

Examples:

(i) Let $A = \{x \in Q; 2 < x^2 < 5\}$ be a set in the usual order. Then A contains an infinite number of lower bounds and upper bounds, but sup. (A) and inf. (A) do not exist.

(ii) Let $X = \{1, 2, 3, 4, 5, 6\}$ be a set in the natural order. Then $A = (2, 3, 4\}$ is a subset of the partially order set X.

Lower bounds of A are 2, 1.

Upper bounds of A are 4, 5, 6.

$\therefore$ sup (A) = 4, inf. (A) = 2.

DEFINITION OF A FUNCTION AND NOTATION

Definition: Function. *A function from a set A into a set B is a relation from A into B such that each element of A is related to exactly one element of the set B. The set A is called the domain of the function and the set B is called the codomain.*

This definition of a function is the standard one that appears in most texts. The reader should note that a function f is a relation from A into B with two important restrictions.

1. Each element in the set A, the domain of f, must be used by the procedure or rule defining f, and
2. The phrase "is related to exactly one element of the set B" means that if $(a, b) \in f$ and $(a, c) \in f$, then $b = c$.

Example 1: *Let $A = \{-2, -1, 0, 1,2\}$ and $B = \{0, 1, 2, 3, 4\}$, and define s as $s = \{(-2, 4), (-1, 1), (0, 0), (1, 1), (2, 4)$, which is a function from A into B.*

Example 2: *Let **R** be the real number. Then $L = \{(x, 3x) \mid x$ Î $\mathbf{R}\}$ is a function from **R** into **R**, or, more simply, L is a function on **R**.*

We will use a different system of notation for functions than the one we used for relations. If f is a function from the set A into the set B, we will write f: $A \rightarrow B$.

The reader is probably more familiar with the procedure for describing functions that is used in basic algebra or calculus courses, for example, y = x^2, f (x) = 2x + 1 and g (x) = 1/x. Here the domain was assumed to be those elements of **R** whose substitutions for x make sense and the codomain was assumed to be **R**. We however, will list the domain and codomain in addition to describing what the function does in order to define a function. The terms *mapping, map and transformation* are also used for functions.

One way to imagine a function and what it does is to think of it as a machine. The machine could be mechanical, electronic, hydraulic, or abstract. Imagine that the machine only accepts certain objects as raw materials or input. The possible raw materials make up the domain. Given some input the machine produces a finished product with depends on the input. The possible finished products that we imagine could come out of this process makeup the codomain.

Example 3: *$f : \mathbf{R} \rightarrow \mathbf{R}$ defined by $f (x) = x^2$ is an alternate (and preferred) description of $f = \{(x, x_2) \mid x \in \mathbf{R}\}$.*

Definition: Image of an Element. *Let f A → B, (read "left be a function from the set A into the set B"). If a ∈ A, then f (a) is used to denote that element of B that a is related to. f(a) is called the image of a, or more precisely, the image of a under. We write f(a) = b to indicate that the image of a is b.*

In example 3, the image of 2 under f is 4; that is f (2) = 4. In example 1, the image of –1 under s is 1; that is, s (–1) = 1.

Definition: Range of a Function. *The range of a function is the set of images of its domain, denoted f(domain). If f : X → Y, then f(X) = [f(a) | a ∈ X} = {b ∈ Y |* ∃ A ∈ x such that f (a) = b}.

Note that the range of a function is a subset of its codomain f(X) is also read as "the image of the set X under the function," or simply "the image of f".

In example 1, s(A) = {0, 1, 4}, 2 and 3 are not images of any element of A. In addition, note that both 1 and 4 are related to more than one element of the domain s(1) = s(–1) = 1 and s(2) = s(–2) = 4. Reread the definition of a function if you feel that this violates the definition of a function.

In example 2, the range of L is equal to its codomain, **R**. If b is any real number, we can demonstrate that is belongs to L (**R**) by finding a real number x for which L (x) = b. By the definition of L, L(x) = 3x, which leads us to the equation 3x = b. This equation always has a solution b/3; thus L (**R**) = **R**.

The formula that we used to describe image of a real number under L. L(x) = 3x is preferred over the set notation for L due to its brevity. Anytime that a function can be described with a rule or formula, we will use this form of a description. In the first example, the image of each element of A is its square. To describe that fact, we write

$$S\ (a) = a^2 (a \in A),$$

or $S: A \to B$ defined by $S\ (a) = a^2$.

There are many ways that a function can be described. The complexity of the function often dictates its representation.

Example 4: *Suppose a survey of 1000 person is done asking how many hours of television each watches per day. Consider the function W: (0, 1, ..., 24) → {0, ..., 1000} defined by W (a) = number of person who gave a response of a hours. This function will probably have no formula such as the ones for s and L above. A bar graph might be the best way to represent W.*

Example 7.1.5. *Consider the function m: **P** → **Q** defined by the set m = {(1, 1), (2, 1/2), (3, 9), (4, 1/4), (5, 25), ...}. No single simple formula could describe m, but if we assume that the pattern given continues we can write*

$$m\ (x) = \begin{cases} x^2 \text{ if x is off;} \\ 1/x \text{ if x is even} \end{cases}$$

INJECTIVE, SURJECTIVE, AND BIJECTIVE FUNCTIONS

Consider the following functions:

Example 1: *Let A = {1, 2, 3, 4} and B = {a, b, c, d} and define f: A → B by*

$f(1) = a$

$f(2) = b$

$f(3) = c$

$f(4) = d$

Example 2: *Let A = {1, 2, 3, 4} and B = {a, b, c, d}, and define g : A → B by*

$g(1) = a$

$g(2) = b$

$g(3) = a$

$g(4) = b$

$g(4) = b.$

The function in the first example gives us more information about the set B than the second function. Since A clearly has four elements, f tells us that the set B contains at least four elements since each element of the set A is mapped onto one and only one element of the set B. The properties that f has and g does not have are the most basic properties that we look for in a function. The following definitions summarize the basic vocabulary for function properties.

COMPOSITION, IDENTITY, AND INVERSE

Now that we have a good understanding of what a function is, our next step is to consider an important operation on functions. Our purpose is not to develop the algebra of functions as completely as we did for the algebra of logic, matrices, and sets, but the reader should be aware of the similarities between the algebra of functions and that of matrices. We first define equality of functions.

Example:

(a) *Let* $f : \{1, 2, 3\} \to \{a, b\}$ *be defined by* $f(1) = a$ $f(2) = a$, *and* $f(3) = b$. *Let* $g : \{a, b\} \to \{5, 6, 7\}$ *be defined by* $g(a) = 5$ *and* $g(b) = 7$. *Then* $g \circ f : \{1, 2, 3\} \to \{5, 6, 7\}$ *is defined by* $(g \circ f)(1) = 5$, $(g \circ f)(2) = 5$ *and* $(g \circ f)(3) = 7$. *For example,* $(g \circ f)(1) = g(f(1)) = g(a) = 5$. *Note that* $f \circ g$ *is not defined. Why?*

(b) *Let* $f: \mathbf{R} \to \mathbf{R}$ *be defined by* $f(x) = x^3$ *and let* $g: \mathbf{R} \to \mathbf{R}$ *be defined by* $g(x) = 3x + 1$. *Then, since* $(g \circ f)(x) = g(f(x)) = g(x^3) = 3x^3 + 1$, *we have* $g \circ f : \mathbf{R} \to \mathbf{R}$ *is defined by* $(g \circ f)(x) = 3x^3 + 1$. *Here* $f \circ g$ *is also defined by* $(f \circ g)(x) = (3x + 1)^3$. *Moreover, since* $3x^3 + 1 \neq (3x + 1)^3$ *for at least one real number,* $g \circ g \neq f \circ g$ *so that the commutative law is not true for functions under the operation of composition. However, the associate law is true for functions under the operation of composition.*

FUNCTION AS A RELATION

Let A and B be two non-empty sets. A relation f from A to B, i.e., a subset of $A \times B$, *is called a function (or a mapping or a map) from A to B if:*

(i) for each $a \in A$ *there exists* $b \in B$ *such that* $(a, b) \in f$,

(ii) $(a, b) \in f$ *and* $(a, c) \in f \Rightarrow b = c$.

Thus, a non-void subset f of $A \times B$ is a function from A to B if each element of A appears in some ordered pair in f and no two ordered pairs in f have the same first element.

If (a, b) $\in$ f, then b is called the image of a under f.

Example: *Let* $A = \{1, 2, 3\}$,

$B = \{2, 3, 4\}$

and f, g and h we three sub-sets of $A \times B$ *as given below :*

$f = \{(1, 2), (2, 3), (3, 4)\}$,

$g = \{(1, 2), (1, 3), (2, 3), (3, 4)\}$,

$h = \{(1, 3), (2, 4)\}$.

Then f is a function from A to B but g and h are not functions from A to B, because 1 $\in$ A has two images 2 and 3 in B and h is not a function from A to B because 3 $\in$ A has no image in B.

KINDS OF FUNCTIONS

If f : A $\rightarrow$ B is a function, then f associates all elements of set A to elements in set B such that an element of set A is associated to a unique element of set B. Following these two conditions we may associate :

(i) different elements of set A to different elements of set B, or

(ii) more than one element of set A may be associated to the same element of set B, or

(iii) there may be some elements is B which do not have their pre-images in A or

(iv) all elements in B may have their pre-images in A.

Corresponding to each of these possibilities we define a type of a function as given below :

One-One Function (Injection) : *A function f : A* $\rightarrow$ *B is said to be a one-one function or an injection if different elements of A have different images in B.*

Thus, f : A $\rightarrow$ B is one-one $\Leftrightarrow$ a $\neq$ b

$\Rightarrow$ f(a) $\neq$ f(b) for all a, b, $\in$ A

$\Leftrightarrow$ f(a) = f(b)

$\Rightarrow$ a = b for all a,

b $\in$ A.

Examples:

(i) A function which associates to each country in the world, its capital, is one-one because different countries have their different

capitals.

(ii) *Let* $X = \{1, 2, 3, 4\}$, $Y = \{1, 4, 9, 16\}$ *and* $f : X \to Y$ *s.t.* $f(x) = x^2$ $\forall x \in X$, *then f is one-one mapping of X into Y, as no two distinct elements of X have the same f-image in Y.*

Let $f : A \to B$ be a function such that A is an infinite set and we wish to check the injectivity of f. In such a case it is not possible to list the images of all elements of set A to see whether different elements of A have different images or not. The following method provides a systematic procedure to check the injectivity of a function.

Method to Check the Injectivity of a Function

(i) Take two arbitrary elements a, b (say) in the domain of f.

(ii) Put $f(a) = f(b)$

(iii) Solve $f(a) = f(b)$. If $f(a) = f(b)$ gives $a = b$ only, then $f : A \to B$ is a one-one function (or an injection) otherwise not.

Note: Let $f : A \to B$ and let $a, b \in A$. Then, $a = b \Rightarrow f(a) = f(b)$ is always true from the definition. But, $f(a) = f(b) \Rightarrow a = b$ is true only when f is injective.

Many-one Function : A function $f : A \to B$ *is said to be a many-one function of two or more elements of set A have the same image is B.*

Thus, $f : A \to B$ is a many one function if there exist $x, y \in A$ such that $x \neq y$ but $f(x) = f(y)$.

In other words, $f : A \to B$ is a many-one function if it is not a one-one function :

Examples:

(i) $A = \{-1, 1, -2, 2\}$ *and* $B = \{1, 4, 9, 16\}$. *Consider* $f : A \to B$ *s.t.* $f(x) = x^2$. *Then* $f(-1) = 1$, $f(1) = 1$, $f(-2) = 4$, $f(2) = 4$.

Clearly 1 and – 1 have the same image. Similarly, 2 and – 2 also have the same image. So, f is a many-one function.

(ii) *Consider a function* $f : Z \to Z$ *given by* $f(x) = |x|$.

Then f is a many-one function because for every $a \in Z$, $a \neq 0$,

$a \neq -a$ *but* $f(a) = f(-a)$ $[\because |a| = |-a|]$.

Onto Function (Surjection) : *A function* $f : A \to B$ *is said to be an onto function or a surjection if every element of B is the f-image of some element of A, i.e., if* $f(A) = B$ *or range of f is the co-domain of f.*

Thus, $f : A \to B$ is a surjection iff for each $b \in B$, $\exists\, a \in A$ such that $f(a) = b$.

Into Function : *A function of $f : A \rightarrow B$ is an into function if there exists an element in B having no pre-image in A.*

In other words, $f : A \rightarrow B$ is into function if it is not an onto function.

Examples:

(i) Let $A = \{-1, 1, 2, -2\}$, $B = \{1, 4\}$ and $f : A \rightarrow B$ be a function defined by $f(x) = x^2$. The f is onto because $f(A) = \{f(-1), f(1), f(2), f(-2)\} = \{1, 4\} = B$.

(ii) A function $f : N \rightarrow N$ defined by $f(x) = 2x$ is not an onto function, because $f(N) = \{2, 4, 6, ...\} \neq N$ (co-domain).

Method for Checking the Surjectivity of a Function : Let $f : A \rightarrow B$ be the given function.

(i) Choose an arbitrary element b in B.

(ii) Put $f(a) = b$.

(iii) Solve the equation $f(a) = b$ for a and obtain a in terms of b. Let $a = g(b)$.

(iv) If for all values of $b \in B$, the values of a obtained from $a = g(b)$ are in A, then f is onto.

If there are some $b \in B$ for which a given by $a = g(b)$, is not in A. Then f is not onto.

Bijection (One-one Onto Function) : *A function $f : A \rightarrow B$ is a bijection if it is one-one as well as onto.*

In other words, a function $f : A \rightarrow B$ is a bijection if :

(i) it is one-one, i.e., $f(x) = f(y) \Rightarrow x = y$ for all $x, y \in A$.

(ii) it is onto, i.e., for all $y \in B$, there exists $x \in A$ such that $f(x) = y$.

Example: *Let A set of even integers and B be the set of odd integers, then the mapping $f : A \rightarrow B$ given by*

$$f(x) = x + 1, \quad \forall x \in A$$

is one-one onto.

One-one into Mapping : *Any mapping which is one-one as well as into is called one-one into mapping.*

Example: *Let X be the set of integers and Y the set of all even integers, then the mapping $f : X \rightarrow Y$, s.t. $f(x) = 2x$, $x \in X$ is an into mapping which is also one-one.*

Many-one into Mapping : *A function which is many one as well as into is called many-one into mapping.*

Example: *If* $X = (x_1, x_2, x_3)$ *and* $Y = (y_1, y_2)$ *and if the function* $f : X \rightarrow Y$, *is defined as* $f(x_1) = y_1$, $f(x_2) = y_1$, $f(x_3) = y_1$, *then it is a many-one into function.*

Many-one Onto Mapping : *A function which is many one as well as onto is called many-one onto mapping.*

Example: *Let* $X = \{a, b, c, d\}$, $Y = \{3, 4, 5\}$ *and* $f(a) = 3$, $f(b) = 4$, $f(c) = 4$, $f(d) = 5$, *then it is many-one onto mapping.*

RECURSION AND RECURRENCE RELATIONS

The Many Faces of Recursion

Consider the following definitions, all of which should be somewhat familiar to you. when reading them, concentrate on how they are similar.

Example: *A very common alternate notation for the binomial coefficient* $\binom{n}{k}$ *is* $C(n, k)$. *We will use the latter notation in this chapter. Here is a recursive definition of binomial coefficients.*

$C(n, k)$ *where* $n\ ^3\ 0$, $k\ ^3\ 0$, *and* $n\ ^3\ k$ *is given by*

$C(n, n) = 1;$

$C(n, 0) = 1;$ *and*

$C(n, k) = C(n - 1, k) + C(n - 1, k - 1)$ *if* $n > k > 0$.

SEQUENCES, OR DISCRETE FUNCTIONS

Definition: Sequence of Integers. *A sequence of integers is a function from the natural numbers into the integers. That is, if S is a sequence of integers,* $S: N \rightarrow Z$. *The image of any natural number k can be written interchangeably as* $S(k)$ *or* S_k *and is called the kth term of S. k itself is called the index or argument.*

Example 1:

(a) The sequence A defined by $A(k) = k^2 - k$, $k \geq 0$, *is a sequence of integers.*

(b) The sequence B defined recursively by $B(0) = 2$ *and* $B(k) = B(k - 1) + 3$ *for* $k \geq 1$ *is a sequence of integers. The terms of B can be computed either by applying the recursion formula or by interation. For example:*

$$B(3) = B(2) + 3$$

$$= (B(1) + 3) + 3$$
$$= ((B\ (0) + 3) + 3) + 3$$
$$= ((2 + 3) + 3) + 3$$
$$= 11;\ or$$
$$B(1) = B\ (0) + 3 = 2 + 3 = 5$$
$$B\ (2) = B\ (1) + 3 = 5 + 8 = 8$$
$$B\ (3) = B(2) + 3 = 8 + 3 = 11$$

(c) *Let C, be the number of strings of zeros and ones with length r having no consecutive zeros. These terms define sequence C of integers.*

Remarks:

(1) A sequence is often called a *discrete function.*

(2) The domain of a sequence is occasionally different from the natural numbers. The most common variation is $\{k \mid k \geq k_0\}$ for some fixed integer k_0. For example, {1, 2, 3, ...} or {–3, –2, –1, 0, 1, 2, ...} could be the domain of a sequence. In real life applications, the domain might be finite. For two integers, l and h, with l < h, the domain can be the domain can be $\{\leq \mid l \leq k \leq h\}$. In Pascal or Ada this set of integers can be specified as the subrange l ≤ h.

(3) The codomain of a sequence can be any set. Fro example, a sequence of complex numbers would have the set of complex numbers as its codomain.

(4) Although, it is important to keep in mind that a sequence is a function, another useful way of visualizing a sequence is as a list. For example, the sequence A could be written as (0, 0, 2, 6, 12, 20, ...). Finite sequence can appear much the same way when they are the input to or output from a computer. The index of a sequence can be thought of as a time variable. Imagine the terms of a sequence flashing on a screen every second. The s_k would be what you see in the kth second. It is convenient to use terminology like this in describing sequences. For example, the terms that precede the kth term of A would be A(0). A(1), ..., A(k – 1). They might be called the *earlier terms.*

A FUNDAMENTAL PROBLEM

Given the definition of any sequence, a fundamental problem that we will concern ourselves with is to devise a method for determining any specific term in a minimum amount of time. Generally, time can be equated with the number of operations needed. In counting operations, the application of a recursive formula would be considered an operation.

Example 2:

(a) *The terms of A in Example 8.2.1. are very easy to computer because of the closed form expression. No matter what term you decide to computer, only two operations need to be performed.*

(b) *How to compute the terms of B is not so clear. Suppose that you wanted to know B (100). One approach would be to apply the definition recursively B (100) = B (99) + 3 = (B (98) + 3)) + 2 = ... The recursion equation for B would be applied 100 times and 100 additions would then follow. To computer B (k) by this method, 2k operations are needed. An iterative computation of B (k) is an improvement: B (1) = 2 + 3 = 5, B (2) = 5 + 3 = 8, ... Only k additions are needed. This still is not a good situation. As k gets large, we take more and more time to computer B (k). The formula B (k) = B (k – 1) + 3 is called a recurrence relation on B. The process of finding a closed form expression for B (k), one that requires no more than some fixed number of operations, is called solving the recurrence relation.*

(c) *The determination of C, is a standard kind of problem in coemptionator One solution is by way of a recurrence relation. In fact many problems in combinatorics are most easily solved by first searching for a recurrence relation and then solving it. The following observation will suggest the recurrence relation that we need to determine* C_k*: If* $k \geq 2$*, then every string of zeros and ones with length k and no two consecutive 0's is either* $1s_{k-1}$ *or* $01s_{k-2}$ *where* s_{k-1} *and* s_{k-2} *are strings with no two consecutive zeros of length k – 1 and k – 2 respectively. From this observation we can see that* $C_k = C_{k-2} + C_{r-1}$ *for* $k \geq 1$*. The terms* $C_n = 1$ *and* $C_1 = 2$ *are easy to determine by enumeration. Now, by iteration, any* C_1 *can be easily determined. For example,* $C_0 = 21$ *can be computed with 5 additions. A closed form expression for* C_k *would be improvement. Note that the recurrence relation for* C_k *is identical to the one for the Fibonacci sequence (Example 8.1.4). Only the basis is different.*

RECURRENCE RELATIONS

In this section we will begin our study of recurrence relations and their solutions. Our primary focus will be on the class of finite order linear recurrence relations with constant coefficients (shortened to finite order linear relations). First, we will examine closed form expressions from which these relations arise. Second, we will present an algorithm for solving them. In later sections we will consider some other common relations and introduce two additional tools for studying recurrence relations: generating functions (8.5) and matrix methods.

Definition: Recurrence Relation. *Let S be a sequence of numbers. A recurrence relation on S is a formula that relates all but a finite number of terms of S to previous terms of S. That is, there is a kn in the domain of S such that if* $k > k_0$, *then S(k) is expressed in terms of some (and possibly all) of the terms that proceed S(k). If the domain of S is {0,1, 2, ...}, the terms S(0), S(1), ..., S(k_0) are not defined by the recurrence formula. Their values are the initial conditions (or boundary conditions, or basis) that complete the definition of S.*

Example 1:

(a) The Fibonacci sequence is defined by the recurrence relation $F_k = F_{k-2} + F_{k-1}$, $k \geq 2$ *and the initial conditions* $F_0 = 1$. *The recurrence relation is called a second-order relation be cause* F_k *depends on the two previous terms of F. Recall that the sequence C in Section 8.2 can be defined with the same recurrence relation, but with different initial conditions.*

(b) The relation $T(k) = 2\ (T(k-1)^2 - kT\ (k-3)$ *is a third-order recurrences relation. If values of T (0), T (1), and T (2) are specified, then T is completely defined.*

(c) The recurrence relation S(n) $= S(\lfloor n/2 \rfloor) + 5, n \geq 0$, *is of infinite order. To determine S (n), you must be go back* $n - \lfloor n/2 \rfloor$ *terms. Since* $n - \lfloor n/2 \rfloor$ *keeps getting larger and larger as n gets large, no finite order can be given to S.*

Example 2:

(a) The Fibonacci sequence is defined by the second-order linear relation $F_i - F_{i-1} - F_{i-2} = 0$.

(b) The relation $P\ (j) + 2P\ (j-3) = j^2$ *is a third-order linear relation.*

(c) The relation $A\ (k) = 2\ (A\ (k-1) + k)$ *can be rewritten as* $A\ (k) - 2A\ (k-1) = 2k$. *Therefore, it is a first-order linear relation.*

SOME COMMON RECURRENCE RELATIONS

In this section we intend to examine a variety of recurrence relations that are not finite order linear with constant coefficients. For each part of this section, we will consider a concrete example, present a solution, and, if possible, examine a more general form of the original relation.

Example1: *Consider the homogeneous first-order linear relation S(n) – nS(n – 1) = 0, n ≥ 1, with initial condition S(0) = 1. Upon close examination of this relation, we see that nth term is n times the (n – 1)st term, which is a characteristic of n factorial. S(n) = n! is a solution of this relation, for if n ≥ 1,*

$$\begin{aligned} S(n) &= n! = (n)\ (n-1) \ldots (2)\ (1) \\ &= (n)\ (n-1)! \\ &= nS(n-1). \end{aligned}$$

In addition, since 0! = 1, the initial condition is satisfied. It should be pointed out that from a computational point of view, our "solution" really isn't much of an improvement since the exact calculation of n! takes n multiplications, which is the operation count for determining S(n) by an iterative method.

If we examine a similar relation, G(k) = 2kG(k – 1), k ³ 0 with G(0) = 1, a table of values for G suggests a possible solution:

k	0	1	2	3	4	5
G(k)	1	2	23	24	210	215

The exponent of 2 in G(n) is growing according to the relation

E(k) = E(k – 1) + k, with E(0) = 0.

Thus $E(k) = \frac{1}{2}k(k+1)$ and $G(k) = 2^{\frac{1}{2}k(k+1)}$.

Note that G(k) could also be written as $(2^0)\,(2^1) \ldots (2^k)$ for k ≥ 0, but this is not a closed from expression.

In general, the relation P(n) = f(n) P(n – 1) n ≥ 0 with P (0) = f (0), where f is a function that is defined for all n ≥ 0, has the "solution".

$$P(n) = f(0)\, f(1) \ldots f(n) = \prod_{k=0}^{n} f(k),\ n \geq 0$$

This product form of P(n) is not a closed form expression because as n grows, the number of multiplications grow. Thus, it is really not a true solution. Often, as for G(n) above, a closed form expression can be obtained from the product form.

Example 2: *(Analysis of a Binary Search Algorithm). Suppose that you intend to use a binary search algorithm on files of zero or more sorted records and that the records are stored in an array, so that you have easy access to each record. A natural question to ask, particularly in an analysis of algorithms course, is "How much time will it take to complete the search?" When a question like this is asked, the time that we refer to* *is often so-called worst-case time. That is, if we were to search through n records, What is the longest amount of time that we will need to complete the search? In order to make an analysis such as this independent of the computer to be used, time is measured by counting the number of steps that are executed. Each step or sequence of steps) is assigned an absolute time, or weight; therefore, our answer will not be in seconds, but in absolute time units. If the steps in two different algorithms are assigned weights that are consistent, then analyses of the algorithms can be used to compare their relative efficiency.*

There are two major steps that must be executed in a call of the binary search algorithm:

(1) If the lower index is less than or equal to the upper index, then the middle of the file is located and its key is compared to the value that you are searching for.

(2) In the worst case, the algorithm must be executed with a file that is roughly half as large as in the previous execution.

If we assume that Step 1 takes one time unit and T (n) is the worst-case time for a file of n records, then

$$T(n) = 1 + T([n/2])$$

For simplicity, we will assume that

$$T(0) = 0,$$

even though the conditions of Step 1 must be evaluated as false if $n = 0$. You might wonder why n/2 is truncated in 8.4a. If n is odd, then $n = 2k + 1$ for some $k \geq 0$, the middle of the file will be the $(k + 1)$st record, and no matter what half of the file the search is directed to, the reduced file will have $k = [n/2]$ records. On the other hand, if n is even, then $n = 2k$ for $k \geq 1$. The middle of the file will be the kth record, and the worst case will occur if we are directed to the k records that come after the middle (the $(k + 1)$st through $(2k)$ th records). Again the reduced file has $[n/2]$ records.

Solution: To determine T (n), the easiest case is when n is a power of two. If we compute T (2m), $m \geq 0$, by iteration, our results are

$$T(1) = 1 + T(0) = 1$$

$$T(2) = 1 + T(1) = 2$$

$$T(4) = 1 + T(2) = 3$$

$$T(8) = 1 + T(4) = 4.$$

The pattern that is established makes it clear that $T(2^m) = m + 1$. This result would seem to indicate that every time you double the size of your file, the search time increases by only one unit.

A more complete solution can be obtained if we represent n in binary form. For each $n \geq 1$, there exists a non-negative integer r such that

$$2r - 1 \quad \leq n < 2r \, (8.4c)$$

For example, if $n = 21$, $24 \leq 21 < 25$; therefore, $r = 5$. If n satisfies, its binary representation requires r digits. For example, $21_{TEN} = 10101_{TWO}$.

In general, $n = (a_1a_2, \ldots a_r)_{TWO}$, where $a_1 = 1$. Note that in this form, [n/2] is easy to describe: it is clear $r - 1$ digit binary number $a_1a_2 \ldots a_{r-1}$. Therefore,

$$\begin{aligned}
T(n) \quad &= T(a_1, \ldots a_{r-1}a_r) \\
&= 1 + T(a_1 \ldots a_{r-1}) \\
&= 1 + (1 + T(a_1 \ldots a_{r-2})) \\
&= 2 + T(a_1 \ldots a_{r-2}) \\
&\;\;\vdots \\
&= (r - 1) + T\,(a_1) \\
&= (r - 1) + 1 \text{ (since } T(1) = 1 \\
&= r.
\end{aligned}$$

From the pattern that we've just established, T(n) reduces to r. A formal inductive proof of this statement is possible. Ho2wever, we expect that most readers would be satisfied with the argument above. Any skeptics are invited to provide the inductive proof. If $n = 21$:

$$\begin{aligned}
T\,(21) \quad &= T\,(10101) = 1 + T\,(1010) \\
&= 1 + (1 + T\,(101)) \\
&= 1 + (1 + (1 + T\,(10)) \\
&= 1 + (1 + (1 + T\,(1))) \\
&= 1 + (1 + (1 + (1 + T(0))))) \\
&= 5.
\end{aligned}$$

Conclusion: $T(n) = r$, where $2r - 1 \geq 1n < 2r$, $n \geq 1$.

A less cumbersome statement of this fact is that for n ³ 1, $T\,(n) = [\log_2 n] + 1$. For example, $T\,(21) = [\log_2 21] + 1 = 4 + 1 = 5$.

GENERATING FUNCTIONS

This section contains an introduction tot eh topic of generating functions and how they are used to solve recurrence relations, among other problems. Methods that employ generating functions are based on the concept that you can take a problem involving sequences and translate it into a problem involving generating functions. Once you've solved the new problem, a translation back to sequence gives you a solution of the original problem.

This section covers:

(a) Definition of a generating function.

(b) Solution of a recurrence relation using generating functions to identify the skills needed to use generating functions.

(c) An introduction and/or review of the skills identified in Point b.

(d) Some applications of generating functions.

Definition: Generating Function of a Sequence. *The generating function of a sequence S with terms* S_0, S_1, S_2 ... *is the infinite sum.*

$$G(S;z) = \sum_{n=0}^{x} S_n z^n = S_0 + S_1 z + S_2 z^2 + S_3 z^3 + \ldots$$

The domain and codomain of generating functions will not be of any concern to us since we will only be performing algebraic operations on them.

Example 1:

(a) If $Sn = 3n,\ n\ ^{3}\ 0$, *then*

$$G(S;z) = 1 + 3z + 9z^2 + 27z^3 + \ldots$$

$$= \sum_{n=0}^{x} 3^n z^n = \sum_{n=0}^{x} (3z)^n$$

We can obtain a closed form expression for G (S;z) by observing that $G(S;z) - 3zG(S;z) = 1$. Therefore,

$$G(S;z) = 1/(1 - 3z)$$

(b) Finite sequences have generating functions. For example, the sequence of binomial coefficients C(n, 0), C (n, 1), ... C(n, n), $n\ ^{3}\ 1$ has generating function

$$G(C(n,); z) = C(n, 0) + C(n, 1)z + \ldots + C(n, n)\, zn$$

$$= \sum_{k=0}^{n} C(n, k) z^k = (1 + z)^n$$

by application of the binomial formula

(c) If $Q(n) = n^2$,

$$G(Q;z) = \sum_{n=0}^{x} n^2 z^n = \sum_{k=0}^{x} k^2 z^k$$

Note that the index that is used in the summation has no significance. Also, note that the lower limit of the summation could start at 1 since $Q(0) = 0$.

Example 2: *If* $S(n) = n$, $T(n) = n^2$, $U(n) = 2^n$, *and* $R(n) = n2^n$,

(a) $(S + T)(n) = n + n^2$

(b) $(U + R)(n) = 2^n + n^{2n} = (1 + n)^{2n}$

(c) $(2U)(n) = 2^{2n} = 2^{n+1} = (U \uparrow)(n)$

(d) $\left(\frac{1}{2}R\right)(n) = \frac{1}{2}n2^n = n2^{n-1}$

(e) $(ST)(n) = nn^2 = n^3$

(f) $(S * T)(n) = \sum_{j=0}^{n} S(j)\,T(n-j) = \sum_{j=0}^{n} j(n-j)^2$

$$= \sum_{j=0}^{n} (jn^2 - 2nj^2 + j^3)$$

$$= n^2 \sum_{j=0}^{n} j - 2n \sum_{j=0}^{n} j^2 + \sum_{j=0}^{n} j^3$$

$$= n^2\,(n(n+1)/2) - 2n((2n+1)(n+1)/6) + ((n(n+1)/2)^2$$

$$= n^2\,(n + 1)\,(n - 1)/12$$

(g) $(U * U)(n) = \sum_{j=0}^{n} U(j)\,U(n-j) = \sum_{j=0}^{n} 2^j 2^{n-j} = (n + 1)^{2n}$

(h) $(S \uparrow)(n) = (n + 1)$

(i) $(S \downarrow)(n) = \max\{0, n - 1)$

(j) $((S \downarrow) \downarrow (n) = \max\{0, n - 2)$

(k) $(U \downarrow)(n) = 2^{n-1}$ if $n > 0$, $(U \downarrow)(0) = 0$

(l) $((U \downarrow) \uparrow (n) = (U\downarrow)(n + 1) = 2n = U(n)$

(m) $((U \downarrow) \downarrow)(n) = \begin{Bmatrix} 0 \text{ if } n = 0 \\ U \uparrow (n-1) \text{ if } n > 0 \end{Bmatrix} = \begin{Bmatrix} 0 \text{ if } n = 0 \\ U(n) \text{ if } n > 0 \end{Bmatrix}$

Note that $(U \downarrow) \uparrow \neq (U \downarrow)\uparrow$.

Definition: If S is a sequence of numbers, define

$S \uparrow p = (S \uparrow (p - 1)) \uparrow$ if $p > 1$ and $S \uparrow 1 = S \uparrow$.

Similarly, define

$S \downarrow p = (S \downarrow (p - 1)) \downarrow$ and $S \downarrow 1 = S \downarrow$.

Note that

$(S \uparrow 2)(k) = ((S \uparrow) \uparrow)(k) = (S \uparrow)(k + 1) = S(k + 2)$

In general,

$$(S \uparrow p)\ (k) = S(p + k), \text{ and}$$

$$(S \downarrow p)\ (k) = \begin{cases} 0 & \text{if } k < p \\ S(k-p) & \text{if } k \geq p \end{cases}$$

Operations on Generating Functions: If

$$G\,(z) = \sum_{k=0}^{\infty} a_k z^k$$

and
$$H\,(z) = \sum_{k=0}^{\infty} b_k z^k$$

are generating functions and c is a real number, then the *sum* G + H, *scalar product cG, product GH, and nominal product zpG,* $p \geq 1$ are generating functions, where

$$(G + H)\,(z) = \sum_{k=0}^{\infty} (a_k + b_k) z^k$$

$$(cG)(z) = c \sum_{k=0}^{\infty} a_k z^k = \sum_{k=0}^{\infty} (ca_k) z^k$$

$$(GH)(z) = \sum_{k=0}^{\infty} c_k z^k, \text{ where } c_k = \sum_{j=0}^{k} a_j b_{k-1}$$

$$(z^p G)(Z) = z^p \sum_{k=0}^{\infty} a_k z^k = \sum_{k=0}^{\infty} a_k z^{k+p}$$

$$= \sum_{n=p}^{\infty} a_{n-p} z^n$$

The last sum is obtained by substituting n – p for k in the previous sum.

Example 3: *If*

$$D(z) = \sum_{k=0}^{\infty} kz^k \ \textit{and}\ H\,(z) = \sum_{k=0}^{x} 2^k z^k$$

$$(D + H)\,(z) = \sum_{k=0}^{x} (k + 2^k) z^k$$

$$(2H)\ (z) = \sum_{k=0}^{x} (2\,2^k)\, z^k$$

$$= \sum_{k=0}^{x} 2^{k+1} z^k = (H(z) - 1)/z$$

$$(zD)\ (z) = z \sum_{k=0}^{x} kz^k = \sum_{k=0}^{x} kz^{k-1}$$

$$= \sum_{k=0}^{x} (k-1)z^k$$

$$= D(z) - \sum_{k=1}^{x} 2^k$$

$$(DH)\ (z) = \sum_{k=0}^{x} \left(\sum_{j=0}^{k} j2^{k-j} \right) 2^k$$

$$(HH)\ (z) = \sum_{k=0}^{x} \left(\sum_{j=0}^{k} 2^j 2^{k-1} 2^k \right)$$

$$= \sum_{k=0}^{x} (k+1)2^k z^k .$$

Note: $D(z) = G(S;z)$, $H(z) = G(U;z)$.

Now, we establish the connection between the operations on sequences and generating functions. Let S and T be sequences and let c be a real number:

$$G(S + T;z) = G(S;z) + G(T;z)$$

$$G(cS;z) = cG(S;z)$$

$$G(S * T;z) = G(S;z)\, G(T;z)$$

$$G(S\uparrow;z) = (G(S;z) - S(0)/z$$

$$G(S\downarrow;z) = zG(S;z).$$

The generating function of the sum of two sequences equals the sum of the generating functions of those sequences. Take the time to write out the other four identities in your own words. From the previous examples, these identities should be fairly obvious, with the possible exception of the last two. We will prove part of the next theorem and leave the interested reader. Note that the there is no operation on generating functions that is related to sequence multiplication; that is, G(ST;z) cannot be simplified.

EXTRA FOR EXPERTS

The remainder of this section is intended for readers who have had, or who intended to take, a course in combinatorics. We do not adivse that it be included in a typical course. The method that was used in Example 8.5.6 is a very powerful one and can be used to solve many problems in combinatorics. We close this section with a general description of the problems that can be solved in this way, followed by some examples.

Consider the situation in which $P_1, P_2, \ldots, P_m$ are n actions that must be taken, each of which result in a well-defined outcome. For each k = 1, 2,

...,m m define X_k to be the set of possible outcomes of P_k. We will assume that each outcome can be quantified in some way and that the quantification of the elements of X_k is defined by the function $Q_k : X_k \to \{0, 1, 2, ...\}$. Thus, each outcome has a non-negative integer associated with it. Finally, define a frequency function F_k ; $\{0, 1, 2, ...\} \to \{0, 1, 2, ...\}$ such that F_k (n) s the number of elements of X_k that have a quantification of n.

Now, based on these assumptions, we can define the problems that can be solved. If a process P is defined as a sequence of processes P_1, P_2, ... P_m as above, and if the outcome of P, which would be an element of $X_1 \times X_2 \times ... \times X_m$, is quantified by $Q(a_1, a_2, ..., a_m) = Q_1(a_1) + ... + Q_m(a_m)$, then the frequency function, F, for P is the convolution of the frequency functions for P_1, P_2, ..., P_m, which has a generating function equal to the product of the generating functions of F_1, F_2, ..., F_m. *I.e.*:

$$G(F; z) = G(F_1;z)\,G(F_2;z) \dots G(F_m;z)$$

Example 1: *Suppose that you roll a die two times and add up the numbers on the top face for each roll. Since the faces on the die represent the integers 1 through 6, the sum must be between 2 and 12. How many ways can any one of the se sums be obtained? Obviously 2 can be obtained only one way, with two 1's. There are two sequences that yield a sum of 3 : 1—2 and 2—1. To obtain all of the frequencies with which is the number 2 through 12 can be obtained, we set up the situation as follows. For j = 1, 2,; Pj is the rolling of the die for the jth time. X = {1, 2, ..., 6} and $Q_j : X_j \to \{0, 1, 2, ...\}$ is defined by $Q_j(x) = x$. Since each number appears on a die exactly once, the frequency function is $F_j(k) = 1$ if $1 \le k \le 6$, and $F_j(k) = 0$ otherwise. The process of rolling the die two times is quantified by adding up the Q_j's; that is, $Q(a_1, a_2) = Q_1(a_1) + Q_2(a_2) = a_1 + a_2$. The frequency function for the process of rolling the die two times is then*

$$\begin{aligned} G(F;z) &= G(F_1;z)\,G(F_2;z) \\ &= (z + z_2 + z_3 + z_4 + z_5 + z_6)^2 \\ &= z_2 + 2z_3 + 3z_4 + 4z_5 + 5z_6 + 6z_7 \\ &\qquad + 5z_8 + 4z_9 + 3z_{10} + 2z_{11} + z_{12} \end{aligned}$$

Now, to obtain F(k), just read the coefficient of z^k.

To apply this method, the crucial step is to decompose a large process in the proper way so that it fits into the general situation that we've described.

Example 2: *Suppose that an organization is divided into three geographic sections, A, B and C. Suppose that an executive committee of 11 members must be selected so that no more than 5 members from any one* *section are on the committee and that Sections A, B and C must have minimum is of 3, 2 and 2 members, respectively, on the committee. Looking at only the number of members from each section on the committee, how many ways can the committee be make up? One example of a valid committee would be 4 A's. 4B's and 3C's.*

Let P_A be the process of deciding *how many* members (not who) from Section A will serve on the committee. $X_A = \{3, 4, 5\}$ and $Q_A(k) = k$. The frequency function, F_A, is defined by $F_A(k) = 1$ if $k \in X_A$, with $F_A(k) = 0$ otherwise. $G(G_A; z)$ is then $z^3 + z^4 + z^5$. Similarly, $G(F_B; z) = z^2 + z^3 + z^4 + z^5 = G(F_c; z)$. Since the committee must have 11 members, our answer will be the coefficient of z_{11} in $G(F_A; z)\, G(F_B; z)\, G(F_C; z)$, which is 10.

MAPPING OR FUNCTION

The concept of mapping of one set into another is of great importance in mathematics. It is not a new concept to any of us as we have been considering mapping from the beginning of our mathematical training. For example, plotting of the relation $y = x^2$ is nothing but to study the particular mapping which takes every real number into its square. The following discussion will make the concept of mapping clear.

Suppose A and B are any two non-empty sets. Let $A = \{a, b, c, d\}$, $B = \{x, y, z\}$. Suppose by some rule or other, we assign to each element of A unique element of B. Suppose a is associated to x, b is associated to y, c is associated to x and d is associated to z. The set of such assignments is called a *'function'* or *'mapping'* from A to B. If we denote this set by f than we write

$$f : A \to B$$

Which is read as *"f is a function of A to B"* or *"f is a mapping from A to B"*.

Loosely speaking, a mapping from one set into another may be defined as given below :

Definition : *Let A and B be two given sets. Suppose there exists a rule denoted by f, which associates to each member of A, a unique member of B. Then f is called a function or a mapping of A to B. The mapping f of A to B is denoted by* $f : A \to B$ *or by* $A \xrightarrow{f} B$.

Further, if $a \in A$, then the element in B which is assigned to a is called the f image of a or the value of the function f for a and is denoted by f(a).

Definition : *If A and B are nom-empty sets then a mapping from A to B is a subset C of* $A \times B$ *such that for every* $a \in A$ *there is a unique* $b \in B$

such that the ordered pair (a, b) is in C. For all practical purposes the following notion of mapping will be used hereafter and thus we arrive at another form of definition.

Definition : *A mapping $f : A \to B$, is a rule which associates any element $a \in A$ with some element $b \in B$, the rule being associate (or map) $a \in A$ with $b \in B$ if $(a, b) \in C$, C being the subset of $A \times B$.*

Note : The rule f should possess the characteristic that there may be some elements of the set B which are not associated to any element of the set A but each element of the set A must be associated to one and only one element of the set B. Two or more elements of the set A may be associated to the same element of the set B but association of one element of A to more than one element in B is not permissible.

Domain, Co-domain and Range of Functions : Let f be a mapping of A into B. Then A is called the *'domain'* of the function f and B the *'co-domain'* of the function f. It is evident from the definition that each element of B need not appear as the image of an element in A. We define the *'range'* of f to consist of all those elements in B which appear as f image of atleast one element in A. There can be more than one elements of A which have the same image in B. The image set f [A] is called the range of f.

Functions Defined as Sets of Ordered Pairs : Let A and B are any two non-empty sets, then a mapping f of A to B is a subset f of $A \times B$ satisfying the following conditions :

(i) for each $a \in A$, $(a, b) \in f$, for some $b \in B$;

(ii) if $(a, b) \in f$ and $(a, b') \in f$, then $b = b'$.

The first condition ensures that we have a rule that assigns to each element $a \in A$ some element $b \in B$. Thus each element in A will have image The second condition guarantees that the image is unique. Accordingly, f is a function from A to B.

Note : If $f : A \to B$, it is important to distinguish between a function f and the value f(x) of f for any element x. While f is a subset of $A \times B$, f(x) is an element of the set B.

Operator : *If the domain and co-domain of a function of are both the same set, say*

$$f : A \to A$$

the f is called an operator or transformation on A.

Following examples will make the notion of a function more clear;

Examples:

(i) Let $A = \{1, 2, 3, 4\}$

and $B = \{1, 2, 3, 4, 5, 6, 7, 8, 9, 10, 11, 12\}$

Now, let f assign to each number in A is square in B. Then f is not a mapping from A to B since no number of B is assigned to the element $4 \in A$.

(ii) *Let* $X = \{p, q, r\}$, $Y = \{1, 2, 3\}$ *and mapping f is as follows :*

$f(p) = 3, f(q) = 1, f(r) = 2,$

then f-image of X is $\{3, 1, 2\}$ *or in other words f-image of X is Y.*

(iii) *Let f be a mapping of N into N such that*

$f(1) = 3; f(2) = 5; f(3) = 7; \ldots$

We can express this mapping by the functional notion as

$f : N \to N;$ *defined by* $f(x) = 2x + 1, \ \forall x \in N.$

(iv) *Let A be the set of countries in the world and B be the set of capital cities then (i) every country has a capital assigned to it, (ii) no country will have two capitals. Thus, f is a function from the set A to B and the image of India under f is New Delhi, i.e., f(India) = New Delhi. Similarly, f(Nepal) = Kathmandu.*

Here, domain of f is the list of countries in the world and the co-domain is the list of capital cities of these countries.

Equal Functions : *Two functions f and g are said to be equal iff :*

(i) the domain of f = domain of g

(ii) the co-domain of f = the co-domain of g and

(iii) f(x) = g(x) for every x belonging to their common domain.

Example : *Let* $A = \{1, 2\}$, $B = \{3, 6\}$, *and* $f : A \to B$ *given by* $f(x) = x^2 + 2$ *and* $g : A \to B$ *given by* $g(x) = 3x$. *Then, we observe that f and g have the same domain and co-domain and also*

$$f(1) = 3 = g(1) \text{ and } f(2) = 6 = g(2).$$

Hence $\quad f = g.$

SOME MISCELLANEOUS EXAMPLES

Example 1: *Prove that the relation R in the set of integers I defined by a R b if a and b are both odd is symmetric and transitive but not reflexive.*

Solution:

1. *R is not Reflexive:* We have $2 \in I$. But 2 is not R-related to 2, since 2 and 2 are not both odd. Therefore R is not reflexive.

2. *R is Symmetric:* Suppose we have a R b. Then a and b are both odd.

Now if a and b are both odd then b and a are both odd *i.e.,* b R a. Thus a R b ⇒ b R a and therefore R is symmetric.

3. *R is Transitive:* Suppose we have a R b and b R c. Then a and b are both odd as well as b and c are both odd. It implies that a and c are both odd *i.e.,* a R c. Thus a R b and b R c ⇒ a R c. Therefore R is transitive.

Example 2: *Show with the help of an example that the union of two transitive relations is not necessarily a transitive relation.*

Solution: Let $R_1 = \{(1,2),(2,1),(1,1),(2,2)\}$. $R_2\{(2,3),(3,2),(2,2),(3,3)\}$ be two relations on the set S = {1, 2, 3}. Obviously both R_1 and R_2 are transitive relations. Now $R_1 \cup R_2$ = {(1, 2), (2, 1), (1, 1), (2, 2), (2, 3), (3, 2), (3, 2), (2, 2), (3, 3)}.

This is not a transitive relation because (1, 2) ∈ $R_1 \cup R_2$ and (2, 3) ∈ $R_1 \cup R_2$ while (1, 3) ∉ $R_1 \cup R_2$.

Example 3: *Prove that the relation "congruence modulo m" is an equivalence relation in the set of integers.*

Solution: Let I be the set of integers. If m is any given positive integer and a, b ∈ I, then we say that a ≡ b (mod m) if m | (a – b) *i.e.,* if m is a divisor of a – b. We shall prove that this defines an equivalence relation in the set I.

Reflexivity: Let a be any integer. Then a – a = 0 and m | 0 because we can write 0 = m. 0. Thus a ≡ a (mod m) ∀ a ∈ I. Therefore the relation is reflexive.

Symmetry: Let a, b ∈ I be such that a ≡ b (mod m).

Then a ≡ b (mod m)

⇒ m | (a – b)

⇒ a – b = km, where k is some integer

⇒ b – a = (–k) m, where –k is also an integer

⇒ m | (b – a)

⇒ b ≡ a (mod m).

Thus, a ≡ b (mod m) ⇒ b ≡ a (mod m). Therefore the relation is symmetric.

Transitivity: Let a, b, c ∈ I be such that

a ≡ b (mod m), b ≡ a (mod m). Then we have

m | (a – b) and m | (b – c)

⇒ a – b = k_1m and b – c = k_2m, where k_1, k_2 are some integers

$\Rightarrow (a - b) + (b - c) = k_1m + k_2m$

$\Rightarrow a - c = (k_1 + k_2)m$, where $k_1 + k_2$ is also an integer

$\Rightarrow m \mid (a - c) \Rightarrow a \equiv c \pmod{m}$.

Thus $a \equiv b \pmod{m}$ and $b \equiv c \pmod{m} \Rightarrow a \equiv c \pmod{m}$. Therefore the relation is transitive.

Since the relation of "congruence modulo m" on the set of integers is reflexive, symmetric and transitive, therefore it is an equivalence relation.

Example 4: *What is the difference between function and relation?*

Let $X = \{1, 2, 3, 4\}$

and $Y = \{1, 5, 9, 11, 15, 16\}$.

Determine which of the following sets are :

(i) relation (ii) function (iii) neither, of X to Y.

(a) $f_1 = \{(x, y) \mid y = x^2, x \in X, y \in Y\}$

(b) $f_2 = \{(1, 1), (2, 11), (3, 1), (4, 15)\}$

(c) $f_3 = \{(1, 5), (2, 9), (3, 1), (4, 5), (2, 11)\}$

(d) $f_4 = \{(1, 1), (2, 7), (3, 5)\}$.

Solution: For difference between function and relation refer

(a) We have $f_1 = \{(1, 1), (3, 9), (4, 16)\}$.

Hence f_1 is a relation of X to Y because $f_1 \subseteq X \times Y$. But f_1 is not a function of X to Y because $2 \in X$ and $2^3 = 4$ which $\notin Y$. Thus under f_1 the image of 2 belonging to X does not exist.

(b) Hence f_2 is a relation of X to Y because $f_2 \subseteq X \times Y$. Also f_2 is a function of X to Y because under f_2 each element of X has a unique image in Y.

(c) Hence, f_3 a relation of X to Y because $f_3 \subseteq X \times Y$. But f_3 is not a function of X to Y because under f_3 the image of $2 \in X$ is not unique. Note the $f_3(2) = 9$ and also $f_3(2) = 11$.

(d) Here f_4 is not a relation of X to Y because $f_4 \not\subseteq X \times Y$. Note that $(2, 7) \in f_4$ but $(2, 7) \notin X \times Y$ because $7 \notin Y$. Also f_4 is not a function of X to Y.

Example 5: *If* $f : R \to R$ *is defined as follows :*

$$f(x) = \begin{cases} 1, \text{ if } x \in Q \\ -1, \text{ if } x \notin Q \end{cases}$$

Find:

(a) $f\left(\frac{1}{2}\right)$, f(π), $f\left(\sqrt{2}\right)$

(b) *Range of f*

(c) *Pre-images of 1 and –1.*

Solution:

(a) It is evident from the definition of f that at every rational point the function attains value 1 and at every irrational point it attains value – 1. So,

$$\frac{1}{2} \in Q \Rightarrow f\left(\frac{1}{2}\right) = 1,\ \pi \notin Q \Rightarrow f(\pi) = -1$$

and $$\sqrt{2} \notin Q \Rightarrow f\left(\sqrt{2}\right) = -1.$$

(b) We have, Range of f = {f(x) : x ∈ R} Also, by definition f(x) attains values 1 and – 1 according as x is rational or irrational and a real number is either rational or irrational.

∴ Range of f = {1, – 1}.

(c) Since f(x) = 1 for all x ∈ Q. Therefore pre-images of 1 are rational numbers, *i.e.*,

$f^{-1}(1) = Q$.

Also, – 1 is the image of every real number which is not rational. So,

$f^{-1}(-1) = R - Q$ = set of irrational numbers.

Example 6: *Let A = {– 2, – 1, 0, 1, 2}. Let the function f : A → R is defined by f(x) = $x^2 + 1$.*

Find the range of f.

Solution: The range of f consists of those elements of R which appear as f-images of different elements of A. So, we calculate the f-image of each element of A.

$$f(-2) = (-2)^2 + 1 = 4 + 1 = 5$$
$$f(-1) = (-1)^2 + 1 = 1 + 1 = 2$$
$$f(0) = (0)^2 + 1 = 0 + 1 = 1$$
$$f(1) = (1)^2 + 1 = 1 + 1 = 2$$
$$f(2) = (2)^2 + 1 = 4 + 1 = 5.$$

The range of f is the set {5, 2, 1, 2, 5}

i.e., the set {1, 2, 5}.

Example 7: *Find the domain for which the function $f(x) = 2x^2 - 1$ and $g(x) = 1 - 3x$ are equal.*

Solution: We have f(x) = g(x)

$\Rightarrow \quad 2x^2 - 1 = 1 - 3x$

$\Rightarrow \quad 2x^2 + 3x - 2 = 0$

$\Rightarrow \quad (x + 2)(2x - 1) = 0$

$\Rightarrow \quad x = -2, 1/2.$

Thus, f(x) and g(x) are equal on the set {–2, 1/2}.

Example 8: *Is g = {(1, 1), (2, 3), (3, 5), (4, 7)} a function? If this is described by the formulae, $g(x) = \alpha x + \beta$, then what values should be assigned to α and β?*

Solution: Since no two ordered pairs in g have the same first component. So, g is a function such that g(1) = 1, g(2) = 3, g(3) = 5 and g(4) = 7.

It is given that $g(x) = \alpha x + \beta$. Therefore g(1) = 1

and $g(2) = 3 \Rightarrow \alpha + \beta = 1$

and $2\alpha + \beta = 3 \Rightarrow \alpha = 2, \beta = -1$.

Example 9: *Show that the mapping $f : I \to I$ defined by $f(x) = x^2$, $x \in I$ where I is the set of positive integers, is one-one into.*

Solution: $f(x) = x^2$ means that the function f is such that f-image of x is x^2. Domain of the mapping is {1, 2, 3, ...} and the range is {1, 4, 9, ...}.

Thus f-image is the subset of its domain, *i.e.*, $\{f(x)\} \subset I$. It is a mapping of I into I. Here two different elements of domain necessarily correspond to different elements of the range so that it is one-one mapping. Hence, it is one-one into mapping.

Example 10: *Show that the function $f : R \to R$ defined by $f(x) = 3x^3 + 5$ for all $x \in R$ is a bijection.*

Solution: *Injectivity* Let x, y be any two elements of R (domain).

Then $\quad f(x) = f(y) \Rightarrow 3x^3 + 5 = 3y^3 + 5$

$\Rightarrow \quad x^3 = y^3 \Rightarrow x = y$

Thus, $f(x) = f(y) \Rightarrow x = y$ for all $x, y \in R$. So, f is an injective map.

Surjectivity : Let y be an arbitrary elements of R (co-domain). Then

$$f(x) = y \Rightarrow 3x^3 + 5 = y \Rightarrow x^3 = \frac{y-5}{3}$$

$$\Rightarrow \qquad x = \left(\frac{y-5}{3}\right)^{1/3}.$$

Thus, we find that for all y ∈ R (co-domain) there exists

$x = \left(\frac{y-5}{3}\right)^{1/3} \in R$ (domain) such that

$$f(x) = f\left[\left(\frac{y-5}{3}\right)^{1/3}\right] = 3\left[\left(\frac{y-5}{3}\right)^{1/3}\right]^3 + 5 = y - 5 + 5 = y.$$

This shows that every element in the co-domain has its pre-image in the domain. So, f is a surjection.

Hence, f is a bijection.

Example 11: *Let* $A = \{x \in R \mid -1 \le x \le 1\} = B$. *Show that* $f : A \to B$ *given by* $f(x) = x|x|$ *is a bijection.*

Solution: *Injectivity* : Let x, y be any two elements in A. Then

$$x \neq y \Rightarrow x|x| \neq y|y| \Rightarrow f(x) \neq f(y)$$

So, $\quad f : A \to B$ is an injective map.

Surjectivity : Clearly, range of f = f(A) = B.

So, $f : A \to B$ is a surjective map. Hence, f is a bijection.

Example 12: *If R is the set of real numbers, discuss the mapping*

$$f : R \to R$$

where $\quad f(x) = x^2, x \in R.$

Solution: If x is any real number then x^2 is also a real number and it will be unique. Thus each element x ∈ R has a unique f-image in R. Therefore, $f : R \to R$.

Since, there is no real number whose square is negative, therefore any negative number in R is not the f-image of any element in R. Consequently f is mapping of R into R.

Also, we see that $(-2)^2 = 4$ and $(2)^2 = 4$. Thus the elements 2 and – 2 in R have the same f-image 4 in R. Hence, f is many-one into mapping of R → R.

Example 13: *Let C and R denote the set of all complex numbers and all real numbers respectively. Then show that* $f : C \to R$ *given by* $f(z) = |z|$ *for all* $z \in C$ *is neither one-one nor onto.*

Solution: *Injectivity* : We find that $z_1 = 1 - i$ and $z_2 = 1 + i$ are two distinct complex numbers such that $|z_1| = |z_2|$, *i.e.*, $z_1 \neq z_2$ but $f(z_1) = f(z_2)$.

This shows that different elements may have the same image. So, f is not an injection, *i.e.*, not one-one.

Surjectivity : f is not a surjection, because negative real numbers in R do not have their pre-images in C. In other words, for every negative real number a there is no complex number $z \in C$ such that $f(z) = |z| = a$. So, f is not a surjection, *i.e.*, not onto.

Hence, $f : C \to R$ is neither one-one nor onto.

Example 14: *Let $A = \{0, 1\}$ and let N be the set of natural numbers. Show that $f : N \to A$ defined by $f(2x) = 0, f(2x + 1) = 1, (x \in N)$ is a many-one onto mapping of N to A.*

Solution: Here we see that each element in A is the f-image of at least one element in N. For example 0 is the f-image of $4 \in N$ and 1 is the f-image of $9 \in N$. Therefore, f is a mapping of N onto A.

Also, we see that the element $1 \in A$ is the f-image of every odd natural number $\in N$. Hence, f is a many-one onto mapping of N to A.

Example 15: *Let R_0 be the set of all non-zero real numbers. Let $f : R_0 \to R_0$ be defined by the formula $f(x) = 1/x$, $x \in R_0$. Show that f is one-one and onto mapping.*

Solution: Let m and n be any two different elements in R_0.

Then $\quad m \neq n \Rightarrow 1/m \neq 1/n$

$$\Rightarrow f(m) \neq f(n).$$

Thus, different elements in R_0 have different f-images in R_0. Hence f is one-one.

Now let y be an arbitrary element in R_0. If y 1/x, we have x = 1/y which is a non-zero real number if y is a non-zero real number. Thus f (1/y) = y. *i e.*, any arbitrary element y in R_0 is the f-image of the element 1/y in R_0. Hence f is onto.

Thus $\quad f : R_0 \to R_0$ is one-one onto.

It should be noted that f (x) = 1/x cannot be a mapping from the set of real numbers to the set of real numbers. Then reason is that the image of 0 will not exist because f (0) = 1/0 and 1/0 is not a real number.

Example 16: *Let C be the set of complex numbers. Prove that the map $f : C \to R$ given by $f(z) = |z|, z \in C$*

is neither one-one nor onto.

Solution: Let $z = x + iy$ be any complex number, where $x, y \in R$ and i $\sqrt{(-1)}$.

Then $| z | = \sqrt{(x^2 + y^2)}$ Also $| z |$ is always a non-negative real number *i.e.,* $| z | \geq 0$.

If m be any negative real number $\in$ R, then there exists no complex number $z \in C$ such that $| z | = m$. Thus m is not the f-image of any complex number $\in$ C. Hence f is not onto but is into.

Also $z_1 = 2 + i3 \in C$ and $z_2 = 2 - i3 \in C$.

Then $| 2 + i3 | = \sqrt{13}$ and $| 2 - i3 | = \sqrt{13}$.

Thus $z_1 \neq z_2$, although $| z_1 | = | z_2 |$ *i.e.,* $f(z_1) = f(z_2)$.

Thus we see that two different complex numbers z_1 and $z_2 \in C$ have the same f-image in R. Hence f is not one-one.

Example 17: *Show that the mapping* $f : I_+ \to I_+$ *defined by* $f(x) = x^2$, $x \in I_+$ *where* I_+ *is the set of positive integers, is one-one into.*

Solution: It is given that f is a mapping from I_+ to I_+ defined by

$$f(x) = x^2 \ \forall \ x \in I_+.$$

We have $\quad I_+ = \{1, 2, 3, 4, ...\}$.

f is one-one. Let $x_1 \ x_2 \in I_+$. We have

$$f(x_1) = f(x_2) \Rightarrow x_1^2 = x_2^2 \text{ [by def. of f]}$$

$$\Rightarrow x_1 = x_2 \Rightarrow \text{f is one-one.}$$

f is into. Now we shall prove that f is into and not onto. We have $2 \in I_+$. Now there exists no $x \in I_+$ such that $x^2 = 2$. Thus $2 \in I_+$ is not the f-image of any $x \in I_+$. Therefore the mapping f is into and not onto.

Example 18: *Classify the following as mappings of* $R \to R$:

(a) $f(x) = \log x$,

(b) $f(x) = +\sqrt{x}$.

(c) $f(x) = \tan x$, $(x \in R)$.

Solution: (a) Let $x \in R$ and let x be a negative real number. Then log x is not a real number, *i.e.,* log x is not an element of R. Thus the negative real numbers in R will have no f-image in R. Also $\log 0 = -\infty$ which is not an element of R. Thus, the real number 0 in R has no f-image in R. Hence f is not a function from R to R. However f is a function from R_+ to R.

(b) Let x be a negative real number. Then $\sqrt{x}$ is not a real number *i.e.,* $\sqrt{x} \notin R$. Thus the negative real numbers in R will have no f-images in R. Hence f is not a function from R to R. If S denotes the set of all non-negative real numbers, then f defined by this formula is a function from S to R.

(c) Let $x = \pi/2$. Then $\tan \pi/2 =$ which is not an element of R. Thus $\pi/2 \in R$ has no f-image in R. In general if $x \in R$ is such that $x = n.\frac{\pi}{2}$ Where n is an odd integer, then x has no f-image in R. Hence f is not a function from R to R.

However, if $X = \{x : x \in R \text{ and } -\pi/2 < x < \pi/2\}$, then f is a function from X to R, Obviously this function will be one-one and onto.

Example 19: *If R is the set of real numbers discuss the mapping*

$$f : R \to R \text{ where } f(x) = x^2,\ x \in R$$

What is the domain and the range of the mapping f ?

Solution: If x is any real number, the x^2 is also a real number and it will be unique. Thus each element $x \in R$ has a unique f-image in R. Therefore $f : R \to R$.

Since there is no real number whose square is negative, therefore any negative number in R is not the f-image of any element in R. Consequently f is a mapping of R into R and not from R onto R.

Also we see that $(2)^2 = 4$ and $(-2)^2 = 4$. Thus the elements 2 and -2 in R have the same f-image 4 in R. Hence f is a many-one into mapping of R to R.

Domain of f: Since $f : R \to R$, therefore domain of f is R.

Range of f: If $x \in R$, then $f(x) = x^2$ is a non-negative real number. Further if y is any non-negative real number, then $\exists$ a real number $\sqrt{y}$ such that $f(\sqrt{y}) = (\sqrt{y})^2 = y$. Thus, every non-negative real number is the f-image of some real number. Therefore the range of f is the set of non-negative real numbers.

Example 20:

Let A = { a, b, c,} and B = {e, f}. Write down all possible functions from A to B.

Solution: While forming a mapping from A to B, each element of A can be associated to an element of B in two ways. Thus we can have $2 \times 2 \times 2$ *i.e.,* 8 distinct mappings from A to B.

These are as given below:

{(a, e), (b, e), (c, e)}, {(a, e), (b, e), (c, f)},

{(a, e), (b, f), (c, e)}, {(a, e), (b, f), (c, f)},

{(a, f), (b, e), (c, e)}, {(a, f), (b, e), (c, f)},

{(a, f), (b, f), (c, e)}, {(a, f), (b, f), (c, f)}.

Example 21: *Each of the following formulas defines a function from R to R. Find the range of each function.*

1. $f(x) = x^3$;
2. $g(x) = \sin x$;
3. $h(x) = x^2 + 1$.

Solution:

1. We know that every real number a has a real cube root $\left(\sqrt[3]{a}\right)$.

   Therefore if a be any arbitrary element $\in$ R, then $f\left(\sqrt[3]{a}\right) = \left(\sqrt[3]{a}\right)^3$

   $= a$ *i.e.,* $\sqrt[3]{a} \in R$ is the pre-image of $a \in R$. Since a is any arbitrary element $\in$ R, therefore the range of f is R. This function will be an onto function.
2. The sine of any real number lies in the closed interval $[-1, 1]$. Also all the numbers in this interval will be the sine of some real numbers. Hence the range of g is the closed interval $[-1, 1]$. This function will be an into function.
3. If we add 1 to the square of each real number, we get the set of numbers which are greater then or equal to 1. Let y be any real number greater than or equal to 1 and let $y = h(x) = x^2 + 1$.

   Then $x = \pm \sqrt{(y-1)}$ are also real numbers.

Thus, every real number which is greater than or equal to 1 is the h-image of some or other real number. Hence the range of h is the infinite interval $(1, \infty)$.

Example 22: *Show that the mapping $f : R \to R$ defined by*

$$f(x) = \cos x \ \forall x \in R$$

is neither one-one nor onto. Modify the domain and co-domain of this mapping so that it may be both one-to-one and onto.

Solution: We have $f : R \to R$ such that

$$f(x) = \cos x \ \forall x \in R.$$

f is not one-one. We have $0, 2\pi \in R$

and $f(0) = \cos 0 = 1$, $f(2\pi) = \cos 2\pi = 1$.

Thus, 0 and 2π are two distinct elements in the domain R of f and they have the same f-image 1 in the co-domain R of f. Therefore f is may-one and not one-one.

f is not onto: We know that if $x \in R$, then $-1 \leq \cos x \leq 1$. Therefore if $y \in$ the co-domain R of f and $y > 1$ or $y < -1$, then there exists no $x \in$ the domain R of f such that $f(x) = \cos x = y$. Therefore the mapping f is into and not onto.

Now let $X = \{x : x \in R \text{ and } 0 \leq x \leq \pi\}$

and $\quad Y = \{y : y \in R \text{ and } -1 \leq y \leq 1\}$.

If we take X as the domain of f and Y as the co-domain of f, then the mapping $f : X \to Y$ such that

$$f(x) = \cos x \ \forall \ x \in X$$

is one-one and onto.

Example 23: *Let R be the set of all real numbers. Using the fact that every cubic equation with real coefficients has a real root, show that $x \to x^2 - x$ defines a mapping of R onto R. Is this a one-one mapping ?*

Solution: If $x \in R$, then $x^3 - x \in R$ and is unique.

Therefore $x \to x^2 - x$ defines a mapping of R to R.

Let y be any arbitrary element $\in R$ *i.e.,* let y be any real number. Then $x^3 - x = y$ is a cubic equation with real coefficients. It will have at least one real root. Thus for any $y \in R$ there exists $x \in R$ such that $x^3 - x = y$. Therefore $x \to x^2 - x$ defines a mapping of R onto R.

Again $\quad 1 \to 1^3 - 1$ *i.e.,* $1 \to 0$

and $\quad -1 \to (-1)^3 - (-1)$

i.e., $\quad -1 \to 0$.

Thus, the two elements 1 and $-1 \in R$ map onto the same element $0 \in R$. Hence the mapping is not one-one.

Example 24:

If S and T are non-empty sets, prove that there exists a one-to-one correspondence between $S \times T$ and $T \times S$.

Solution:

If $a \in S$ and $b \in T$, then the ordered pair $(a, b) \in S \times T$ and the ordered pair $(b, a) \in T \times S$. Let f be a mapping from $S \times T$ to $T \times S$ defined by the formula

$$f(a, b) = (b, a) \ \forall \ (a, b) \in S \times T.$$

Here $f(a, b)$ denotes the image under the mapping f of the element $(a, b) \in S \times T$.

Obviously the mapping f is well-defined.

f is one-one. Let (a, b), (c, d) $\in$ S $\times$ T. Then f (a, b) = f (c, d)

$\Rightarrow$ (b, a) = (d, c) [by def. of f]

$\Rightarrow$ b = d, a = c

$\Rightarrow$ (a, b) = (c, d)

$\Rightarrow$ f is one-one.

f is onto: Let (y, z) be any element of T $\times$ S. Then y $\in$ T, z $\in$ S Therefore (z, y) $\in$ S $\times$ T. We have f (z, y) = (y, z).

Thus, (y, z) T $\times$ S $\Rightarrow \exists$ (z, y) $\in$ S $\times$ T such that f (z, y) = (y, z). Therefore f is onto.

Thus, f is a one-one function from S $\times$ T onto T $\times$ S. Therefore f gives a one-to-one correspondence between S $\times$ T and T $\times$ S.

Example 25: *If the mapping $f : I \to I$ be defined by $f(x) = x^2$ where I is the set of integers, evaluate $f^{-1}(16)$ and $f^{-1}(-3)$. Does the inverse mapping exist? If so, find it.*

Solution: Let $f^{-1}(16) = x$ where $x \in I$

$$16 = f(x) = x^2$$

$$\therefore \quad x = 4 \text{ or } -4$$

Hence, $f^{-1}(16) = \{-4, 4\}$

Also, since there is no integer whose square is – 1, it follows that $f^{-1}(-3) = \phi$, the empty set.

Under the given mapping, the elements – 4 and 4 have the same image 16. Accordingly, the given mapping is not one-one. Hence the inverse mapping does not exist.

Example 26:

If S and T are non-empty sets, prove that there exists a one-to-one correspondence between S $\times$ T and T $\times$ S.

Solution: (a) Let x be an element of f^{-1} (A $\cup$ B), then

$x \in f^{-1}(A \cup B)$

$\Rightarrow$ $f(x) \in A \cup B$

$\Rightarrow$ $f(x) \in A$ or $f(x) \in B$

$\Rightarrow$ $x \in f^{-1}(A)$ or $x \in f^{-1}(B)$

$\Rightarrow$ $x \in \{f^{-1}(A) \cup f^{-1}(B)\}$

$\therefore \quad f^{-1}(A \cup B) \subset \{f^{-1}(A) \cup \{f^{-1}(B)\}$ ...(1)

Again, let y be an element of $f^{-1}(A) \cup f^{-1}(B)$, then

$$y \in f^{-1}(A) \cup f^{-1}(B)$$

$$\Rightarrow \quad y \in f^{-1}(A) \text{ or } y \in f^{-1}(B)$$

$$\Rightarrow \quad f(y) \in A \text{ or } f(y) \in B$$

$$\Rightarrow \quad f(y) \in A \cup B$$

$$\Rightarrow \quad y \in f^{-1}(A \cup B)$$

Therefore $f^{-1}(A) \cup f^{-1}(B) \subset f^{-1}(A \cup B)$ (2)

(1) and (2), imply.

$$f^{-1}(A \cup B) = f^{-1}(A) \cup f^{-1}(B).$$

Similarly, 2nd result can be proved.

Example 27: *If the map $f : R \to R$ be given by $f(x) = 4x - 1$ and the map $g : R \to R$ be given by $g(x) = x^3 + 2$, find (g of) x and (f og) x, R being the set of real numbers.*

Solution: We have,

$$(gof)x = g[f(x)] = g(4x - 1) \text{ as } f(x) = 4x - 1$$

$$= (4x - 1)^3 + 2 \text{ as } g(x) = x^3 + 2$$

$$= 64x^3 - 4x^2 + 12x + 1.$$

Also

$$(fog)x = f[g(x)] = f(x^3 + 2)$$

$$= 4(x^3 + 2) - 1$$

$$= 4x^3 + 7.$$

Example 28: *Let the functions $f : R \to R$ and $g : R \to R$ be defined by $f(x) = 2x$, $g(x) = x^2 + 2$, $\forall x \in R$. Check the functions f and g for being*

(i) one-to-one

(ii) onto.

Find the formulae defining the functions $f \circ g$ and $g \circ g$ and obtain the values of $(f \circ g)(2)$ and $(g \circ g)(1)$.

Solution: The mapping f is both one-to-one and onto as shown below.

f is one-to-one: Let $x_1, x_2 \in R$. Then

$$f(x_1) = f(x_2)$$

$$\Rightarrow 2x_1 = 2x_2 \Rightarrow x_1 = x_2.$$

$\therefore$ The mapping f is one-to-one.

f is onto: Let y be any element of R. Then y/2 is also an element of R and we have

$$f(y/2) = 2.(y/2) = y.$$

Thus, each element in R is the f-image of some element in R. Hence the mapping f is onto.

The mapping g is neither one-to-one nor onto as shown below.

g is not one-to-one: We have $1 \in R$ and $-1 \in R$. By the definition of the mapping g, we have

$$g(1) = 1^2 + 2 = 3,$$

$$g(-1) = (-1)^2 + 2 = 3.$$

Thus, 1 and –1 are two distinct elements in R and we have g (1) = g (–1). Therefore the mapping g is not one-to-one.

The mapping g is not onto: We have $-5 \in R$ and there exists no $x \in R$ such that $g(x) = x^2 + 2 = -5$. Therefore the mapping g is not onto.

To find the formula for the mapping $f \circ g : R \to R$.

If $x \in R$, then we have

$$(f \circ g)(x) = f[g(x)] = f(x^2 + 2) = 2(x^2 + 2)$$

$$= 2x^2 + 4.$$

$\therefore$ $f \circ g : R \to R$ is defined by the formula

$$(f \circ g)(x) = 2x^2 + 4, \forall x \in R.$$

Using this formula, we have

$$(f \circ g)(2) = 2.(2)^2 + 4 = 12.$$

Now to find the formula defining the mapping $g \circ g : R \to R$.

If $x \in R$, then we have

$$(g \circ g)(x) = g[g(x)] = g(x^2 + 2)$$

$$= (x^2 + 2)^2 + 2 = x^4 + 4x^2 + 6.$$

$\therefore$ $g \circ g : R \to R$ is defined as

$$(g \circ g)(x) = x^4 + 4x^2 + 6, \forall x \in R.$$

$$(g \circ g)(1) = 1^4 + 4.1^2 + 6 = 11.$$

Example 29: *If* $f : X \to Y$ *and* $g : Y \to Z$ *are any two mappings, show that if* $g \circ f : Y \to Z$ *is one-to-one, then f is one-to-one.*

Solution: Let x_1, x_2 be any two elements of X.

Then $f(x_1) = f(x_2)$

$\Rightarrow g[f(x_1)] = g[f(x_2)]$

$\Rightarrow (g \circ f)(x_1) = (g \circ f)(x_2)$

$\Rightarrow x_1 = x_2$, because the mapping g o f is given to be one-to-one.

Hence the mapping f is one-to-one.

Example 30: *Let f : R → R be given by the formula* $f(x) = x^2$, *(x ∈ R) and g : R → R be give by the formula g (x) = x + 3, (x ∈ R). Calculate (f o g) (2) and (g o f) (2). Hence show that*

$$f \circ g \neq g \circ f.$$

Solution: We have $(f \circ g)(2) = f[g(2)] = f(2 + 3)$

$-f(5) = 5^2 = 25.$

Also $(g \circ f)(2) = g[f(2)] = g(2^2)$

$= g(4) = 4 + 3 = 7.$

Now both f o g and g o f are mappings from R to R. Since 2 ∈ R is such that (f o g) (2) ≠ (g o f) (2), therefore the mappings f o g and g o f are not equal. Hence f o g ≠ g o f.

Example 31: *Let A = {1, 2, 3, 4, 5} and let the functions*

$$f : A \to A,\ g : A \to A$$

be defined as

$f(1) = 3, f(2) = 5, f(3) = 3,$

$f(4) = 1, f(5) = 2,$

$g(1) = 4, g(2) = 1,$

$g(3) = 1, g(4) = 2,$

$g(5) = 3.$

Find the composite functions g o f and f o g.

Solution: We have,

$(g \circ f)(1) = g[f(1)] = g(3) = 1$

$(g \circ f)(2) = g[f(2)] = g(5) = 3$

$(g \circ f)(3) = g[f(3)] = g(3) = 1$

$(g \circ f)(4) = g[f(4)] = g(1) = 4$

$(g \circ f)(5) = g[f(5)] = g(2) = 1.$

Also $(f \circ g)(1) = f[g(1)] = f(4) = 1$

$$(f \circ g)(2) = f[g(2)] = f(1) = 3$$
$$(f \circ g)(3) = f[g(3)] = f(1) = 3$$
$$(f \circ g)(4) = f[g(4)] = f(2) = 5$$
$$(f \circ g)(5) = f[g(5)] = f(3) = 3.$$

Example 32: *Let the functions $f : R \rightarrow R$, $g : R \rightarrow R$ be defined by*

$$f(x) = 2x + 1,\ g(x) = x^2 - 2.$$

Find the formulae for $g \circ f$ and $f \circ g$.

Solution: Let us first find the formula for $(g \circ f) : R \rightarrow R$.

We have $(g \circ f)(x) = g[f(x)] = g(2x + 1)$

$$= (2x + 1)^2 - 2 = 4x^2 + 4x - 1.$$

Now let us find the formula for $f \circ g$. We have

$(f \circ g)(x) = f[g(x)] = f(x^2 - 2) = 2(x^2 - 2) + 1 = 2x^2 - 3.$

Example 33: *If $f : R \rightarrow R$ be defined by $f(x) = |x|$, then prove that $f \circ f = f$.*

Solution: Since $f : R \rightarrow R$, therefore the composite mapping $f \circ f$ is also a mapping from R to R *i.e.,* $f \circ f : R \rightarrow R$.

Now if x be any element of R, we have

$$(f \circ f)(x) = f[f(x)] = f(|x|)$$
$$= ||x|| \quad |x| = f(x).$$

Thus we have $(f \circ f)(x) = f(x), \forall x \in R$.

Hence be the definition of the equality of two mappings,

we have $\quad f \circ f = f.$

Example 34: *Give an example to show that composition of two functions is not in general commutative.*

Solution: Consider the two mappings f and g from R to R given. These mappings f and g are such that $f \circ g \neq g \circ f$.

Hence, the composite of mappings is not a commutative operation.

Example 35: *If $f : R \rightarrow R : f(x) = |x|$, then prove that $f \circ f = f$.*

Solution: $(f \circ f)(x) = f[f(x)] = f(|x|)$

$$= ||x|| = |x| = f(x)$$

$$\therefore \quad f \circ f = f$$

Example 36: *If the mappings f and g are given by*

$$f = \{(1, 2), (3, 5), (4, 1)\}$$

$$g = \{(2, 3), (5, 1), (1, 3)\}$$

then write down pairs in the mappings (f og) and (g of).

Solution: Here, range (f) = {2, 5, 1} and dom (g) = {2, 5, 1}

∴ Range (f) ⊂ dom (g), so (gof) is defined.

Also, dom (gof = dom(f) = {1, 3, 4}

Now, (gof) (1) = g[f(1)] = g(2) = 3,

(gof) (3) = g[f(3)] = g(5) = 1,

(gof) (4) = g[f(4)] = g(1) = 3.

∴ gof = {(1, 3), (3, 1), (4, 3)}.

Also, range (g) = {3, 1}, dom (f) = {1, 3, 4}.

Since range (g) ⊂ dom (f), so (fog) is also defined.

Also dom (fog) = dom (g) = {2, 5, 1}

Now, (fog) (2) = f[g(2)] = f(3) = 5;

(fog) (5) = f[g(5)] = f(1) = 2;

(fog) (1) = f[g(1)] = f(3) = 5.

∴ fog = {(2, 5), (5, 2), (1, 5)}.

Example 37: *Decide whether or not the following are functions from A → B where A = {1, 2, 3, 4, 5}, B = {a, b, c, d, e}. If they are functions give the range of each. If they are not, tell why?*

(a) f = {(1, a), (2, b), (3, b), (5, c)}

(b) g = {(1, c), (5, d), (3, a), (2, b), (1, d), (4, a)}

(c) h = {(5, a), (1, c), (4, b), (3, c), (2, d)}

Solution:

(a) Since the element 4 ∈ A is not associated to any element ∈ B, therefore f is not a function from A → B.

(b) The element 1 ∈ A is associated to two different elements c and d ∈ B. Therefore, g is not a function from A → B.

(c) Each element of A is associated to a unique element of B. Therefore h is a function from A → B. The range of h is the set of the h-images of all elements of A. Thus range of h = h(A) = {a, c, b, c, d} = B.

Example 38: *Let R be the set of all real numbers. Using the fact that every cubic equation with real coefficients has a real root, show that $x \to x^2 - x$ defines a mapping of R onto R. Is this a one-one mapping ?*

Solution: If $x \in R$, then $x^3 - x \in R$ and is unique.

Therefore $x \to x^2 - x$ defines a mapping of R to R.

Let y be any arbitrary element $\in$ R *i.e.,* let y be any real number. Then $x^3 - x = y$ is a cubic equation with real coefficients. It will have at least one real root. Thus for any $y \in R$ there exists $x \in R$ such that $x^3 - x = y$. Therefore $x \to x^2 - x$ defines a mapping of R onto R.

Again $\quad 1 \to 1^3 - 1$ *i.e.,* $1 \to 0$

and $\quad -1 \to (-1)^3 - (-1)$

i.e., $\quad -1 \to 0.$

Thus, the two elements 1 and $-1 \in R$ map onto the same element $0 \in R$. Hence the mapping is not one-one.

Example 39: *Let $X = \{x : x \in R$*

and $\quad -\pi/2 \leq x \leq \pi/2$ *i.e.,*

let $\quad X = [-\pi/2, \pi/2]$

and $\quad Y = (y : y \in R$

and $\quad -1 \leq y \leq 1\}$ *i.e., let* $Y = [-1, 1]$.

Show that the function $f : X \to Y$ defined by

$$f(x) = \sin x, \ (x \in X', \text{ is one-one onto.}$$

Also give the inverse mapp $f^{-1} : Y \to X$.

Solution: Let m and n be any two different real numbers lying in the closed interval $[-\pi/2, \pi/2]$. We know that any two different real numbers lying in the closed interval $[-\pi/2, \pi/2]$ have not the same sine.

$\therefore \quad m \neq n \Rightarrow \sin m \neq \sin n$

$\Rightarrow \quad f(m) \neq f(n)$. Hence f is one-one.

Again if y is any arbitrary real number lying in the closed interval $[-1, 1]$, $\exists$ a real number x lying in the closed interval $[-\pi/2, \pi/2]$ such that is n x = y.

Thus, every element y in Y is the f-image of some element x in X. Hence f is onto.

Thus $f : X \to Y$ is one-one onto, therefore f has an inverse function $f^{-1} : X \to Y$.

Let y be the image of x under the function f. Then

$$y = f(x) = \sin$$

Consequently, x will be the image of y under the inverse function f^{-1} *i.e.*,

$$x = f^{-1}(y).$$

Solving for x in terms of y in the equation y = sin x, we get

$$x = \sin^{-1} y.$$

Thus $f^{-1}(y) = \sin^{-1} y$, $(y \in Y)$ is the formula defining the inverse function $f^{-1} : Y \to X$.

Example 40: *If $f : R \to R$ is defined as follows :*

$$f(x) = \begin{cases} 1, \text{ if } x \in Q \\ -1, \text{ if } x \notin Q \end{cases}$$

Find: (a) $f\left(\frac{1}{2}\right)$, $f(\pi)$, $f\left(\sqrt{2}\right)$

(b) *Range of f*

(c) *Pre-images of 1 and –1.*

Solution:

(a) It is evident from the definition of f that at every rational point the function attains value 1 and at every irrational point it attains value – 1. So,

$$\frac{1}{2} \in Q \Rightarrow f\left(\frac{1}{2}\right) = 1, \pi \notin Q \Rightarrow f(\pi) = -1$$

and $$\sqrt{2} \notin Q \Rightarrow f\left(\sqrt{2}\right) = -1.$$

(b) We have, Range of f = $\{f(x) : x \in R\}$ Also, by definition f(x) attains values 1 and – 1 according as x is rational or irrational and a real number is either rational or irrational.

$\therefore$ Range of f = $\{1, -1\}$.

(c) Since $f(x) = 1$ for all $x \in Q$. Therefore pre-images of 1 are rational numbers, *i.e.*,

$f^{-1}(1) = Q.$

Also, – 1 is the image of every real number which is not rational. So,

$f^{-1}(-1) = R - Q$ = set of irrational numbers.

Example 41: *Let A be the set of all triangles in a plane. Let R be the relation in A defined as xRy iff x is congruent to y, $x \in A$, $y \in A$. Then R is an equivalence relation.*

Solution: Hence, we observe that

1. xRx, for every $x \in A$, since every triangle is congruent to itself. Thus R is reflexive.
2. $xRy \Rightarrow yRx$, since if triangle x is congruent to triangle y then y is congruent to x. Thus r is symmetric.
3. xRy and $yRx \Rightarrow xRz$, since if triangle x is congruent to y and triangle y is congruent to z, the triangle x is congruent to z. Thus R is transitive.

Since R is reflexive, symmetric and transitive, therefore R is an equivalence relation.

Note: In a similar way we can prove that the relation of similarity in the set of all triangles in a plane is an equivalence relation.

Example 42: *Prove that the relation defined by 'is perpendicular to in the set of straight lines in a plane is symmetric but neither reflexive nor transitive.*

Solution: Let R stands for "is perpendicular to". Let L be the set of straight lines in a plane.

1. *Reflexivity :* Since no straight line is perpendicular to itself, hence relation is not reflexive, *i.e.*,

   a R a for $a \in L$

2. *Symmetry :* If straight line a is $\perp$ to straight line b then b is also $\perp$ to a *i.e.*,

   $$a \, R \, b \Rightarrow b \, R \, a \text{ for } a, b \in L.$$

   Hence relation is symmetric.

3. *Transitivity :* If for a, b, c, $\in L$, $a \perp b$ and $b \perp c$ (it may be parallel).

   Hence a R b, b R c does not implied a R c $\forall$ a, b, c $\in$ L.

   Hence relation is not transitive.

Example 43: *If I be the set of integers and if R be defined over I by "a R b iff a – b is an even integer" where a, b $\in$ I, then show that the relation R is an equivalence relation.*

Solution:

(i) Reflexivity : Since O = a – a is even.

Hence a R a $\forall$ a $\in$ I

Therefore, R is reflexive over I.

(ii) *Symmetry* : Since a – b is even then b – a = – (a – b) is also even and hence a R b ⇒ b R a.

Therefore, R is symmetric in I.

(iii) *Transitivity* : a R b and b R c

⇒ (a – b) and (b – c) are even numbers

⇒ (a – b) + (b – c) is even

⇒ (a – c) is even

∴ a R b and b R c ⇒ a R c.

Therefore, R is transitive in I.

Hence R is an equivalence relation.

Example 44: *If I the set of integers then show that relation R in I such that a R b iff a – b is divisible by m (positive integer) is an equivalence relation.*

Solution: (i) *Reflexivity* : For each a ∈ I, a = a = 0 which is divisible by m, so a R a Therefore, R is reflexive.

(ii) *Symmetry* : Let a R b for a, b, ∈ I,

i.e., a – b is divisible by m. Then as a – b = – (b – a)

(b – a) is also divisible by m.

Hence a R b ⇒ b R a so that R is symmetric.

(iii) *Transitivity* : For a, b, c ∈ I, Let a R b, b R c, *i.e.*, let (a – b), (b – c) be divisible by m. Then as

(a – b) + (b – c) = a – c,

a – c is also divisible by m.

Hence, a R b, b R c ⇒ a R c, *i.e.*, R is transitive, showing that R is an equivalence relation.

Example 45: *Which of the following relations in the set of real numbers are equivalence relations ?*

1. *a R b iff* $|a| \leq b$,
2. *a R b iff* $|a| \geq |b|$
3. *a R b iff* $|a| \neq |b|$.

Solution: Let E denote the set of real numbers.

1. The given relation R on the set E is not reflexive.

For example –6 ∈ E. We have $|-6| = 6$ and the statement $6 \leq -6$ is not true. Thus –6 is not R-related to –6 because the statement $|-6| \leq -6$ is not true.

Thus, there exists elements in E which are not R-related to themselves. Therefore the relation r is not reflexive. Hence it is not an equivalence relation.

2. The given relation R on the set E is not reflexive. For example $3 \in E$. We have $|3| = 3$. The statement $|3| > |3|$ is false. Thus 3 is not R-related to 3 because the statement $|3| > |3|$ is not true.

   Thus, there exist element in E which are not R-related to themselves. Therefore the relation R on the set E is not reflexive. Hence it is not an equivalence relation.

3. The given relation R on the set E is not reflexive. For example $4 \in E$. The statement $|4| \neq |4|$ is false and so 4 is no R-related to itself. Since the relation R on the set E is not reflexive, therefore it cannot be an equivalence relation.

Example 46: *Show that the relation R in the set of non-zero integers I_0 defined by a R b if $a^b = b^a$, $(a, b, \in I_0)$ is reflexive and symmetric.*

Solution:

1. *R is Reflexive:* We have $\forall\ a \in I_0$, $a^a = a^a$ *i.e.,* a R a. Therefore R is reflexive.
2. *R is Symmetric:* Suppose we have a I_0 b. Then $a^b = b^a$. Now $a^b = b^c$ implies $b^a = a^b$ *i.e.,* b R a. Thus, a R b $\Rightarrow$ b R a. Therefore R is symmetric.

Example 47: *Let the relation R in the set of real numbers be defined as a R b if and only if $1 + ab > 0$. Show that this relation is reflexive and symmetric but not transitive.*

Solution: Let S denote the set of all real numbers. Let R be a relation in S defined as a R b iff $1 + ab > 0$.

1. *R is Reflexive:* Let a be any real number.

   Then $1 + aa = 1 + a^2 > 0$, since $a^2 \geq 0$.

   Thus a R a $\forall\ a \in S$. Therefore R is reflexive.

2. *R is Symmetric:* Let a, b be any two real numbers. Then

   a R b $\Rightarrow 1 + ab > 0$

   $\Rightarrow 1 + ba > 0.$ $\qquad [\because\ ab = ba]$

   $\Rightarrow$ b R a.

   $\therefore$ R is symmetric.

3. *R is not Transitive:* Consider three real numbers

$$1, -\frac{1}{2}, -4$$

We have $1 + 1.\left(-\frac{1}{2}\right) = \frac{1}{2} > 0.$

$\therefore \quad 1\ R - \frac{1}{2}.$

Further $1 + \left(-\frac{1}{2}\right)(-4) = 3 > 0.$

$\therefore \quad -\frac{1}{2}\ R - 4.$

But $1 + 1(-4) = -3$ which is not greater than 0. Therefore 1 is not R-related to –4.

Thus $1\ R - \frac{1}{2}, -\frac{1}{2}\ R - 4$ and 1 is not R-related to –4.

$\therefore$ R is not transitive.

Example 48: *Let I be the set of all integers. Let a relation a R b, (a, b ∈ I) be defined if a – b is an even integer. Show that is an equivalence relation.*

Solution: Do yourself.

Example 49: *Give an example of a relation which is:*

1. *Symmetric and reflexive but not transitive.*
2. *Symmetrıc and transitive but not reflexive.*
3. *Reflexive but neither symmetric nor 'transitive.*

Solution: Consider the set S = {1, 2, 3}. Then

1. R_1 = {(1, 1), (2, 2), (3, 3), (2, 3), (3, 2), (1, 2), (2, 1)} is a relation on S such that R_1 is reflexive and symmetric but not transitive.

   Observe that (1, 2), ∈ R_1, (2, 3) ∈ R_1 but (1, 3) ∉ R_1 and so R_1 is not transitive.
2. R_2 = {(1, 2), (2, 2), (1, 2), (2, 1)} is a relation on S such that R_2 is symmetric and transitive but not reflexive. Observe that (3, 3) ∉ R_3 and so R_2 is not reflexive.
3. R_3 = {(1, 1), (2, 2), (3, 3), (1, 2), (2, 3)} is a relation on S such that R_3 is reflexive but is neither symmetric nor transitive.

Example 50: *In the set N of all natural numbers, the relation R defined by aRb iff a divides b is a partial order relation.*

Solution: We have, "a $\in$ N, a is a divisor of a *i.e.,* aRa. Therefore R is reflexive.

Again, if a is a divisor of b then b cannot be a divisor of a unless a = b. Thus aRb and bRa $\Rightarrow$ a = b. Therefore R is anti-symmetric.

Finally a is a divisor of b and b is a divisor of c implies a is a divisor of c. Therefore R is transitive.

Since R is reflexive, anti-symmetric and transitive, therefore R is a partial order relation.

Example 51: *Prove that the relation of similarity in the set of all triangles in a plane is an equivalence relation.*

Solution: Let A be the set of all triangles in a plane. Let R be the relation in A defined as x R y if and only if the triangle x is similar to the triangle y, x $\in$ A, y $\in$ A.

R is Reflexive: Let x $\in$ A. Since every triangle is similar to itself, therefore by our definition of R, we have x R x.

Thus x R x $\forall$ x $\in$ A. Therefore R is reflexive.

R is Symmetric: Let x, y $\in$ A be such that x R y. We have x R y $\Rightarrow$ triangle x is similarly to triangle y [by def. of R]

$\Rightarrow$ triangle y is similar to triangle x

$\Rightarrow$ y R x [by def. of R].

Thus x r y $\Rightarrow$ y R x. Therefore R is symmetric.

R is Transitive: Let x, y, z $\in$ A be such that x R y and y R z. We have x R y and y R z

$\Rightarrow$ triangle x is similar to triangle y and triangle y is similar to triangle z

$\Rightarrow$ triangle x is similar to triangle z

$\Rightarrow$ x R z [by def. of R].

Thus, x R y and y R z $\Rightarrow$ x R z. Therefore R is transitive.

Since R is reflexive, symmetric and transitive therefore R is an equivalence relation.

Example 52: *Show that the relation "greater than" denoted by > in the set of natural numbers N is transitive but is neither reflexive nor symmetric.*

Solution:

1. *R is not Reflexive:* We have 3 $\in$ N, but 3 is not greater than 3 *i.e.,* 3 is not R-related to 3. Therefore R is not reflexive.

2. *R is not Symmetric:* We have $4 \in N$, $2 \in N$, 4 is greater than 2 *i.e.*, 4 R 2 but 2 is not greater than 4 *i.e.*, $(2, 4) \notin R$. Therefore R is not symmetric.
3. *R is Transitive:* Suppose a R b and b R c. Then $a > b$ and $b > c$. Now $a > b$ and $b > c$ implies $a > c$ *i.e.*, a R c. Therefore R is transitive.

Example 53: *Show that corresponding to an equivalence relation R defined in a set S, for any two members be and c of the same equivalence class, b has the relation R to c.*

Solution: Suppose b and c are any two members of the equivalence class $[a] = \{x : x\ Ra, x \in S, a \in S\}$.

Then we have b R c and c R a.

Now c R a $\Rightarrow$ a R c since R is symmetric :

Again bRa and aRc $\Rightarrow$ b R c, since r is transitive. Hence the result.

Example 54: *Given that R is a relation in a set A and R^{-1} is its inverse relation, prove that*

1. *if R is reflexive, then R^{-1} is reflexive,*
2. *if R is symmetric, then R^{-1} is symmetric,*
3. *if R is transitive, then R^{-1} is transitive.*

Solution:

1. $\forall\ a \in A$, $(a, a) \in R$ since R is reflexive.

Now $(a, a) \in R \Rightarrow (a, a) \in R^{-1}$.

Thus $\forall\ a \in A$, $(a, a) \in R^{-1}$ and therefore R^{-1} is reflexive.

2. If $(a, b) \in R^{-1}$, then $(b, a) \in R$.

Since R is symmetric, therefore

$$(b, a) \in R \Rightarrow (a, b) \in R \Rightarrow (b, a) \in R^{-1}.$$

Thus $(a, b) \in R^{-1} \Rightarrow (b, a) \in R^{-1}$ and therefore R^{-1} is symmetric.

3. Let (a, b) and $(b, c) \in R^{-1}$. Then $(c, b) \in R$ and $(b, a) \in R$. since R is transitive, therefore

$(c, b) \in R$ and $(b, a) \in R$

$\Rightarrow (c, a) \in R$

$\Rightarrow (a, c) \in R^{-1}$.

Thus $(a, b) \in R^{-1}$ and $(b, c) \in R^{-1}$

$\Rightarrow (a, c) \in R^{-1}$.

Hence R^{-1} is transitive.

Thus, we can say that if R is an equivalence relation in A, then R^{-1} is also an equivalence relation in A.

Example 55: *Which of the following relations in the set of real numbers are equivalence relations.*

1. a R b if | a | = | b |,
2. a R b if | a | ≥ | b |
3. a R b if a – b ≥ 0?

Solution:

1. We have, ∀ a ∈ E. | a | = | a | *i.e.,* a R a.

   Therefore R is reflexive.

   Again | a | = | b |

   ⇒ | b | = | a | *i.e.,* a R b ⇒ b R a.

   Therefore R is symmetric.

   Finally | a | = | b | and | b | = | c |

   ⇒ | a | = | c |

   i.e., a R b and b R c

   ⇒ a Rc. Therefore R is transitive.

   Hence R is an equivalence relation.
2. We have | 8 | ≥ | 7 |, but | 7 | is not ≥ | 8 |. Thus, 8 R 7 but 7 is not R-related to 8. Therefore R is not symmetric. Hence R is not an equivalence relation.
3. We have 4 – 3 ≥ 0; but 3 – 4 is not ≥ 0. Thus 4 R 3 but 3 is not R-related to 4. Therefore, R is not symmetric. Hence R is not an equivalence relation.

Example 56: *Show that if R and R' be symmetric relations in a set A, then R ∪ R' is also a symmetric relation in A.*

Solution: Since R and R' are relations in A, therefore R ⊆ A × A and R' ⊆ A × A. Hence R ∪ R' ⊆ A × A and therefore R ∪ R' is also a relation in A.

Let (a, b) ∈ R ∪ R'.

Now (a, b) ∈ R ∪ R'

⇒ (a, b) ∈ R or (a, b) ∈ R'

$\Rightarrow$ (b, a) $\in$ R or (b, a) $\in$ R' [$\because$ R and R' are symmetric]

$\Rightarrow$ (b, a) $\in$ R $\cup$ R'.

Thus we have shown that

(a, b) $\in$ R $\cup$ R'

$\Rightarrow$ (b, a) $\in$ R $\cup$ R'.

Hence R $\cup$ R' is symmetric.

Example 57: *Consider the set N × N, the set of ordered pairs of natural numbers. Let R be the relation in N × N which is defined by (a, b) R (c, d) if a + d = b + c.*

Prove that R is an equivalence relation.

Solution:

1. *R is Reflexive:* $\forall$ (a, b) $\in$ N × N, we have a + b = b + a *i.e.*, (a, b) R (a, b). Therefore R is reflexive.
2. *R is Symmetric:* Suppose (a, b) R (c, d) and (c, d). Then a + d = b+c, which implies that c + b = d + a *i.e.*, (c, d) R (a, b). Hence, R is symmetric.
3. *R is Transitive:* Now suppose (a, b) R (c, d) and (c, d) R (e, f). Then a + d = b + c and c + f = d + e.

   Thus, (a + d) + (c + f) = (b + c) + (d + e). Subtracting c + d from both sides, we get a + f = b + e.

$\therefore$ (a, b) R (e, f) and hence r is transitive.

Since R is reflexive, symmetric and transitive, therefore R is an equivalence relation and therefore induces a partition of N × N.

Example 58: *Let α be a mapping of a set S into a set T. Then if we define a R b for a $\in$ S and b $\in$ S, provided α (a) = α (b), prove that r is an equivalence relation.*

Solution: α is a mapping from S into T. If a $\in$ S, then by α (a) we mean the image of a under the mapping α.

1. *R is Reflexive.* Let a be any element of S.

   Then α (a) = α (a).

   Thus α (a) = α (a) $\forall$ a $\in$ S.

$\therefore$ a R a $\forall$ a $\in$ S and so R is reflexive.

2. *R is Symmetric.* Let a, b be any two elements of S. Then a R b

   $\Rightarrow$ α (a) = α (b)

   $\Rightarrow$ α (b) = α (a)

$\Rightarrow$ b R a.

$\therefore$ R is symmetric.

3. *R is Transitive.* Let a, b, c be any three elements of S.

Then a R b $\Rightarrow \alpha(a) = \alpha(b)$

and b R c $\Rightarrow \alpha(b) = \alpha(c)$.

Now $\alpha(a) = \alpha(b)$, $\alpha(b) = \alpha(c)$

$\Rightarrow \alpha(a) = \alpha(c) \Rightarrow$ a R c.

Thus a R b and b R c

$\Rightarrow$ a R c and so R is transitive.

Since R is reflexive, symmetric and transitive, therefore R is an equivalence relation.

Example 59: *Consider the set N × N, the set of all ordered pairs of natural numbers. Let R be the relation in N × N which is defined by (a, b) R (c, d) if and only if ad = bc.*

Prove that R is an equivalence relation and therefore induces a partition of N × N.

Solution:

1. *R is Reflexive:* $\forall$ (a, b) $\in$ N × N, we have ab = ba *i.e.,* (a, b) R (a, b). Therefore R is reflexive.
2. *R is Symmetric:* Suppose (a, b) R (c, d). Then ad = bc, which implies cb = da. Thus (c, d) R (a, b) and R is symmetric.
3. *R is Transitive:* Now suppose (a, b) R (c, d) and (c, d) R (e, f). Then ad = bc and cf = de.

Thus (ad) (cf) = (bc) (de).

Dividing both sides by dc, we get

af = be *i.e.,* (a, b) R (e, f).

Therefore R is transitive.

Hence R is an equivalence relation.

Example 60: *Show that the identity relation on a set S is an equivalence relation.*

Solution: Let R be the identity relation on a set S.

Then R = {(a, a) : a $\in$ S}. To prove that R is an equivalence relation in S.

R is Reflexive: Let a be any element of S. Then by definition of R, we have (a, a) ∈ R ⇒ a R a.

Thus a R a ∀ a ∈ S. Therefore R is reflexive.

R is Symmetric: Let a, b, ∈ S be such that a R b. Then

(a, b) ∈ R.

Therefore we must have a = b and thus, a R b ⇒ b R a. So R is symmetric.

R is Transitive: Let a, b, c ∈ S be such that a R b and b R c. Then (a, b) ∈ R and (b, c) ∈ R. Therefore, we must have a = b and b = c. From this we get a = c and so we have (a, c) ∈ R *i.e.,* we have a R c. Thus, a R b and b R c ⇒ a R c. Therefore R is transitive.

Hence R is an equivalence relation on S.

Example 61: *If R and S are equivalence relations in a set X, prove that R ∩ S is an equivalence relation in X.*

Solution: Since R and S are relations in X, therefore R ⊆ X × X and S ⊆ X × X. Hence R ∩ S ⊆ X × X. Therefore R ∩ S is also a relation in X.

R ∩ S is reflexive. We have

(a, a) ∈ R ∀ a ∈ X. [∵ R is reflexive]

Also (a, a) ∈ S ∀ a ∈ X. [∵ S is reflexive]

∴ ∀ a ∈ X, we have

(a, b) ∈ R ∩ S. Therefore R ∩ S is reflexive.

R ∩ S is symmetric. Let (a, b) ∈ R ∩ S.

Now (a, b) ∈ R ∩ S ⇒ (a, b) ∈ R and (a, b) ∈ S

⇒ (b, a) ∈ R and (b, a) ∈ S. [∵ R and S are symmetric]

⇒ (b, a) ∈ R ∩ S.

Therefore R ∩ S is symmetric.

R ∩ S is transitive. We have

(a, b) ∈ R ∩ S and (b, c) ∈ R ∩ S

⇒ [(a, b) ∈ R and (a, b) ∈ S]

and [(b, c) ∈ R and (b, c) ∈ S]

⇒ [(a, b) ∈ R and (b, c) ∈ R]

and [(a, b) ∈ S and (b, c) ∈ S]

⇒ (a, c) ∈ R and (a, c) ∈ S [∵ R and S are transitive]

$\Rightarrow$ $(a, c) \in R \cap S$. Therefore $R \cap S$ is transitive.

Since $R \cap S$ is reflexive, symmetric and transitive, therefore $R \cap S$ is an equivalence relation.

Example 62: *Let S be the set of all point in a plane. Let R be a relation such that for any two points a and b, a R b if b is within one inch from a. Show that R is reflexive and symmetric but, not transitive.*

Solution:

1. *R is Reflexive:* Let a be any arbitrary point $\in$ S. Then distance of a from a is zero and therefore a is within one inch from a. Hence $\forall$ $a \in S$, we have a R a. Thus R is reflexive.
2. *R is Symmetric:* Suppose we have a R b *i.e.,* b is within one inch from a . Now the distance of a from b is equal to the distance of b from a. Therefore if b is within one inch from a, then a is also within one inch from b. So a R b implies b R a. Therefore R is symmetric.
3. *R is not Transitive:* Suppose, we have a R b and b R c. Then b is within one inch from a and c is within one inch from b. Suppose a, b and c are in the same straight line and b lies between a and c. Let the distance of b from a be 3/4 inch and the distance of c from b be also 3/4 inch. Then the distance of c from a is 3/4 + 3/4 *i.e.,* 1½ inches. Thus c is not within one inch from and therefore a is not R-related to c. Hence R is not transitive.

Example 63: *Prove that a relation R on a set A is symmetric iff*

$$R = R^{-1}.$$

Solution: First, let R be a symmetric relation on set A. Then we have to prove that $R = R^{-1}$. In order to prove this we have to prove that $R \subset R^{-1}$ and $R^{-1} \subset R$.

Now, $(a, b) \in R \Rightarrow (b, a) \in R$ ($\because$ R is symmetric)

$\Rightarrow (a, b) \in R^{-1}$ (by def. of inverse relation)

Thus, $(a, b) \in R \Rightarrow (a, b) \in R^{-1}$ for all $a, b \in A$.

So, $R \subset R^{-1}$ ...(i)

Now, let (x, y) be an arbitrary element of R^{-1}. Then

$(x, y) \in R^{-1} \Rightarrow (y, x) \in R$ (by def. of inverse relation)

$\Rightarrow (x, y) \in R$ ($\because$ R is symmetric)

Thus, $(x, y) \in R^{-1} \Rightarrow (x, y) \in R$ for all $x, y \in A$.

So $\quad R^{-1} \subseteq R$ ...(ii)

Thus, from (i) and (ii), we get $R = R^{-1}$. *Conversely,* let R be a relation on set A such that $R = R^{-1}$. Then we have to prove that R is a symmetric relation on set A.

Let $\quad (a, b) \in R$. Then

$(a, b) \in R \Rightarrow (b, a) \in R^{-1}$ (by def. of inverse relation)

$\Rightarrow (b, a) \in R,$ $\quad (\because R = R^{-1})$

Thus, $\quad (a, b) \in R \Rightarrow (b, a) \in R$ for all $a, b \in A$.

So, R is a symmetric relation on A.

Hence, R is symmetric iff $R = R^{-1}$.

Example 64: *Let a relation R_1 on the set R of real numbers be defined as $(a, b) \in R_1 \Leftrightarrow 1 + ab > 0$ for all $a, b \in R$. Show that R_1 is reflexive and symmetric but not transitive.*

Solution: (i) *Reflexivity* : Let a be an arbitrary element of R. Then

$a \in R_1 \Rightarrow 1 + a, a = 1 + a^2 > 0$ $\quad (\because a^2 > 0$ for all $a \in R)$

$\Rightarrow (a, a) \in R_1$ $\quad$ (by def. of R_1)

Thus, $(a, a) \in R_1$ for all $a \in R$. So R_1 is reflexive on R.

(ii) *Symmetry* : Let $(a, b) \in R_1$, Then

$(a, b) \in R_1 \Rightarrow 1 + ab > 0 \Rightarrow 1 + ba > 0$

$\Rightarrow (b, a) \in R_1$ $\quad$ (by def. of R_1)

Thus, $\quad (a, b) \in R_1 \Rightarrow (b, a) \in R_1$ for all a,

$b \in R$. So, R_1 is symmetric on R.

(iii) *Transitivity* : We observe that $(1, 1/2) \in R_1$ and $(1/2, 1) \in R_1$ but $(1, -1) \notin R_1$ because $1 + 1 \times (-1) = 0 \not> 0$.

So, R_1 is not transitive on R.

Example 65: *Let N denote the set of all natural numbers and R be the relation on N × N defined by $(a, b)\ R\ (c, d) \Leftrightarrow ad\ (b + c) = bc\ (a + d)$. Check whether R is an equivalence relation on N × N.*

Solution: (i) *Reflexivity* : Let (a, b) be an arbitrary element of N × N. Then,

$(a, b) \in N \times N \Rightarrow a, b \in N$

$\Rightarrow a\ b\ (b + a) = ba\ (a + b)$

$\Rightarrow (a, b)\ R\ (a + b)$

Thus, (a, b) R (a, b) for all (a, b) $\in$ N $\times$ N. So, R is reflexive on N $\times$ N.

(ii) *Symmetry* : Let (a, b), (c, d) $\in$ N $\times$ N be such that (a, b) R (c, d). Then

$$(a, b)\ R\ (c, d) \Rightarrow ad\ (b + c) = bc\ (a + d)$$

(by comm. of add. and mult. on N)

$$\Rightarrow (c, d)\ R\ (a, b)$$

Thus, (a, b) R (c, d) $\Rightarrow$ (c, d) R (a, b) for all (a, b), (c, d) $\in$ N $\times$ N. So, R is symmetric on N $\times$ N.

Transitivity : Let (a, b), (c, d), (e, f) $\in$ N $\times$ N such that (a, b) R (c, d) and (c, d) R (e, f). Then

$$(a, b)\ R\ (c, d) = ad\ (b + c) = bc\ (a + d)$$

$$\Rightarrow \frac{b + c}{bc} = \frac{a + d}{ad} \Rightarrow \frac{1}{b} + \frac{1}{c} + \frac{1}{a} + \frac{1}{d} \qquad \text{...(i)}$$

and (c, d) R (e, f) $\Rightarrow$ ef (d + e) = de (e + f)

$$\Rightarrow \frac{d + e}{de} = \frac{e + f}{ef} \Rightarrow \frac{1}{d} + \frac{1}{e} = \frac{1}{e} + \frac{1}{f} \qquad \text{...(ii)}$$

Adding (i) and (ii), we get

$$\left(\frac{1}{b} + \frac{1}{c}\right) + \left(\frac{1}{d} + \frac{1}{e}\right) = \left(\frac{1}{a} + \frac{1}{d}\right) + \left(\frac{1}{c} + \frac{1}{f}\right)$$

$$\Rightarrow \quad \frac{1}{b} + \frac{1}{e} = \frac{1}{a} + \frac{1}{f} \Rightarrow \frac{b+e}{be} = \frac{a + f}{af}$$

$$\Rightarrow \quad af\ (b + e) = be\ (a + f) \Rightarrow (a, b)\ R\ (e, f)$$

Thus, (a, b) R (c, d) and (c, d) R (e, f)

$\Rightarrow$ (a, b) R (e, f) for all (a, b), (c, d), (e, f) $\in$ N $\times$ N. So, R is transitive on N $\times$ N.

Hence, R being reflexive, symmetric and transitive is an equivalence relation on N $\times$ N.

Congruence Modulo m : Let m be an arbitrary but fixed integer. Two integers a and b are said to be congruence modulo m if a – b is divisible by m and we write a $\equiv$ b (mod m).

Thus, a $\equiv$ b, (mod m) $\Leftrightarrow$ a – b is divisible by m.

For example, 18 $\equiv$ 3 (mod 5) because 18-3 = 15 which is divisible by 5. But 25 $\not\equiv$ 2 (mod 4) because 4 is not a divisor of 25-2 = 23.

Examples 66: *Prove that the relation 'congruence modulo m' on the set Z of all integers is an equivalence relation.*

Solution: (i) *Reflexivity* : Let a be an arbitrary integer. Then

$$a - a = 0 = 0 \times m \Rightarrow a = a \text{ is divisible by } m$$

$$\Rightarrow a \equiv a \pmod{m}$$

Thus, $a \equiv a \pmod{m}$ for all $a \in Z$. so, "congruence modulo m" is reflexive.

(ii) *Symmetry* : Let a , b, $\in$ Z such that $a \equiv b \pmod{m}$

Then, $a \equiv b \pmod{m}$

$$\Rightarrow a - b \text{ is divisible by } m$$

$$\Rightarrow a - b = \lambda m \text{ for } \lambda \in Z.$$

$$\Rightarrow b - a = (-\lambda) m \Rightarrow b = a \text{ is divisible by } m$$

$$\Rightarrow b \equiv a \pmod{m}$$

So, "congruence modulo m" is symmetric on Z.

(iii) *Transitivity* : Let a, b, c $\in$ Z such that

$a \equiv b \pmod{m}$ and $b \equiv c \pmod{m}$. Then

$a \equiv b \pmod{m} \Rightarrow a - b$ is divisible by m

$$\Rightarrow a - b = \lambda_1 m \text{ for some } \lambda_1 \in Z$$

$b \equiv c \pmod{m} \Rightarrow b - c$ is divisible by m

$$\Rightarrow b - c = \lambda_2 m \text{ for some } \lambda_2 \in Z$$

$$\therefore \quad (a - b) + (b - c) = \lambda_1 m + \lambda_2 m = (\lambda_1 + \lambda_2) m$$

$$\Rightarrow \quad (a - c) = \lambda_3 m, \text{ where } \lambda_3 = \lambda_1 + \lambda_2 \in Z$$

$$\Rightarrow \quad a \equiv c \pmod{m}$$

Thus, $a \equiv b \pmod{m}$ and $b \equiv c \pmod{m}$

$$\Rightarrow \quad a \equiv c \pmod{m}.$$

So, 'congruence modulo m' is transitive on Z.

Hence, 'congruence modulo m' is an equivalence relation on Z.

Examples 67: *Consider a set* $A = \{p, q, r\}$ *and the relation R on A defined by*

$R = \{(p, p), (p, q), (q, r), (r, r)\}$ find :

(a) Reflexive (R);

(b) Symmetric (R); and

(c) Transitive (R).

Solution: (a) The reflexive closure on R is obtained by adding all diagonal pairs of A × A to R which are not currently in R. Hence

reflexive (R) = R ∪ {(q, q)}

= {(p, p), (p, q), (q, q), (q, r) (r, r)}

(b) The symmetric closure on R is obtained by adding all the pairs in R^{-1} to R which are not currently in R. Hence.

Symmetric (R) = R ∪ {q, p), (r, q)}

= {(p, p), (p, q), (q, p), (q, r), (r, q) (r, r)}

(c) The transitive closure on R, since A has three elements, is obtained by taking the union of R with R^2 = RoR and R^3 = RoRoR. Now,

R^2 = RoR = {(p, p), (p, q), (p, r), (q, r), (r, r)}

R^3 = RoRoR = {(p, p), (p, q), (p, r), (q, r), (r, r)}

Hence, transitive (R) = R ∪ R^2 ∪ R^3

= {(p, p), (p, q), (p, r), (q, r), (r, r)}

Examples 68: *If A = {1, 2, 3, 4, 5, 6, 7}, which of the following two is a partition giving rise to an equivalence relation? Why?*

(i) A_1 = {1, 3, 5}, A_2 = {2}, A_3 = {4, 7}

(ii) B_1 = {1, 3, 5, 7}, B_2 = {3}, B_3 = {4, 6}

Solution: Since A is not the union of A_1, A_2 and A_3, therefore sets A_1, A_2, A_3 do not form a partition of A.

Clearly, B_1, B_2 and B_3, are disjoint sets such that their union is A. So, these sets form a partition of A.

Examples 69: *Show that in the set N of all natural numbers, the relation R defined by a R b if a divides to is a partial order relation.*

Solution: (i) We have ∀ a ∈ N, a is a divisor of a, *i.e.*, a R a. Therefore, R is reflexive.

(ii) Again, if a is a divisor of b then b cannot be a divisor of a unless a = b. Thus, a R b and b R a ⇒ a = b. Therefore, R is anti-symmetric.

(iii) Finally, a is a divisor of b and b is a divisor of c implies a is a divisor of c. Therefore R is transitive.

Since R is reflexive, anti-symmetric and transitive, therefore R is a partial order relation.

Example 70: *Let R → R defined by f(x) = ax + b, where a, b, x ∈ R and a ≠ 0. Prove that f is invertible.*

Solution: f is one-one for

$$x_1, x_2 \in R, f(x_1) = f(x_2)$$

$$\Rightarrow \quad ax_1 + b = ax_2 + b \Rightarrow ax_1 = ax_2$$

$$\Rightarrow \quad x_1 = x_2.$$

f is onto :

Let y ∈ R such that

$$y = f(x) \Rightarrow y = ax + b$$

$$\Rightarrow \quad ax = y - b \text{ and } a \neq 0 \in R$$

$$\Rightarrow \quad x = \frac{1}{a}(y - b) \in R$$

∴ Given $y \in R$, ∃ some $x = \frac{1}{a}(y - b) \in R$ s.t. $f(x) = y$

∴ $f : R \to R$ is both one-one and onto hence f is invertible.

Example 71: *Let S be a non-empty set and ∗ be a binary operation on S defined by* $x * y = x : x, y \in S$.

Determine whether ∗ is commutative and associative.

Solution: Let x, y ∈ S. Then

$$x * y = x \text{ and } y * x = y.$$

Thus if x and y are distinct elements of S, we have

$$x * y \neq y * x.$$

∴ the operation on S defined by ∗ is not commutative.

Again let x, y, z be any three elements of S. Then

$$(x * y) * z = x * z = x$$

and $x * (y * z) = x * y = x$.

Thus $(x * y) * z = x * (y * z)\ \forall\ x, y, z \in S$.

Hence the operation on S defined by ∗ is associative.

Example 72: *Find whether the following algebraic structures have identity element or not:*

1. (N, +) 2. (N, ·) 3. (I, +); 4. (I, ·); 5. (R, ·);
6. (P (S), ∪); 7. (P (S), ∩).

Solution:

1. The algebraic structure (N, +) does not possess identity element. For ordinary addition of numbers, the number 0 is identity and $0 \notin N$.

2. The algebraic structure (N, ·) possesses identity element and it is 1. We have $1 \in N$ and

$$1a = a = a1 \ \forall \ a \in N.$$

3. The algebraic structure (I, +) possesses identity element and it is 0. We have $0 \in I$ and

$$0 + a = a = a + 0 \quad \forall \ a \in I.$$

4. The algebraic structure (I, ·) possesses identity element and it is 1. We have $1 \in I$ and $1a = a = a1 \ \forall \ a \in I$.

5. The algebraic structure (R, ·) possesses identity element and it is 1.

6. The algebraic structure (P (S), ∪) possesses identity element and it is the null set ∅. We have

   $\varnothing \in P(S)$ because $\varnothing \subseteq S$.

   Also $\quad \varnothing \cup A = A = A \cup \varnothing, \ \forall \ A \in P(S)$.

7. The algebraic structure (P (S), ∩) possesses identity element and it is the set S itself. We have

   $$S \in P(S) \text{ because } S \subseteq S.$$

   Also $\quad S \cap A = A = A \cap S, \ \forall \ A \in P(S)$ *i.e.*, $\forall \ A \subseteq S$

Example 73: *Define binary operation. Show that the relation o given by $a \text{ o } b = a^2$ is a binary operation on the set of natural numbers. Is this binary operation associative.*

Solution: Let a, b, ∈ N where N is the set of natural numbers. Then a^b is a unique natural numbers. Thus,

$$a \text{ o } b = a^b \in N, \ \forall \ a, b \in N.$$

∴ 'o' is a binary operation on the set N.

Now let a, b, c, ∈ N. Then

$$(a \text{ o } b) \text{ o } c = (a^b) \text{ o } c = (a^b) = a^{bc} \qquad ...(1)$$

and $a \text{ o } (b \text{ o } c) = a \text{ o } (b^c) = (a)^{bc}$ ...(2)

From (1) and (2), we observe that it is not necessary that $a \text{ o } (b \text{ o } c) = (a \text{ o } b) \text{ o } c \ \forall \ a, b, c \in N$. Hence, the operation on N defined by 'o' is not associative.

For a concrete example, take $2, 2, 3 \in N$.

We have $\quad (2 \text{ o } 2) \text{ o } 3 = (2) \text{ o } 3 = 4 \text{ o } 3 = 4^3 = 64$

and $\quad 2 \text{ o } (2 \text{ o } 3) = 2 \text{ o } (2^3) = 2 \text{ o } 8 = 2^8 = 256.$

Thus $\quad (2 \text{ o } 2) \text{ o } 3 \neq 2 \text{ o } (2 \text{ o } 3).$

Example 74: *Consider the binary operation* $*$: $Q \times Q \to Q$ *which 1 defined by* $a * b = a + b + ab$, *for every* $a, b, \in Q$.

1. *Is* $*$ *commutative?*
2. *Is* $*$ *associative?*
3. *Find the identity element for* $*$.
4. *Do any of the elements in* Q *have an inverse and what is it?*

Solution:

1. We have $a * b = a + b + ab$

   and $b * a = b + a + ba.$

   But $a + b = b + a$ and $ab = ba$.

$\therefore$ $a * b = b * a$ and thus $*$ is commutative.

2. We have $a * (b * c) = a * (b + c + bc)$

   $= a + (b + c + bc) + a (b + c + bc)$

   $= a + b + c + bc + ab + ac + abc.$

   Also $(a * b) * c = (a +.b + ab) * c$

   $= (a + b + ab) + c + (a + b + ab) c$

   $= a + b + c + ab + ac + bc + abc.$

$\therefore$ $a * (b * c) = (a * b) * c$ and so $*$ is associative.

3. Let e be the identity element for $*$. Then for every $a \in Q$, we must have $a * e = e * a = a$.

   But $*$ is commutative, therefore $a * e = e * a$.

   Now $a * e = a, (\forall a \in Q)$

   $\Rightarrow a + e + ae = a \Rightarrow e + ae = 0 \Rightarrow e (1 + a) = 0$

   $\Rightarrow e = 0$, since $1 + a \neq 0$, for every $a \in Q$.

   Now $0 \in Q$ and we have

   $0 * a = 0 + a + 0.a = a = a * 0 \ \forall a \in Q.$

   Hence 0 is the identity element.

4. Since 0 is the identity element, therefore for a to have an inverse b, we must have $a * b = 0$.

   Now $a * b = 0 \Rightarrow a + b + ab = 0 \Rightarrow a + b (a + 1) = 0$

   $\Rightarrow a = - b (a + 1) \Rightarrow b = - \dfrac{a}{a + 1}$, if $a \neq - 1$.

   Thus if $a \neq - 1$, then a has an inverse and it is $-a/(a + 1)$.

Example 75: *Let N_0 and N_e denote the set of all odd natural numbers and the set of all even natural numbers respectively:*

1. *Is addition a binary operation on N_0?*
2. *Is multiplication a binary operation on N_0?*
3. *Is addition a binary operation on N_e? If yes, find whether this operation has identity element or not.*

Solution:

1. The sum of two odd natural numbers is an even natural number. Thus if $x, y \in N_0$, then $x + y \notin N_0$. Therefore addition is not a binary operation on the set N_0.
2. The product of two odd natural numbers is also an odd natural number and is unique. Thus,

   $x, y \in N_0, \forall x, y \in N_0$.

   Therefore multiplication is a binary operation on the set N_0.
3. The sum of two even natural numbers is an even natural number and is unique. Thus

   $x + y \in N_e, \forall x, y \in N_e$.

   Therefore addition is a binary operation on the set N_e.

However, the set N_e does not possess identity element for addition because the number 0 which is identity for ordinary addition of numbers is not an element of the set N_e.

Example 76: *Let f be a function defined from the set X to the set Y and let A, B be the subsets of Y, then*

(i) $f^{-1}(A \cup B) = f^{-1}(A) \cup f^{-1}(B)$

(ii) $f^{-1}(A \cap B) = f^{-1}(A) \cap f^{-1}(B)$.

Example 77: *If $f : X \to Y$ and $A, B \subseteq X$. Then prove that*

$$f(A \cup B) = f(A) \cup f(B).$$

Solution: Let y be any arbitrary element of $f(A \cup B)$

Then $\quad y \in f(A \cup B)$

$\Rightarrow \exists\, x \in A \cup B$ such that $f(x) = y$

$\Rightarrow \exists\, x \in A$ or $x \in B$ such that $f(x) = y$

$\Rightarrow y \in f(A)$ or $y \in f(B)$

$\Rightarrow y \in f(A) \cup f(B)$.

$\therefore$ f (A $\cup$ B) $\subseteq$ f (A) $\cup$ f (B). ...(1)

Again let y be any arbitrary element of f (A) $\cup$ f (B).

Then y $\in$ f (A) $\cup$ f (B)

$\Rightarrow$ y $\in$ f (A) or y $\in$ f (B)

$\Rightarrow$ $\exists$ x $\in$ A or x $\in$ B such that f (x) = y

$\Rightarrow$ $\exists$ x $\in$ A $\cup$ B such that f (x) = y

$\Rightarrow$ y $\in$ f (A $\cup$ B)

$\therefore$ f (A) $\cup$ f (B) $\subseteq$ f (A $\cup$ B). ...(2)

From (1) and (2), we conclude that

f (A $\cup$ B) = f (A) $\cup$ f (B).

Example 78: *Let X = {x : x $\in$ R*

and $-\pi/2 \leq x \leq \pi/2$ *i.e.,*

let $X = [-\pi/2, \pi/2]$

and *Y = (y : y $\in$ R*

and $-1 \leq y \leq 1\}$ *i.e., let Y = [–1, 1].*

Show that the function f : X → Y defined by

f (x) = sin x , (x $\in$ X', is one-one onto.

Also give the inverse mapp f^{-1} : Y → X.

Solution: Let m and n be any two different real numbers lying in the closed interval [– π/2, π/2]. We know that any two different real numbers lying in the closed interval [– π/2, π/2] have not the same sine.

$\therefore$ m $\neq$ n $\Rightarrow$ sin m $\neq$ sin n

$\Rightarrow$ f (m) $\neq$ f (n). Hence f is one-one.

Again if y is any arbitrary real number lying in the closed interval [–1, 1], $\exists$ a real number x lying in the closed interval [– π/2, π/2] such that is n x = y.

Thus, every element y in Y is the f-image of some element x in X. Hence f is onto.

Thus f : X → Y is one-one onto, therefore f has an inverse function f^{-1} X → Y.

Let y be the image of x under the function f. Then

y = f (x) = sin

Consequently, x will be the image of y under the inverse function f^{-1} *i.e.*,

$$x = f^{-1}(y).$$

Solving for x in terms of y in the equation y = sin x, we get

$$x = \sin^{-1} y.$$

Thus $f^{-1}(y) = \sin^{-1} y$, $(y \in Y)$ is the formula defining the inverse function $f^{-1} : Y \rightarrow X$.

Example 79: *Decide whether or not the following are functions from A to B where A = {1, 2, 3, 4, 5} and B = {a, b, c, d, e}.*

If they are functions, give the range of each. If they are not, tell, why?

1. f = ({1, a), (2, b), (3, b), (5, e)}.
2. g = {(1, e), (5, d), (3, a), (2, b), (1, d), (4, a)}.
3. h = {(5, a), (1, e), (4, b), (3, c), (2, d)}.

Solution:

1. Since the element $4 \in A$ is not associated to any element $\in B$, therefore f is not a function from A to B.
2. The element $1 \in A$ is associated to two different elements e and $d \in B$. Therefore g is not a function from A to B.
3. Each element of A is associated to a unique element of B. Therefore h is a function from $A \rightarrow B$. The range of h is the set of the h-images of all elements of A. So range of h = h (A) = {a, e, b, c, d} = B.

Example 80: *Let A = (–2, –1, 0, 1, 2}. Let the function $f : A \rightarrow R$ be defined by the promulas $f(x) = x^2 + 1$. Find the range of f.*

Solution: The range of f consists of those elements of R which appear as f-image of different elements of A. So we calculate the f-image of each element of A.

$$f(-2) = (-2)^2 + 1 = 5,\ f(-1) = (-1)^2 + 1 = 2,$$

$$f(0) = (0)^2 + 1 = 1,\ f(1) = (1)^2 + 1 + 1 = 2.$$

$$f(2) = (2)^2 + 1 = 4 + 1 = 5.$$

Thus, the range of f is the set {5, 2, 1, 2, 5}, *i.e.*, the set {5, 2, 1}.

Example 81: *Let N be the set of natural numbers and A be the set of even natural numbers.*

Let $f : N \rightarrow A$ be defined by the formula $f(x) = 2x$, $x \in N$. Show that the mapping f is one-one onto. Find the formula ·hat defines the inverse function f^{-1}.

Solution: First to prove that f is a one-one mapping.

Suppose m and n are any two different elements $\in$ N.

Then $m \neq n \Rightarrow 2m \neq 2n \Rightarrow f(m) \neq f(n)$.

Thus different elements belonging to N have different f-images in A. Hence f is one-one.

Now to prove the f is an onto mapping. Let y be any arbitrary element in A *i.e.,* let y be any even natural number. Then $f(y/2) = y$ and y/2 is a natural number *i.e.,* $y/2 \in N$. Thus each element in A is the f-image of some element in N. Hence f is onto.

Since $f : N \to A$ is one-one onto, therefore f has an inverse function $f^{-1} : A \to N$.

Let y be the image of x under the function f. Then

$$y = f(x) = 2x.$$

Consequently, x will be the image of y under the inverse function f^{-1}

i.e., $$x = f^{-1}(y).$$

Solving for x in terms of y in the equation $y = 2x$, we get

$$x = y/2.$$

Then $$f^{-1}(y) = y/2.$$

Hence $f^{-1}(y) = y/2$, $(y \in A)$ is a formula defining the inverse function $f^{-1} : A \to N$.

Example 82: *Let S be the set of all triangles and R_+ be the set of positive real numbers. Prove that the map $f : S \to R_+$ given by*

$$f(\Delta) = \text{area of the } \Delta,\ (\Delta \in S), \text{ is many-one and onto.}$$

Solution: Let y be any arbitrary element in R_+ *i.e.,* let y be any positive real number. Then $\exists$ a triangle whose area is equal to y. Thus, every element in R_+ is the f-image of some element in S. Therefore f is onto.

Again there can be two or more triangles which have the same area. Therefore f is many-one.

Hence $f : S \to R_+$ is many-one onto.

Example 83: *Let Q be the set of rational numbers. Let $f : Q \to Q$ be defined by*

$$f(x) = 2x + 3,\ (x \in Q).$$

Show that f is one-one and onto. Also find a formula that defines the inverse function f^{-1}.

Solution: Let m and n be any two different elements in Q.

Then $m \neq n \Rightarrow 2m \neq 2n$

$$\Rightarrow 2m + 3 \neq 2n + 3$$

$$\Rightarrow f(m) \neq f(n).$$

Thus, different elements in Q have different f-images in Q. Hence f is one-one.

Let y be any arbitrary element in Q. If y = 2x + 3, we have

$$x = (y - 3)/2 \text{ which is also a rational number.}$$

Thus $\left(\frac{y-3}{2}\right)$ = y *i.e.,* any arbitrary element y in Q is the f-image of the element (y – 2)/2 ∈ Q. Hence f is onto

Since f : Q → Q is one-one onto, therefore f has an inverse function $f^{-1} : Q \to Q$.

Let y be the image of x under the function f. Then

$$y = f(x) = 2x + 3.$$

Consequently, x will be the image of y under the inverse function f^{-1} *i.e.,* $x = f^{-1}(y)$.

Solving for x in terms of y in the equation y = 2x + 3, we get

$$x = (y - 3)/2.$$

Thus, $f^{-1}(y) = (y - 3)/2$, (y ∈ Q) is the formula defining the inverse function $f^{-1} : Q \to Q$.

Note: In order to prove that the mapping f is one-one, we can also argue like this:

Let m and n be any two elements in Q. Then

$$f(m) = f(n)$$

$$\Rightarrow 2m + 3 = 2n + 3$$

$$\Rightarrow 2m = 2n \Rightarrow m = n.$$

Therefore f is one-one.

Example 84: *Decide whether or not the following are functions from A → B where A = {1, 2, 3, 4, 5}, B = {a, b, c, d, e}. If they are functions give the range of each. If they are not, tell why?*

(a) f = {(1, a), (2, b), (3, b), (5, c)}

(b) g = {(1, c), (5. d), (3, a), (2, b), (1, d), (4, a)}

(c) h = {(5, a), (1, c), (4, b), (3, c), (2, d)}

Solution:

(a) Since the element $4 \in A$ is not associated to any element $\in B$, therefore f is not a function from $A \to B$.

(b) The element $1 \in A$ is associated to two different elements c and d $\in B$. Therefore, g is not a function from $A \to B$.

(c) Each element of A is associated to a unique element of B. Therefore h is a function from $A \to B$. The range of h is the set of the h-images of all elements of A. Thus range of h = h(A) = {a, c, b, c, d} = B.

EXERCISES

1. Prove that the function $f : N \to N$, defined by $f(x) = x^2 + x + 1$ is one-one but not onto.
2. Let f = {(3, 1), (9, 3) (12, 4)} and g = {1, 3), (3, 3), (4, 9) (5, 9)}. Show that fog and gof are both defined. Also, find fog and gof.
3. Let A = {a, b, c} B = {u, v, w} and let f and g be two functions from A to B and from B to A respectively defined as.

   f = {(a, v), (b, u), (c, w)},

   g = {(u, b), (v, a), (w, c)}.

   Show that f and g both are bijections and find fog and gof.
4. Find fog(2) and gof(1) when:

   $f : R \to R$ $f(x) = x^2 + 8$ and $g : R \to R : g(x) = 3x^3 + 1$
5. Let R^+ be the set of all non-negative real numbers. If $f : R^+ \to R^+$ and $g : R^+ \to R^+$ are defined as $f(x) = x^2$ and $g(x) = +\sqrt{x}$. Find fog and gof. Are they equal functions?
6. Let $A = \{x \in R \mid -1 \le x \le 1\}$ and $f : A \to A$, $g : A \to A$ be two functions defined by $f(x) = x^2$ and $g(x) = \sin(\pi x/2)$: Show that g^{-1} exists but f^{-1} does not exits. Also find g^{-1}.
7. If $f : R \to R$ be defined by $f(x) = x^3 - 3$, then prove that f^{-1} exists and find a formula for f^{-1}. Hence, find f^{-1} (24) and f^{-1} (5).
8. Let A and B be two sets each with finite number of elements. Assume that there is an injective map from A to B and that there is an injective map from B to A. Prove that there is a bijection from A to B.
9. If $f : Q \to Q$, $g : Q \to Q$ are two functions defined by $f(x) = 2x$ and $g(x) = x + 2$. Show that f and g are bijection maps. Verify that $(g\,of)^{-1} = f^{-1}og^{-1}$.

10. If $f : A \to A$, $g : A \to A$ are two bijections then prove that
   (i) fog is an injection
   (ii) fog is a surjection.
11. Let $f : R \to R$ is given by $f(x) =- (x + 1)^2 - 1$, $x \geq -1$. Show that f is invertible. Also find the set $S = \{x : f(x) = f^{-1}(x)\}$.

   [**Hint :** $f(x) = y \Rightarrow x = \sqrt{(y-1)} - 1$]

   $\Rightarrow f^{-1}(y) \sqrt{y-1} - 1$. Now $f(x) = f^{-1}(x)$

   $\Rightarrow (x + 1)^2 - 1 = \sqrt{x-1} - 1$

   $\Rightarrow \sqrt{x-1} \{(x + 1)^{2/3} - 1\} = 0$

   $\Rightarrow x + 1 = 0$ or $(x + 1)^{3/2} = 1$

   $\Rightarrow x = 0, -1\}$
12. Find : (i) 200 (mod 20),
   (ii) 10 (mod 3)
   (iii) –347 (mod 6),
   (iv) 555 (mod 11)
13. Find : (i) 3! (3! + 2!),
   (ii) 30!/28!,
   (iii) 6!/5!
14. Let p and q be integers and suppose M (p, q) is defined recursively by

$$M(p, q) = \begin{cases} 5 \text{ if } p < q \\ M(p-q, q+2) + a \text{ if } p \geq q \end{cases}$$

   Find M (2, 7), M (5, 3) and M (15, 2).
15. By definition of the Ackermann function, find A (3, 1) and A (2, 3)
16. For the Ackermann function, prove that A (2, 3) = 2x = 3.
17. Find the value of :
   (i) $\lceil 6 \rceil$, (ii) $\lceil -8 \rceil$
   (iii) $\lfloor 8.3 \rfloor$ (iv) $\lfloor -8.7 \rfloor$
18. Let $f(x) = \lfloor x/2 \rfloor + \lfloor x/3 \rfloor$ for $x \in N$. Calculate f(x) for $0 \leq x \leq 10$ and for x = 73.
19. Find $\lfloor 5/2 \rfloor$, $\lfloor (5/2)^2 \rfloor$ and $(\lfloor 5/2 \rfloor)^2$.

20. Use the definition of O notation prove that
    (i) $7x^3 - 3x^2$ is $O(x^3)$
    (ii) $\lceil x^2 \rceil$ is $O(x^2)$
    (iii) $1^2 + 2^2 + \ldots + n^2$ is $O(x^3)$.
21. If $f(x) = 4x^3 - 3x^2$ and $g(x) = x^4$. Prove that f and g are of the same order.
22. For any two sets A and B, prove that $A' - B' = B - A$.
23. If $A \cup B = A \cup C$ and $A \cap B = A \cap C$, then show that $B = C$.
24. If $f(x) = 3x^2 + 4x + 1$ and $g(x) = x^2$ for $x \geq 1$.
    Show that $f(x) = \Theta\, g(x)$.
25. Show that the functions f and g defined by $f(n) = 4n^4 - 3n^2$ and $g(n) = n^4$, where n is a positive integer, have the same orders.
26. Define a function as a set of ordered pairs.
27. What is the fundamental difference between a relation and a function? Is every relation a function?
28. Let $A = \{-2, -1, 0, 1, 2\}$ and $f : A \to Z$ be a function defined by $f(x) = x^2 - 2x - 3$. Find
    (a) range of f, *i.e.* f(A)
    (b) pre-images of 6, –3 and 5.
29. If a function $f : R \to R$ be defined by

$$f(x) = \begin{cases} 3x - 2, & x < 0, \\ 1, & x = 0, \\ 4x + 1, & x > 0, \end{cases}$$

    Find f(1), f(–1), f(0), f(2)
30. Let $f : R \to R$ and $g : C \to C$ be two functions defined as $f(x) = x^2$ and $g(x) = x^2$. Are they equal functions?
31. Classify the following functions as injection, Surjection or bijection:
    (i) $f : R \to R,\quad f(x) = |x|$
    (ii) $f : Z \to Z,\quad f(x) = x^2 + x$
    (iii) $f : Z \to Z,\quad f(x) = x = 5$
    (iv) $f : R \to R,\quad f(x) = \sin x$
    (v) $f : R \to R,\quad f(x) = x^3 + 1$
    (vi) $f : R \to R,\quad f(x) = x^3 - x$
    (vii) $f : R \to R,\quad f(x) = \sin^2 x + \cos^2 x$

(viii) $f : Q-\{3\} \to Q$, $f(x) = \dfrac{2x+3}{x-3}$.

(ix) $f : Q \to Q$, $f(x) = x^3 + 1$

(x) $f : R \to R$, $f(x) = 5x^3 + 4$

32. Show that the function $f : N \to N$ given by

$f(n) = n - (-1)^n$ for all $n \in N$ is one-one and onto.

33. If sets $A = \{(x, y): x^2 + y^2 = 1\}$ and $B = \{(x, y): x + y = 1$, then find $A \cap B$.

34. For any two sets A and B, show that $A \times B$ and $B \times A$ have one element in common iff A and B have one element in common.

35. If A and B are any subsets, then prove that $A \cap (B - A) = \phi$.

36. Prove that:

(i) $A \supseteq B \Rightarrow (A - C) \supseteq (B - C)$

(ii) $A \subseteq B \Rightarrow A \cup B = B$ and $A \cap B = A$

37. Prove that:

(i) $A - B\ \phi \Leftrightarrow A \subseteq B$

(ii) $A' \subseteq B \Leftrightarrow A \cup B = X$, the universal set.

38. The graph of a mapping $f{:}X \to V$ is a subset of the product $X \times Y$. What properties characterize the graphs of mappings among all subsets of X X V?

39. Let X and Y be non-empty sets. If A_1 and A_2 are subsets of X, and B_1 and B_2 subsets of Y, show the following:

$(A_1 \times B_1) \cap (A_2 \times B_2) = (A_1 \cap A_2) \times (B_1 \cap B_2)$;

$(A_1 \times B_1) - (A_2 \times B_2) = (A_1 - A_2) \times (B_1 - B_2)$
$\cup (A_1 \cap A_2) \times (B_1 - B_2) \cup (A_1 - A_2) \times (B_1 \cap B_2)$.

40. Let X and Y be non-empty sets, and let A and B be rings of subsets of X and Y, respectively. Show that the class of all finite unions of sets of the form $A \times B$ with $A\ \varepsilon\ A$ and $B\ \varepsilon\ B$ is a ring of subsets of $X \times Y$.

41. Under what conditions would each of the following be true?

(a) $A \cup B = \phi$ (b) $A \cup \phi = \phi$,

(c) $A \cap U = U$, (d) $A \cup \phi = U$,

(e) $A \cap B = A$, (f) $A \cup A = U$,

(g) $A \cup B = A \cap B$ (h) $A \cap B = \phi$.

42. If A = {a, b}, B {2, 3}, C {3, 4}, find (i) $A \times (B \cup C)$, (ii) $A \times (B \cap C)$.

43. For any two sets A and B, prove the following:

    (i) $A \cap (A' \cup B) = A \cap B$

    (ii) $A - (A - B) = A \cap B$

    (iii) $A \cap (A \cup B)' = \phi$

    (iv) $A - B = A \Delta (A \cap B)$

44. A market research group conducted a survey of 1000 consumers and reported that 720 consumers liked product A and 450 consumer liked product B. What is the least number that must have liked both products?

45. Of the members of three athletic teams in a certain school, 21 are in the basket ball team, 26 in hockey team and 29 in the football team, 14 play hockey and basket ball, 15 play hockey and football, 12 play foot ball and basket ball and 8 play all the three games. How many members are there in all?

46. Define cartesian product of two sets. If A, B and C are sets and $A \subset B$, then prove that $A \times C \subset B \times C$.

47. Using mathematical induction, prove the following.

    (i) $1^2 + 2^2 + 3^2 + \ldots\ldots + n^2 = 1/6\ n\ (n + 1)\ (2n + 1)$

    (ii) $1 . 2 + 2 . 3 + \ldots\ldots + n\,(n + 1) = n/3\ (n + 1)\ (n + 2)$

    (iii) $\frac{1}{1,3} + \frac{1}{3,5} + \frac{1}{5,7} + \ldots\ldots + \frac{1}{(2n-1)\,(2n+1)} = n/2n + 1$

    (iv) $\frac{1}{2} + \frac{1}{4} + \frac{1}{8} + \ldots\ldots + \frac{1}{2^n} = 1 - \frac{1}{2^n}$

    (v) $2^n > n,\ n \in N$

    (vi) $2^n > 3^n,\ n \in N$

48. Use mathematical induction to prove the following.

    (i) n (n + 1) (n + 2) is a multiple of 6.

    (ii) $3^{2n} - 1$ is divisible by 8.

    (iii) $10^n + 3.4^{n+2} + 5$ is divisible by 9

    (iv) $9^n - 8n - 1$ is a multiple of 64.

    (v) for all positive integers n, prove that :

    $\frac{n^7}{7} + \frac{n^5}{5} + \frac{2n^3}{3} - \frac{n}{105}$ is an integer.

49. Shourya is industrious. All the first class students are industrious. Is Shourya first class student?

50. Define a relation. When a relation R on a set A is known as symmetric, reflexive, transitive and antisymmetric? Give an example for each.

51. Show that in the set of all real numbers, the relation 'greater than' is transitive but not reflexive.

52. Show that the relation R in the set of natural numbers N defined by a R b if a divides b, is reflexive and transitive but not symmetric'.

53. Give an example of the relation which is.

    (a) reflexive, symmetric but not transitive.

    (b) symmetric, transitive but not reflexive.

    (c) symmetric but neither transitive nor reflexive.

    (d) neither symmetric nor reflexive, nor transitive.

54. If R and S are equivalence relations on a set A, prove that $R \cap S$ is an equivalence relation in A.

55. Which of the following relations in the set of real numbers are equivalence relations

    (a) $a R b$ if $|a| = |b|$,

    (b) $a R b$ if $|a| \geq |b|$,

    (c) $a R b$ if $a - b \geq 0$?

56. S is the set of real numbers and a R b, if $a = \pm b$, determine whether R is an equivalence relation?

57. Prove that if a relation R is transitive then its inverse relation R^{-1} is also transitive.

58. Find all the partitions of {a, b, c}.

59. Let $f: X \to Y$ be an arbitrary mapping. Define a relation in X as follows: $x_1 \sim x_2$ means that $f(x_1) = f(x_2)$. Show that this is an equivalence relation and describe the equivalence sets.

60. In the set R of all real numbers, let $x \sim y$ mean that $x - y$ is an integer. Show that this is an equivalence relation and describe the equivalence sets.

61. Let I be the set of all integers, and let m be a fixed positive integer. Two integers a and 6 are said to be *congruent* modulo m—symbolized by $a \equiv b \pmod{m}$—if $a - 6$ is exactly divisible by m, *i.e.*, if $a - 6$ is

an integral multiple of m. Show that this is an equivalence relation, describe the equivalence sets, and state the number of distinct equivalence sets.

62. Let X = {1, 2, 3, 4, 5, 6, 7, 8, 9} be any set and its three subsets be given by,

A = {1, 4, 7, 8}, B = {4, 6, 8, 9}, and C = {3, 4, 5, 7}, then find

(i) $A \cap (B - C)$, (ii) $A - (B \cup C)$

(iii) $A' \cap (B' - C')$ (iv) $A \cup (B \cap C)$.

63 If A = {a, b, c, d, e}, B = {a, c, e, g} and C = {b, e, f, g}, then verify that:

(i) $(A \cup b) \cap C = (A \cap C) \cup (B \cap C)$;

(ii) $A - (B \cup C) = (A - B) \cap (A - C)$;

(ii) $A \cap (B - C) = (A \cap B) - (A \cap C)$;

64. Give an example of three sets A, B and C such that :

$A \cap B \neq \phi$, $B \cap C \neq \phi$, $A \cap C \neq \phi$, and $A \cap B \cap C \neq \phi$.

65. The set X consists of all points within and on the unit circle $x^2 + y^2 = 1$, whereas the set Y consists of all point on and inside the rectangular boundary x = 0, x = 1, y = – 1 and y = 1. Determine the sets $X \cup Y$ $X \cap Y$. Illustrate your answer by diagrams.

66. For any sets A, B and C prove that:

(i) $A - B = A \cap B'$

(ii) $A - (A \cap B) = (A \cap B')$

(iii) $A \cap (B - A = \phi$

(iv) $(A - B) \cup (B - A) = (A \cup B) - (A \cap B)$

67. For any sets A, B, C prove that:

(i) $A - (B \cup C) = (A - B) \cap (A - C)$

(ii) $A - (B \cap C) = (A - B) \cup (A - C)$

(iii) $A \cap (A' \cup B) = A \cap B$.

68. For any sets A and B prove that:

(i) $A \cup B = A \cap B \Leftrightarrow A = B$.

(ii) $A \cup B = \phi \Leftrightarrow A = \phi$ and $B = \phi$

69. Prove that:

(i) $A - B\ \phi \Leftrightarrow A \subseteq B$

(ii) $A' \subseteq B \Leftrightarrow A \cup B = X$, the universal set.

70. Prove that:

(i) $A \supseteq B \Rightarrow (A - C) \supseteq (B - C)$

(ii) $A \subseteq B \Rightarrow A \cup B = B$ and $A \cap B = A$

71. If $A \cup B = A \cup C$ and $A \cap B = A \cap C$, then show that $B = C$.

72. On the real line, if $A =]0, 3[$ and $B =]1, 4]$, then find A', B', $A \cup B$, $A \cap B$ and $A - B$.

73. If $A = \{x \in R: |x - 3| <\}$ and $B = \{x \in R: |x| \leq 2\}$, find $A \cup B$, $A \cap B$, $A - B$ and $B - A$.

74. Prove or disprove the following:

    (i) $P(A) \cap P(B) = P(A \cap B)$

    (ii) $(A \cup B) - C = A \cup (B - C)$

    (iii) $x \in (A \cap B')' \Rightarrow x \in B$

    (iv) $A \cup B = A \cup C \Leftrightarrow B = C$

75. For any three sets A, B and C prove that:

    (i) $A - (B - C) = (A - B) \cup (A \cap C)$

    (ii) $A \cap (B - C) = (A \cap B) - C$.

2

COMBINATORICS

INTRODUCTION

Counting occurs not only in highly sophisticated applications of mathematics to engineering and computer science out also in many basic applications. Techniques for counting are important in mathematics and in computer science, especially in the analysis of algorithms. In day-to-day life, we often come across problems of counting.

If the problem is simple and small, then the counting can actually be done by listing all of them. For example, if we want to find how many odd numbers are there between 10 and 25, then we can actually write all the odd numbers between 10 and 25 and count them. However, if we want to find how many odd numbers are there in a given set of 10,000 numbers, then it is almost impossible to write all these numbers and count them.

Example: *A person is to complete a true false questionnaire consisting of 10 question. How many different ways are there to answer the questionnaire? Since each question can be answered either of 2 ways (true or false) and there are a total of 10 questions, there are* $2 \cdot 2 \cdot 2 \cdot 2 \cdot 2 \cdot 2 \cdot 2 \cdot 2 \cdot 2 \cdot 2 = 2^{10}$ *different ways of answering the questionnaire. The reader is encouraged to visualize the tree diagram of this example.*

We formulize the procedures developed in the previous examples with the following rule and its extension.

RULE OF PRODUCTS

Rule of Products: *If two operations must be performed and if the first operation can always be performed* p_1 *different ways and the second operation can always be performed* p_2 *different ways, then there are* p_1p_2 *different ways that the two operations can be performed.*

Note: It is important that p_2 does not depend on the option that is chosen in the first operation. Another way of saying this is that p_2 is independent of the first operation. If p_2 is dependent on the first operation, then the rule of products does not apply.

Extended Rule of Products

The rule of products can be extended to include sequences of more than two operations. If n operations just be performed and the number of options for each operation are p_1, p_2... and p_n respectively, then the n operations can be performed.

$$p_1 \times p_2 \times ... \times p_n \text{ ways}$$

Example: *A questionnaire contains 4 questions that have 2 possible answers and 3 questions with 5 possible answers. There are 2 · 2 · 2 · 2 · 5 · 5 · 5 = $2^4 5^3$ = 2000 different ways to answer the questionnaire.*

Many counting problems involve selecting a subset of a set and placing the subset in order. We may wish to know how many different ways we can arrange or order, 3 different objects, for example the letters a, b and. Certainly abc, bac, and cba are 3 such arrangements. In fact, there are 3 · 2 · 1 = 6 different arrangements, or orders, of the elements in the set A = {a, b, c}.

PERMUTATIONS

Definition: Permutation. *If A is a set a permutation of A is an ordering of the elements of A.*

Example 1: *The alphabetical ordering of the players of a baseball team is one permutation of the set of players. Other orderings of the player's names might be done by batting average, age, or height. The information that determines the ordering is called the key. We would expect that each key would give a different permutation of the names. If there are 25 players on the team, there are 25 · 24 · 23 · ... · 3 · 2 · 1 different permutations of the players.*

Example 2: *The selection of the president, secretary, and treasurer for a club is a permutation of three members of the club. The set that is being permuted is the set of officers. In this case, the officers are not put into positions 1, 2 and 3; their positions are determined by the offices they hold.*

Before we develop a formula for permutations of k elements taken from a set of n elements, we look at some useful notation.

FUNDAMENTAL PRINCIPLES OF COUNTING

(i) **Multiplication Principle :** If an operation can be performed in 'm' different ways; following which a second operation can be performed in 'n' different ways, then the two operations in succession can be performed in m × n ways. This can be extended to any finite number of operations.

Note: For AND → '×' (multiply)

(ii) **Addition Principle :** If an operation can be performed in 'm' different ways and another operation, which is independent of the first operation, can be performed in 'n' different ways. Then either of the two operations can be performed in (m + n) ways. This can be extended to any finite number of mutually exclusive operations.

Note: For OR → '+' (Addition)

There is a set theoretical interpretation of the above two counting principles. Suppose n(A) denotes the number of elements in the set A and n(B), the number of elements in set B, them:

(i) **Addition Principle :** If A and B are disjoint sets, then

$n(A \cup B) = n(A) + n(B)$

(ii) **Multiplication Principle :** Let A × B be the Cartesian product of sets A and B. Then

$n(A \times B) = n(A) . n(B).$

THE FACTORIAL

The continued product of first is natural numbers is called the "n factorial" and is denoted by n! or $\underline{|n}$.

i.e., $n! = 1 \times 2 \times 3 \times ... \times (n - 1) \times n.$

Thus $3! = 1 \times 2 \times 3 = 6;$ $4! = 1 \times 2 \times 3 \times 4 = 24$, etc.

clearly, n! is defined for positive integers only.

Zero Factorial

We define $0! = 1$.

Note: Factorials of proper fractions or negative integers are not defined. Factorial n is defined only for whole numbers.

Deduction

$$n! = 1 \times 2 \times 3 \times 4 .... \times (n - 1) \times n$$
$$= [1 \times 2 \times 3 \times 4 \times ... \times (n - 1)] \times n$$
$$= [(n -)!]\ n$$
$$\therefore \quad n! = n\ [(n - 1)!]$$

for example : $10! = 10\ (9!)$

$8! = 8\ (7!)$ and $3! = 3\ (2!)$

THE PIGEONHOLE PRINCIPLE

If n pigeons are assigned to m pigeonholes, and m < n, then atleast one pigeonhole contains two or more pigeons.

Suppose each pigeonhole contains at most 1 pigeon. Then at most m pigeons have been assigned. But since m < n, not all pigeons have been assigned pigeonholes. This is a contradiction. Hence, at least one pigeonhole contains two or more pigeons.

THE EXTENDED PIGEONHOLE PRINCIPLE

If n pigeonholes are occupied by kn + 1 or more pigeons, where k is a positive integer, then at least one pigeon hole is occupied by k + 1 or more pigeons.

DERAGEMENTS

If n things are arranged in a row, the number of ways in which they can be deranged so that no one of them occupies its original place is

$$n!\left(1-\frac{1}{1!}+\frac{1}{2!}-\frac{1}{3!}+\ldots+(-1)^n\cdot\frac{1}{n!}\right)$$

Note: If r things go to wrong place out of n things then (n – r) things go to original place (Here r < n).

If D_r = No. of ways, if all n things go to wrong place

and D_r = No. of ways, if r things go to wrong place

Then $D_n = {}^nC_{n-r}\, D_r$

Where $$D_r = r!\left(1-\frac{1}{1!}+\frac{1}{2!}-\frac{1}{3!}+\ldots+(-1)^n\cdot\frac{1}{r!}\right)$$

THE INCLUSION-EXCLUSION PRINCIPLE

Let A and B be any finite sets.

Then $n(A \cup B) = n(A) + n(B) - n(A \cap B)$

Clearly, to find the number $n(A \cup B)$ of elements in the union $A \cup B$, we add n(A) and n(B) and then subtract $n(A \cap B)$, *i.e.*, we *include* n(A) and n(B) and *exclude* $n(A \cap B)$.

This principle holds for any number of sets.

For any three sets A, B and C we have

$$n(A \cup B \cup C) = n(A) + n(B) + n(C) - n(A \cap B) - n(B \cap C) - n(C \cap A) + n(A \cap B \cap C).$$

BINOMIAL THEOREM

If x and a are real numbers then for all $n \in \mathbf{N}$.

$$(x+a)^n = {}^nC_0\, x^n a^0 + {}^nC_1\, x^{n-1} a^1 + {}^nC_2\, x^{n-2} a^2 + \ldots + {}^nC_r\, x^{n-r} a^r + \ldots + {}^nC_{n-1}\, x^1 a^{n-1} + {}^nC_n\, x^0 a^n$$

i.e., $(x + a)^n = \sum_{r=0}^{n} {}^nC_r\, x^{n-r}\, a^r$

Properties of The Binomial Coefficients

1. In the expansion of $(1 + x)^n$ the coefficients of terms equidistant from the beginning and end are equal.
2. The sum of the binomial coefficients in the expansion of $(1 + x)^n$ is 2^n.

   i.e., $C_0 + C_1 + C_2 + \ldots + C_n = 2^n$

   or $\sum_{r=0}^{n} {}^nC_r = 2^n$
3. The sum of the coefficients of the odd terms in the expansion of $(1 + x)^n$ is equal to the sum of the coefficients of the even terms and each is equal to 2^{n-1}.

   i.e., $C_0 + C_2 + C_4 + \ldots = C_1 + C_3 + C_5 + \ldots = 2^{n-1}$.
4. ${}^nC_r = \frac{n}{r}.\, {}^{n-1}C_{r-1} = \frac{n}{r}.\frac{n-1}{r-1}\, {}^{n-2}C_{r-2}$
5. $C_0 - C_1 + C_2 - C_3 + C_3 + C_4 \ldots + (-1)\, {}^nC_n = 0$.
6. The number of ways (or combinations) of n different things reflecting atleast one of then is ${}^nC_1 + {}^nC_2 + {}^nC_3 + \ldots + {}^nC_n = 2^n - 1$.

MULTIMONIAL THEOREM

(i) If there are l objects of one kind, m objects of second kind, n objects of third kind and so on; then the number of ways choosing r objects out of these objects (*i.e.*, $l + m + n + \ldots$) is the coefficient of x^r in the expansion of

$$(1 + x + x^2 + \ldots x^l)\,(1 + x + x^2 + \ldots x^m)\,(1 + x + x^2 + \ldots x^n) \ldots$$

Further if one object of each kind is to be included, then the number of ways of choosing r objects out of these $l + m + n + \ldots$ objects is the coeff. of x^r in the expansion of

$$(x + x^2 + x^3 + \ldots x^l)\,(x + x^2 + x^3 + \ldots x^m)\,(x + x^2 + x^3 + \ldots x^n) \ldots .$$

(ii) If there are l objects of one kind, m objects of second kind, n objects of third kind and so on, then the number of possible arrangement/permutations of r objects out of l + m + n + ... objects is the coefficient of x^r in the expansion of r!

$$\left(1+\frac{x}{1!}+\frac{x^2}{2!}+\ldots+\frac{x^l}{l!}\right)$$

$$\left(1+\frac{x}{1!}+\frac{x^2}{2!}+\ldots+\frac{x^m}{m!}\right)$$

$$\left(1+\frac{x}{1!}+\frac{x^2}{2!}+\ldots+\frac{x^m}{n!}\right)$$

HOW TO FIND NUMBER OF SOLUTIONS OF THE EQUATION

Let the equation be

$$\alpha + 2\beta + 3\gamma + \ldots + q\theta = n \qquad \ldots(1)$$

(i) If zero included then number of solutions of (1)

$= $ coefficient of x^n in $(1 + x + x^2 + \ldots)\,(1 + x^2 + x^4 + \ldots)\,(1 + x^3 + x^6 + \ldots)$

$\ldots.\ (1 + x^q + x^{2q} + \ldots)$

$= $ coefficient of x^n in $(1 + x)^{-1}\,(1 + x^2)^{-1}\,(1 + x^3)^{-1}\ \ldots.\ (1 + x^q)^{-1}$

(ii) If zero excluded then the number of solutions of (1)

$= $ coefficient of x^n in $(x + x^2 + x^3 + \ldots)\,(x^2 + x^4 + x^6 + \ldots)\,(x^3 + x^6 + x^9 + \ldots)$

$\ldots.\ (x^q + x^{2q} + \ldots)$

$= $ coefficient of x^n in $x^{1+2+3+\ldots+q}\,(1 - x)^{-1}\,(1 - x^3)^{-1}\ \ldots\ (1-x^q)^{-1}$

$= $ coefficient of $x^{n-\frac{q(q+1)}{2}}$ in $(1-x)^{-1}\,(1-x^2)^{-1}\,(1-x^3)^{-1}\ \ldots\ (1-x^n)^{-1}$

COMBINATIONS

Each of the different groups or selections which can be made by some or all of a number of given things without reference to the order of the things in each group is called a combination.

DIFFERENCE BETWEEN A PERMUTATION AND COMBINATION

(i) In a combination only selection is made whereas in a permutation not only a selection is made but also an arrangement in a definite order is considered.

(ii) in a combination, the ordering of the selected objects is immaterial whereas in a permutation, the ordering is essential. For example, ab and ba are same as combinations but different as permutations.

(iii) Practically to find the permutations of n different items, taken r at a time, we first select r items from n items and then arrange them. So, usually the number of permutations exceeds the number of combinations.

(iv) Each combination corresponds to many permutations. For example, the six permutations ABC, ACB, BCA, BAC, CBA and CAB correspond to the same combination ABC.

Note: Generally we use the word 'arrangements' for permutations and the word 'selections' for combinations.

Notation: The number of all combinations of n objects, taken r at a time is generally denoted by C(n, r) or ^nC_r or $\binom{n}{r}$.

Thus, ^nC_r or C(n, r) = Number of ways of selecting r objects from n objects.

Important Results

(1) $$^nC_r = \frac{n!}{r!(n-r)!} \quad (0 \le r \le n)$$

$$= \frac{^nP_r}{r!}$$

$$= \frac{n(n-1)(n-2)\ldots(n-r+1)}{r(r-1)(r-2)\ldots 2.1},$$

$n \in N$ and $r \in W$.

If $r > n$, then $^nC_r = 0$.

(i) ^nC_r is a natural number

(ii) $^nC_0 = {}^nC_n = 1$, $^nC_1 = n$

(iii) $^nC_r = {}^nC_{n-1}$

(iv) $^nC_r + {}^nC_{r-1} = {}^{n+1}C_r$

(v) $^nC_x = {}^nC_y \Leftrightarrow x = y$ or $x + y = n$

(vi) $n.\ {}^{n-1}C_{r-1} = (n - r+1)\ {}^nC_{r-1}$

(vii) If n is even then the greatest value of ^nC_r is $^nC_{n/2}$

(viii) If n is odd then the greatest value of

^nC_r is $^nC_{(n+1)/2}$ or $^nC_{(n-1)/2}$.

(ix) ${}^{n}C_{r} = n/r.\ {}^{n-1}C_{r-1}$

(x) $$\frac{{}^{n}C_{r}}{{}^{n}C_{r-1}} = \frac{n-r+1}{r}$$

(2) The number of combinations of n different things taken r at a time, when k particular objects occur is ${}^{n-k}C_{r-k}$. If k particular objects never occur is ${}^{n-k}C_{r}$.

(3) The number of ways in which a composite number N can be resolved into two factors which are relatively prime (or coprime) to each other is equal to 2^{n-1} where n is the number of different factors in N.

PERMUTATIONS

The arrangements in a definite order of a number of objects taking some or all of them at a time are called *permutations*.

For example, consider arranging the digits 1, 2, 3. The possible arrangements are 123, 132, 231, 213, 312, 321. There are 6 permutations.

Let n and r be positive integers such that $1 \le r \le n$. Then the number of all permutations of n items, taken r at a time is denoted by ${}^{n}P_{r}$ or P(n, r).

Some Important Results

(1) The number of permutations of n different things, taking r at a time is denoted by ${}^{n}P_{r}$ or P(n, r) or A(n, r) then

$$ {}^{n}P_{r} = \frac{n!}{(n-r)!} \quad (0 \le r \le n)$$

$$= n(n-1)(n-2) \ldots (n-r+1),\ n \in \mathbf{N} \text{ and } r \in \mathbf{W}.$$

Note: (i) The number of permutations of n different things taken all at a time = ${}^{n}P_{n} = n!$.

(ii) ${}^{n}P_{0} = 1$, ${}^{n}P_{1} = n$
and ${}^{n}P_{n-1} = {}^{n}P_{n} = n!$

(iii) $P_{n} = n!$, $P_{4} = 4! = {}^{4}P_{4}$.

(iv) $P_{n} = n!$, $P_{4} = 4! = {}^{4}P_{4}$.

(2) The number of permutations of n things taken all at a time, p are alike of one kind, q are alike of another kind and r are alike of a third kind and the rest $n - (p + q + r)$ are all different is

$$\frac{n!}{p!\, q!\, r!}$$

(3) The number of permutations of n different things taken r at a time when each thing may be repeated any number of times is n^r.

(4) *Number of permutations under certain conditions:*

(i) Number of permutations of n different things, taken r at a time, when a particular things to be always included in each arrangement, is

$$r.\ {}^{n-1}P_{r-1}.$$

(ii) Number of permutations of n different things, taken r at a time, when a particular thing is never taken in each arrangement is

$${}^{n-1}P_r$$

(iii) Number of permutations of n different things, taken all at a time, when m specified things always come together is

$$m! \times (n - m + 1)!$$

(iv) Number of permutations of n different things, taken all at a time, when m specified things never come tougher is

$$n! \times (n - m + 1)!$$

Circular Permutations

(i) Arrangements Round a Circular Table

Consider five persons A, B, C, D, E on the circumference of a circular table in order which has no head now, shifting A, B, C, D, E one position in anticlockwise direction we will get arrangements as follows:

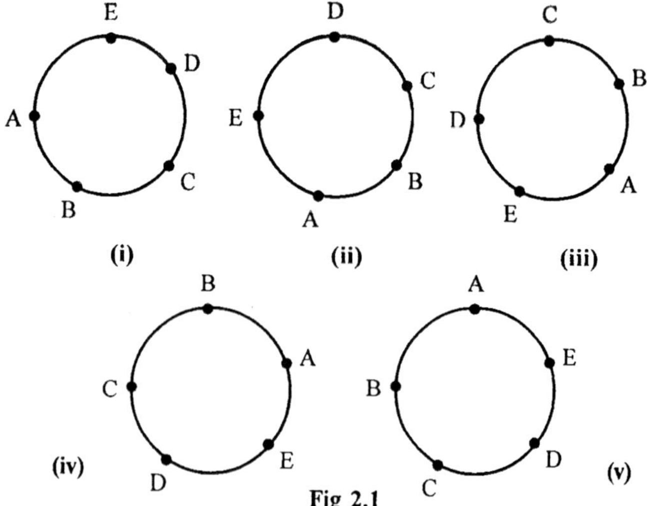

Fig 2.1

We see that arrangements in all figures are different.

∴ *The number of circular permutations of n different things taken all at a time is $(n - 1)!$, if clockwise and anticlockwise orders are taken as different.*

(ii) Arrangements of Beads of Flowers (all different) Around a Circular Necklace or Garland

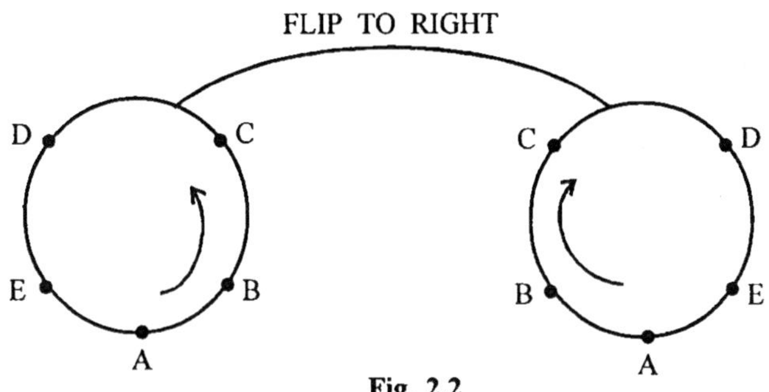

Fig. 2.2

Consider five beads A, B, C, D, E in a necklace or five flowers A, B, C, D, E in a garland etc. If the necklace or garland on the left is turned over we obtain the arrangement on the right, *i.e.*, anticlockwise and clockwise order of arrangement is not different we will get arrangements as follows:

The number of circular permutations of n different things taken all at a time is $1/2\ (n - 1)!$ if clockwise and anticlockwise orders are taken as not different.

Number of Circular Permutations of n Different Things Taken r at a Time

Case I: *If clockwise and anticlockwise orders are taken as different, then the required number of circular permutations.*

$$= ({}^nP_r)/r.$$

Case II: *If clockwise and anticlockwise orders are taken as not different, then the required number of circular permutations*

$$= ({}^nP_r)/(2r)$$

SOLVED EXAMPLES

Example 1: *There are 6 multiple choice questions in an examination. How many sequence of answers are possible, if the first three questions have 4 choices each and the next three have 5 each?*

Solution: Here we have to perform 6 jobs of answering 6 multiple choice questions. Each one of the first three questions can be answered in 4 ways and each one of the next three can be answered in 5 different ways. So, the total number of different sequences = $4 \times 4 \times 4 \times 5 \times 5 \times 5 = 8000$.

Example 2: *There are 4 students for physics, 6 students for chemistry and 7 students for Mathematics-Goldmedal. In how many ways are of these Goldmedals be awarded?*

Solution: Physics, chemistry and Mathematics Goldmedals can be awarded in 4, 6 and 7 ways respectively.

Example 3: *In how many ways can a cricket team be selected from a group of 25 players containing 10 batsmen, 8 bowlers, 5 all-rounders and 2 wicket keepers? Assume that the team of 11 players requires 5 batsmen, 3 all-rounders, 2 bowlers and 1 wicket keeper.*

Solution: The selection of team will be :

(i) Selection of 5 batsmen out of 10 can be done in ${}^{10}C_5$ ways.

(ii) Selection of 3 all-rounders out of 5 can be done in ${}^{5}C_3$ ways.

(iii) Selection of 2 bowlers out of 8 can be done in ${}^{8}C_2$ ways

(iv) Selection of 1 wicket keeper out of 2 can be done in ${}^{2}C_1$ ways.

$\therefore$ The team can be selected is

$${}^{10}C_5 \times {}^{5}C_3 \times {}^{8}C_2 \times {}^{2}C_1 = 141120 \text{ ways.}$$

Example 4: *There are 25 students in a class in which 15 boys and 10 girls. The class teacher selects either a boy or a girl for monitor of the class. In how many ways the class teacher can make this selection?*

Solution: Since there are 15 ways to select a boy. Similarly, there are 10 ways to select a girl.

Hence by the fundamental principle of addition, either a boy or a girl can be selected in $15 + 10 = 25$ ways.

Example 5: *For the post of 5 officers, there are 23 applicants, 2 posts are reserved for SC candidates and there are 7 SC candidates among the applicants. In how many ways can the selection be made?*

Solution: Clearly, there are 7 SC candidates and 16 other candidates. We have to select 2 out of 7 SC candidates and 3 out of 16 other candidates. This can be done in

$${}^{7}C_2 \times {}^{16}C_3 = 11760 \text{ ways.}$$

Example 6: *There are 10 points in a plane, no three of which are in the same straight line, excepting 4 points, which are collinear. Find*

(i) number of straight lines obtained from the pairs of these points;

(ii) number of triangles that can be formed with the vertices as these points.

Solution: (i) Number of straight lines formed joining the 10 point, taking 2 at a time = $^{10}C_2 = \frac{10!}{2!\,8!} = 45$

Number of straight lines formed by joining the four points, taking 2 at a time = $^4C_2 = \frac{4!}{2!2!} = 6$

But 4 collinear points, when joined pairwise give only one line.

∴ Required number of straight line = 45 – 6 + 1 = 40.

(ii) Number of triangles formed by joining the points taking 3 at a time

$= {}^{10}C_3 = \frac{10!}{3! \times 7!} = 120$

Number of triangles formed by joining 4 points, taken 3 at a time

$= {}^4C_3 = 4,$

But 4 collinear points cannot form a triangle when taken 3 at a time. Hence.

Required number of triangles = 120 – 4 = 116.

Example 7: *From a class of 25 students, 10 are to be chosen for an excursion party. There are 3 students who decide that either all of them will join or none of them will join. In how many ways can they be chosen?*

Solution: *When three particular students join the excursion party:*

In this case, we have to choose 7 students from the remaining 22 students. This can be done in $^{22}C_7$ ways.

When three particular students do not join the excursion party.

In this case, we have to choose 10 students from the remaining 22 students. This can be done in $^{22}C_{10}$ ways

Hence, the required number of ways = $^{22}C_7 + {}^{22}C_{10}$ = 817190.

Example 8: *In how many ways the number 8100 can be split in two factors which are relatively prime (or coprime)?*

Solution: Here N = 8100 = $2^2 . 3^3 . 5^2 . 7^1$ Co-prime means consecutive primes.

Here co-primes are 2, 3, 5, 7.

∴ n = 4 (number of different factors in N).

Hence number of ways in which a composite number N can be resolved into two factors which are relatively prime (or co-prime)

$= 2^{4-1} = 8.$

Example 9: *Show that if any five numbers from 1 to 8 are chosen, then two of them will add to 9.*

Solution: Let us construct four different sets containing two numbers that add up to 9 as follows:

$$A_1 = \{1, 8\}, A_2 = \{2, 7\};$$
$$A_3 = \{3, 6\}, A_4 = \{4, 5\};$$

Each of the five numbers chosen must belong to one of these sets. Since there are only four sets, then according to the pigeonhole principle, two of the chosen numbers belong to the some set. These numbers add up to 9.

Example 10: *Assume that there are 10 distinct pairs of gloves in a drawer. Show that if you choose 11 single gloves at random from the drawer, you are certain to have a pair.*

Solution: The 10 distinct pairs constitute 10 pigeonholes. The 11 single gloves correspond to 11 pigeons. Therefore, there must be atleast one pigeonhole with two gloves and thus you will certainly have drawn at least one pair of globes.

Example 11: *Let L be a list of the 26 letters in English alphabet which are not necessarily in alphabetical order. (a) show that L has a sublist consisting of four or more consecutive consonants. (b) Assuming L begins with a vowel, show that L has a sublist consisting of five or more consecutive consonants.*

Solution: (a) The five letters partition L into n = 6 sublists (pigeonholes) of consecutive consonants. Here k + 1 = 4 and so k = 3. Hence nk + 1 = 6 (3) + 1 = 19 < 21. Hence some sublist has at least 4 begins with a vowel,

(b) Since L begins with a vowel, the remainder of the vowels partition L into n = 5 sublists. Here k + 1 = 5 ⇒ k = 4.

Hence kn + 1 = 4 × 5 + 1 = 21

Thus some sublist has atleast 5 consecutive consonants.

Example 12: *A student is allowed to select at most n books from a collection of (2n + 1) books. If the total number of ways in which he can select a book is 63, find the value of n.*

Solution: Given that the student selects at most n books from a collection of (2n + 1) books. It means that he selects one book or two books or three books or .... or n books. Hence by the given hypothesis

$$^{2n+1}C_1 + {}^{2n+1}C_2 + {}^{2n+1}C_3 + ... + {}^{2n+1}C_n = 63 \qquad ...(1)$$

But we know that

$$^{2n+1}C_0 + {}^{2n+1}C_1 + {}^{2n+1}C_2 + ... + {}^{2n+1}C_{2n+1} = 2^{2n+1}$$

Now, $\quad {}^{2n+1}C_0 = {}^{2n+1}C_{2n+1} = 1$

Then, $\quad 2 + ({}^{2n+1}C_1 + {}^{2n+1}C_2 + {}^{2n+1}C_3 + ... + {}^{2n+1}C_n)$

$+ ({}^{2n+1}C_{n+1} + {}^{2n+1}C_{n+2} + {}^{2n+1}C_{n+3} + ... + {}^{2n+1}C_{2n-1} + {}^{2n+1}C_{2n})$

$\Rightarrow \quad 2 + ({}^{2n+1}C_1 + {}^{2n+1}C_2 + {}^{2n+1}C_3 + ... + {}^{2n+1}C_n)$

$+ ({}^{2n+1}C_{n-1} + {}^{2n+1}C_{n-2} + ... + {}^{2n+1}C_2 + {}^{2n+1}C_1) = 2^{2n+1}$

[$\because$ ${}^{2n+1}C_r$]

$\Rightarrow \quad 2 + 2\,({}^{2n+1}C_1 + {}^{2n+1}C_2 + {}^{2n+1}C_3 + ... + {}^{2n+1}C_n) = 2^{2n+1}$

$\Rightarrow \quad 2 + 2 \,.\, 63 = 2^{2n+1}$ [from com (1)]

$\Rightarrow \quad 1 + 63 = 2^{2n}$

$\Rightarrow \quad 2^6 = 2^{2n}$

$\Rightarrow \quad 6 = 2n$

$\therefore \quad n = 3.$

Example 13: *Find the number of combinations and permutations of 4 letters taken from the word* ***Examination****.*

Solution: There are 11 letters

A, A; I, I; N, N; E, X, M, T, O.

Then number of combinations

$= \text{coefficient of } x^4 \text{ in } (1 + x + x^2)^3 (1 + x)^5$

[$\because$ 2A's, 2I's, 2N's, 1E, 1 X, 1M, 1T and 1O

$= \text{coefficient of } x^4 \text{ in } \{(1 + x)^3 + x^6 + 3(1 + x)^2 x^2 + 3(1 + x) x^4$
$(1 + x)^5$

$= \text{coefficient of } x^4 \text{ in } \{(1 + x)^8 + x^6 . (1 + x)^5 + 3x^2 (1 + x^7) + 3x^4$
$+ x)^6\}$

$= {}^8C_4 + 0 + 3 \,.\, {}^7C_2 + 3$

$$= \frac{8.7.6.5}{1.2.3.4} + 3 \,.\, \frac{7.6}{1.2} + 3$$

$= 70 + 63 + 3 = 136.$

Number of permutations

$$= \text{coefficient of } x^4 \text{ in } 4!\left(1 + \frac{x}{1!} + \frac{x^2}{2!}\right)^2 \left(1 + \frac{x}{1!}\right)^5$$

$$= \text{coefficient of } x^4 \text{ in } 4!\left(1 + x + \frac{x^2}{2}\right)^3 (1 + x)^5$$

= coefficient of x^4 in

$$4!\left\{(1 + x)^3 + \frac{x^6}{8} + \frac{3}{2}(1 + x)^2\, x^2 + \frac{3}{4}\, x^4\,(1 + x)\right\}(1 + x)^5$$

= coefficient of x^4 in

$$4!\left\{(1 + x)^8 + \frac{x^6}{8}(1 + x)^5 + \frac{3}{2}\, x^2\,(1 + x)^7 + \frac{3}{4}x^4\,(1 + x)^6\right.$$

$$= 4!\left\{{}^8C_4 + 0 + \frac{3}{2}\,.\,{}^7C_2 + \frac{3}{4}\right\}$$

$$= 24\left\{\frac{8.7.6.5}{1.2.3.4} + \frac{3}{2}\,.\,\frac{7.6}{1.2} + \frac{3}{4}\right\}$$

$= 8 \,.\, 7 \,.\, 6 \,.\, 5 + 6(3 \,.\, 7 \,.\, 6) + 6.3$

$= 1680 + 756 + 18 = 2454$

Example 14: *Find the number of non-negative integral solutions of* $x_1 + x_2 + x_3 + 4x_4 = 20$

Solution: Number of non-negative integral solutions of the given equation

= coefficient of x^{20} in $(1 - x)^{-1}\,(1 - x)^{-1}\,(1 - x)^{-1}\,(1 - x^4)^{-1}$

= coefficient of x^{20} in $(1 - x)^{-3}\,(1 - x^4)^{-1}$

= coefficient of x^{20} in $(1 - {}^3C_1\, x + {}^4C_2\, x^2 + {}^5C_3\, x^3 + {}^6C_4\, x^4 + \ldots$
$+ {}^{10}C_8\, x^8 + \ldots\, {}^{14}C_{12}\, x^{12} + \ldots + {}^{18}C_{16}\, x^{16} + \ldots\, {}^{22}C_{20}\, x^{20} + \ldots)$
$(1 + x^4 + x^8 + x^{12} + x^{16} + x^{20} + \ldots)$

$= 1 + {}^6C_4 + {}^{10}C_8 + {}^{14}C_{12} + {}^{18}C_{16} + {}^{22}C_{20}$

$= 1 + {}^6C_2 + {}^{10}C_2 + {}^{14}C_2 + {}^{18}C_2 + {}^{22}C_2$

$$= 1 + \left(\frac{6.5}{1.2}\right) + \left(\frac{10.9}{1.2}\right) + \left(\frac{14.13}{1.2}\right) + \left(\frac{18.17}{1.2}\right) + \left(\frac{22.21}{1.2}\right)$$

$= 1 + 15 + 45 + 91 + 153 + 231$

$= 536.$

Example 15: *In a group of 1000 people, there are 750 who can speak Hindi and 400 who can speak Punjabi. How many can speak both Hindi and Punjabi.*

Solution: Let H and P be the set of those people who can speak Hindi and Punjabi respectively, then according to the problem, we have

$$n(H \cup P) = 1000, n(H) = 750, n(P) = 400.$$

By inclusion-exclusion principle, we have

$$n(H \cup P) = n(H) + n(P) - n(H \cap P)$$

$\Rightarrow$ $1000 = 750 + 400 - n(H \cap P)$

$\therefore$ $n(H \cap P) = 150$

$\therefore$ Number of people speaking Hindi and Punjabi both is 150.

Example 16: *A survey of 500 television watchers produced the following information: 285 watch football, 195 watch hockey 115 watch basketball, 45 watch football and basket ball, 70 watch football and hockey, 50 watch hockey and basketball, 50 do not watch any of the three games. How many watch all the three games?*

Solution: Let F, H and B be the sets of television watchers who watch Football, Hockey and Basket ball respectively. Then according to the problem, we have

$$n(U) = 500, n(F) = 285, n(H) = 195, n(B) = 115, n(F \cap B) = 45,$$

$$n(F \cup H) = 70, n(H \cap B) = 50 \text{ and } n(F' \cup H' \cup B') = 50,$$

Where U is the set of all the television watchers.

Since $n(F' \cup H' \cup B') = n(U) - n(F \cup H \cup B)$

$\Rightarrow$ $50 = 500 - n(F \cup H \cup B)$

$\Rightarrow$ $n(F \cup H \cup B) = 450$

By inclusion-exclusion principle,

$$n(F \cup H \cup B) = n(F) + n(H) + n(B) - n(F \cap H) - n(H \cap B) - n(B \cap F) + n(F \cap H \cap B).$$

$\Rightarrow$ $450 = 285 + 195 + 115 - 70 - 50 - 45 + n(F \cap H \cap B)$

$\therefore$ $n(F \cap H \cap B) = 20$

Which is the number of those who watch all the three games.

Hence by the fundamental principle of addition, number of ways of awarding one of the three Goldmedals = 4 + 6 + 7 = 17 ways.

Example 17: *How many three digit odd numbers can be formed by using the digits 1, 2, 3, 4, 5, 6, if:*

(i) the repetition of digits is not allowed?

(ii) the repetition of digits is allowed?

Solution: For a number to be odd, we must have 1, 3 or 5 at the unit's place. So, there are 3 ways of filling the unit's place.

(i) Since the rejection of digits is not allowed, the ten's place can be filled with any of the remaining 5 digits in 5 ways. Now, four digits are left. So, hundred's place can be filled in 4 ways.

So, required number of numbers = $3 \times 5 \times 4 = 60$.

(ii) Since the repetition of digits is allowed, so each of the ten's and hundred's place can be filled in 6 ways.

Hence, required number of numbers = $3 \times 6 \times 6 = 108$.

Example 18: *If* $^{56}P_{r+6} : {}^{54}P_{r+3} = 30800 : 1$, *find* $^{r}P_{2}$.

Solution: We have

$$\frac{^{56}P_{r+6}}{^{54}P_{r+3}} = \frac{30800}{1}$$

$$\Rightarrow \quad \frac{56!}{(50-r)!} \times \frac{(51-r)!}{54!} = \frac{30800}{1}$$

$$\Rightarrow \quad 56.55\,(51-r) = 30800$$

$$\Rightarrow \quad r = 41.$$

$$\therefore \quad {}^{r}P_{2} = {}^{41}P_{2} = 41.40 = 1640$$

Example 19: *Prove that* $^{n}P_{r} = {}^{n-1}P_{r} + r.\,{}^{n-1}P_{r-1}$.

Solution: R.H.S. $= {}^{n-1}P_{r} + r.\,{}^{n-1}P_{r-1}$

$$= \frac{(n-1)!}{(n-1-r)!} + r.\frac{(n-1)!}{(n-1-r+1)!}$$

$$= \frac{(n-r).(n-1)!}{(n-r)!} + \frac{r.(n-1)!}{(n-r)!}$$

$$= \frac{(n-1)!}{(n-r)!}[n-r+r] = \frac{n\,(n-1)!}{(n-r)!}$$

$$= \frac{n!}{(n-r)!} = {}^{n}P_{r} = \text{L.H.S.}$$

Example 20: *There are m men and n monkeys (n > m). If a man have any number of monkeys, in how many ways may every monkey have a master?*

Solution: The first monkey can select his master by m ways, and after that the second monkey can select his master again by m ways, so can the third And so on.

All monkeys can select master by

$$= m \times m \times m \text{ ... upto n times}$$

$$= (m)^n \text{ ways.}$$

Example 21: *How many permutations can be made out of the letters of the word* ***Triangle****? How many of these will begin with T and end with E?*

Solution: The word *Triangle* has eight different letters, which can be arranged themselves in 8! ways.

∴ Total number of permutations

$$= 8! = 40320$$

Again when T is fixed at the first place and E at the last place, the remaining six can be arranged in 6! ways.

Example 22: *In how many ways 5 days and 3 girls can be seated in a row so that no two girls are together?*

Solution: The 5 boys can be seated in a row in $^5P_5 = 5!$ ways. in each of these arrangements 6 places are created, shown by the cross-marks, as given below

$$\times B \times B \times B \times B \times B \times$$

Since no two girls are to sit together, so we may arrange 3 girls in 6 places. This can be done in $^6P_3$ ways, *i.e.*, 3 girls can be seated in $^6P_3$ way.

Hence the total number of seating arrangements

$$= {}^5P_5 \times {}^6P_3 = 5! \times 6 \times 5 \times 4 = 14400.$$

Example 23: *A person writes greeting card to six friends and addresses the corresponding envelopes. In how many ways can the greeting cards be placed in the envelopes so that (ii) at least two of them are in the wrong envelopes, (ii) all the cards are in the wrong envelopes.*

Solution: (i) The number of ways in which atleast two of them are in the wrong envelopes

$$= \sum_{r=2}^{6} {}^nC_{n-r} \text{ Dr}$$

$$= {}^nC_{n-2}\, D_2 + {}^nC_{n-3}\, D_3 + {}^nC_{n-4}\, D_4 + {}^nC_{n-5}\, D_5 + {}^nC_{n-6}\, D_6$$

Here n = 6

$$= {}^6C_4 \,.\, 2!\left(1 - \frac{1}{1!} + \frac{1}{2!}\right) + {}^6C_3 \,.\, 3!\left(1 - \frac{1}{1!} + \frac{1}{2!} - \frac{1}{3!}\right) + {}^6C_2 \,.\, 4!$$

$$\left(1 - \frac{1}{1!} + \frac{1}{2!} - \frac{1}{3!} + \frac{1}{4!}\right) + {}^6C_1 \,.\, 5!\left(1 - \frac{1}{1!} + \frac{1}{2!} - \frac{1}{3!} + \frac{1}{4!} - \frac{1}{5!}\right)$$

$$= 15 + 40 + 135 + 264 + 265$$

$$= 719.$$

(ii) The number of ways in which all letters be placed in wrong envelopes

$$= 6!\left(1 - \frac{1}{1!} + \frac{1}{2!} - \frac{1}{3!} + \frac{1}{4!} - \frac{1}{5!} + \frac{1}{6!}\right)$$

$$= 720\left(\frac{1}{2} - \frac{1}{6} + \frac{1}{24} - \frac{1}{120} + \frac{1}{720}\right)$$

$$= 360 - 120 + 30 - 6 + 1 = 265$$

Example 24: *If A and B be two sets containing 3 and 6 elements respectively, what can be the minimum number of elements in $A \cup B$? Find also, the maximum number of elements in $A \cup B$.*

Solution: By inclusion-exclusion principle

$$n(A \cup B) = n(A) + n(B) - n(A \cap B).$$

Now, $n(A \cup B)$ is minimum or maximum according as $n(A \cap B)$ is maximum or minimum respectively.

Case I: If $n(A \cap B)$ is minimum,

i.e., $n(A \cap B) = 0$ such that

$A = \{a, b, c, d, e, f\}$

and $B = \{g, h, i\}$.

Then $[n(A \cup B)]_{max}. = n(A) + n(B)$

$= 6 + 3 = 9.$

Case II: If $n(A \cap B)$ is maximum,

i.e., $n(A \cap B) = 3$ such that

$A = \{a, b, c, d, e, f\}$

and $B = \{b, d, e\}$

Then $[n(A \cup B)]_{min}. = n(A) + n(B) - n(A \cap B)$

$= 6 + 3 - 3 = 6.$

Example 25: *How many words can be formed from the letters of the word '**Daughter**' so that*

(i) the vowels always come together?

(ii) the vowels never come together?

Solution: There are 8 letters in the word 'Daughter', including 3 vowels (A, U, E) and 5 consonants (D, G, H, T, R)

(i) Considering three vowels as one letter, we have 6 letters which can be arranged $^6P_6 = 6!$ ways. But corresponding each way of these arrangements, the vowels A, U, E can be put together in 3! ways.

$= 6! \times 3! = 720 \times 6 = 4320$

Example 26: *In how many ways can 9 examination papers be arranged so that the best and the worst papers are never together?*

Solution: The number of arrangements in which the best and worst paper never come together can be obtained by subtracting from the total number of arrangements, the number of arrangements in which the best and worst come together.

The total number of arrangements of 9 papers $= {}^9P_9 = 9!$

considering the best and the worst paper as one paper, we have 8 papers which can be arranged in $^8P_8 = 8!$ ways. But the best and worst papers can be put together in 2! ways. So, the number of permutations in which the best and the worst papers can be put together

$$= (2! \times 8!)$$

Hence, the number of ways in which the best and the worst papers never come together

$$= 9! - 2 \times 8! = 9 \times 8! - 2 \times 8!$$

$$= 7 \times 8! = 282240.$$

Example 27: *When a group photograph is taken, all the seven teachers should be in the first row and all the twenty students should be in the second row. If the two corners of the second row are reserved for the two tallest students, interchangeable only between them, and if the middle seat of the front row is reserved for the principal, how many arrangements are possible?*

Solution: Since the middle seat of the front row is reserved for the principal, the remaining 6 teachers can be arranged in the front row in $^6P_6 = 6!$ ways.

The two corners of the second row are reserved for the two tallest students. They can occupy these two places in 2! ways. The remaining 18 students in 18! ways.

Hence, by the fundamental principle of counting, the total number of arrangements

$$= 6! \times (18! \times 2!)$$
$$= 18! \times 1440.$$

Example 28: *A code word is to consist of two distinct English alphabets followed by two distinct numbers from 1 to 9. For example, PK 25 is a code word. How many such code words are there? How many of them end with an even integer?*

Solution: There are 26 English alphabets. So, first two places can be filled in ${}^{26}P_2$ ways. In last two places we have to use two distinct numbers from 1 to 9. So, last two place can be filled in ${}^{9}P_2$ ways. Hence, by the fundamental principle of counting, the total number of code words

$$= {}^{26}P_2 \times {}^{9}P_2 = 650 \times 72$$
$$= 46800$$

Now, we have to find the number of code words ending with an even integer. in this case, the code word can have any of the number 2, 4, 6, 8 at the extreme right position. So the extreme right position can be filled in 4 ways. Now, next left position can be filled with any one of the remaining 8 digits in 8 ways and the two extreme left positions can be filled in by two English alphabets in ${}^{26}P_2$ ways.

Hence, the total number of code words which end with an even integer

$$= 4 \times 8 \times {}^{26}P_2 = 4 \times 8 \times 650$$
$$= 20800.$$

Example 29: *How many arrangements can be mode with the letters of the word '**Mathematics**'? In how many of them vowels are together?*

Solution: There are 11 letters in the word *Mathematics* of which two are M's, two are A's, two are T's and all other are distinct. So,

Required number of arrangements

$$= \frac{11!}{2!2!2!} = 4989600$$

There are 4 vowels A, E, A, I. Considering these four vowels as one letter we have 8 letters (M, T, H, M, T, C, S and one letter obtained by combining all vowels), out of which M and T occur twice and the rest al' different.

These 8 letters can be arranged in $\frac{8!}{2! \times 2!}$ ways.

But the four vowels can be put together in 4!/2! ways (as A occur twice)

Hence, the total number of arrangements in which vowels are always together

$$= \frac{8!}{2! \times 2!} \times \frac{4!}{2!} = 10080 \times 12$$

$$= 120960$$

Example 30: *How many numbers greater than a million can be formed with the digits 2, 3, 0, 3, 4, 2, 3?*

Solution: Any number greater than a million will contain all the seven digits.

Now, we have to arrange these seven digits, out of which 2 occurs twice, 3 occurs thrice and the rest are distinct.

The number of such arrangements

$$= \frac{7!}{2! \times 3!} = 420$$

These arrangements also include those number which contain 0 at the million's place

Keeping 0 fixed at the millionth place, we have 6 digits out of which 2 occurs twice, 3 occurs thrice and the rest are distinct. These 6 digits can be arranged in $\frac{6!}{2! \times 3!} = 60$ ways.

Hence, the number of required number = 420 – 60 = 360.

Example 31: *In the different permutations of the word, 'EXAMINATION' are listed as in dictionary. How many items are there in the list before the first word starting with E?*

Solution: In a dictionary the words at each stage are arranged in alphabetical order. In the given problem we have to find the total number of words starting with A, because the very next word will start with E.

For finding the number of words starting with A, we have to find the number of arrangements of the remaining 10 letters, EXAMINATION, of which these are 2 I's, 2 M's and the others each of its own kind.

The number of such arrangements

$$= \frac{10!}{2!\ 2!} = 907200$$

Hence, the required number of items

$= 907200.$

Example 32: *In how many ways 5 rings of different types can be worn in 4 fingers?*

Solution: The first ring can be work in any of the 4 fingers. So, there are 4 ways of wearing it. Similarly, each one of the other rings can be worn in 4 ways.

Hence, the requisite number of ways

$$= 4 \times 4 \times 4 \times 4 \times 4 = 4^5.$$

Example 33: *How many 4-digit number are there, when a digit may be repeated any number of times?*

Solution: In a four digit number 0 can not be placed at thousand's place. So, thousand's place can be filled with any digit from 1 to 9. Thus, thousand's place can be filled in 9 ways.

Since repetition of digits is allowed, therefore each of the remaining 3 places can be filled in 10 ways by using the digits from 0 to 9.

Hence, the required number of numbers

$$= 9 \times 10 \times 10 \times 10 = 9000.$$

Example 33(a): *If 20 persons were invited for a party, in how many ways can they and the host be seated at a circular table ? In how many of these ways will two particular persons be seated on either side of the host?*

Solution: (i) Clearly, there are 21 persons, including the host, to be seated round a circular table. These 21 persons can be seated round a circular table in $(2! - 1)! = 20!$ ways.

(ii) Let P_1, P_2 be two particular persons and H be the host. These two particular persons can be seated on either side of the host in the following two ways : (1) P_1 H P_2 and (ii) P_2 H P_1.

Consider the two particular persons and the host as one person, we have 18 persons in all. These 19 persons can be seated round a circular table in $(19 - 1)!. = 18!$ ways. But two particular persons can be seated on either side of the host in 2 ways. So, the number of ways of seating 21 persons at a circular table with two particular persons on either side of the host = $18! \times 2$.

Example 33(b): *A round table conference is to be hold between 20 delegates of 2 countries. In how many ways can they be seated if two particular delegates are :*

(i) always together? (ii) never together?

Solution: (i) Let D_1 and D_2 be two particular delegates. Considering D_1 and D_2 as one of delegate, we have 19 delegates in all. These 19 delegates can be seated round a circular table in $(19 - 1)! = 18!$ ways. But two particular delegates can arrange among themselves in 2! ways. Hence, the total number of ways $= 18 \times 2! = 2 \times (18!)$.

(ii) To find the number of ways in which two particular delegates never sit together, we subtract the number of ways in which they sit together from the total number of seating arrangements of 20 persons. Clearly 20 persons can be seated round a circular table in $(20 - 1)! = 19!$ ways.

Hence, the required number of seating arrangements

$$= 19! - 2 \times 18!$$

$$= 17 \times 18!$$

Example 33(c): *Three boys and three girls are to be seated around a table in a circle. Among them, the boy X does not want any girl neighbour and the girl Y does not want any boy neighbour. How many such arrangements are possible?*

Solution: Let B_1, B_2 and X be three boys and G_1, G_2 and Y three X does not want any girl neighbour. Therefore boy X will have his neighbours as boys B_1 and B_2 as shown in Fig 12.3. Similarly, girl Y has her neighbours as girls G_1 and G_2 as shown in Fig. 2.3. But the boys B_1 and B_2 can be arranged among themselves in 2! ways and the girls G_1 and G_2 can be arranged among themselves in 2! ways.

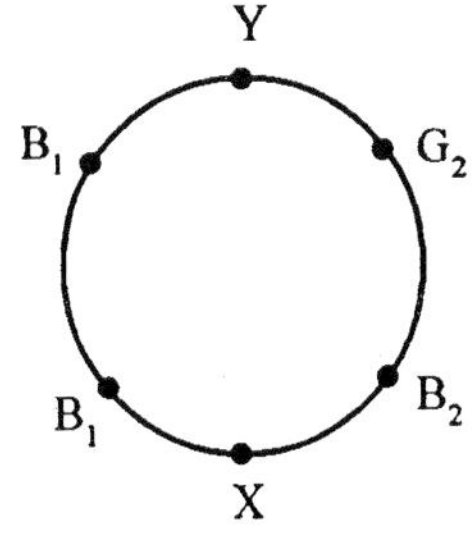

Fig. 2.3

Hence, the required number of arrangements $= 2! \times 2! = 4$.

Example 34: *Find the number of ways in which 8 different flowers can be strung to form a garland so that 4 particular flowers are never separated.*

Solution: Considering 4 particular flowers as one flower, we have five flowers which can be strung to form a garland in 4! ways. But 4 particular flowers can be arranged in 4! ways. Thus, the required number of ways $= 4! \times 4! = 576$.

Example 35: *Evaluate* ${}^{47}C_4 + \sum_{j=0}^{3} {}^{50-j}C_3 + \sum_{k=0}^{5} {}^{56-k}C_{53-k}$.

Solution: We have

$${}^{47}C_4 + \sum_{j=0}^{3} {}^{50-j}C_3 + \sum_{k=0}^{5} {}^{56-k}C_{53-k}$$

$$= {}^{47}C_4 + \left({}^{50}C_3 + {}^{49}C_3 + {}^{48}C_3 + {}^{47}C_3\right)$$
$$+ \left({}^{56}C_{53} + {}^{55}C_{52} + {}^{54}C_{51} + {}^{53}C_{50} + {}^{52}C_{49} + {}^{51}C_{48}\right)$$
$$= {}^{47}C_4 + \left({}^{47}C_3 + {}^{48}C_3 + {}^{49}C_3 + {}^{50}C_3\right)$$
$$+ \left({}^{56}C_3 + {}^{55}C_3 + {}^{54}C_3 + {}^{53}C_3 + {}^{52}C_3 + {}^{51}C_3\right)$$
$$[\because {}^{n}C_r = {}^{n}C_{n-r}]$$
$$= \left({}^{47}C_4 + {}^{47}C_3\right) + \left({}^{48}C_3 + {}^{49}C_3 + {}^{50}C_3\right) + \left({}^{51}C_3 + {}^{52}C_3 + \ldots {}^{56}(\right.$$
$$[\because {}^{n}C_r + {}^{n}C_{r-1} = {}^{N+1}C_e]$$
$$= \left({}^{48}C_4 + {}^{48}C_3\right) + {}^{49}C_3 + {}^{50}C_3 + \ldots + {}^{56}C_3$$
$$= {}^{57}C_4$$

Example 36(a): *Prove that product of r consecutive positive integers is divisible by r!.*

Solution: Let r consecutive positive integers be (m), (m + 1), (m + 2), ..., (m + r – 1), where $m \in N$.

$$\therefore \text{Product} = m(m+1)(m+2)\ldots(m+r-1)$$
$$= \frac{(m-1)!\,m(m+1)(m+2)\ldots(m+r-1)}{(m-1)!}$$
$$= \frac{(m+r-1)!}{(m-1)!}$$
$$= r!\,\frac{(m+r-1)!}{r!\,(m-1)!}$$
$$= r!\,.\,{}^{m+r-1}C_r$$

which is divisible by r!, as ${}^{m+r-1}C_r$ is a natural number.

Example 36(b): *If* ${}^{n+1}C_{r+1} : {}^{n}C_r : {}^{n-1}C_{r-1} = 11 : 6 : 3$, *then find the value of n and r.*

Solution: Here, $\dfrac{{}^{n+1}C_{r+1}}{{}^{n}C_r} = \dfrac{11}{6}$

$$\Rightarrow \quad \frac{n+1}{r+1}\cdot\frac{{}^{n}C_r}{{}^{n}C_r} = \frac{11}{6}$$

$$\left[\because {}^{n}C_r = \frac{n}{r}\,{}^{n-1}C_{r-1}\right]$$

$$\Rightarrow \quad \frac{n+1}{r+1} = \frac{11}{6}$$

$$\Rightarrow \quad 6n - 11r = 5 \qquad ...(1)$$

and $$\frac{{}^{n}C_{r}}{{}^{n-1}C_{r-1}} = \frac{6}{3}$$

$$\Rightarrow \quad \frac{n}{r} \cdot \frac{{}^{n-1}C_{r-1}}{{}^{n-1}C_{r-1}} = \frac{2}{1}$$

$$\Rightarrow \quad n = 2r \qquad ...(2)$$

Salving (1) and (2), we get n = 10, r = 5.

Example 36(c): *Three gentlemen and three ladies are candidates for two vacancies. A voter has to vote for two candidates. In how many ways can one cast his vote?*

Solution: Clearly, there are 6 candidates and a voter has to vote for any two of them. So, the required number of ways is the number of ways selecting 2 out of 6, *i.e.*, ${}^{6}C_{2}$.

Hence, the required number of ways

$$= {}^{6}C_{2} = \frac{6!}{2!4!} = 15.$$

Example 36(d): *A question paper has two parts. Part A and Part B, each containing 10 questions. If the student has to choose 8 from Part A and 5 from Part B, in how many ways can he choose the questions?*

Solution: There are 10 questions in Part A of which 8 questions can be chosen in ${}^{10}C_{8}$ ways. Similarly, 5 questions can be chosen from Part B containing 10 questions in ${}^{10}C_{5}$ ways.

Hence, the total number of ways of selecting 8 questions from Part A and 5 from Part B

$$= {}^{10}C_{8} \times {}^{10}C_{5} = \frac{10!}{8!\,2!} \times \frac{10!}{5!\,5!}$$

$$= 11340$$

Example 36(e): *A committee of 12 is to be formed from 9 women and 8 men. In how many ways this can be done if atleast five women have to be included in a committee? In how many of these committees (i) the women are in majority (ii) the men are in majority?*

Solution: There are 9 women and 8 men. A committee of 12, consisting of atleast 5 women, can be formed by choosing.

(i) 5 women and 7 men

(ii) 6 women and 6 men

(iii) 7 women and 5 men

(iv) 8 women and 4 men

(v) 9 women and 3 men

∴ Total number of ways of forming the committee

$$= {}^9C_5 \times {}^8C_7 + {}^9C_6 \times {}^8C_6 + {}^9C_7 \times {}^8C_5 + {}^9C_8 \times {}^8C_4 + {}^9C_9 \times {}^8C_3$$

$$= 126 \times 8 + 84 \times 28 + 36 \times 56 + 9 \times 70 + 1 \times 56 = 6062.$$

(i) Women are in majority in (iii), (iv) and (v) cases.

So, total number of committees in which women are in majority

$$= {}^9C_7 \times {}^8C_5 + {}^9C_8 \times {}^8C_4 + {}^9C_9 \times {}^8C_3$$

$$= 36 \times 56 + 9 \times 70 + 1 \times 56 = 2702.$$

(ii) Men are in majority in only (i) case.

So, total number of committees in which men are in majority

$$= {}^9C_5 \times {}^8C_7 = 126 \times 8$$

$$= 1008.$$

Example 37: Computer $\dfrac{10!}{6!\,4!}$

Solution: $\dfrac{10!}{6!\,4!} = \dfrac{10 \times 9 \times 8 \times 7 \times 6!}{6! \times 4 \times 3 \times 2 \times 1}$

$$= \frac{10 \times 9 \times 8 \times 7}{4 \times 3 \times 2 \times 1} = 210$$

Example 38: *If* $\dfrac{1}{9!} + \dfrac{1}{10!} = \dfrac{x}{11!}$, *find x.*

Solution: $\dfrac{1}{9!} + \dfrac{1}{10!} = \dfrac{x}{11!}, \Rightarrow \dfrac{1}{9!} + \dfrac{1}{10 \times 9!} = \dfrac{x}{11 \times 10 \times 9!}$

$$\Rightarrow \frac{1}{9!}\left[1 + \frac{1}{10}\right] = \left(\frac{x}{11 \times 10}\right) \times \frac{1}{9!}$$

$$\Rightarrow 1 + \frac{1}{10}\ \frac{x}{11 \times 10} \quad \Rightarrow \quad \frac{11}{10} = \frac{x}{11 \times 10}$$

$$\Rightarrow x = 11 \times 11 = 121.$$

***Example 39(a):** If* $\frac{n!}{2!\,(n-2)!}$ *and* $\frac{n!}{4!\,(n-4)!}$ *are in the ratio 2 : 1, find the value of n.*

Solution: We have

$$\frac{n!}{2!\,(n-2)!} \times \frac{4!\,(n-4)!}{n!} = \frac{2}{1}$$

$$\Rightarrow \frac{4!\,(n-4)!}{2!\,(n-2)!} = \frac{2}{1}$$

$$\Rightarrow \frac{4!\,(n-4)!}{2!\,(n-2)\times(n-3)\times(n-4)!} = \frac{2}{1}$$

$$\Rightarrow (n-2)\,(n-3) = 6$$

$$\Rightarrow n^2 - 5n = 0$$

$$\Rightarrow n = 0, 5$$

But for n = 0, (n – 2)! and (n – 4)! are not meaningful. So, n = 5.

***Example 39(b):** Prove inequalities* $(n!)^2 \le n^n \,.\, n! < (2n)!$ *for al positive integer n.*

Solution: We have

$$(n!)^2 = (n!)\,(n!) = (1\,.\,2\,.\,3\,.\,4\,....\,(n-1)\,n)\,(n!)$$

Now,

$$\left.\begin{array}{c} 1 \le n \\ 2 \le n \\ 3 \le n \\ \cdots\cdots \\ \cdots\cdots \\ \cdots\cdots \\ (n-1) \le n \\ n \le n \end{array}\right| \Rightarrow 1\,.\,2\,.\,3\,...\,(n-1)n \le n\,.\,n\,.\,n\,....\,n$$

$$\Rightarrow \quad n! \le n^n \le (n!)\,(n!) \le n^n\,(n!)$$

$$\Rightarrow \quad (n!)^2 \le n^n \le (n!) \qquad ...(1)$$

We have

$$(2n!) \le = 1\,.\,2\,.\,3\,...\,(n-1)n\,(n+1)\,(n+2)\,...\,(2n-1)\,(2n)$$

or $\quad (2n)! = n!\,(n+1)\,(n+2)\,..\,(2n-1)\,(2n)$

Now,

$$\left.\begin{array}{c} n+1>n \\ n+2>n \\ n+3>n \\ \cdots\cdots \\ \cdots\cdots \\ n+(n-1)>n \\ n+n>n \end{array}\right] \Rightarrow (n+1)(n+2)(n+3)\ldots(2n-1)(2n)>n^n$$

$$\Rightarrow \quad n!\,(n+1)\,(n+2)\,..\,(2n-1)\,(2n) > n!\,n^n$$

$$\Rightarrow \quad (2n)! > n!\,n^n \Rightarrow n!\,n^n < (2n)! \;..\; (-2)$$

From (1) and (2), we get

$$(n!)^2 \le n^n\,(n!) < (2n)!$$

Example 40: *Prove that 33! is divisible by 2^{15}. What is the largest integer n such that 33! divisible by 2^n?*

Solution: Let $E_2(n)$ denotes the index of 2 in n. Then

$$\begin{aligned} E_2(33!) &= E_2(1\,.\,2\,.\,3\,.\,4\ldots 32.33) \\ &= E_2(2\,.\,4\,.\,6\,.\,8\ldots 30.32) \\ &= 16 + E_2(1\,.\,2\,.\,3\,.\ldots 15.16) \\ &= 16 + 8 + E_2(1\,.\,2\,.\,3\,.\ldots 8) \\ &= 16 + 8 + E_2(2\,.\,4\,.\,6\,.\ldots 8) \\ &= 16 + 8 + 4 + E_2(1\,.\,2\,.\,3\,.\,4) \\ &= 16 + 8 + 4 + E_2(2\,.\,4) \\ &= 16 + 8 + 4 + 3 = 31. \end{aligned}$$

Thus exponent of 2 in 33! is 31,

i.e., $\quad 33! = 2^{31} \times$ an integer

This shows that 33! is divisible by 2^{15} and the largest integer n such that 33! is divisible by 2^n is 31.

Example 41: *A hall has 12 gates. In how many ways can a man enter the hall through one gate and come out through a different gate?*

Solution: Since there are 12 ways of entering into the hall. After enering into the hall, the man come out through a different gate in 11 ways.

Hence, by the fundamental principle of multiplication, total number of ways is 12 × 11 = 132 ways.

Example 42: *Five persons entered the lift cabin on the ground floor of an 8-floor house. Suppose each of them can leave the cabin independently at any floor beginning with the first. Find the total number of ways in which each of the five persons can leave the cabin (i) at any one of the 7 floors (ii) at different floors.*

Solution: Let P_1, P_2, P_3, P_4, P_5 be fine persons.

(i) P_1 can leave the cabin at any of the seven floors, So, P_1 can leave the cabin in 7 way. Similarly, each of P_2, P_3, P_4, P_5 can leave the cabin in 7 ways. Thus the total number of ways in which each of the five persons can leave the cabin at any of the seven floors is $7 \times 7 \times 7 \times 7 \times 7 = 7^5$.

(ii) P_1 can leave the cabin at any of the seven floors. So, P_1 can leave the cabin in 7 ways. Now, P_2 can leave the cabin at any of the remaining 6 floors. So, P_2 can leave the cabin in 6 ways. Similarly, P_3, P_4 and P_5 can leave the cabin in 5, 4 and 3 ways respectively. Thus, the total number of ways in which each of the five persons can leave the cabin at different floors is $7 \times 6 \times 5 \times 4 \times 3 = 2520$.

EXERCISES

1. Prove that ${}^nC_r + 2\,{}^nC_{r-1} + {}^nC_{r-2} = {}^{n+2}C_r$.
2. If $(n + 2)! = 60\,[(n - 1)!]$, find n
3. A person wants to buy one fountain pen, one ball pen and one pencil from a stationary shop. If there are 10 fountain pen varieties, 12 ball pen varieties and 5 pencil varieties, in how many ways can he select these articles?
4. There are four parcels and five post-offices. In how many different ways can the parcels be sent by registered post?
5. Twelve students compete in a race. In how many ways first three prizes be given?
6. If $P(15, r-1) : P(16, r-2) = 3 : 4$, find r.
7. From among the 36 teachers in a school, one principal and one vice-principal are to be appointed. In how many ways can this be done?
8. From a group of 15 cricket players, a team of 11 players is to be chosen. In how many ways can this be done?
9. How many 3-digit numbers are there, with distinct digits, with each digit odd?

10. There are 10 professors and 20 students out of whom a committee of 2 professors and 3 students is to be formed. Find the number of ways in which this can be done. Further find in how many of these committees

    (i) A particular professor is included.

    (ii) A particular student is included.

    (iii) A particular student is excluded.

11. In how many ways can 11 members of a committee sit at a round table so that the secretary and joint secretary are always the neighbours of the president?

12. In how many ways can 6 Hindus and 6 muslims sit around a round table so that two muslims may never sit together?

13. A student has to answer 10 questions, choosing at least 4 from each of part A and part B. If there are 6 questions in part A and 7 in part B, in how many ways can the student choose 10 questions?

14. Show that in any set of eleven integers, there are two whose difference is divisible by 10.

15. If ${}^nC_4$, ${}^nC_5$ and ${}^nC_6$ are in A.P., then find n.

16. Of the members of three athletic teams in a certain school, 21 are on the basketball team, 26 on hockey team and 29 on the football team. 14 play hockey and basketball, 15 play hockey and football, 12 play football and basketball and 8 play all the thee games. How many members are there in all?

17. How many words, with or without meaning, can be formed by using all the letters of the word '*Delhi*', using each letter exactly once?

18. If a denotes the number of permutations of (x + 2) things taken all at a time, b the number of permutations of x things taken 11 at a time and c to number of permutations of x – 11 things taken all at a time such that a = 182 bc, find the value of x.

19. Show that in a group of 13 children, there must be at least two children who were born in the same month.

20. Find the minimum number of students in a class to be sure that four out of them are born in the same month.

21. In how many ways can a lawn tennis mixed double be made up from seven married couples if no husband and wife play in the same set?

33. How many different words can be formed with the letters of word '*Sunday*'? How many of the words begin with N? How many begin

with N and end in Y?

23. If $^{15}C_{3r} = {}^{15}C_{r+3}$, find r

24. How many words can be formed with the letters of the word '*Parallel*' so that all L's do not come together?

25. How many number of four digits can be formed with the digits 1, 3, 3, 0?

26. If $^{28}C_{2r} : {}^{24}C_{2r-4} = 225 : 11$, find r.

27. In how many ways can the letters of the word '*Arrange*' be arranged so that the two R's are never together?

28. In how many ways can 7 letters be posted in 4 letter boxes?

29. In how many ways can a garland of 20 different flowers be made?

3

LOGICS

INTRODUCTION

We shall study the algebra of statements or sentences. A statement, in practice, is constructed by means of words. Also we know that a word has more than one meaning, so there is a possibility of interpreting a group of words in more than one way and thereby creating a confusion in the meaning of a statement.

We shall remove this confusion or ambiguity by developing the algebra of statements, which will in turn simplifying the complicated statements. We use symbolic language to express mathematical statements and analysis of this symbolic language is the *logic*. Study of logic is very important in discrete mathematics as it provides the theoretical basis for many areas of computer science as artificial intelligence, digital logic design etc. Here we discuss a few of the basic ideas and define some of the logical concepts that are useful in computer science.

PROPOSITIONS AND LOGICAL OPERATORS

Propositions

Definition: Proposition. *A proposition is a sentence to which one and only one of the terms true or false can be meaningful applied.*

Example: *"Four is even," "$4 \in \{1,3,5\}$," and "$43 \geq 21$" are propositions.*

In traditional logic, a declarative statement with a definite truth value is considered a proposition. Although, our ultimate aim is to discuss mathematical logic, we won't separate ourselves completely from the traditional setting. This is natural because the basic assumptions, or postulates, of mathematical logic are modeled after the logic we use in everyday speech, we expect that logical propositions contain connectives like the word *and*. The statement "Black holes exist and Mars supports life}" is a proposition and, hence, must have a definite truth value. Whatever that truth value is, it should be the same as the truth value of "Mars supports life and black holes exist.".

Logical Operators

There are several ways in which we commonly combine simple statements into compound ones. The words *and, or, not, if ... then*, and *if and only if* can be added to on e or more propositions to create a new proposition. To avoid any confusion, we will precisely define each one's meaning and introduce its standard symbol. With the exception of negation (*not*), all of the operators act on pairs of propositions. Since each proposition has two possible truth values, there are four ways that truth can be assigned to two propositions. In defining the effect that a logical operator has on two propositions, the result must be specified for all four cases. The most convenient way of doing this is with a truth table, which we will illustrate by defining the word *and.*

TRUTH TABLES AND PROPOSITIONS GENERATED BY A SET

Consider the compound proposition $c : (p \wedge q) \vee (\sim q \wedge r)$, where p, q, and r are propositions. This is an example of a proposition generated by p, q, and r. We will define this terminology later in the section. Since each of the three simple propositions has two possible truth values, it follows that there are eight different combinations of truth values that determine a value for c. These values can be obtained from a truth table for c. To construct the truth table, we build c from p, q and r and from the logical operators. The result is Table 3.1. Strictly speaking, the first three columns and the last column make up the truth table for c. The other columns are work space needed to build up to c.

Table 3.1: Truth Table for c

p	q	r	$(p \wedge q)$	$\sim q$	$(\sim q \vee r)$	c
0	0	0	0	1	0	0
0	0	1	0	1	1	1
0	1	0	0	0	0	0
0	1	1	0	0	0	0
1	0	0	0	1	0	0
1	0	1	0	1	0	1
1	1	0	1	0	0	1
1	1	1	1	0	0	0

Note that the first three columns of the truth table are an enumeration of the eight three-digit binary integers. This standardizes the order in which the cases are listed. In general, if c is generated by n simple propositions, then the truth table for c will have 2^n rows with the first n columns being an enumeration of the n digit binary integers. At a glance we can see that for exactly four of the eight cases, c will be true. For example, if p and r are true and q is false (the sixth case), then c is true.

Let S be any set of propositions. We will give two definitions of a proposition generated by S. The first is a bit imprecise, but should be clear. The second definition is called a *recursive definition.* If you find it confusing, use the first definition and reread the second occasionally.

Definition: Proposition Generated by S.

(1) *A proposition generated by S is any valid combination of propositions in S with conjunction, disjunction, and negation.*

(2) (a) *If p Î S, then p is a proposition generated by S.*

(b) If x and y are propositions generated by S, then so are (x), ~x, (x) ∨ (y) and (x) ∧ (y).

Note: We have not included the conditional and biconditional in the definition because they can both be obtained from conjunction, disjunction, and negation, as we will see later.

If S is a finite set, then we may use slightly different terminology. For example, if S = {p, q, r}, we might say that a proposition is generated by p, q, and r instead of {p, q, r}. One other variation that we will use is that the parentheses that are added when taking a disjunction or conjunction will be dropped if the lack of them causes no confusion. For example, the conjunction of p and q ∧ r will be written p ∨ (q ∧ r) instead of (p) ∧ (q ∨ r). Note that dropping both sets would be confusing; in fact it would be incorrect. It is customary to use the following hierarchy for interpreting propositions, with parentheses overriding this order:

First: Negation

Second: Conjunction

Third: Disjunction

Within any level of the hierarchy, work from left to right. Using these rules, p ∧ q ∨ r is taken to mean (p ∧ q) ∨ r. These precedence rules are universal and are exactly those used in many computer languages such as Pascal.

Example: *A few shortened expressions and their fully parenthesized versions:*

(a) $p \wedge q \wedge r$ is $((p) \wedge (q) \wedge r$

(b) $\sim p \vee \sim r$ is $(\sim p) \vee (\sim r)$.

(c) $\sim\sim p$ is $\sim(\sim p)$.

A proposition generated by a set S need not include each element of S in its expression. For example $\sim q \wedge r$ is a proposition generated by p, q, and r. In this context, its truth table is the first three columns and the sixth column of the truth table for $(p \wedge q) \vee (\sim q \wedge r)$.

METHODS OF PROOF FOR SET

There are a variety of ways that we could attempt to prove that the distributive law for intersection over union is true; *i.e.*, that for any three sets A, B and C, $A \cap (B \cup C) = (A \cap B) \cup (A \cap C)$. We start with a common "non -proof" and then work towards more acceptable methods.

EXAMPLES AND COUNTER EXAMPLES

We could, for example, let A = {1, 2}, B = {5, 8, 10} and C = {3, 2, 5} and determine whether the distributive law is true. Obviously, in doing this we will have only determined that the distributive law is true for this *one* example. It does *not* prove the distributive law for all possible sets A, B and C and hence is an *invalid* method of proof. However, trying a few examples has considerable merit insofar as it makes us more comfortable with the statement in question, and indeed if the statement is *not* true for the example, we have disproved the statement.

Definition: Counter-example. *An example which disproves a statement is called a Counter-example.*

Example: *From basic algebra we learned that multiplication is distributive over addition. Is addition distributive over multiplication; i.e. is $a + (b \times c) = (a + b) \times (a + c)$? If we choose the values $a = 3$, $b = 4$, and $c = 1$, we find that $3 + (4 \times 1) \neq (3 + 4)\ (3 + 1)$. Therefore, this set of value; serves as a Counter-example to a distributive law of addition over multiplication.*

PROOF USING VENN DIAGRAMS

In this method, we illustrate both sides of the statement via a Venn diagram and determine whether both Venn diagrams give us the same "picture." The advantage of this method is that it is relatively quick and mechanical. The disadvantage is that it is workable only if there are a small number of sets under consideration. Also, the method *illustrates* rather than proves facts. Many mathematicians do not consider it a valid method of proof.

PROOF USING SET-MEMBERSHIP TABLES

Let A be a subset of a universal set U and let u ∈ U. To use this method we note that exactly one of the following is true; u ∈ A or u ÿ A. Denote the situation where u ∈ A by 1 and that where u ∉ A by 0. Working with two sets, A and B, and if u ∈ U, there are four possible outcomes of "where u can be." What are they? The set-membership table for A ∪ B is:

A	B	A ∪ B
0	0	0
0	1	1
1	0	1
1	1	1

This table illustrates that u ∈ A ∪ B if and only if u ∈ A or u ∈ B.

In order to prove the distributive law via a set-membership table, write out the table for each side of the set statement to be proved and note that if S and T are two columns in a table, then the set statement S is equal to the set statement T if and only if corresponding entries in each column are the same.

To prove A ∩ (B ∪ C) = (A ∩ B) ∪ (A ∩ C), first note that the statement involves three sets, A, B and C. So there are $2^3 = 8$ possibilities for the membership of an element in the sets.

A	B	C	B ∪ C	A ∩ B	A ∩ C	A ∩ (B ∪ V)	(A ∩ B) ∪ (A ∩ C)
0	0	0	0	0	0	0	0
0	0	1	1	0	0	0	0
0	1	0	1	0	0	0	0
0	1	1	1	0	0	0	0
1	0	0	0	0	0	0	0
1	0	1	1	0	1	1	1
1	1	0	1	1	0	1	1
1	1	1	1	1	1	1	1

Since each entry in Column 7 is the same as the corresponding entry in Column 8, we have shown that A ∩ (B ∪ C) = (A ∩ B) ∪ (A ∩ C) for any sets A, B and C. The main advantage of this method is that it is mechanical. The main disadvantage is that it is reasonable to use only for a relatively small number of sets. If we are trying to prove a statement involving five set, there are $2^5 = 32$ rows! Also, this method tends to distract a person from learning and understanding the core concepts of the subject matter, namely, definitions and theorems.

PROOF USING DEFINITIONS

This method involves using definitions and basic concepts to prove the given statement. This procedure forces one to learn, relearn, and understand basic definitions and concepts. It helps individuals to focus their attention on the main ideas of each topic and therefore is the most useful method of proof. One does not learn a topic by memorizing or occasionally glancing at core topics, but by using them in a variety of contexts. The word *proof* panics most people; however, everyone can become comfortable with proofs. Do not expect to prove every statement immediately. In fact, it is not our purpose to prove every theorem or fact encountered, only those which illustrate methods and/or basic concept. Throughout the text we will focus in on main techniques of proofs. Let's illustrate by proving the distributive law.

PARTITIONS OF SETS

When confronted by a complicated task the human mind will frequently "divide and conquer"; that is, subdivide the task into subproblems and solve each part separately. A task or set can be subdivided or partitioned, in many different ways, depending on what the observer would like to accomplish.

Example 1: *Consider the set of students in a classroom. How can the instructor partition this set? The instructor could partition it into subsets, or blocks, where each block contain students; (a) in the same row, or (b) who have the same colour eyes, or (c) in specific weight categories, or (d) in specific height categories, etc.*

One could also think of the concept of partitioning a set as a "packaging problem." How can one "package" a carton of, say, twenty-four cans? We, could use: four six-packs, three eight-packs, two twelve-packs , etc. In all cases: (a) the sum of all cans in all packs must be twenty-four, and (b) a can must be in one and only one pack.

Definition: Partition. *Let A be a set, A partition of A is any set of nonempty subsets (or blocks)* A_1, A_2, ... *of A such that:*

(a) $A1 \cup A2 \cup .... = A$, and

(b) *the subsets* A_i *are mutually disjoint; that is,* $A_1 \cap A_j = f$ *for* $i \neq j$.

Example 2: *Let* $A = \{a, b, c\}$. *Then* $\{\{a\}, \{b, c\}\}$ *is a partition of A. We see that we have partitioned A into two blocks, namely* $\{a\}$ *and* $\{b, c\}$. *Note* *how our definition of a partition allows for the possibility that A can be broken up into an infinite number of blocks. Of course, if A is finite, as in Example 4.3.2., the number of blocks can be no larger than #A.*

Example 3: *Two examples of partitions of Z are* $\{\{n\} \mid n \in Z\}$ *and* $\{\{n \mid n \in Z, n < 0\}, \{0\} \{n \mid n \in Z, n > 0\}\}$. *The set of subsets* $\{\{n \in Z \mid n \geq 0\}, \{n \in Z \mid n \geq 0\}\}$ *is not a partition because the two subsets have a non-empty intersection A second example of a non-partition is* $\{\{n \in \mathbf{Z} : \mid n \mid = k\} : k = -1, 0, 1, 2, \ldots\}$. *One of the blocks,* $\{n \in \mathbf{Z} : \mid n \mid = -1\} = \phi$.

THE DUALITY PRINCIPLE

We observed that each of the set laws labelled 1 through 9 had an analogue 1′ through 9′. We notice that each of the laws in Column 2 can be obtained from the corresponding law in Column 1 by replacing $\cup$ by $\cap$, $\cap$ by $\cup$, ϕ by U, U by ϕ, and leaving the complement as it is stated.

Definition: Duality Principle for Sets. *Let S be any identity involving sets and the operations c,* $\cap$, *and U. If* S^* *is obtained from S by making the substitutions* $\cap \to \cup$, $\cup \to \cap$, $\phi \to U$, $U \to \phi$, *then the Statement* S^* *is also true and it is called the dual of the Statement S.*

Example: *The dual of* $(A \cap B) \cup (A \cap B^c) = A$ *is* $(A \cup B) \cap (A \cup B^c) = A$.

One should not underestimate the importance of this concept. It gives us a whole second set of identities, theorems, and concepts. For example, we can write the dual of minset and minset normal form to obtain what is called *maxset* and *maxset normal form.*

Statement

If a sentence can be judged to be true or false but not both, it is called a *statement or proposition.* In other words, a sentence for which the question, "Is it true?" or "Whether it is true or false?" has a meaning, is called a *statement.* It is important to note that *every sentence is not a statement.*

Examples: *Let us consider the following sentences:*

(i) What is the time by your watch?

(ii) Girls are pretty.

(iii) $\sqrt{3}$ *is an irrational number.*

(iv) There is a life on the Mars.

(v) Buck up! boys, buck up.

(vi) How are you?

(vii) Delhi is the capital of India.

Now, we will examine each of the sentences mentioned above.

We notice that the sentences (iii), (iv) and (vii) are statements because in these cases we have answer to the question "Is it true?" In sentence (iii) "Is it true that $\sqrt{3}$ is an irrational number?" has an answer. The answer can be yes or no to such questions. Similarly in sentences (iv) and (vii), the question:

Is there life on the Mars?

Is Delhi the capital of India? have answers.

These answers can be affirmative or negative, we are not concerned with that, but the important thing is that the question "Is the sentence true?" should have an answer but it is not necessary to obtain it. Thus sentences (iii), (iv) and (vii) are *statements.* On the other hand the sentences:

Girls are pretty

What is the time by your watch

Buck up! boys, buck up

How are you?

have no answer to the question "Is the sentence true?, viz.

Is "What is time by your watch? true?

is "The girls are pretty" true?

have no meaning and, therefore, they are *not statements.*

Truth Value of a Statement

We know that every statement is a sentence, which is either true or false. The truth or falsity of a statement is called its *truth value.* We assign to the statement p, the letter **T** when p is true and the letter **F**, when it is false. Both **T** and **F** are called the *truth values* of the statement p.

Equivalent Statements

If the truth values of two statements are identical, then they are equivalent, *i.e.*, if p and q are two statements, then p and q are equivalent statements if p is **T** and q is also **T** or if p is **F** and q is also **F**. The equivalent statements are denoted by p = q or p $\Leftrightarrow$ q.

Example:

Let the statements p and q be as follows:

p: n is an even integer

q: n + 1 is an odd integer.

Now, if n is an even number, then we know that n + 1 is an odd number, therefore p $\Leftrightarrow$ q. Hence p and q are equivalent statements.

Simple Statement

A statement p is said to be ***simple*** if it has one subject and one predicate.

Compound Statement

A statement is said to be *compound statement* if it is formed of two or more than two simple statements. The simple statements are called the components of the compound statement. The compound statement is formed by connecting the simple statements with the help of the words *'and' 'or'*, *'if' ... 'then'*.

Example:

If p and q are two statements such that

p: Gunjan is an intelligent girl

q: Gunjan will join M.C.A.

Now, p and q are two simple sentences and they can be combined in a number of ways to form a *Compound* sentences such as:

(i) Gunjan is an intelligent *girl and* she will join M.C.A.

(ii) Gunjan is intelligent *or she* will join M.C.A.

(iii) If Gunjan is intelligent *then* she will join M.C.A.

(iv) Gunjan is an intelligent *girl if and only if* she joins M.C.A.

LOGIC

We use symbolic language to express mathematical statements and adjudge the truth or falsity of these statements through valid reasoning.

The analysis of this symbolic language may be termed as logic.

We usually denote statements by small letter p, q, r etc. It is clear that for a given statement p, exactly one of the following must hold:

(i) p is true;

(ii) p is false.

MATHEMATICAL SYSTEM

A mathematical system consists of:

(i) ***A set or universe U.***

(ii) ***Definitions:*** *Sentences that explain the meaning of concepts that relate to the universe are known as definitions. Any term used in describing the universe itself is said to be undefined. All definitions are given in terms of these undefined concepts of objects.*

(iii) ***Axioms:*** *Assertions about the properties of the universe and rules for creating and justifying more assertions. These rules always include the system of logic.*

(iv) ***Theorem:*** *the additional assertions mentioned above.*

Example:

In the logical system, the universe consists of propositions. The axioms are the truth tables for the logical operators and the key definitions are those of equivalence and implication.

Theorem:

A true proposition derived from axioms of mathematical system is called a theorem.

Proof:

All the theorems can be expressed in terms of a finite number of propositions, $p_1, p_2, ..., p_n$, called the *premises,* and a proposition C, called the *conclusion*. These theorems take the form

$$p_1 \wedge p_2 \wedge ... \wedge p_n \Rightarrow C$$

or more simply,

$$p_1, p_2, ..., \text{ and } p_n \text{ imply } C.$$

When a theorem is stated, it is assumed that the axioms of the system are true. In addition, any previously proven theorem can be considered an extension of the axioms and can be used in demostrating that the new theorem is true. When the proof is complete, the new theorem can be used to prove subsequent theorems.

PROOFS

A proof of a theorem is a finite sequence of logically valid steps that demostrate that the premises of a theorem imply the conclusion.

Proofs in Propositional Calculus (Logical System)

As deseribed earlier, a theorem is a proposition that can be proved to be true. An argument that establishes truth of a theorem is called a proof.

Valid Arguments

An argument is a sequence of statements. All statements but then final one are called premises (or assumption or hypothesis). The final statement is called conclusion.

An argument is said to be logically valid, if and only if the conjunction of the premises implies the conclusion. This means that if the premises are all true, the conclusion must also be true. However, if one or more of the premises is false, so that the conjunction of all the premises is false, then the conclusion may be either true or false.

To test the validity of an argument, the following procedure may be adopted:

(i) Identify the premises and conclusion of the argument.

(ii) Construct a truth table showing the truth values of all premises and the conclusion.

(iii) Find the rows (known as *critical rows*) in which all the premises are true.

(iv) In each critical row, determine. Whether the conclusion of the argument is also true.

   (a) If in each critical row the conclusion is also true, then the argument from is valid.

   (b) If there is at least one critical row in which the conclusion is false, the argument form is invalid.

RULES OF INFERENCE

The rules of inference are criteria for determining the validity of an argument. Any conclusion which is arrived by following the rules of inference is called a valid conclusion, and the argument is called valid argument. Generally, for a proof we use two fundamental rules of inference.

Rule 1: *If the statement p is assumed as true and also the statement $p \to q$ is accepted as true, then q must be true.*

Symbolically,

$$p \to q$$

$$p$$

$$\therefore q$$

In this presentation, the assertions above the horizontal line are the *premises or hypotheses* while the assertion below the line is the *conclusion.* The rule depicted is known as *modus ponens* or the *rule of detachment*. The validity of the argument can also seen from the truth table. For this we construct a truth table for the premises and conclusion.

Truth Table

		Premises	Conclusion	
p	q	p ⇒ q	p	q
T	T	T	T	T
T	F	F	T	F
F	T	T	F	T
F	F	T	F	F

It is clear from the truth table that there is only one case in which both premises are true (first case), and that in this case the conclusion is also true. Hence the argument is valid.

Another way of stating that the above argument is valid is that $[(p \Rightarrow q) \wedge p] \Rightarrow q$ is tautology.

Rule 2: Whenever the two implications $p \Rightarrow q$ and $q \Rightarrow r$ are accepted as true then the implication $p \Rightarrow r$ is accepted as true.

Symbolically:

$$p \Rightarrow q$$
$$q \Rightarrow r$$
$$\therefore\ p \Rightarrow r$$

This argument is known as a *hypothetical syllogism.*

Truth Table

p	q	r	p ⇒ q	q ⇒ r	p ⇒ r
T	T	T	T	T	T
T	T	F	T	F	F
T	F	T	F	T	T
T	F	F	F	T	F
F	T	T	T	T	T
F	T	F	T	F	T
F	F	T	T	T	T
F	F	F	T	T	T

It is clear from the first, fifth, seventh and eighth rows of the truth table that both premises are true. Since in each case the conclusion is also true, the argument is valid.

This rule may also be described as:

$$(p \Rightarrow q) \wedge (q \Rightarrow r)$$
$$\Rightarrow (p \Rightarrow r)$$

is a tautology.

Additional Valid Argument Forms

There are other valid inferences. Some of them are:

Modus Tollens

The argument of the from

$$\begin{array}{l} p \Rightarrow q \\ \quad\ \sim q \\ \therefore\ \sim p \end{array}$$

This argument is called modus tollens which means "method of denying". It can easily be established by using a truth table.

Addition

The following argument form is valid.

$$\begin{array}{l} \quad p \\ \therefore\ p \vee q \end{array}$$

This form is used for making generalizations. If p is true, then more generally, p or q is true for any other statement q.

Disjunctive Syllogism

The following statement form is valid

$$\begin{array}{l} p \vee q \\ \quad \sim q \\ \therefore\ p \end{array}$$

According to this argument, when there are two possibilities and one can rule one out, the other must be the case.

METHODS OF PROOF

Direct Proof

A direct proof is a proof in which the truth of the premises of a theorem are shown to directly imply the truth of the theorem's conclusion.

Example: *For example the direct proof of the theorem:* $p \rightarrow r,\ q \rightarrow s,\ p \vee q \Rightarrow s \vee r$ *is*

Step	Proposition	Justification
(1)	$p \vee q$	Premise
(2)	$\sim p \to q$	(1) conditional rule
(3)	$q \to s$	premise
(4)	$\sim p \to s$	(2), (3), chain rule
(5)	$\sim s \to p$	(4), conditional rule
(6)	$p \to r$	premise
(7)	$\sim s \to r$	(5), (6), chain rule
(8)	$s \vee r$	(7), conditional rule

Indirect Proofs

Consider a theorem $P \Rightarrow C$, where P represents $p_1 \wedge p_2 \wedge ..., \wedge p_n$, the premises. The method of indirect proof is based an the equivalence $P \to C \Rightarrow \sim (P \wedge \sim C)$.

This logical law states that if $P \Rightarrow C$, then $P \wedge \sim C$ is always false, *i.e.*, $P \wedge \sim C$ is a contradiction. This means that a valid method of proof is to negate the conclusion of a theorem and add this negation to the premises. If a contradiction can be implied from this set of propositions, the proof is complete. Indirect proofs can often more convenient than direct proofs.

Conditional Conclusion

The conclusion of a theorem is often a conditional proposition. The condition of the conclusion can be included as a premise in the proof of the theorem. The object of the proof is then to prove the consequence of the conclusion. This rule is justified by the logical law

$$p \to (h \to c) \Leftrightarrow (p \wedge h) \to C$$

NORMAL FORMS

By comparing truth tables, we can easily conclude whether two logical expressions P and Q are equivalent. But if the number of variables increases, the process becomes tedious. For example.

$a, a \to b, b \to c, ..., x \to y, y \to z \Rightarrow z$ is a theorem in propositional calculus. However, suppose that we wrote such a program and we had to write the truth table for

$$(a \wedge (a \to b) \wedge ... \wedge (y \to z)) \to z.$$

The truth table will have 2^{26} cases. At one thousand cases per second, it would take approximately 18 hours to verify the theorem.

A better method is to transform the expressions P and Q to some standard forms of expressions P' and Q' such that a simple comparison of P' and Q' shows whether P and Q are equivalent. The standard forms are called *normal forms or cononical forms*. There are two types of normal forms:

Dijunctive Normal Forms

In a logical expression, a product of the variables and their negations is called an *elementary product*. For example $p \wedge \sim q$, $\sim p \wedge \sim q$, $\sim p \wedge q$ are elementary products. A sum of the variables and their negations is called an *elementary sum*. For example $\sim p \vee q$, $\sim p \vee \sim q$, $p \vee \sim q$ are elementary sums. The elementary sums or products satisfy the following properties:

(i) An elementary sum is identically true if an only if it contains at least one pair of factors in which one is the negation of the other.

(ii) An elementary product is identically false if and if it contains at least one pair of factors in which one is negation of the other.

A logical expression is said to be in disjunctive normal form if it is the sum of elementary products. For example, $p \vee (q \wedge r)$ and $p \vee (\sim q \wedge r)$ are in disjunctive normal form.

Conjunctive Normal Form

A logical expression is said to be in conjunctive normal form if it consists of a product of elementary sum.

PROPOSITIONS OVER A UNIVERSE

Let U *be a non-empty set. A proposition over* U *is a sentence that contains a variable that can take on any value in* U *and which has a definite truth value as a result of any such substitution.*

Truth Set: If p(n) is a proposition over U, the truth set of p(n) is $T_{p(n)} = \{a \in U \mid p(a) \text{ is true}\}$.

Example: *The truth set of the proposition* $\{a, b\} \cap A = \phi$ *taken as a proposition over the power set of* $\{a, b, c, d\}$ *is* $\{\phi, \{c\}, \{d\}, \{c, d\}\}$.

Tautology and Contradiction: *A proposition over* U *is a tautology if its truth set is* U. *It is a contradiction if its truth set is empty.*

Example: $(p + 1)(p - 1) = p^2 - 1$ *is a tautology over the rationals,* $x^2 - 3 = 0$ *is a contradiction over the rationals.*

Equivalence: Two propositions are equivalent if $p \Rightarrow q$ is a tautology. In terms of truth sets, this means that p and q are equivalent if $T_p = T_q$.

Example: $n + 3 = 7$ *and* $n = 4$ *are equivalent propositions over the integers.*

Implification: If p and q are propositions over U, p implies q if $p \to q$ is a tautology. Since the truth set of $p \to q = T_p' \cap T_q$, then $p \Rightarrow q$. When $T_p \subset T_q$.

Example: Over the natural numbers: $n \leq 3 \Rightarrow n \leq 6$ since $\{0, 1, 2, 3,\} \subset \{0, 1, 2, 3, 4, 5, 6,\}$.

QUANTIFIERS

If p(n) is a proposition over a universe U, its truth set $T_{p(n)}$ is equal to subset of U. In many cases, we are most concerned with whether $T_{p(n)}$ is empty or not. In other cases, we might be interested in whether $T_{p(n)} = U$, *i.e.*, p(n) is a tautology. Since the conditions $T_{p(n)} \neq \phi$ and $T_{p(n)} = U$ are very important, we have a special system of notation for them, which are called *quantifiers.*

THE EXISTENTIAL QUANTIFIER

If p(x) is a proposition over U with $T_{p(n)} \neq \phi$, we say "There exists an n in U such that p(n) is true". We abbreviate this sentence with the symbols $(\exists\, n)_U\ (p(n))$. $\exists$ is called the *existential quantifier*. Symbol $\exists$ denotes 'there exists'.

Example: *Consider the sentence "there exists x such that $x^2 = 3$". This sentence can be written as*

$(\exists\, x \subset R)\ P(x)$

or $\exists\, x\, P(x)$

where $P(x)$ "$x^2 = 3$".

This statement is called an *existential statement.*

The Universal Quantifier

If p(x) is a proposition over U with $T_{p(n)} = U$, we say "for all n in U, p(n) (is true)". We abbreviate this proposition with the symbol $(\forall\, n)_U\ (p(n))$. $\forall$ is termed as the *universal quantifier* and it denotes *'for all'*.

Example:

Consider the sentence "All human beings are mortal".

Let P(x) denote "x is mortal".

Then the above sentence can be written as

$(\forall\, x \in S)\ P(x)$

or $\forall\, x\, P(x)$

This statement is called *universal statement.*

Translating Sentences into Logical Expressions

The logical operators and quantifiers can be used to express English sentences into logical expressions. Let us consider the statement.

Every bird can fly.

We translate this logically as

For every x, if x is bird then x can fly.

Using B for the bird and F for the predicate can fly, we can write

For every x, $B(x) \Rightarrow F(x)$

or $\forall x, B(x) \Rightarrow F(x)$.

Statements containing words like every, each and every one indicate universal quantifier. Sentences of this type must be reworded such that they start with for every x, which is then translate to x.

Again, let us consider the sentence

Some men are genius

We translate this as

There exist men who are genius.

Let p be the property is genius. Then the sentence can be written as $\exists x\, p(x)$.

Negation of Quantified Statements

When we negate a quantified proposition the existential and universal quantifiers complement one another.

Example: *Consider the statement "All students in the class have taken a course in mathematics".*

This statement can be written as

$$\forall x\, p(x)$$

Where p(x) is the statement "x has taken a course in mathematics". Its negation will be

"It is not the case that all students in the class have taken a course in mathematics".

This is equivalent to

"There is a student in the class who has not taken a course in mathematics".

This can be written as

$$\exists\, x \sim p(x)$$

Therefore, we get the following equivalence

$$\sim \forall\, x\, p(x) \equiv \exists\, x \sim p(x).$$

Thus, the negation of a universal statement is logically equivalent to an existential statement.

Similarly, we can show that the negation of a existential statement is logically equivalent to a universal statement.

Multiple Quantifiers

If a proposition has more than one variable, then we can quantify it more than once. For example, p (x, y): $(x + y)^2 = x^2 + 2xy + y^2$ is a tautology over the set of all pairs of real numbers because it is true for each pair (x, y) in **R** × **R**. Another way to look at this proposition is as a proposition with two variables.

The assertion that p (x, y) is a tautology could be quantified as

$$(\forall\, x)_{\mathbf{R}}\ (\forall\, y)_{\mathbf{R}}\ (p\ (x, y))\ \text{or}$$

$$(\forall\, y)_{\mathbf{R}}\ (\forall\, x)_{\mathbf{R}}\ (p\ (x, y))$$

In general, multiple universal quantifiers can be arranged in any order without logically changing the meaning of the resulting proposition.

The same is true for multiple existential quantifiers, for example, p (x, y): x + y = 6 and x – y = 2 is a proposition over **R** × **R**.

$$(\exists\, x)_{\mathbf{R}}\ (\exists\, y)_{\mathbf{R}}\ (x + y = 6 \text{ and } x - y = 2)$$

and $$(\exists\, y)_{\mathbf{R}}\ (\exists\, x)_{\mathbf{R}}\ (x + y = 6 \text{ and } x - y = 2)$$

are equivalent.

Thus, we have

$$\forall\, x\, \forall\, y\, p(x, y) \equiv \forall\, y\, \forall\, x\, p(x, y) \qquad ...(1)$$

$$\exists\, x\, \exists\, y\, p(x, y) \equiv \exists\, y\, \exists\, x\, p(x, y) \qquad ...(2)$$

Both the sides of (1) are true if and only if p(x, y) is true for all possible pairs x and y and false if there is a pair x, y for p(x, y) is false. Both sides of (2) are true if there is a single pair of x, y that makes p(x, y) true and false if p(x, y) is false for every pair x, y.

When existential and universal quantifiers are mixed, the order can not be exchanged without possibly changing the meaning of the proposition.

For example: The statement $\exists\, x\, \forall\, y\, p(x, y)$ and $\forall\, y\, \exists\, x\, p(x, y)$ are not logically equivalent.

LOGICAL CONNECTIVES

Negation of a Statement or Contradiction

Associated with every statement is another statement called its negation. In other words, the statement having meaning contradictory to the given statement p is called the negation or contradiction of p and is denoted by '~ p' *i.e.*

'~ p' ⇒ implies not p or negative of p.

It is important to note that the negation of a *true* statement is *false* and that of a *false* statement is *true*.

i.e., if p is true then ~ p is false

if p is false then ~ p is true

Example: *The negation of the statement*

p: $\sqrt{5}$ is an irrational number

is ~ p: $\sqrt{5}$ is not an irrational number.

The following truth table expresses the relation between the truth values of the statement p and those of its negation.

p	~p
T	F
F	T

In the above table p is the statement and ~ p is the contradiction or negation of p. The truth values of p are stated is the column under p and that of ~ p are stated in the column under ~ p.

Theorem :

Prove that for any statement p, ~ (~p) = p. (Law of double negation).

Proof:

We shall prove that the statements p and ~ (~p) are equivalent. Let us prepare the truth table for these two.

Truth Table

p	~p	~(~p)
(1)	(2)	(3)
T	F	T
F	T	F

The table shows that if p is **T** ⇒ ~ (~p) is also T

and if p is **F**

⇒ ~ (~p) is also F.

Hence, columns (1) and (3) show that p and ~ (~p) are equivalent statements.

Hence ~ (~p) = p.

Conjunction

If the compound statement is formed by connecting the two simple statements with the help of the word *'and'* then, *'and'* is called the *conjunction* of the statements.

Example: *If p and q are two statements such that*

p: Shourya is an intelligent boy

q: Shourya will join M.B.B.S.

These two statements give rise to the compound sentence 'Shourya is an intelligent boy and he will join M.B.B.S.

In this compound sentence *and* is the conjunction for p and q.

Truth Table for p ∧ q (p and q)

If p and q denote two statements then the conjunction of p and q is denoted by p ∧ q, and is read as p and q.

The statement p ∧ q is true if and only if both p and q are true. In all other cases it is false. In other words.

if p is true and q is true then p ∧ q is true,

if p is true and q is false then p ∧ q is false,

if p is false and q is true then p ∧ q is false,

if p is false and q is false then p ∧ q is false,

This can be represented by following truth table.

Truth Table for p ∧ q

p	q	p ∧ q
T	T	T
T	F	F
F	T	F
F	F	F

Disjunction $\vee$ (or)

If the compound statement is obtained by connecting the two simple statements with the help of the word *or*, then the word *or* is called the *disjunction* of the statements. If p and q are two statements, then $p \vee q$ denotes the *disjunction* of p and q. The symbol $p \vee q$ is read as p or q.

Example:

If p stands for 'I shall purchase a book' and q stands for 'I shall purchase a pencil' then $p \vee q$ = *I shall purchase a book or a pencil.*

Truth Table for $p \vee q$

The statement $p \vee q$ will be true if either

(i) p is true, or

(ii) q is true, or

(iii) both p and q are true.

If both p and q are false, then the statement $p \vee q$ is false. The truth table for $p \vee q$ is as follows:

Truth Table for $p \vee q$

p	q	$p \vee q$
T	T	T
T	F	T
F	T	T
F	F	F

Implication $\Rightarrow$ or Conditional Statement

A conditional statement has two simple statements connected by the word "*if, ... then*". If p and q are two statements, the word "*if, ... then*" is symbolically written as $p \Rightarrow q$. It is read as p implies q.

Example: *A father declared, "If my son stands first then I shall buy a watch for him".*

The part 'If my son stands first' is called the *antecedent* and 'I shall buy a watch for him' is called the *consequent* in the above conditional statement. If we denote antecedent by p and the consequent by q then conditional statement is expressed by writing $p \Rightarrow q$. Now there are four possibilities, namely.

(i) the son stands first and his father buys a watch for him,

(ii) the son does not stand first and the father buys him a watch,

(iii) the son stands first but the father does not buy a watch for him,

(iv) the son does not stand first and the father does not buy him a watch,

It is clear that in all the four cases the father breaks his promise only in case (iii).

Therefore it is the case when the conditional is false. In all other cases if is true. Thus if p is true and q is false then $p \Rightarrow q$ is false otherwise it is true in all other cases. The truth table of $p \Rightarrow q$ is given as follows:

Truth Table for $p \Rightarrow q$

p	q	$p \Rightarrow q$
T	T	T
F	T	T
T	F	F
F	F	T

Double Implication $\Leftrightarrow$ or Biconditional or Equivalence

A biconditional contains the connective **'if and only if'** and has two conditions, thus $p \Leftrightarrow q$ is same in the meaning as $p \Rightarrow q$ and $q \Rightarrow p$.

Example: *In the example given for conditional had the father promised "I shall buy a watch for my son if and only if he stands first", he would surely have meant that he would not buy a watch if his son does not stand first. As such in addition to case (iii), case (ii) as well would go against his promise and will make the conditional a false statement.*

Thus the statement $p \Leftrightarrow q$ is true if p and q have the same truth values and is false if they have the opposite truth values. The truth table for $p \Leftrightarrow q$ is as given below:

Truth Table for $p \Leftrightarrow q$ (or)
$(p \Rightarrow q) \wedge (q \Rightarrow p)$

p	q	$p \Leftrightarrow q$
T	T	T
F	T	F
T	F	F
F	F	T

Logically Equivalent Statements

Two statements are said to be 'logically equivalent' if both have the identical truth values, *i.e.*, in each row of the truth table both statements must have same truth values.

Logically equivalent statements are expressed by writing the symbol ≡ in between or sometimes by = if there is no confusion.

Theorem (De Morgan's Law)

If p and q are two statements, then prove that

$$(a)\ \sim(p \wedge q) = (\sim p) \vee (\sim q)$$

$$(b)\ \sim(p \vee q) = (\sim p) \wedge (\sim q)$$

Proof:

(a) Let us form the truth table:

Truth Table

p (1)	q (2)	p ∧ q (3)	~(p ∧ q) (4)	~p (5)	~q (6)	(~p) ∨ (~q) (7)
T	T	T	F	F	F	F
T	F	F	T	F	T	T
F	T	F	T	T	F	T
F	F	F	T	T	T	T

In the above table columns (4) and (7) are identical and thus the statements ~ (p ∧ q) and (~p) ∧ (~q) are equivalent statements.

Hence $\sim(p \wedge q) = (\sim p) \vee \sim(q)$

(b) Let us construct the following truth table

Truth Table

p (1)	q (2)	p ∨ q (3)	~(p ∨ q) (4)	~p (5)	~q (6)	(~p) ∧ (~q) (7)
T	T	T	F	F	F	F
T	F	T	F	F	T	F
F	T	T	F	T	F	F
F	F	[illegible]	T	T	T	T

In the above table we notice that columns (4) and (7) are identical, and therefore, the statements $\sim(p \vee q)$ and $(\sim p) \wedge (\sim q)$ are equivalent statements.

Hence $\sim (p \vee q) = (\sim p) \wedge (\sim q)$.

ARGUMENT

An argument is a statement which declares that the given set of propositions $p_1, p_2, ..., p_n$ yield a new proposition Q. Then argument is expressed as

$$p_1, p_2, p_3, ..., p_n \vdash Q$$

or $$p_1 \wedge p_2 \wedge p_3 \wedge ... \wedge p_n \vdash Q$$

The symbol $\vdash$ is known as *turnstile*. The proposition $p_1, p_2, p_3, ..., p_n$ are called *'premises'* (or *assumptions*) and Q is called the *'conclusion'*.

Such an argument is true, *i.e.*, valid when Q is true, *i.e.*, when all the premises $p_1, p_2, p_3, ..., p_n$ are true. It may so happen that p_1, p_2 being true (in the truth table) but conclusion is not true, the argument is false *i.e.*, not valid.

LAWS OF ALGEBRA OF PROPOSITION

Idempotent laws	$p \vee p \equiv p$	$p \wedge p \equiv p$
Associative laws	$(p \vee q) \vee r \equiv p \vee(q \vee r)$	$(p \wedge q)\wedge r \equiv p \wedge(q\wedge r)$
Commutative laws	$p \vee q \equiv q \vee p$	$p \wedge q \equiv q \wedge p$
Distributive laws	$p \vee (q \wedge r) \equiv (p \vee q) \wedge (p \wedge r)$	
		$p\wedge(q\vee r) \equiv (p\wedge q)\vee(p\wedge r)$
Identity laws	$p \vee t \equiv p$	$p \wedge t \equiv p$
	$p \vee t \equiv t$	$p \wedge f \equiv f$
Complement laws	$p \vee \sim p \equiv t$	$p \wedge \sim p \equiv f$
	$\sim \sim p \equiv p$	$\sim t \equiv f, \sim f \equiv t$
De Morgan's laws	$\sim(p \vee q) \equiv \sim p \wedge \sim q$	$\sim (p \wedge q) \equiv \sim p \vee \sim q$

TAUTOLOGY AND FALLACY

Prime Statement

A statement is said to be a prime statement if it does not contain any connectives.

Tautology: A statement is said to be a tautology if its truth value is T irrespective of the truth or falsity of its prime statements. A tautology is generally denoted by t.

Fallacy or Contradiction: A statement is said to be a contradiction or a fallacy if its truth value is F irrespective of the truth or falsity of its prime statements. A fallacy is generally denoted by f.

Remark: It is obvious from above definitions that if a statement is a fallacy then its negation is a tautology and vice - versa.

Logically True Statement: A statement is logically true if it is derivable from a tautology. For example, the statement is $p \vee \sim p$ is a tautology and as such it is logically true.

SOLVED EXAMPLES

Example 1: *Represent the argument.*

If this number is divisible by 4, then it is divisible by 2.

This number is not divisible by 2. ...

This number is not divisible by 4.

symbolically and determine whether the argument is valid.

Solution: Let

p: The number is divisible by 4.

q: It is divisible by 2.

The argument may be written as

$$\begin{array}{ll} & p \Rightarrow q \\ & \sim q \\ \therefore & \sim p \end{array}$$

Thus by modus tollens the argument is valid

Example 2: *Represent the argument.*

Either Gunjan is not guilty or Rashmi is telling the truth. ...

Rashimi is not telling the truths

Therefore Gunjan is not guilty.

symbolically and determine whether the argument is valid.

Solution: Let

p: Gunjan is not guilty

q: Rashmi is telling the truth

The argument can be written as

$$p \vee q$$

$$\sim q$$
$$\therefore \quad p$$

Thus by disjunctive syllogism, the argument is valid.

Example 3: *Prove that s is a valid conclusion from the premises* $p \Rightarrow q$, $p \Rightarrow r$, $\sim (q \wedge r)$ *ad* $s \vee p$.

Solution: To prove the theorem we have the following table:

1.	$p \Rightarrow q$	Premise (given)
2.	$p \Rightarrow r$	Premise (given)
3.	$(p \Rightarrow q) \wedge (p \Rightarrow r)$	From 1 and 2
4.	$\sim(q \wedge r)$	Premise given)
5.	$\sim q \vee \sim r$	De Morgan's law from 4
6.	$\sim p \vee \sim p$	Using 3 and 5
7.	$\sim p$	Idempotent law from 6
8.	$s \vee p$	Premise (given)
9.	s	Disjunctive syllogism from 7 and 8

Thus s is valid from the given premises.

Example 4: *Prove the validity of the following argument "If I get the admission and work hard then I will get first division. If I get first division, then I will be happy. I will not be happy.*

Therefore, either I will not get the admission or I will not work hard".

Solution: Let

p: I get the admission

q: I work hard

q: I get first division

s: I will be happy.

Then the above argument can be written in symbolic for as

$$(p \wedge q) \Rightarrow r$$
$$r \Rightarrow s$$
$$\sim s$$

Therefore,

1.	$(p \wedge q) \Rightarrow r$	Premise (given)
2.	$r \Rightarrow s$	Premise (given)

3.	$(p \wedge q) \Rightarrow s$	Hypothetical syllogism by 1 and 2
4.	$\sim s$	Premise (given)
5.	$\sim(p \wedge q)$	Modus tollens by 3 and 4
6.	$\sim p \vee \sim q$	Conclusion.

Hence the argument is valid.

***Example 5:** In a certain country it is found that weather follows the following rules:*

If it is fine today, then it is windy tomorrow

If it is calm today, then it is hot tomorrow

If it is fine tomorrow, then it is cold tomorrow

Each day is either hot or cold, wet or fine and calm or windy. Forecast tomorrow's weather if today is fine, calm and cold.

Solution: The argument is as follows:

(i) fine today $\Rightarrow$ windy tomorrow

today is fine, $\therefore$ tomorrow is windy

(ii) calm today $\Rightarrow$ hot tomorrow

today is calm, $\therefore$ tomorrow is hot

The truth table for $p \Rightarrow q$ and $\sim q \Rightarrow \sim p$ are same, so that proposition $p \Rightarrow q$ and $\sim q \Rightarrow \sim p$ are equivalent. In other words $p \Rightarrow q \equiv \sim q \Rightarrow \sim p$.

$\therefore$ fine tomorrow $\Rightarrow$ cold tomorrow

$\equiv \sim$(cold tomorrow) $\Rightarrow \sim$ (fine tomorrow)

$\equiv$ hot tomorrow $\Rightarrow$ wet tomorrow

(iii) hot tomorrow $\Rightarrow$ wet tomorrow

tomorrow is hot, $\therefore$ tomorrow is wet.

The forecast is hot, wet and windy.

***Example 6:** Let p be "He is tall" and q be "He is handsome". Write each of the following statements in symbolic form using p and q.*

(i) It is false that he is short or handsome

(ii) He is tall or he is short and handsome

(iii) He is tall and handsome

(iv) It is not true that he is short or not handsome

(v) He is neither tall nor handsome

(vi) He is tall but not handsome.

Solution:

(i) $\sim(\sim p \vee q)$,

(ii) $p \vee (\sim p \wedge q)$,

(iii) $p \wedge q$,

(iv) $\sim(\sim p \vee \sim q)$,

(v) $\sim p \wedge \sim q$,

(vi) $p \wedge \sim q$.

Example 7: *Prove that product of two odd integers is an odd integer.*

Solution: Let p and q are two odd integers. Then there exist two integers m and n, so that $p = 2m + 1$ and $q = 2n + 1$. Then

$$pq = (2m + 1)(2n + 1) = 4mn + 2m + 2n + 1$$
$$= 2(2mn + m + n) + 1 \text{ which is odd.}$$

Example 8: *Simplify the following statements:*

(i) $\sim\sim p$,

(ii) $\sim(p \vee \sim q)$,

(iii) $\sim(\sim p \wedge q)$,

(iv) $\sim(\sim p \vee \sim q)$,

(v) $(p \vee q) \wedge \sim p$

Solution:

(i) $\sim\sim p = p$ ($\therefore$ negative of a negative is positive)

(ii) $\sim(p \vee \sim q) = \sim p \wedge \sim\sim q = \sim p \wedge q$ ($\because \sim\sim q = q$)

(iii) $\sim(\sim p \wedge q) = \sim\sim p \vee \sim q = p \vee \sim q$ ($\because \sim\sim p = p$)

(iv) $\sim(\sim p \vee \sim q) = \sim\sim p \wedge \sim\sim q = p \wedge q$

(v) $(p \vee q) \wedge \sim p = \sim p \wedge (p \vee q)$ (Commutative law)

$= (\sim p \wedge p) \vee (\sim p \vee q)$ (Distributive law)

$= f \vee (\sim p \wedge q) = \sim p \wedge q.$

Example 9: *Show by means of a truth table that* $\sim(p \Rightarrow q) = p \wedge \sim q$

Solution:

Let us construct the truth table for the given proposition

$$\sim(p \Rightarrow q) = p \wedge \sim q$$

Truth Table

p (1)	q (2)	$p \Rightarrow q$ (3)	$\sim(p \Rightarrow q)$ (4)	$\sim q$ (5)	$p \wedge \sim q$ (6)
T	T	T	F	F	F
T	F	F	T	T	T
F	T	T	F	F	F
F	F	T	F	T	F

The given statement is valid as the truth values under column (4) and column (6) are alike. Hence $\sim (p \Rightarrow q) = p \wedge \sim q$.

Example 10: *Simplify the following statements:*

(i) $p \vee (p \wedge q)$

(ii) $\sim(p \vee q) \wedge (\sim p \wedge q)$

Solution:

(i) $p \vee (p \vee q) = (p \wedge t) \vee (p \wedge q)$ (Identity law) $(\because\ p = p \vee t)$

$= p \wedge (t \vee q)$ (Distributive law)

$= p \wedge t = p$ $(\because\ t \vee q = t)$

(ii) $\sim (p \vee q) \vee (\sim p \wedge q)$

$= (\sim p \wedge \sim q) \vee (\sim p \wedge q)$ (De Morgan's law)

$= \sim p \wedge (\sim q \vee q)$ (Distributive law)

$= \sim p \wedge t = \sim p$ (Complement law)

Example 11: *Show that the statement (p Ù q) Þ p is a tautology.*

Solution: Let us prepare the truth table for the statement $(p \wedge q) \Rightarrow p$.

Truth Table

p (1)	q (2)	$p \wedge q$ (3)	$(p \wedge q) \Rightarrow p$ (4)
T	T	T	T
T	F	F	T
F	T	F	T
F	F	F	T

In the above table we notice that column (4) under $(p \wedge q) \Rightarrow p$ has all its entries as T.

Hence (p ∧ q) ⇒ is a tautology.

Example 12: *Prove that the statement [(p ⇒ q) ∧ (q ⇒ r)] ⇒ (p ⇒ r) is a tautology*

Solution: Let us construct the truth table for the given proposition.

Truth Table

p	q	r	(p⇒q)	(q⇒r)	(p⇒r)	[p⇒ r∧q ⇒r]	[p⇒q∧q⇒r] ⇒ p ⇒ r
(1)	(2)	(3)	(4)	(5)	(6)	(7)	(8)
T	T	T	T	T	T	T	T
T	T	F	T	F	F	F	T
T	F	T	F	T	T	F	T
T	F	F	F	T	F	F	T
F	T	T	T	T	T	T	T
F	T	F	T	F	T	F	T
F	F	T	T	T	T	T	T
F	F	F	T	T	T	T	T

Since the column (8) contains all its entries as T, therefore, the given proposition is a tautology.

Example 13: *Let p be "It is cold" and q be "It is raining". Give a simple verbal sentence which describes each of the following statements:*

(i) ~p; (ii) p ∨ q,

(iii) q ∨ p,

(iv) q ⇔ p, (v) p ∧ q,

(vi) p ⇒ ~q, (vii) ~~q,

(viii) ~p ∧ ~q,

(ix) p ⇔ q.

Solution:

(i) It is not cold

(i) It is cold or it is raining

(ii) It is cold or it is not cold

(iii) It is raining or it is not cold

(iv) It is raining if and only if it is cold

(v) It is cold and raining

(vi) It is cold then it is not raining

(vii) It is raining

(viii) It is not cold and it is not raining

(ix) It is cold if and only if it is raining

Example 14(a): *Prove by means of a truth table*

$$p \Rightarrow (q \wedge r) = (p \Rightarrow q) \wedge (p \Rightarrow r)$$

Solution: Let us construct the truth table for the given proposition.

Truth Table

p	q	r	$q \wedge r$	$p \Rightarrow (q \wedge r)$	$p \Rightarrow q$	$p \Rightarrow r$	$(p \Rightarrow q) \wedge (p \Rightarrow r)$
(1)	(2)	(3)	(4)	(5)	(6)	(7)	(8)
T	T	T	T	T	T	T	T
T	T	F	F	F	T	F	F
T	F	T	F	F	F	T	F
T	F	F	F	F	F	F	F
F	T	T	T	T	T	T	T
F	T	F	F	T	T	T	T
F	F	T	F	T	T	T	T
F	F	F	F	T	T	T	T

Hence we notice that the truth values of columns (5) and (8) are alike, therefore the two statements are equivalent.

Hence, $p \Rightarrow (q \wedge r) = (p \Rightarrow q) \wedge (p \Rightarrow r)$.

Example 14(b): *Prove that* $\sqrt{3}$ *is irrational by giving a proof by contradiction.*

Solution: Let $\sqrt{3}$ is a rational. Under assumption that $\sqrt{3}$ is rational, there exist integers p and q such that $\sqrt{3} = p/q$. Where p and q have no common factors. Squaring both sides, we get

$$3 = p^2/q^2 \Rightarrow 3q^2 = p^2$$

Hence p^2 is a multiple of 3, and therefore odd. This implies p is even.

Hence p = 3k for some integer k.

Then $3q^2 = (3k)^2 \Rightarrow q^2 = 3k^2$.

Thus q^2 is odd, q is odd. But now p and q have a common factor of 3, which is a contradiction to the statement that p and q have no common factors.

Hence our initial assumption that √3 is rational is false. Thus √3 is irrational.

Example 15: *By means of truth table, prove that*

$$p \Rightarrow q = (p \Rightarrow q) \wedge (q \Rightarrow p)$$

Solution: Let us construct the truth table for the given proposition.

Truth Table

p	q	$p \Leftrightarrow q$	$p \Rightarrow q$	$q \Rightarrow p$	$(p\Rightarrow q)\wedge (q \Rightarrow p)$
(1)	(2)	(3)	(4)	(5)	(6)
T	T	T	T	T	F
T	F	F	F	T	F
F	T	F	T	F	F
F	F	T	T	T	T

The truth values of columns 3 and 6 are alike, so the given proposition is true.

Example 16: *Prove that proposition ~[p ∧ (~p)] is a tautology.*

Solution: Let us prepare the truth table for the given proposition.

Truth Table

p	~p	p ∧ (~p)	~[p ∧ (~p)
(1)	(2)	(3)	(4)
T	F	F	T
F	T	F	T

Since the column (4) contains T everywhere, therefore this proposition is a tautology.

Example 17: *By means of a truth table, prove.*

$$p \vee (q \wedge r) = (p \vee q) \wedge (p \vee r).$$

Solution: Let us form the truth table for the given proposition.

Truth Table

p	q	r	q ∧ r	p ∨ (q ∧ r)	p ∨ q	p ∨ r	(p ∨ q) ∧ (p ∨ r)
(1)	(2)	(3)	(4)	(5)	(6)	(7)	(8)
T	T	T	T	T	T	T	T
T	T	F	F	T	T	T	T
T	F	T	F	T	T	T	T
T	F	F	F	T	T	T	T
F	T	T	T	T	T	T	T
F	T	F	F	F	T	F	F
F	F	T	F	F	F	T	F
F	F	F	F	F	F	F	F

Since the truth values in columns (5) and (8) are identical, therefore the corresponding compound propositions are also identical.

Example 18(a): *Let A(x): x is an integer, B (x): either positive or negative. Express the statement "Any integer is either positive or negative" using quantifiers.*

Solution: The given sentence can be written as

For all x, if x is an integer, then x is either positive or negative

i.e., $(\forall x)(A(x) \Rightarrow B(x))$

Example 18(b): *Test the validity of the following argument: "If shourya studies then he will not fail in B. Tech. examination. If he does not play, then he will study. He failed in B. Tech. Therefore he played."*

Solution: We symbolize the given statement as follows:

p: Shourya studies

q: He failed in B. Tech. Entrance Examination.

r: He plays

Now the given argument is as follows:

$$p \Rightarrow \sim q, -r \Rightarrow p, q \vdash r$$

Let us now prepare the following truth table:

Truth Table

line	p (1)	q (2)	r (3)	~q (4)	~r (5)	p ⇒ ~q (6)	~r ⇒ p (7)
1.	T	T	T	F	F	F	T
2.	T	T	F	F	T	F	T
3.	T	F	T	T	F	T	T
4.	T	F	F	T	T	T	T
5.	F	T	T	F	F	T	T
6	F	T	F	F	T	T	F
7.	F	F	T	T	F	T	T
8.	F	F	F	T	T	T	F

The premises $p \Rightarrow \sim q$, $\sim r \Rightarrow p$ and q are simultaneously only in line 5.

Thus in that case the conclusion r is also true. Hence the argument is valid.

Example 19(a): *Prove that compound proposition is a tautology*

$$[(p \Rightarrow q) \wedge p] \Rightarrow q.$$

Solution: Let us prepare the following truth table.

Truth Table

p (1)	q (2)	p ⇒ q (3)	(p ⇒ q) ∧ p (4)	[(p ⇒ q) ∧ p] ⇒ q (5)
T	T	T	T	T
T	F	F	F	T
F	T	T	F	T
F	F	T	F	T

Since all the entries in the 5th column are T, therefore

$[(p \Rightarrow q) \wedge p] \Rightarrow q$ is a tautology.

Example 19(b): *Obtain a conjunctive normal from of*

$$[q \vee (p \wedge q)] \wedge \sim [(p \vee r) \wedge q]$$

Solution:

$$[q \vee (p \wedge q)] \wedge \sim [(p \vee r) \wedge q]$$
$$\equiv [q \vee (p \wedge r)] \wedge [\sim(p \vee r) \vee \sim q]$$
$$\equiv [q \vee (p \wedge r)] \wedge [(\sim p \wedge \sim r) \sim q]$$
$$\equiv (q \vee p) \wedge (q \vee r) \wedge (\sim q \vee \sim q) \wedge (-r \wedge \quad q)$$

This is the required conjunctive normal form.

Example 20: *Verity whether the following statements are tautology or fallacies.*

(i) $(p \wedge q) \Rightarrow (p \vee q)$

(ii) $\sim(p \vee q) \Leftrightarrow (\sim p \wedge \sim q)$

(iii) $[(p \Rightarrow q) \wedge (q \Rightarrow p)] \Leftrightarrow p \Leftrightarrow q$

(iv) $[(p \vee q) \vee r] \Leftrightarrow [(p \vee (q \vee r)]$

Solution: Let us construct the truth tables for the given propositions:

(i) Truth Table

p (1)	q (2)	$p \wedge q$ (3)	$p \vee q$ (4)	$(p \wedge q) \Rightarrow (p \vee q)$ (5)
T	T	T	T	T
T	F	F	T	T
F	T	F	T	T
F	F	F	F	T

Since all the entries in column 5 are T, therefore it is a tautology.

(ii) Truth Table

			(A)			(B)	
p (1)	q (2)	$p \vee q$ (3)	$\sim(p \vee q)$ (4)	$\sim p$ (5)	$\sim q$ (6)	$(\sim p \wedge \sim q)$ (7)	$A \Leftrightarrow B$ (8)
T	T	T	F	F	F	F	T
T	F	T	F	F	T	F	T
F	T	T	F	T	F	F	T
F	F	F	T	T	T	T	T

Since all the entries in the column 8 are T's therefore it is a tautology.

(iii) **Truth Table**

p	q	$p \Rightarrow q$	$q \Rightarrow p$	(A) $(p\Rightarrow q)\wedge(q\Rightarrow p)$	(B) $p \Leftrightarrow q$	$A \Leftrightarrow B$
(1)	(2)	(3)	(4)	(5)	(6)	(7)
T	T	T	T	T	T	T
T	F	F	T	F	F	T
F	T	T	F	F	F	T
F	F	T	T	T	T	T

Since all the entries in column (7) are T's, therefore it is a tautology.

(iv) **Truth Table**

p	q	r	$p\vee q$	(A) $(p\vee q)\vee r$	$q \vee r$	(B) $p\vee(q\vee r)$	$A \Leftrightarrow B$
(1)	(2)	(3)	(4)	(5)	(6)	(7)	(8)
T	T	T	T	T	T	T	T
T	T	F	T	T	T	T	T
T	F	T	T	T	T	T	T
T	F	F	T	T	F	T	T
F	T	T	T	T	T	T	T
F	T	F	T	T	T	T	T
F	F	T	F	T	T	T	T
F	F	F	F	F	F	F	T

Since the columns (5) and (7) are identical so, we conclude that

$$(p \vee q) \vee r \Leftrightarrow p \vee (q \vee r)$$

Since all the entries in column 8 are T's so the given statement is a tautology.

***Example 21:** Verify whether the following statements are tautology or fallacies:*

(i) $[(p \Rightarrow q) \wedge (q \Rightarrow r)] \Rightarrow (p \Rightarrow r)$

(ii) $p \Rightarrow [(q \vee r) \wedge \sim (p \Rightarrow \sim r)$

(iii) $(p \Rightarrow q) \Rightarrow [(q \Rightarrow r) \Rightarrow (p \Rightarrow q)]$

Solution: Let us construct the truth tables for all the given propositions.

(i) Truth Table

p	q	r	p ⇒ q	q ⇒ r	(X) (p⇒q)∧(q⇒r)	(Y) p⇒r	X ⇒ Y
(1)	(2)	(3)	(4)	(5)	(6)	(7)	(8)
T	T	T	T	T	T	T	T
T	T	F	T	F	F	F	T
T	F	T	F	T	F	F	T
T	F	F	F	T	F	F	T
F	T	T	T	T	T	T	T
F	T	F	T	F	T	T	T
F	F	T	T	T	T	T	T
F	F	F	T	T	T	T	T

Since all the entries in column (8) are T's, so it is a tautology.

(ii) Truth Table

p	q	r	(X) q ∨ r	~r	(Y) p⇔~r	~(p⇔~r)	x∧y	p⇔x∧y
(1)	(2)	(3)	(4)	(5)	(6)	(7)	(8)	(9)
T	T	T	T	F	F	T	T	T
T	T	F	T	T	T	F	F	F
T	F	T	T	F	F	T	T	T
T	F	F	F	T	F	T	T	T
F	T	T	T	F	F	T	T	T
F	T	F	T	T	T	F	F	T
F	F	T	T	F	F	T	T	T
F	F	F	F	T	F	T	T	T

Since all the entries in the column (9) are not T's, so the given statement is not a tautology.

(iii) **Truth Table**

p	q	r	(X) $p \Rightarrow q$	(Y) $q \Rightarrow r$	$Y \Rightarrow X$	$X \Rightarrow (Y \Rightarrow X)$
(1)	(2)	(3)	(4)	(5)	(6)	(7)
T	T	T	T	T	T	T
T	T	F	F	F	T	T
T	F	T	F	T	F	T
T	F	F	F	T	F	T
F	T	T	T	T	T	T
F	T	F	T	F	T	T
F	F	T	T	T	T	T
F	F	F	T	T	T	T

Since all the entries in the column 7 are T's, so the given statement is a tautology.

Example 22(a): *By means of a truth table show that proposition* $(p \wedge q) \wedge \sim(p \vee q)$ *is a contradiction.*

Solution:

Let us construct the truth table for the given proposition.

Truth Table

p	q	$p \wedge q$	$p \vee q$	$\sim(p \vee q)$	$(p \wedge q) \wedge \sim(p \vee q)$
(1)	(2)	(3)	(4)	(5)	(6)
T	T	T	T	F	F
T	F	F	T	F	F
F	T	F	T	F	F
F	F	F	F	T	F

Since all the entries in the column (6) are F, so the given proposition is a contradiction.

Example 22(b): *Show that the following argument is invalid:*

If Vipin solved this problem, then he obtained the answer 7

Vipin obtained the answer 7

Therefore, Vipin solved this problem correctly.

Solution: Let

p: Vipin solved this problem

q: Vipin obtained the answer 7.

Then this argument is of the form: if $p \Rightarrow q$ and q, then p. This argument is faulty because the conclusion can be false even though $p \Rightarrow q$ and q are true. That is, in the implication $[(p \Rightarrow q) \wedge q] \Rightarrow p$ is not a tautology. It is possible, Vipin obtained the correct answer 7 by luck, guessing or prior knowledge but the arguments and intermediate steps are wrong. Hence the argument is invalid.

Example 22(c): *Obtain the disjunctive normal forms of the following:*

(a) $p \vee (\sim p) \Rightarrow (q \vee (q \Rightarrow \sim r)))$

(b) $p \Rightarrow (p \Rightarrow q) [(\vee \sim(\sim q \vee \sim p)]$

Solution:

(a) $p \vee (\sim p) \Rightarrow (q \vee (q \Rightarrow \sim r)))$

$$\equiv p \vee (\sim p \Rightarrow (q \vee (\sim q \vee \sim r)))$$

$$\equiv p \vee p \vee q \vee \sim q \vee -r$$

$$\equiv p \vee q \vee \sim q \vee r$$

Which is the required disjunctive normal form.

(b) $p \Rightarrow ((p \Rightarrow q) \wedge \sim (\sim q \vee \sim p)$

$$\equiv \sim p \vee ((p \Rightarrow q \wedge \sim (\sim q \vee -p))$$

$$\equiv \sim p \vee ((\sim p \vee q) \wedge \sim (\sim q \vee -p))$$

$$\equiv \sim p \vee ((\sim p \vee q) \wedge (q \wedge p)$$

$$\equiv \sim p \vee [(\sim p \wedge (q \wedge p)) \vee (q \wedge p))]$$

$$\equiv \sim p \vee [(\sim p \wedge \sim p \sim q)] \vee (q \wedge p)$$

$$\equiv \sim p \vee (p \wedge q)$$

Which is the required disjunctive normal form.

Example 22(d): *Obtain a conjunctive normal from of*

$$[q \vee (p \wedge q)] \wedge \sim [(p \vee r) \wedge q]$$

Solution:

$$[q \vee (p \wedge q)] \wedge \sim [(p \vee r) \wedge q]$$

$$\equiv [q \vee (p \wedge r)] \wedge [\sim(p \vee r) \vee \sim q]$$

$$\equiv [q \vee (p \wedge r)] \wedge [(\sim p \wedge \sim r) \sim q]$$

$$\equiv (q \vee p) \wedge (q \vee r) \wedge (\sim q \vee \sim q) \wedge (-r \wedge \sim q)$$

This is the required conjunctive normal form.

Example 23: *If $A = \{1, 2, 3, ..., 9\}$. Determine the truth value of each of the following statements :*

(a) $(\exists x \in A), x + 4 = 10$

(b) $(\forall x \in A), x + 4 < 15$

(c) $(\exists x \in A), x + 4 > 15$.

Solution:

(a) True, for if $x = 6$, then $6 + 4 = 10$

(b) True, for every number is A satisfies $x + 4 < 15$

(c) False, for every number is A, $x + 4 > 15$ is false.

Example 24: *Let A(x): x is an integer, B (x): either positive or negative. Express the statement "Any integer is either positive or negative" using quantifiers.*

Solution: The given sentence can be written as

For all x, if x is an integer, then x is either positive or negative

i.e., $(\forall x) (A (x) \Rightarrow B (x))$

Example 25(a): *Let A(x): x is businessman, B(x): x is dishonest K(x): x is successful. Express the following using quantifiers.*

(a) There exists a businessman

(b) Some businessmen are dishonest

(c) Some businessmen are not successful.

Solution:

(a) $(\exists x) (A (x))$

(b) There exists an x such that x is businessman and x is dishonest.

$$(\exists x) (A (x) \wedge B (x))$$

(c) There exists an x such that x is businessman and x is not successful.

$$(\exists x) (A (x) \wedge \sim K (x)).$$

Example 25(b): *Negate the statement for all real numbers x. if x > 4 then $x^2 > 16$.*

Solution: Let P(x) and Q(x) denote "x > 4" and "$x^2 > 16$"

Then the given statement can be written as

$$\forall\, x\, (P(x) \Rightarrow Q(x))$$

This is equivalent to

$$\forall\, (x\, (\sim P(x) \vee \sim Q(x))$$

The negation of this statement is

$$\exists\, x\, (P(x) \wedge \sim Q(x))$$

There exist a real number x such that x > 4 and $x^2 \leq 16$.

Example 26: *Represent the argument.*

If shourya studies hard, then he gets first division.

Shourya studied hard. ... He got first division, symbolically and determine whether the argument is valid.

Solution: Let

p: shourya studies hard,

q: shourya gets first division

The argument may be written symbolically as

$$p \Rightarrow q$$

$$p$$

$$\therefore q$$

Hence, by modus ponens the argument is valid.

Example 27: *Prove that for every positive integer n, $n^3 + n$ is even.*

Solution: *When n is even:* Then n = 2k for some positive integer k.

Now $n^3 + n = (2k)^3 + 2k = 8k^3 + 2k$

$= 2\,(4k^3 + k)$ which is even.

When n is odd: Then n = 2k + 1 for some positive integer k.

Now $n^3 + n = (8k^3 + 12k^2 + 6k + 1) + (2k + 1)$

$= 8k^3 + 12k^2 + 8k + 2$

$= 2\,(4k^3 + 6k^2 + 4k + 1)$

Which is even

Hence the sum $n^3 + n$ is even.

Example 28: *By means of truth table, show that*

$$p \rightarrow (q \vee r) = (p \rightarrow q) \wedge (p \rightarrow r)$$

Solution: Let us prepare the truth table for the given proposition.

Truth Table

				(A)		(B)	
p	q	r	q ∨ r	p→(q∨r)	p→q	p→r	(p→q)∨(p→r)
(1)	(2)	(3)	(4)	(5)	(6)	(7)	(8)
T	T	T	T	T	T	T	T
T	T	F	T	T	T	F	T
T	F	T	T	T	F	T	T
T	F	F	F	F	F	F	F
F	T	T	T	T	T	T	T
F	T	F	T	T	T	T	T
F	F	T	T	T	T	T	T
F	F	F	F	T	T	T	T

Since all the entries in columns (5) and (8) are identical, therefore

$$p \rightarrow (q \vee r) = (p \rightarrow q) \vee (p \rightarrow r).$$

Example 29: *Represent the argument.*

If it rains today, then we will not play cricket today.

If we don't play cricket today, then we will play cricket tomorrow. ....

Therefore, if it rains today, then we will play cricket tomorrow,

symbolically and determine whether the argument is valid.

Solution: Let

p: It is raining today

q: We will not play cricket today

r: We will play cricket tomorrow.

The argument is of the form

$$p \Rightarrow q$$

$$q \Rightarrow r$$

$$\therefore \quad p \Rightarrow r$$

Hence the argument is a hypothetical syllogism and thus the argument is valid.

Example 30: *Prove that √3 is irrational by giving a proof by contradiction.*

Solution: Let $\sqrt{3}$ is a rational. Under assumption that $\sqrt{3}$ is rational, there exist integers p and q such that $\sqrt{3} = p/q$. Where p and q have no common factors. Squaring both sides, we get

$$3 = p^2/q^2 \Rightarrow 3q^2 = p^2$$

Hence p^2 is a multiple of 3, and therefore odd. This implies p is even. Hence $p = 3k$ for some integer k. Then $3q^2 = (3k)^2 \Rightarrow q^2 = 3k^2$. Thus q^2 is odd, q is odd. But now p and q have a common factor of 3, which is a contradiction to the statement that p and q have no common factors.

Hence our initial assumption that $\sqrt{3}$ is rational is false. Thus $\sqrt{3}$ is irrational.

EXERCISES

1. Check the validity of the following argument:

   (a) "If I study, then I will pass in examination. If I do not go to cinema, then I will study, But I failed in examination. Therefore, I went to cinema".

   (b) "If today is Monday, then Yesterday was Sunday. Yesterday was Sunday. Today is Monday".

   (c) "If I try hard and I have a talent, then I will become a scientist. If I become scientist, then I will be happy. Therefore, if I will not be happy, then I did not try hard or I do not have talent".

   (d) "If I drive to work then I will arrive in time. I do not drive to work. Therefore, I will not arrive in time".

2. Show that each of the following inferences is fallacy:

   (a) If the client is guilty, then he was at the scene of the crime. The client was at the scene of the crime. Hence the client is not guilty.

   (b) If today is Ankit's birthday, then today is July 18. Today is July 18. Hence today is Ankit's birthday.

3. If we denote the statement 'I purchased a car' by p, then write the following statements.

   (a) p, (b) $\sim(\sim p)$

4. Prove that $\sqrt{5}$ is irrational.
5. Prove by contradiction that the difference of any rational number and any irrational number is irrational.
6. Express the following statements in words:

   (a) $p \wedge q$, (b) $(\sim p) \wedge q$, (c) $(\sim p) \wedge (\sim q)$, (d) $(\sim p) \vee (\sim q)$

   Where the statements p and q are given by

   p: I shall purchase a tape recorder

   q: I shall not purchase a car.
7. Let p be the statement "He is tall" and q be "He is handsome". Give a simple verbal sentence which describes each of the following statements.

   (i) $p \wedge \sim q$, (ii) $p \vee (\sim p \wedge q)$, (iii) $\sim(\sim p \vee \sim q)$.
8. If the truth values of the statements p, q, r are T, F, T respectively, then give the truth values of the following statements:

   (i) $p \vee q$,

   (ii) $p \vee (\sim r)$

   (iii) $(\sim p) \vee (\sim q)$,

   (iv) $(p \vee q) \wedge r$, (v) $\sim(p \vee r)$, (vi) $\sim(p) \wedge (\sim q)$
9. By means of a truth table, prove that:

   (i) $\sim(p \Leftrightarrow q) \equiv \sim p \Leftrightarrow q \equiv p \Leftrightarrow \sim q$

   (ii) $p \vee (q \wedge r) \equiv (p \vee q) \wedge (p \vee r)$

   (iii) $p \Rightarrow (q \wedge r) \equiv (p \Rightarrow q) \wedge (p \Rightarrow r)$

   (iv) $(p \Leftrightarrow q) \Leftrightarrow r \equiv p \Leftrightarrow (q \Leftrightarrow r)$

   (v) $p \vee q \equiv (p \downarrow q) \downarrow (p \downarrow q) \equiv \sim(p \downarrow q)$
10. Prove the following:

    (i) Conjunction or disjunction of a statement with itself is equivalent to the statement.

    (ii) the double negation of a statement is equivalent to the statement.

    (iii) a statement which implies own negation is self-contradiction.

    (iv) a logically true statement and a self-contradiction implies every statement.
11. Test the validity of:

(a) "If the train is late, I shall miss my appointments; if it is not late, I shall miss the train; but either it will be late or not late, therefore, in any case, I shall miss my appointment.

(b) "On my son's birthday, I bring his toys. Either it is my son's birthday or I work late in college; I did not bring my son's toys today; Therefore, today I worked late".

12. Construct the truth tables for:

(a) $(\sim p) \wedge q$, (b) $\sim(p \wedge q)$

(c) $p \vee (\sim q)$, (d) $\sim[p \vee (\sim q)]$

(e) $(\sim p) \wedge (\sim q)$

13. Prove that the proposition $[\sim p \wedge (\sim p)]$ is a tautology.

14. Show that the statement $p \wedge \sim p$ is a fallacy.

158. Prove De Morgan's Law

$\sim(p \wedge q) \Leftrightarrow (\sim p) \vee (\sim q)$

Also show that the given statement is a tautology.

16. Make an appropriate truth table and test the validity of the following arguments.

"If Piyush is a junior he is taking English. Piyush is junior, therefore, he is taking English".

17. Show that $t \Rightarrow s$ is a valid conclusion from the given premises

$(p \wedge q) \vee (r \Rightarrow s)$,

$t \Rightarrow r$, $\sim (p \wedge q)$

18. Show that s is a valid conclusion from the given premises

$p \Rightarrow -q$, $q \vee r$,

$-s \Rightarrow p$, $\sim r$,

9. Consider the following statement $\forall$ integers n, n^2 is odd then n is odd:

Which of the following are equivalent ways of expressing this statement.

(a) Given any integer whose square is odd, that integer is itself odd.

(b) Any integer with an odd square is odd.

(c) All integers have odd squares and are odd.

(d) All odd integers have odd squares.

(e) For all integers, there are some whose square is odd.

(f) If the square of an odd integer is odd, then that integer is odd.

20. A tautology is a statement which is always true Using truth tables, show that $(p \wedge q) \Rightarrow p$ and $p \Rightarrow (p \vee q)$ are both tautologies where p, q are any two statements.

21. Show that the statement

$$p \vee (q \wedge r) \Leftrightarrow (p \vee q) \wedge (p \vee r),$$

where p, q, r are statements, is a tautology.

22. Prove that:

(a) $p \Rightarrow q = (\sim p) \Rightarrow (\sim q)$

(b) $\sim (p \Rightarrow q) = p \wedge (\sim q)$

(c) $p \Rightarrow q = (\sim p) \vee q$

(d) $[(p \rightarrow q) \wedge \sim q] \rightarrow \sim p$.

23. Rewrite the following argument using quantifiers, variables, and predicate symbols:

(a) There is a student who likes mathematics but not commerce

(b) Some men are genius

(c) Some numbers are not rational

(d) Not all birds can fly

(e) All birds can fly.

24. Write negations for each of the following:

(a) $x \in R$ if $x (x + 1) > 0$ then $x > 0$ or $x < -1$.

(b) Real number x, if $x > 2$, then $x^2 > 4$

4

MATRIX

INTRODUCTION

A one-dimensional array is called a vector and a two-dimensional or n-dimensional array is called a matrix. Matrices provide a means of storing large quantities of information in such a way that each element can be identified and manipulated, if necessary.

A large systems of linear equations can be expressed in matrix form which can be analysed and solved by computer. It is necessary for the computer engineers to learn the matrix analysis in order to apply it in many areas. Data is frequently arranged in *arrays, i.e.*, sets whose elements are indexed by one or more subscripts.

BASIC DEFINITIONS

Definition: Matrix. *A matrix is a rectangular array of elements of the form*

$$A = \begin{bmatrix} A_{11} & A_{12} & A_{13} & \cdots & A_{1n} \\ A_{21} & A_{22} & A_{23} & \cdots & A_{2n} \\ A_{31} & A_{32} & A_{33} & \cdots & A_{3n} \\ . & . & . & . & . \\ A_{m1} & A_{m2} & A_{m3} & \cdots & A_{mn} \end{bmatrix}$$

A convenient way of describing a matrix in general is to designate each entry via its position in the array. That is, the entry A_{32} is the entry in the third row and fourth column of the matrix A. since it is rather cumbersome to write out the large rectangular array above each time we wish to discuss the generalized form of a matrix, it is common practice to replace the above by $A = [A_{ij}]$. We will assume that each entry Aij $(1 \le i \le m,\ 1 \le j \le n)$ is a real number. However, entries can come from any set, for example, the set of complex numbers.

Definitions: Order. *The matrix A above has m rows and n columns. It therefore, is called an m × n (read "m by n") matrix, and it said to be of order m × n.*

We will use $M_{m \times n}$ (**R**) to stand for the set of all m × n matrices whose entries are real numbers.

Example 1: $A = \begin{bmatrix} 2 & 3 \\ 0 & -5 \end{bmatrix}$,

$$B = \begin{bmatrix} 0 \\ 1/2 \\ 15 \end{bmatrix}$$

and $$D = \begin{bmatrix} 1 & 2 & 5 \\ 6 & -2 & 3 \\ 4 & 2 & 8 \end{bmatrix}$$

are 2 × 2, 3 × 1, and 3 × 3 matrices respectively.

Since we now understand what a matrix looks like, we are in a position to investigate the operations of matrix algebra for which users have found the most applications.

Example 2: *First we ask ourselves: Is the matrix*

$A = \begin{bmatrix} 1 & 2 \\ 3 & 4 \end{bmatrix}$ *equal to the matrix*

$B = \begin{bmatrix} 1 & 2 \\ 3 & 5 \end{bmatrix}$*? Next, is the matrix*

$A = \begin{bmatrix} 1 & 2 & 3 \\ 4 & 5 & 6 \end{bmatrix}$ *equal to the matrix*

$B = \begin{bmatrix} 1 & 2 \\ 4 & 5 \end{bmatrix}$*? Why not? We formalize in the following definition.*

Definition: Equality. *The matrix A is said to be equal to the matrix B (written A = B) if and only if:*

(1) *A and B have the same order, and*

(2) Corresponding entries are equal: that is, $A_{ij} = B_{ij}$ for all i and j.

MATRIX

A matrix is an arrangement of numbers in rows and columns. A matrix A having m rows and n columns is typically written as

$$A = \begin{bmatrix} a_{11} & a_{12} & \cdots & a_{1n} \\ a_{21} & a_{22} & \cdots & a_{2n} \\ \cdots & \cdots & \cdots & \cdots \\ a_{m1} & a_{m2} & \cdots & a_{mn} \end{bmatrix}_{m \times n}$$

The horizontal lines are called rows and the vertical lines columns.

The numbers $a_{11}, a_{12}, \ldots, a_{mn}$ belonging to the matrix are called its *elements.*

A matrix having m rows and n columns is said to be of order m × n (read as 'm by n'). The order may be written on right of the matrix, as shown above.

Notations : Matrices are denoted by capital letters such as A, B, C, ..., X, Y, Z and their elements by small letters a, b, c,..., a_{11}, a_{12}, etc.

There are different notations of enclosing the elements constituting a matrix in common use, viz. [ ], ( ) and || ||, but we shall use the first one throughout the chapter.

The suffixes of the element a_{ij} depict that the element lies in ith row and jth column. Note that we always write row number first and column number afterwards. Also, note that, for the sake of brevity, the matrix given above may also be written as $A = [a_{ij}]_{m \times n}$.

Example 1: *Marks obtained by two students, say, Piyush and Nitish, in Commerce, Mathematics and Statistics are as follows :*

	Commerce	***Mathematics***	***Statistics***
Piyush	*65*	*78*	*80*
Nitish	*55*	*82*	*75*

These marks may be represented by the following rectangular array enclosed by a pair of square brackets [ ]:

$$\begin{bmatrix} 65 & 78 & 80 \\ 55 & 82 & 75 \end{bmatrix}$$

This rectangular array consists of two rows and three columns. The first row indicates the marks obtained by Piyush in Commerce, Mathematics and Statistics respectively and the second by Nitish in the three respective subjects.

The first column refers to the marks obtained by Piyush and Nitish in Commerce, the second column in Mathematics and the third in Statistics.

Such a rectangular array is matrix representation. Since in this matrix we have two rows and three columns, the order of this matrix is 2 × 3.

Sub-Matrix

A matrix which is obtained from a given matrix by deleting any number of rows or columns is called a *sub-matrix* of the given matrix.

For example, the matrix $\begin{bmatrix} 2 & 3 \\ 9 & 3 \end{bmatrix}$ is a sub-matrix of $\begin{bmatrix} 1 & 2 & 3 \\ 4 & 5 & 6 \\ 7 & 9 & 3 \end{bmatrix}$.

Addition of Matrices

Two matrices A and B are conformable for addition, if they are comparable, *i.e.*, B has the same number of rows and the same number of columns as A. Their sum, denoted by A + B, is defined to be the matrix obtained by adding the corresponding elements of A and B.

For example, if $A = \begin{bmatrix} 1 & 2 & 5 \\ 3 & 2 & 2 \end{bmatrix}$

and $$B = \begin{bmatrix} 2 & 3 & 0 \\ 3 & 3 & 7 \end{bmatrix},$$ we have

$$A + B = \begin{bmatrix} 2+1 & 3+2 & 0+5 \\ 3+3 & 3+1 & 7+2 \end{bmatrix}$$

$$= \begin{bmatrix} 3 & 5 & 5 \\ 6 & 4 & 9 \end{bmatrix}.$$

In general, if $A = [a_{ij}]_{m \times n}$ and $B = [b_{ij}]_{m \times n}$, we get $A + B = [a_{ij} + b_{ij}]_{m \times n}$, which is a matrix obtained by adding the elements in the corresponding positions. Thus, from

$$A = \begin{bmatrix} a_{11} & a_{12} & \dots & a_{1n} \\ a_{21} & a_{22} & \dots & a_{2n} \\ \dots & \dots & \dots & \dots \\ a_{m1} & a_{m2} & \dots & a_{mn} \end{bmatrix} \text{ and}$$

$$B = \begin{bmatrix} b_{11} & b_{12} & \dots & b_{1n} \\ b_{21} & b_{22} & \dots & b_{2n} \\ \dots & \dots & \dots & \dots \\ b_{m1} & b_{m2} & \dots & b_{mn} \end{bmatrix},$$

We get

$$A + B = \begin{bmatrix} a_{11}+b_{11} & a_{12}+b_{12} & \dots & a_{1n}+b_{1n} \\ a_{21}+b_{21} & a_{22}+b_{22} & \dots & a_{2n}+b_{2n} \\ \dots & \dots \quad \dots & \dots & \dots \quad \dots \quad \dots \\ a_{m1}+b_{m1} & a_{m2}+b_{m2} & \dots & a_{mn}+b_{mn} \end{bmatrix}.$$

ADDITION AND SCALAR MULTIPLICATION

Example 1: *Concerning addition, it seems natural that if*

$$A = \begin{bmatrix} 1 & 0 \\ 2 & -1 \end{bmatrix}$$

and $$B = \begin{bmatrix} 3 & 4 \\ -5 & 2 \end{bmatrix},$$

then

$$A + B = \begin{bmatrix} 1+3 & 0+4 \\ 2+(-5) & (-1)+2 \end{bmatrix}$$

$$= \begin{bmatrix} 4 & 4 \\ -3 & 1 \end{bmatrix}.$$ *If however,*

$$A = \begin{bmatrix} 1 & 2 & 3 \\ 0 & 1 & 2 \end{bmatrix}$$

and $$B = \begin{bmatrix} 3 & 0 \\ 2 & 8 \end{bmatrix},$$ *can we find A + B?*

Example 2: *If* $c = 3$ *and if* $A = \begin{bmatrix} 1 & -2 \\ 3 & 5 \end{bmatrix}$ *and we wish to find cA, it seems natural to multiply each entry of A by 3,*

$$\text{so that } 3A = 3\begin{bmatrix} 1 & -2 \\ 3 & 5 \end{bmatrix}$$

$$= 3\begin{bmatrix} 3 & -6 \\ 9 & 15 \end{bmatrix}.$$

OPERATIONS ON MATRICES

Multiplication of a Matrix by a Scalar

Let $A = [a_{ij}]$ be an $m \times n$ matrix and let k be any real number (called scalar). Then the product of k and A denoted by kA is defined to be the $m \times n$ matrix whose (i, j)th element is k a_{ij}, *i.e.*,

$$kA = \begin{bmatrix} ka_{11} & ka_{12} & \dots & ka_{1n} \\ ka_{21} & ka_{22} & \dots & ka_{2n} \\ \dots & \dots & \dots & \dots \\ ka_{m1} & ka_{m2} & \dots & ka_{mn} \end{bmatrix}$$

Thus, if $A = \begin{bmatrix} 2 & 3 \\ 4 & 5 \end{bmatrix}, 3A = \begin{bmatrix} 6 & 9 \\ 12 & 15 \end{bmatrix}.$

Thus, we notice that, so get the scalar product, each element of the given matrix is multiplied by the given scalar.

Remarks:

(i) The product of a matrix with a scalar is commutative, *i.e.*, kA = Ak.

(ii) If k = – 1, (– 1) A = [– a_{ij}]. Generally (– 1) A is denoted by – A and is called the negative of matrix A. Thus, – [a_{ij}] = [– a_{ij}].

The following properties of scalar multiplication can be easily verified:

(i) If A and B are comparable matrices and k is any scalar, we have k(A + B) = kA + kB.

(ii) If k and *l* are any two scalars and A is any marix, we have (k + *l*) A = kA + *l*A.

(iii) If k and *l* are any scalars, we have k(*l*A) = (k*l*) A.

MULTIPLICATION OF MATRICES

A definition which is more awkward to motivate (and we will not attempt to do so here) is the product of two matrices. The reader will see in further illustrations and concepts that if we define the product of matrices the following way, we will obtain a very useful algebraic system which is quite similar to elementary algebra.

Example 1: *Let A = a 3 × 2 matrix* $\begin{bmatrix} 1 & 0 \\ 3 & 2 \\ -5 & 1 \end{bmatrix}$

and B = a2 × 1 matrix $\begin{bmatrix} 6 \\ 1 \end{bmatrix}$.

Then $AB = \begin{bmatrix} 1 & 0 \\ 3 & 2 \\ -5 & 1 \end{bmatrix} \begin{bmatrix} 6 \\ 1 \end{bmatrix}$

$$= a\ 3 \times 1\ matrix \begin{bmatrix} (1)(6)+(0)(1) \\ (3)(6)+(2)(1) \\ (-5)(6)+(1)(1) \end{bmatrix} = \begin{bmatrix} 6 \\ 20 \\ -29 \end{bmatrix}.$$

Remarks:

(1) The product AB is defined only if A is $m \times \underline{n}$ matrix and B is an $\underline{n} \times p$ matrix; that is, the two "inner" numbers must be the same. Furthermore, the order of the product matrix AB is the "outer" numbers, in this case $m \times p$.

(2) It is wise to first obtain the order of the product matrix. For example, if A is a 3×2 matrix and B is a 2×2 matrix, then AB is a 3×2 matrix of the form

$$AB = \begin{bmatrix} C_{11} & C_{12} \\ C_{21} & C_{22} \\ C_{31} & C_{32} \end{bmatrix}$$

Then to obtain, for example, C_{31}, we multiply corresponding entries in the third row of A times the first column of B and add the results.

Example 2:

Let $\quad A = \begin{bmatrix} 1 & 0 \\ 0 & 3 \end{bmatrix}$ *and* $B = \begin{bmatrix} 3 & 0 \\ 2 & 1 \end{bmatrix}$

Then $\quad AB = \begin{bmatrix} (1)(3)+(0)(2) & (1)(0)+(0)(1) \\ (0)(3)+(3)(2)+ & (0)(0)+(3)(1) \end{bmatrix}$

$$= \begin{bmatrix} 3 & 0 \\ 6 & 3 \end{bmatrix}$$

Note: $\quad BA = \begin{bmatrix} 3 & 0 \\ 2 & 3 \end{bmatrix} \neq AB.$

Remarks:

(1) An $n \times n$ matrix is called a *square matrix.*

(2) If A is a square matrix, AA is defined and is denoted by A^2, and $AAA = A^3$.

Similarly, $AAA \ldots A = A^n$,

where A is multiplied by itself n times

(3) The $m \times n$ matrices each of whose entries is 0 is denoted by $0_{m \times n}$ or simply 0, when no confusion arises.

SPECIAL TYPES OF MATRICES

We have already investigated one special type of matrix, namely the zero matrix, and found that it behaves in matrix algebra in an analogous fashion to the real number 0; that is, as the additive identity. We will now investigate the properties of a few other special matrices.

Definition: Diagonal Matrix. *A square matrix D is called a diagonal matrix if* $D_{ij} = 0$ *whenever* $i \neq j$;

Example 1:

$$A = \begin{bmatrix} 1 & 0 & 0 \\ 0 & 2 & 0 \\ 0 & 0 & 5 \end{bmatrix},$$

$$B = \begin{bmatrix} 3 & 0 & 0 \\ 0 & 0 & 0 \\ 0 & 0 & -5 \end{bmatrix},$$

and $I = \begin{bmatrix} 1 & 0 & 0 \\ 0 & 1 & 0 \\ 0 & 0 & 1 \end{bmatrix}$ *are all diagonal matrices.*

In Example 5.4.1, the 3 × 3 diagonal matrix I whose diagonal entries are all 1's has the singular property that for any other 3 × 3 matrix A we have AI = IA = A. For example.

Example 2:

If $A = \begin{bmatrix} 1 & 2 & 5 \\ 6 & 7 & -2 \\ 3 & -3 & 0 \end{bmatrix}$, *then*

$$AI = \begin{bmatrix} 1 & 2 & 5 \\ 6 & 7 & -2 \\ 3 & -3 & 0 \end{bmatrix} \text{ and}$$

$$IA = \begin{bmatrix} 1 & 2 & 5 \\ 6 & 7 & -2 \\ 3 & -3 & 0 \end{bmatrix}$$

In other words, the matrix I behaves in matrix algebra like the real number I; that is, as a multiplicative identity. In matrix algebra the matrix I is called simply the *identity matrix*. Convince yourself that if A is any $n \times n$ matrix $AI = IA = A$.

LAWS OF MATRIX ALGEBRA

The following is a summary of the basic laws of matrix operations. Assume that the indicated operations are defined; that is, that the orders of the matrices A, B and C are such that the operations make sense.

(1) $A + B = B + A$.

(2) $A + (B + C) = (A + B) + C$.

(3) $c(A + B) = cA + cB$, where $c \in \mathbf{R}$.

(4) $(c_1 + c_2)A = c_1A + c_2A$ where $c_1, c_2 \in \mathbf{R}$.

(5) $c_1(c_2A) = (c_1c_2)A$, where $c_1, c_2 \in \mathbf{R}$.

(6) $0A = \mathbf{0}$, where $\mathbf{0}$ is the zero matrix.

(7) $0A = \mathbf{0}$, where 0 is on the left is the number 0.

(8) $A + \mathbf{0} = A$.

(9) $A + (-1)A = 0$.

(10) $A(B + C) = AB + AC$.

(11) $(B + C)A = BA + CA$

(12) $A(BC) = (AB)C$.

Example: *If we wished to write out each of the above laws carefully, we would specify the orders of the matrices. For example, Law 10 should read:*

Remarks:

(1) We notice the absence of the "law" AB = BA. Why?

(2) Is it really necessary to have *both* a right (No. 11) and a left (No. 10) distributive law? Why?

(3) What does Law 8 define? What does Law 9 define?

Some Special Types of Matrices

(i) **Row Matrix :** If a matrix has only one row, it is called a *row matrix or row vector.* Thus, any $1 \times n$ matrix is called a row matrix, for example,

$$A = [a_1\ a_2\ a_3\ \dots\ a_n]$$

is a row matrix of [illegible] $\times$ n.

(ii) **Column Matrix :** A matrix consisting of only one column is called a *column matrix or column vector.* In other words, any m × 1 matrix is called a column matrix, for example

$$A = \begin{bmatrix} a_1 \\ a_2 \\ \vdots \\ a_m \end{bmatrix}$$

is a column matrix of order m × 1.

(iii) **Zero or Null Matrix :** If every element of an m × n matrix is zero, the matrix is called a *zero matrix or null matrix* of order m × n, and is denoted by $0_{m \times n}$ or 0_{mn} or 0 simply. For example,

$$\begin{bmatrix} 0 & 0 & 0 & 0 \\ 0 & 0 & 0 & 0 \end{bmatrix}$$

is a zero matrix of order 2 × 4.

(iv) **Square Matrix :** Any matrix in which the number of rows is equal to the number of columns is called a *Square matrix.* Thus any n × n matrix is a square matrix of order n. Generally, we denote the order of a square matrix by a single number n, rather than n × n.

Remark: The elements a_{ij} for which i = j in $A = [a_{ij}]_{n \times n}$ are called the *diagonal elements* and the line along which the elements a_{11}, a_{22}, ..., a_{nn} lie is called the *leading diagonal* or *principal diagonal* or *diagonal* simply. In a square matrix the pair of elements a_{ij} and a_{ji} are said to be *conjugate elements.*

(v) **Diagonal Matrix :** A square matrix in which all elements except those in the leading diagonal are zero, is called a *diagonal matrix.* Thus, a diagonal matrix of order n will be :

$$A = \begin{bmatrix} a_{11} & 0 & 0 & \dots & 0 \\ 0 & a_{22} & 0 & \dots & 0 \\ \dots & \dots & \dots & \dots & \dots \\ 0 & 0 & 0 & \dots & a_{nn} \end{bmatrix}$$

Sometimes a diagonal matrix of order n with diagonal elements a_{11}, a_{22},..., a_{nn} is denoted by

$A = \text{diag}(a_{11}\ a_{22}\ \dots\ a_{nn})$.

(vi) **Scalar Matrix :** A diagonal matrix whose diagonal elements are all equal is called a *scalar matrix.* For example,

$$\begin{bmatrix} 5 & 0 & 0 \\ 0 & 5 & 0 \\ 0 & 0 & 5 \end{bmatrix}$$

is a scalar matrix.

(vii) **Identity or Unit Matrix :** A scalar matrix in which each of its diagonal elements is unity is called an *identity or unit matrix.*

Thus, a square matrix $A = [a_{ij}]_{n \times n}$ is called an identity matrix, if

$$a_{ij} = \begin{cases} 1, \text{ when } i = j, \\ 0, \text{ when } i \neq j. \end{cases}$$

An identity matrix of order n is denoted by I_n. Thus, $I_2 = \begin{bmatrix} 1 & 0 \\ 0 & 1 \end{bmatrix}$ is a unit matrix or order 2.

(viii) **Single Element Matrix :** A matrix having only one element is called a *single element matrix.* Thus, any matrix [a] is a single element matrix. For example, [3] is a single element matrix.

(ix) **Triangular Matrix :** If every element above or below the leading diagonal is zero, the matrix is called a *triangular matrix.* If the zero elements lie below the leading diagonal, the matrix is called *upper triangular matrix;* if the zero elements lie below the leading diagonal, the matrix is called *lower triangular matrix.* The matrices A_1 and A_2 given below are the examples of upper and lower triangular matrices respectively :

$$A_1 = \begin{bmatrix} a_{11} & a_{12} & a_{13} & \dots & a_{1n} \\ 0 & a_{22} & a_{23} & \dots & a_{2n} \\ 0 & 0 & a_{33} & \dots & a_{3n} \\ \dots & \dots & \dots & \dots & \dots \\ 0 & 0 & 0 & \dots & a_{nn} \end{bmatrix} \text{(upper triangular matrix)}$$

$$A_2 = \begin{bmatrix} a_{11} & 0 & 0 & \dots & 0 \\ a_{21} & a_{22} & 0 & \dots & 0 \\ a_{31} & a_{32} & a_{33} & \dots & 0 \\ \dots & \dots & \dots & \dots & \dots \\ a_{n1} & a_{n2} & a_{n3} & \dots & a_{nn} \end{bmatrix} \text{(lower triangular matrix)}$$

EQUALITY OF MATRICS

Two matrices are called comparable, if each of them consists of as many rows and columns as the other.

Two matrices $A = [a_{ij}]$ and $B = [b_{ij}]$ are said to be equal, if (i) they have the same order and (ii) have equal corresponding elements throughout ($a_{ij} = b_{ij}$ every i and j).

The equality of matrices A and B is denoted by writing A = B.

Thus, the matrics $\begin{bmatrix} 1 & 7 \\ 3 & 5 \end{bmatrix}$ and $\begin{bmatrix} 1 & 2 & 3 \\ 4 & 5 & 9 \end{bmatrix}$ are not comparable while

$\begin{bmatrix} 1 & 7 & 8 \\ 3 & 5 & 4 \end{bmatrix}$ and $\begin{bmatrix} 1 & 2 & 6 \\ 3 & 2 & 9 \end{bmatrix}$ are comparable but not equal.

The matrices $\begin{bmatrix} 1 & 5 & 9 \\ 3 & 4 & 12 \end{bmatrix}$ and $\begin{bmatrix} 1 & 5 & 3\times 3 \\ 3 & 2\times 2 & 3\times 4 \end{bmatrix}$ are equal.

Properties of Matrix Addition

Suppose A, B, C are three matrices of the same order $m \times n$. Then the matrix addition has following properties :

1. ***Associativity***

   $A + (B + C) = (A + B) + C.$

   i.e., the addition of matrices is *associative.*

2. ***Commutativity***

   $A + B = [a_{ij}] + [b_{ij}] = [a_{ij} + b_{ij}]$

   $= [b_{ij} + a_{ij}] = [b_{ij}] + [a_{ij}]$

   $= B + A$

   i.e., matrix addition is *commutative.*

3. ***Distributive law***

   $m(A + B) = mA + mB$ (m being an arbitrary scalar), because

   $m(A + B) = m[a_{ij} + b_{ij}]$

   $= m[a_{ij}] + m[b_{ij}] = mA + mB.$

4. ***Existence of additive identity***

   Let A be any $m \times n$ matrix, and 0 the $m \times n$ null matrix. Now, we have

   $A + 0 = 0 + A = A$

   i.e., the null matrix is the identity for the matrix addition.

5. ***Existence of additive inverse***

   –A is the additive inverse of A, because

   $(-A) + A = [-a_{ij}] + [a_{ij}]$

$= [- a_{ij} + a_{ij}] = 0 = A + (- A)$

Thus, for any matrix A, there exists a unique additive inverse – A.

6. ***Cancellation law***

$A + B = A + C \Rightarrow [a_{ij} + b_{ij}] = [a_{ij} + c_{ij}]$

$\Rightarrow a_{ij} + b_{ij} = a_{ij} + c_{ij}$

$\Rightarrow b_{ij} = c_{ij}$

$\Rightarrow [b_{ij}] = [c_{ij}]$

$\Rightarrow B = C.$

Thus is said to be left cancellation.

Similarly, right cancellation, namely,

$B + A = C + A \Rightarrow B = C$ can be proved.

INVERSE OF MATRIX

If, for a given square matrix A of order $n \times n$, there exists a matrix B such that $AB = BA = I_n$ (where I_n is a unit matrix of order n), the square matrix B is said to be an inverse of A. We write B as A^{-1}, read as 'A inverse'. A matrix having an inverse is called an invertible matrix.

From the definition given above, we see that we can talk of an inverse of a square matrix only. Also, we find that, if B be an inverse of A, A is also an inverse of B.

We already know that

$$A.(\text{adj } A) = |A| \, I$$

or $$A\left(\frac{\text{adj } A}{|A|}\right) = I, \qquad \text{provided } |A| \neq 0.$$

Hence, $$A^{-1} = \frac{\text{adj } A}{|A|}, \qquad \text{if } |A| \neq 0.$$

Thus, we find another form of the inverse or reciprocal of the matrix A, which is quite suggestive of the procedure for finding an inverse.

A^{-1} is said to be the invere of A because it possesses the property $AA^{-1} = A^{-1} A = I$.

Note : We have

$$|A| \, |A^{-1}| = |AA^{-1}| = |I| = 1.$$

Hence, $$|A^{-1}| = |A|^{-1}$$

It is very natural that one may have the following questions in his mind regarding the inverse of a matrix;

(i) Does every square matrix possess an inverse?

(ii) If 'no', how to know whether a given matrix is invertible.

(iii) Can there be more than one inverse of a matrix?

(iv) If 'no', how one can proceed to determine the inverse of an invertible matrix.

The answer of the first question is obvious, if we look into the following example :

Let us consider the matrix

$$A = \begin{bmatrix} 0 & 0 \\ 0 & 0 \end{bmatrix}.$$

If B be any 2 × 2 square matrix, whatsoever, we find that

$$AB = BA = 0.$$

Thus, we notice that there cannot be any matrix B for which AB = BA = I_2. Therefore A is not invertible. Hence, we conclude that a square matrix may have or may not have an inverse. Regarding second and third querries, the following theorem will show that a matrix cannot have more than one inverse and the necessary and sufficient conditions for the existence of the inverse of a matrix is laid down in the next theorem. So far as the fourth question is concerned, a method has already been suggested earlier after the definition of the inverse of a matrix. No doubt, because of the importance of the concept of the inverse of a matrix, there exist many methods for finding out the inverse of a matrix. We shall consider one more method in a subsequent section.

Theorem 1:

The inverse of a matrix is unique.

Proof:

If possible, let B and C be two inverses of a square matrix A. Since B is an inverse of A, we have

$$AB = BA = I \quad ...(i)$$

Again, since C is an inverse of A, we have

$$AC = CA = I \quad ...(ii)$$

From (i), we have

$$C(AB) = CI = C \quad ...(iii)$$

Also, from (ii), we have

$(CA)\,B = IB = B$ ...(iv)

We know that $C(AB) = (CA)\,B$.

Therefore, from (iii) and (iv) it follows that

$B = C$

i.e., the inverse is unique.

Theorem 2:

A square matrix A has an inverse, if and only if $|A| \neq 0$.

Proof:

The condition is necessary.

Let B be the inverse of the matrix A, then

$AB = I.$

Therefore, $|A|\,|B| = |I| = 1.$

Hence, $|A| \neq 0.$

The condition is sufficient. Suppose $|A| \neq 0$. Let us assume that

$$B = \frac{\text{adj } A}{|A|}$$

$$AB = A.\left(\frac{\text{adj } A}{|A|}\right)$$

$$= \frac{1}{|A|}(A.\text{adj } A)$$

$$= \frac{|A|I}{|A|} = I.$$

Similarly, $BA = I$

$\therefore\ AB = BA = I.$

Hence, A has an inverse.

SYSTEM OF LINEAR EQUATIONS

A system of linear equations may have unique solution, infintely many solutions or no solution. The following are the simple examples of these different types of systems :

(i) $3x + 4y = 12$

$3x - 2y = 0$

On solving, we get $x = \frac{4}{3}$ and $y = 2$. Thus, this system has unique solution, *i.e.*, only one value of each unknown.

(ii) $2x + 4y = 6$

$3x + 6y = 6$

Here, $x = 3 - 2y$ satisfies both the equations. Substituting any value of y in $x = 3 - 2y$, we will get the corresponding value of x. Thus, there are infinite pairs of the values of x and y satisfying the system.

(iii) $2x + y = 10$

$4x + 2y = 15$

The system, has no solution, *i.e.*, there is no pair of the values of x and y satisfying the sysem.

The system of linear equations having unique solution or infintely many solutions is called a *consistent* system, and a system having no solution is called an *inconsistent* system.

A system of linear equation can be solved with the help of determinants and/or matrices. The next section gives the method of solving the system with the help of determinants.

MINORS

Consider the determinant of a square matrix A,

$$|A| = \begin{vmatrix} a_{11} & a_{12} & a_{13} \\ a_{21} & a_{22} & a_{23} \\ a_{31} & a_{32} & a_{33} \end{vmatrix}.$$

When we delete any one row and any one column of |A|, we get a 2 × 2 determinant. For example, if we strike off the row and column passing through a_{11}, *i.e.*, the first row and first column, we get the determinant as

$$\begin{vmatrix} a_{22} & a_{23} \\ a_{32} & a_{33} \end{vmatrix}$$

This determinant is called the minor of the element a_{11} in determinant A.

Thus, the minor of an element in the determinant of a square matrix may be defined as a determinant which is left after deleting the row and column in which the element lies. The number of minors in a determinant will be equal to the number of elements therein. The following is the list of all nine minors in |A|.

The minors of a_{11}, a_{12} and a_{13} are

$$\begin{vmatrix} a_{22} & a_{23} \\ a_{32} & a_{33} \end{vmatrix}, \begin{vmatrix} a_{21} & a_{23} \\ a_{31} & a_{33} \end{vmatrix} \text{ and } \begin{vmatrix} a_{21} & a_{22} \\ a_{31} & a_{32} \end{vmatrix} \text{ respectively.}$$

The minors of a_{21}, a_{32} and a_{33} are

$$\begin{vmatrix} a_{12} & a_{13} \\ a_{32} & a_{33} \end{vmatrix}, \begin{vmatrix} a_{11} & a_{13} \\ a_{31} & a_{33} \end{vmatrix} \text{ and } \begin{vmatrix} a_{11} & a_{12} \\ a_{31} & a_{32} \end{vmatrix} \text{ respectively.}$$

The minors of a_{31}, a_{32} and a_{33} are

$$\begin{vmatrix} a_{12} & a_{13} \\ a_{22} & a_{23} \end{vmatrix}, \begin{vmatrix} a_{11} & a_{13} \\ a_{21} & a_{23} \end{vmatrix} \text{ and } \begin{vmatrix} a_{11} & a_{12} \\ a_{21} & a_{22} \end{vmatrix} \text{ respectively.}$$

In general, the determinant obtained by striking off the ith row and jth column of a matrix $A = [a_{ij}]_{n \times n}$ is called the minor of a_{ij} in $|A|$. The minor of element a_{ij} is designated by M_{ij}.

ELEMENTARY ROW OPERATIONS

The following operations performed on a matrix are called elementary row operations :

(i) Interchanging any two rows.

(ii) Replacing a row by a non-zero scalar product of the same row.

(iii) Replacing any row by the sum of that row and a scalar multiple of some other row.

The above operations may respectively be denoted by the symbols :

(i) $R_i^N = R_j$ and $R_j^N = R_i$

(ii) $R_i^N = kR_i$

(iii) $R_i^N = R_i + kR_j$

(where R_i^N is the new ith row, R_i is the old ith row and k is a scalar).

FINDING INVERSE THROUGH AUGMENTED MATRIX

For finding the inverse of matrix A, an augmented matrix is made in the form |A|I|, where I is the identity matrix of A' s order. Then the row operations are performed on [A|I] such that A becomes the identity matrix. The corresponding version of I is A^{-1}. For quick results, the following scheme of row operations may be adopted :

(a) Transform one column completely to the desired form before moving on to the next column.

(b) While transforming any column, first the element 1 should be brought at the desired place using row operation (ii) given above.

(c) The form of the previously transformed column should not be allowed to change by the subsequent operations.

DETERMINANTS

A determinant also is an arrangement of numbers in rows and columns; but is always has a square form, and can be reduced to a single value. Thus, a determinant is distinct from a matrix in the sense that the determinant is always in the square shape and it has a numerical value, whereas the matrix is not always in the square shape and it has a no single value attached to it.

The arrangement of the numbers of determinant is enclosed within two vertical parallel lines. Like a square matrix, an n × n determinant is generally called the determinant of order n. Thus, the following are the examples of the determinants of order 1, 2 and 3 respectively :

$$|a_1|, \begin{vmatrix} a_{11} & a_{12} \\ a_{21} & a_{22} \end{vmatrix}, \begin{vmatrix} a_{11} & a_{12} & a_{13} \\ a_{21} & a_{22} & a_{23} \\ a_{31} & a_{32} & a_{33} \end{vmatrix}$$

With each square matrix, we can associate a determinant which is formed exactly by the same array of elements. For example, the determinant of matrix

$$A = \begin{bmatrix} 2 & 4 \\ 3 & 1 \end{bmatrix} \text{ is given by } |A| = \begin{vmatrix} 2 & 4 \\ 3 & 1 \end{vmatrix}.$$

It may be noted that A is only an array of four numbers in rows and columns with no single value associated with it, where as |A| has a value.

Finding Value of a Determinant

Determinant of Order One

The value of the determinant of order one is the number of which the determinant is formed. Thus,

$$|a_{11}| = a_{11},\ |10| = 10,\ |-16| = -16.$$

It may be noted that the absolute value or modulus is also written in the same way. A modulus is not a determinant. As seen above the determinant of – 16 is – 16, whereas the modulus of – 16 is 16.

Determinant of Order Two

The value of the determinant of order two is found as under :

$$\begin{vmatrix} a_{11} & a_{12} \\ a_{21} & a_{22} \end{vmatrix} = a_{11}\, a_{22} - a_{12}\, a_{21}$$

Thus, the value is equal to the product of the elements on the prime diagonal minus the product of other two elements.

Example: $\begin{vmatrix} 2 & 4 \\ 3 & 1 \end{vmatrix} = 2 \times 1 - 4 \times 3 = -10$

Determinant of Order Three

The value of the determinant of order three is found by expanding the determinant by any row or any column. The technique of expansion may be applied to a determinant of order 2 also but it is specially useful in the case of the determinants of higher order. For example, let us have a determinant

$$\Delta = \begin{vmatrix} a_{11} & a_{12} & a_{13} \\ a_{21} & a_{22} & a_{23} \\ a_{31} & a_{32} & a_{33} \end{vmatrix}$$

If we decide to find the value of Δ by expanding it by 1st row, the expansion will be

$$\Delta = a_{11}\begin{vmatrix} a_{22} & a_{23} \\ a_{32} & a_{33} \end{vmatrix} - a_{12}\begin{vmatrix} a_{21} & a_{23} \\ a_{31} & a_{33} \end{vmatrix} + a_{13}\begin{vmatrix} a_{21} & a_{22} \\ a_{31} & a_{32} \end{vmatrix}.$$

The first term of the expansion is a_{11} multiplied by the determinant obtained by deleting the row and column in which a_{11} lies. The second term is a_{12} multiplied by the determinant which is left after eliminating the row and column in which a_{12} lies. The third term is a_{13} multiplied by the determinant left after deleting the row and column in which a_{13} lies. These terms have been joined by using alternate plus and minus signs. a_{11}, a_{12} and a_{13} are the successive terms of the first row by which the determinant has been expanded. Similarly we can expand it by any other row or any column, taking care of the fact the signs needed for adding the terms will follow the following pattern .

$$\begin{vmatrix} + & - & + \\ - & + & - \\ + & - & + \end{vmatrix}$$

Thus, by expanding the determinant by, say, second column, we have

$$\Delta = -a_{12}\begin{vmatrix} a_{21} & a_{23} \\ a_{31} & a_{33} \end{vmatrix} + a_{22}\begin{vmatrix} a_{11} & a_{13} \\ a_{31} & a_{33} \end{vmatrix} - a_{32}\begin{vmatrix} a_{11} & a_{13} \\ a_{21} & a_{23} \end{vmatrix}$$

The value of the determinant will be the same irrespective of the row or column selected for expansion. The value in the case is

$$\Delta = a_{11}a_{22}a_{33} - a_{31}a_{22}a_{13} + a_{12}a_{23}a_{31} - a_{32}a_{23}a_{11} + a_{13}a_{21}a_{32} - a_{33}a_{21}a_{12}.$$

The values of the determinants of higher order will be found by using the similar expansion. the expansion of a 4 × 4 determinant will first give four determinants of order 3 and then each of these will been expanded into the determinants of order 2 and finally the final value will be obtained.

Example: *Find the value of determinant*

$$\begin{vmatrix} 3 & -5 & 8 \\ 6 & -4 & -3 \\ 4 & 2 & 0 \end{vmatrix}$$ *by expanding it by*

(i) second row and (ii) third column.

Solution:

(i) Expanding by the second row,

$$\begin{vmatrix} 3 & -5 & 8 \\ 6 & -4 & -3 \\ 4 & 2 & 0 \end{vmatrix} = -6\begin{vmatrix} -5 & 8 \\ 2 & 0 \end{vmatrix} + (-4)\begin{vmatrix} 3 & 8 \\ 4 & 0 \end{vmatrix} - (-3)\begin{vmatrix} 3 & -5 \\ 4 & 2 \end{vmatrix}$$

$= -6(-16) - 4(-32) + (26)$
$= 96 + 128 + 78 = 302.$

(ii) Expanding by the third column,

$$\begin{vmatrix} 3 & -5 & 8 \\ 6 & -4 & -3 \\ 4 & 2 & 0 \end{vmatrix} = \begin{vmatrix} 6 & -4 \\ 4 & 2 \end{vmatrix} - (-3)\begin{vmatrix} 3 & -5 \\ 4 & 2 \end{vmatrix} + 0\begin{vmatrix} 3 & -5 \\ 6 & -4 \end{vmatrix}$$

$= 8(28) + 3(26) + 0$

$= 224 + 78 = 302$, same as before.

Properties of Determinants

The following are the important properties of determinans. The students are advised to verify these properties on their own.

(i) If any two rows (or columns) of a determinant are interchanged, the sign of the determinant is changed, the absolute value remaining unaltered. For example,

$$\begin{vmatrix} a_1 & a_2 & a_3 \\ b_1 & b_2 & b_3 \\ c_1 & c_2 & c_3 \end{vmatrix} = -\begin{vmatrix} a_1 & a_3 & a_2 \\ b_1 & b_3 & b_2 \\ c_1 & c_3 & c_2 \end{vmatrix}.$$

In this example the second and third columns have been interchanged.

(ii) If every element in any row (or column) of a determinant is multiplied by the same scalar c, the determinant thus obtained is c times the original determinant. Thus,

$$\begin{vmatrix} a_1 & ca_2 & a_3 \\ b_1 & cb_2 & b_3 \\ c_1 & cc_2 & c_3 \end{vmatrix} = c\begin{vmatrix} a_1 & a_2 & a_3 \\ b_1 & b_2 & b_3 \\ c_1 & c_2 & c_3 \end{vmatrix}.$$

(iii) If in a determinant rows are changed into columns into rows, the value of the determinant remains unchanged. Thus,

$$\begin{vmatrix} a_1 & a_2 & a_3 \\ b_1 & b_2 & b_3 \\ c_1 & c_2 & c_3 \end{vmatrix} = \begin{vmatrix} a_1 & b_1 & c_1 \\ a_2 & b_2 & c_2 \\ a_3 & b_3 & c_3 \end{vmatrix}.$$

(iv) If any two rows (or columns) of a determinant are identical, the value of the determinant is zero. Thus,

$$\begin{vmatrix} a_1 & b_1 & c_1 \\ a_1 & b_1 & c_1 \\ a_2 & b_2 & c_2 \end{vmatrix} = 0, \begin{vmatrix} 3 & 9 & 5 \\ 2 & 6 & 7 \\ 1 & 3 & 6 \end{vmatrix} = 3\begin{vmatrix} 3 & 3 & 5 \\ 2 & 2 & 7 \\ 1 & 1 & 6 \end{vmatrix} = 3 \times 0 = 0.$$

(v) If each element of any row or any column is the sum (or difference) of two quantities, the determinant can be expressed as the sum (or difference) of two determinants of the same order, as given below:

$$\begin{vmatrix} a_1 & a_2+\alpha & a_3 \\ b_1 & b_2+\beta & b_3 \\ c_1 & c_2+\gamma & c_3 \end{vmatrix}$$

$$= \begin{vmatrix} a_1 & a_2 & a_3 \\ b_1 & b_2 & b_3 \\ c_1 & c_2 & c_3 \end{vmatrix} + \begin{vmatrix} a_1 & \alpha & a_3 \\ b_1 & \beta & b_3 \\ c_1 & \gamma & c_3 \end{vmatrix}.$$

(vi) If any row (or column) or a multiple thereof is added to or subtract from any other row (or column), the value of the determinant remains unchanged. Thus,

$$\begin{vmatrix} a_1 & a_2 & a_3 \\ b_1 & b_2 & b_3 \\ c_1 & c_2 & c_3 \end{vmatrix} = \begin{vmatrix} a_1 & a_2 & a_3 + ka_2 \\ b_1 & b_2 & b_3 + kb_2 \\ c_1 & c_2 & c_3 + kc_2 \end{vmatrix}.$$

Boolean Product of Two Matrices

Let $A = [a_{ij}]$ be an $m \times n$ Boolean matrix and $B = [b_{ij}]$ be an $n \times p$ Boolean matrix. Then the Boolean product of A and B is defined by

$$C = [c_{ij}],$$

where C is a Boolean matrix of order $m \times p$, where

$$c_{ij} = (a_{i1} \wedge b_{ij}) \vee (a_{i2} \wedge b_{2j}) \vee \ldots \vee (a_{in} \wedge b_{nj})$$

Note : The Boolean product of two Boolean matrices is the usual definition of matrix product except that the addition is replaced with the operation $\vee$ and multiplication with $\wedge$.

BOOLEAN OR ZERO-ONE MATRIX

Let $A = [a_{ij}]$ be a matrix whose elements are the bits 0 and 1 subject to the boolean operations $\vee$ and $\wedge$, which operate on pairs of bits defined by

$$b_1 \wedge b_2 = \begin{cases} 1, & \text{if } b_1 = b_2 = 1 \\ 0, & \text{otherwise} \end{cases}$$

$$b_1 \vee b_2 = \begin{cases} 1, & \text{if } b_1 = 1 \text{ or } b_2 = 1 \\ 0, & \text{otherwise} \end{cases}$$

Then A is called a *Boolean matrix*. Boolean matrices are generally used to represent descrete structure in relation and graph theory.

TRANSPOSE OF MATRIX

The matrix obtained by interchanging the rows and the columns of a given matrix A is called the transpose of the matrix A and is denoted by A' or A^T. For example, the transpose of

$$A = \begin{bmatrix} 2 & 3 & 4 & -1 \\ 3 & 5 & 7 & 9 \\ 1 & 0 & 2 & 3 \end{bmatrix} \text{ is given by}$$

$$A' = \begin{bmatrix} 2 & 3 & 1 \\ 3 & 5 & 0 \\ 4 & 7 & 2 \\ -1 & 9 & 3 \end{bmatrix}$$

Note : From the definition, it is clear that

(i) The transpose of an $m \times n$ matrix is an $n \times m$ matrix.

(ii) The (i, j) th element of A' is the (j, i) th element of A.

Properties of Transpose

(i) The transpose of the transpose of a matrix is the original matrix. Thus, $(A')' = A$.

(ii) The transpose of the sum of matrices is the sum of their individual transposes. Thus,

$(A + B)' = A' + B'$, A and B being comparable.

(iii) If k is any complex number, we have $(kA)' = kA'$.

(iv) The transpose of the product of matrices is equal to the product of the transpose of the individual matrices, taken in the reverse order. Thus,

$(AB)' = B'A'$ and $(ABC)' = C'B'A'$

These properties may be verified easily by the students.

Symmetric Matrix

A square matrix $A = [a_{ij}]$ is said to be symmetric, if $a_{ij} = a_{ji}$ for all values of i and j. In other words, A is symmetric, if $A' = A$. For example, the matrices

$$\begin{bmatrix} a & h & g \\ h & b & f \\ g & f & c \end{bmatrix}$$

and

$$\begin{bmatrix} 1 & -3 & 5 \\ -3 & 2 & 7 \\ 5 & 7 & 3 \end{bmatrix}$$

are both symmetric.

Skew-Symmetric Matrix

A square matrix $A = [a_{ij}]$ is said to be Skew-symmetric, if $a_{ij} = -a_{ji}$ for all value of i and j. Thus, A is Skew-symmetric, if $A' = -A$, for example, the matrix.

$$\begin{bmatrix} 0 & h & g \\ -h & 0 & f \\ -g & -f & 0 \end{bmatrix}$$ is Skew-symmetric.

Note : (i) For diagonal element,

$a_{ii} = -a_{ii} \Rightarrow a_{ii} = 0.$

Thus, every diagonal element of a skew-symmetric matrix is zero.

(ii) If k is a scalar and A is a skew-symmetric matrix, kA is also skew-symmetric.

Orthogonal Matrix

A square matrix A is said to be an orthogonal matrix, if

$$A'A = AA' = 1,$$

where I is the unit matrix.

CONJUGATE OF A MATRIX

A matrix obtained by replacing each element of a matrix by its complex conjugate is said to be its conjugate matrix. Symbolically, the conjugate of a matrix A is denoted by $\overline{A}$.

Thus, if $A = [a_{ij}]$, we have matrix $\overline{A} = \left[\bar{a}_{ij}\right]$, where $\bar{a}_{ij}$ is the complex conjugate of a_{ij}. For example, if

$$A = \begin{bmatrix} 1+i & 3i \\ 2 & 1-2i \end{bmatrix}, \text{ we have}$$

$$\overline{A} = \begin{bmatrix} 1-i & -3i \\ 2 & 1+2i \end{bmatrix}.$$

Notes :

1. To find complex conjugate, replace i by – i.
2. The elements of a matrix are real numbers, if and only if $\overline{A} = A$.

Conjugate Transpose of a Matrix

The conjugate of the transpose of matrix is said to be the conjugate transpose of the matrix. The term 'tranjugate' is also used for conjugate transpose. We denote the tranjugate of matrix A by A^{θ}. Thus,

$$\left(\overline{A}\right) = A^{\theta}.$$

For example, if

$$A = \begin{bmatrix} 1+i & 3i \\ 2 & 1-2i \end{bmatrix}, \text{ we have}$$

$$A^{\theta} = \begin{bmatrix} 1-i & 2 \\ -3i & 1+2i \end{bmatrix}.$$

Notes :

(i) Evidently, $(\overline{A'}) = (\overline{A})' = A^{\theta}$.

(ii) If we write the tranjugate of $(\overline{A'})$, we get back A, *i.e.*, $(A^{\theta})^{\theta} = A$.

(iii) If all elements of A are real, we have $A^{\theta} = A'$.

(iv) $(kA)^{\theta} = \overline{k}A^{\theta}$, k being a scalar.

HERMITIAN AND SKEW-HERMITIAN MATRICES

Hermitian Matrix : A square matrix is said to be hermitian matrix, if its conjugate tranpose is equal to the matrix itself.

Thus, any square matrix $A = [a_{ij}]$ is hermitian,

if $A^{\theta} = A$., *i.e.*,

If $a_{ij} = \overline{a}_{ji}$ for all i and j.

For example, the matrix

$$A = \begin{bmatrix} a & \alpha+i\beta & \gamma+i\delta \\ \alpha-i\beta & b & x+iy \\ \gamma-i\delta & x-iy & c \end{bmatrix}$$

is hermitian.

Skew-hermitian Matrix : A square marix $A = [a_{ij}]$ is said to be skew-hermitian if $A^{\theta} = -A$, *i.e.*, if $a_{ij} = -\overline{a}_{ji}$ for all i and j. For example, the matrix.

$$A = \begin{bmatrix} i & x-iy & 2 \\ -x+iy & -3i & \alpha+i\beta \\ -2 & -\alpha+i\beta & 0 \end{bmatrix}$$

is a skew hermitian matrix.

Note : For the diagonal elements in a skew-hermitian, we note that

$$a_{ii} = -\overline{a}_{ii} \text{ or } a_{ii} + \overline{a}_{ii} = 0$$

so that a_{ii} is either purely imaginary or zero, *i.e.*, every diagonal element of a skew-hermitian matrix is either zero or a purely imaginary number.

Some Properties

(i) If A and B are two matrices such that these are conformable for addition, we have
$\left(\overline{A+B}\right) = \overline{A} + \overline{B}$.

(ii) If A and B are two matrices conformable for multiplication, we have
$\overline{(AB)} = \overline{A}, \overline{B}$.

(iii) If A and B are any two matrices conformable for addition, we have
$(A + A)^{\theta} = A^{\theta} + B^{\theta}$.

(iv) If A and B are any two matrices conformable for multiplication, we have $(AB)^{\theta} = B^{\theta}A^{\theta}$.

This is known as the reversal law for tranjugate.

(vi) Every square matrix can be uniquely expressed as the sum of a hermitian and a skew-hermitian matrix.

Multiplication of Matrices

The multiplication of one matrix by another is possible, if and only if nmumber of columns of the first matrix is equal to the number of rows of the second. The resulting matrix will have the number of rows equal to those in the first matrix and the number of columns equal to those in the second. Thus, if matrix A is of order m × n and B is of order n × p, the product AB is possible, *i.e.*, the matrices A and B are conformable for multiplication in the order A, B. The order of the resulting matrix AB will be m × p. The (i, k)th element (*i.e.*, the element lying in ith row and kth column) of AB is given by

$$a_{i1}\, b_{1k} + a_{i2}\, b_{2k} + \ldots + a_{in}\, b_{nk} = \sum_{j=1}^{n} a_{ij}\, b_{jk}\,.$$

Thus, to obtain the (i, k)th element of the product AB, we multiply the elements of the ith row of A by the corresponding elements of the kth column of B and add the products thus obtained. The resulting sum is the (i, k)th element of AB.

If AB is denoted by $C = [c_{ij}]$, *i.e.*, $AB = [c_{ij}]$, we have

$$\begin{bmatrix} a_{11} & \cdots & a_{1j} & \cdots & a_{1n} \\ \cdots & \cdots & \cdots & \cdots & \cdots \\ a_{i1} & \cdots & a_{ij} & \cdots & a_{in} \\ \cdots & \cdots & \cdots & \cdots & \cdots \\ a_{m1} & \cdots & a_{mj} & \cdots & a_{mn} \end{bmatrix} \begin{bmatrix} b_{11} & \cdots & b_{ik} & \cdots & b_{ip} \\ \cdots & \cdots & \cdots & \cdots & \cdots \\ b_{ji} & \cdots & b_{jk} & \cdots & b_{jp} \\ \cdots & \cdots & \cdots & \cdots & \cdots \\ b_{n1} & \cdots & b_{nk} & \cdots & b_{np} \end{bmatrix}$$

$$= \begin{bmatrix} c_{11} & \cdots & c_{1k} & \cdots & c_{1p} \\ \cdots & \cdots & \cdots & \cdots & \cdots \\ c_{i1} & \cdots & c_{ik} & \cdots & c_{ip} \\ \cdots & \cdots & \cdots & \cdots & \cdots \\ c_{m1} & \cdots & c_{mk} & \cdots & c_{mp} \end{bmatrix}$$

where $c_{ik} = \sum_{j=1}^{n} a_{ij}\, b_{jk}$.

Putting $i = 1, 2, \ldots, m$

and $k = 1, 2, 3, \ldots, p$,

all the elements of C will be found.

In the product AB, A is said to be pre-multiplier or pre-factor while B is said to be post-multiplier or post-factor. It is to be noted that in multiplying one matrix by another, unlike ordinary number, the placement of matrices as prefactor and postfactor is very important. Thus, AB is not the same as BA.

To find the product of two matrices, the procedure explained in the following example may be adopted for convenience.

Example: *Find the product AB, if*

$$A = \begin{bmatrix} 2 & 0 & 1 \\ 2 & 4 & 3 \end{bmatrix}$$

and

$$B = \begin{bmatrix} 1 & 2 & 5 \\ 3 & 2 & 1 \\ 1 & 0 & 4 \end{bmatrix}.$$

Is it possible to find BA?

Solution: The matrix A is of order 2×3 and B is of order 3×3. Hence, A and B are conformable for multiplication in the order A, B but not in the order B, A. Thus, AB is possible but not BA. The matrix AB will be of the order 2×3. To find AB, we shall proceed as follows :

$$\begin{matrix} 5 & 1 & 4 \\ 2 & 2 & 0 \\ 1 & 3 & 1 \end{matrix}$$

$$\begin{bmatrix} 2 & 0 & 1 \\ 2 & 4 & 3 \end{bmatrix} \begin{bmatrix} 1 & 2 & 5 \\ 3 & 2 & 1 \\ 1 & 0 & 4 \end{bmatrix} = \begin{bmatrix} 3^1 & 4^3 & 14^5 \\ 17^2 & 12^4 & 26^6 \end{bmatrix}$$

Write the matrices A and B in that order as given in the L.H.S. above. Then bring the first column of matrix B over matrix A in the row form 1 3 1 Multiply the elements of this 'row' with the corresponding elements of the 1st row of matrix A and add the products.

Thus, we get $1 \times 2 + 3 \times 0 + 1 \times 1 = 3$. Put the value 3 at the place marked 1 in the resulting matrix. Similarly, multiply the elements of 1, 3, 1 with the corresponding elements of the second row of matrix A and add the products. Thus, we get $1 \times 2 + 3 \times 4 + 1 \times 3 = 17$. Put this value at the place marked 2 in the resulting matrix. The first column of the resulting matrix AB is now complete.

As the next step, bring the second column of matrix B over matrix A in the row form 2 2 0 and do the multiplications and additions similar to those explained above. Thus, we get $2 \times 2 + 2 \times 0 + 0 \times 1$, *i.e.*, 4 which is to be put at the place marked 3, and $2 \times 2 + 2 \times 4 + 0 \times 3$, *i.e.*, 12 which is to be put at the placed marked 4. The second column of the resulting matrix AB is now complete.

As the third step, bring the third column of matrix B over matrix A in the row form 5 1 4 and do the similar operations to write the third column of the resulting matrix AB. Thus, $5 \times 2 + 1 \times 0 + 4 \times 1$, *i.e.*, 14 is to be placed at the location marked 5, and $5 \times 2 + 1 \times 4 + 4 \times 3$, *i.e.*, 26 is to be placed at the location marked 6.

Thus, we get

$$AB = \begin{bmatrix} 3 & 4 & 14 \\ 17 & 12 & 26 \end{bmatrix}.$$

Note : While doing the matrix multiplication, the process of bringing each column of the second matrix over the first is to be done only mentally.

PROPERTIES OF MATRIX MULTIPLICATION

1. **Matrix Multiplication is not Commutative :** To verify the above statement, let us take an example. Consider the matrices

$$A = \begin{bmatrix} 1 & 1 \\ 0 & 0 \end{bmatrix}, B = \begin{bmatrix} 0 & 1 \\ 0 & 0 \end{bmatrix}.$$

It can easily found that

$$AB = \begin{bmatrix} 0 & 1 \\ 0 & 0 \end{bmatrix},$$

while $$BA = \begin{bmatrix} 0 & 0 \\ 0 & 0 \end{bmatrix}$$

so that $AB \neq BA$.

This shows that matrix multiplication is not commutative. Actually speaking, for a given pair of matrices A and B, the products AB and BA may not be even comparable. For example, if A is an $m \times n$ matrix and B is an $n \times m$ matrix, AB would be an $n \times n$ matrix and BA would be an $m \times n$ matrix.

It may also happen that for a pair of matrices A and B the product AB may be defined but the product BA may not be defined. For example, if A is an $m \times n$ matrix and B is an $n \times p$ matrix, AB would be an $m \times p$ matrix, but it is not meaningful to talk of BA unless $m = p$.

Notes:

1. **Multiplication of a Matrix by a Unit Matrix :** If A is a square matrix of order $n \times n$ and I is the unit matrix of the same order, we get

   $AI = A = IA$.

2. **Multiplication of a Matrix by itself :** The product A.A is defined, if the number of columns is equal to the number of rows of A, *i.e.*, if A is a square matrix and in that case $A.A. = A^2$ will also be a square matrix of the same type. Also,

   $A.A.A. = A^2.A = A^3$.

   Similarly, A.A.A. ...n times $= A^n$.

   Note : If I is a unit matrix, we have $I = I^2 = I^3 - ... = I^n$.

3. It is worthwhile to note that the statement 'matrix multiplication is not commutative' does not mean that there are no matrices A and B such that $AB = BA$. It simply means that generally $AB \neq BA$. Thus we wish to convey that there do exist some pairs of matrices A and B for which $AB = BA$.

4. It is also to be noted that in matrices, $AB = 0$ need not always imply that either $A = 0$ or $B = 0$. This will be clear, if we consider the matrices,

   $$A = \begin{bmatrix} 1 & 1 \\ 1 & 1 \end{bmatrix}, B = \begin{bmatrix} 1 & 0 \\ -1 & 0 \end{bmatrix}.$$

   For these matrices, $AB = \begin{bmatrix} 0 & 0 \\ 0 & 0 \end{bmatrix}$, but none of A and B is a zero matrix.

   Note 3 : The familiar cancellation law of multiplication for numbers fails to be true for matrix multiplication.

Below we give the properties which hold good for matrices.

5. **Associative Law :** Let A, B and C be the matrices of suitable size for the products A(BC) and (AB) C to exist. Then, A(BC) = (AB) C.
6. **Distributive Law :** A(B + C) = AB + AC, (left distributive) and (B + C) D = BD + CD (right distributive), provided that the matrices A, B, C and D are of the sizes that they are conformable for the operations involved so that the above relations are meaningful.

SOLVED EXAMPLES

Example 1: *For a square matrix A, prove, that (A + A') is symmetric while (A – A') is skew-symmetric, where A' denotes the transpose of A.*

Solution: We know that a matrix A will be symmetric if A' = A and skew-symmetric if A' = – A.

Now,

$$(A + A')' = A' + (A')' \qquad [\because (A + B)' = A' + B']$$

$$= A' + A$$

$$= A + A' \qquad [\because (A')' = A]$$

Since (A + A')' = (A + A') is a symmetric matrix.

Again,

$$(A + A')' = A' - (A')'$$

$$= A' - A$$

$$= -(A - A')$$

Since (A – A')' = – (A – A'),

(A – A') is a skew-symmetric matrix.

Example 2: *Prove that every square matrix can be expressed uniquely as a sum of a symmetric matrix and a skew-symmetric matrix.*

Solution:

Let A be a square matrix; then we can write

$$A = \frac{1}{2}(A + A') + \frac{1}{2}(A - A')$$

$$= P + Q,$$

where $P = \dfrac{A + A'}{2}$

and $\quad Q = \dfrac{A - A'}{2}$

We shall show that P is symmetric and Q is skew-symmetric *i.e.*,

$P' = P$ and $Q' = -Q$.

Now, $\quad P = \dfrac{A + A'}{2}$

$\therefore \quad P' = \dfrac{1}{2}(A + A')' = \dfrac{1}{2}[A' + (A')']$

$= \dfrac{1}{2}(A' + A) \qquad [\because (A')' = A]$

$= \dfrac{1}{2}(A + A') = P.$

Hence, P is symmetric.

Again, $\quad Q = \dfrac{1}{2}(A - A')$

$\therefore \quad Q' = \dfrac{1}{2}(A - A')' = \dfrac{1}{2}[A' - (A')']$

$= \dfrac{1}{2}[A' - A] = -\dfrac{1}{2}(A - A') = -Q$

$\therefore \quad Q' = -Q.$

Hence, Q is skew-symmetric.

$\therefore$ A = P + Q = a symmetric matrix + a skew-symmetric matrix.

Uniqueness : Let, if possible, A = R + S be another representation of where R is symmetric and S is skew-symmetric.

Then, we have $\quad A' = (R + S)' = R' + S'$

$= R - S \qquad [\because R' = R \text{ and } S' = -S]$

Now $\quad A = R + S$

and $\quad A' = R - S.$

$R = \dfrac{1}{2}(A + A') = P$

and $\quad S = \dfrac{1}{2}(A - A') = Q.$

Hence every square matrix can uniquely be represented as sum of a symmetric matrix and a skew-symmetric matrix.

Example 3(a): *Every square matrix can be uniquely expressed as P + iQ, where P and Q are hermitian.*

Solution: Let A be a square matrix. Then we can write

$$A = \frac{1}{2}\left(A + A^{*}\right) + \frac{i}{2i}\left(A - A^{*}\right)$$

$$= P + iQ$$

where $\quad P = \frac{1}{2}\left(A + A^{*}\right)$ and $Q = \frac{1}{2i}\left(A - A^{*}\right) \quad$ ...(i)

Now, $\quad P^{*} = \left[\frac{1}{2}\left(A + A^{*}\right)\right]^{*} = \frac{1}{2}\left[A^{*} + \left(A^{*}\right)^{*}\right]$

$$= \frac{1}{2}\left(A^{*} + A\right) = \frac{1}{2}\left(A + A^{*}\right) = P$$

and $\quad Q^{*} = \left[\frac{1}{2i}\left(A - A^{*}\right)\right]^{*} = \left(\frac{1}{\overline{2i}}\right)\left[A^{*} - \left(A^{*}\right)^{*}\right]$

$$= -\frac{1}{2i}\left(A^{*} - A\right) = \frac{1}{2i}\left(A - A^{*}\right) = Q$$

Hence $P^{*} = P$ and $Q^{*} = Q$, *i.e.*, P and Q both are hermitian, Hence any square matrix A is expressible as P + iQ where P and Q are hermitian.

Uniqueness : To prove the uniqueness of the representation, let us suppose that another representation of the form

$$A = R + iS \quad \text{...(ii)}$$

is possible, where R and S are both hermitian, *i.e.*, $R^{*} = R$ and $S^{*} = S$.

Then $\quad A^{*} = (R + i\,S)^{*} = R^{*} + (i\,S)^{*}$

$$= R^{*} - i\,S^{*}$$

$$= R - i\,S$$

...(iii)

from (ii) and (iii), we get

$$R = \frac{1}{2}\left(A + A^{*}\right) = P$$

and $S = \frac{1}{2i}\left(A - A^{*}\right) = Q$

Hence the representation is unique.

Example 3(b): *Prove that the matrix* $A = \begin{bmatrix} 1 & 1-i & 2 \\ 1+i & 3 & i \\ 2 & -i & 0 \end{bmatrix}$ *is hermitian.* *k is a complex number, verify if kA is hermitian?*

Solution: We have

$$A' = \begin{bmatrix} 1 & 1+i & 2 \\ 1-i & 3 & -i \\ 2 & i & 0 \end{bmatrix}$$

and
$$A^{*} = \begin{bmatrix} 1 & 1-i & 2 \\ 1+i & 3 & i \\ 2 & -i & 0 \end{bmatrix} = A$$

Since $A^{*} = A$ Hence A is hermitian.

Now for second part, we have

$$(kA)^{*} = (\overline{kA})' = \bar{k}(\bar{A})' = \bar{k}A^{*} \neq kA^{*}$$

because $\bar{k} \neq k$ as k is a complex number. Hence kA is not hermitian.

Example 3(c): *If X, Y are two matrices given by the equations*

$$X + Y = \begin{bmatrix} 1 & -2 \\ 3 & 4 \end{bmatrix}$$

and $$X - Y = \begin{bmatrix} 3 & 2 \\ -1 & 0 \end{bmatrix},$$ *find X, Y.*

Solution: We have

$$X + Y = \begin{bmatrix} 1 & -2 \\ 3 & 4 \end{bmatrix}$$

$$X - Y = \begin{bmatrix} 3 & 2 \\ 1 & 0 \end{bmatrix}$$

By adding equations (i) and (ii),

$$2X = \begin{bmatrix} 1 & -2 \\ 3 & 4 \end{bmatrix} + \begin{bmatrix} 3 & 2 \\ -1 & 0 \end{bmatrix} = \begin{bmatrix} 1+3 & -2+2 \\ 3-1 & 4+0 \end{bmatrix}$$

$\therefore$
$$X = \frac{1}{2}\begin{bmatrix} 4 & 0 \\ 2 & 4 \end{bmatrix} = \begin{bmatrix} 2 & 0 \\ 1 & 2 \end{bmatrix}$$

From equation (i),

$$Y = \begin{bmatrix} 1 & -2 \\ 3 & 4 \end{bmatrix} - X = \begin{bmatrix} 1 & -2 \\ 3 & 4 \end{bmatrix} - \begin{bmatrix} 2 & 0 \\ 1 & 2 \end{bmatrix}$$

$$= \begin{bmatrix} 1-2 & -2-0 \\ 3-1 & 4-2 \end{bmatrix} = \begin{bmatrix} -1 & -2 \\ 2 & 2 \end{bmatrix}.$$

Example 3(d): *Write down the products AB and BA of the two matrices A and B, where*

$$A = [1 \quad 2 \quad 3 \quad 4]$$

and $B = \begin{bmatrix} 1 \\ 2 \\ 3 \\ 4 \end{bmatrix}.$

Solution: Since A is a 1 × 4 matrix and B is a 4 × 1 matrix, AB will be a 1 × 1 matrix

$$AB = [1 \quad 2 \quad 3 \quad 4] \times \begin{bmatrix} 1 \\ 2 \\ 3 \\ 4 \end{bmatrix}$$

$$= [1.1 + 2.2 + 3.3 + 4.4] = [30]$$

BA will be a 4 × 4 matrix.

$$BA = \begin{bmatrix} 1 \\ 2 \\ 3 \\ 4 \end{bmatrix} [1 \quad 2 \quad 3 \quad 4]$$

$$= \begin{bmatrix} 1\times1 & 2\times1 & 3\times1 & 4\times1 \\ 1\times2 & 2\times2 & 3\times2 & 4\times2 \\ 1\times3 & 2\times3 & 3\times3 & 4\times3 \\ 1\times4 & 2\times4 & 3\times4 & 4\times4 \end{bmatrix}$$

$$= \begin{bmatrix} 1 & 2 & 3 & 4 \\ 2 & 4 & 5 & 8 \\ 3 & 6 & 9 & 12 \\ 4 & 8 & 12 & 16 \end{bmatrix}.$$

Example 4: *If* $A = \begin{bmatrix} a & b \\ c & d \end{bmatrix}$

and $I = \begin{bmatrix} 1 & 0 \\ 0 & 1 \end{bmatrix}$, *show that*

$$A^2 - (a + d)\, A = (bc - ad)\, I.$$

Solution:

$$A^2 = A.A = \begin{bmatrix} a & b \\ c & d \end{bmatrix} \times \begin{bmatrix} a & b \\ c & d \end{bmatrix}$$

$$= \begin{bmatrix} a^2 + bc & ab + bd \\ ac + cd & bc + d^2 \end{bmatrix}$$

$$A^2 - (a + d)\ A = \begin{bmatrix} a^2 + bc & ab + bd \\ ac + cd & bd + d^2 \end{bmatrix} - (a + d) \begin{bmatrix} a & b \\ c & d \end{bmatrix}$$

$$= \begin{bmatrix} a^2 + bc & ab + bd \\ ac + cd & bc + d^2 \end{bmatrix} - \begin{bmatrix} a^2 + ad & ab + bd \\ ac + cd & ad + d^2 \end{bmatrix}$$

$$= \begin{bmatrix} bc - ad & 0 \\ 0 & bc - ad \end{bmatrix} = (bc - ad) \begin{bmatrix} 1 & 0 \\ 0 & 1 \end{bmatrix}$$

$$= (bc - ad)\ I.$$

Example 5: $A = \begin{bmatrix} 1 & 2 \\ 3 & 4 \end{bmatrix}, B = \begin{bmatrix} 1 & 0 \\ 2 & -3 \end{bmatrix}$

and $C = \begin{bmatrix} 1 & -1 \\ 0 & 1 \end{bmatrix}$, show that A (B + C) = AB + AC.

Solution: We have

$$B + C = \begin{bmatrix} 1 & 0 \\ 2 & -3 \end{bmatrix} + \begin{bmatrix} 1 & -1 \\ 0 & 1 \end{bmatrix}$$

$$= \begin{bmatrix} 1+1 & 0-1 \\ 2+0 & -3+1 \end{bmatrix} = \begin{bmatrix} 2 & -1 \\ 2 & -1 \end{bmatrix}$$

$$\therefore \quad A\ (B + C) = \begin{bmatrix} 1 & 2 \\ 3 & 4 \end{bmatrix} \times \begin{bmatrix} 2 & -1 \\ 2 & -2 \end{bmatrix}$$

$$= \begin{bmatrix} 2+4 & -1-4 \\ 6+8 & -3-8 \end{bmatrix} = \begin{bmatrix} 6 & -5 \\ 14 & -11 \end{bmatrix}$$

Again,

$$AB = \begin{bmatrix} 1 & 2 \\ 3 & 4 \end{bmatrix} \times \begin{bmatrix} 1 & 0 \\ 2 & -3 \end{bmatrix}$$

$$= \begin{bmatrix} 1+4 & 0-6 \\ 3+8 & 0-12 \end{bmatrix} = \begin{bmatrix} 5 & -6 \\ 11 & -12 \end{bmatrix}$$

and $$AC = \begin{bmatrix} 1 & 2 \\ 3 & 4 \end{bmatrix} \times \begin{bmatrix} 1 & -1 \\ 0 & 1 \end{bmatrix}$$

$$= \begin{bmatrix} 1+0 & -1+2 \\ 3+0 & -3+4 \end{bmatrix} = \begin{bmatrix} 1 & 1 \\ 3 & 1 \end{bmatrix}.$$

$$\therefore \quad AB + BC = \begin{bmatrix} 5 & -6 \\ 11 & -12 \end{bmatrix} + \begin{bmatrix} 1 & 1 \\ 3 & 1 \end{bmatrix}$$

$$= \begin{bmatrix} 6 & -5 \\ 14 & -11 \end{bmatrix}$$

From (i) and (ii), we have

$$A(B + C) = AB + AC.$$

Example 6(a): *If* $A = \begin{bmatrix} 0 & 1 \\ 1 & 0 \end{bmatrix}$ *and* $B = \begin{bmatrix} 0 & -i \\ i & 0 \end{bmatrix}$

where $i^2 = -1$,

verify $(A + B)^2 = A^2 + B^2$.

Solution:

$$A + B = \begin{bmatrix} 0 & 1 \\ 1 & 0 \end{bmatrix} + \begin{bmatrix} 0 & -i \\ i & 0 \end{bmatrix}$$

$$= \begin{bmatrix} 0 & 1-i \\ 1+i & 0 \end{bmatrix}$$

$$\therefore \quad (A+B)^2 = \begin{bmatrix} 0 & 1-i \\ 1+i & 0 \end{bmatrix} \times \begin{bmatrix} 0 & 1-i \\ 1+i & 0 \end{bmatrix}$$

$$= \begin{bmatrix} 0+1-i^2 & 1-i^2+0 \\ 0+0 & 1-i^2+0 \end{bmatrix}$$

$$= \begin{bmatrix} 1-(-1) & 0 \\ 0 & 1-(-1) \end{bmatrix} = \begin{bmatrix} 2 & 0 \\ 0 & 2 \end{bmatrix}$$

Again, $$A^2 = \begin{bmatrix} 0 & 1 \\ 1 & 0 \end{bmatrix} \times \begin{bmatrix} 0 & 1 \\ 1 & 0 \end{bmatrix} = \begin{bmatrix} 0+1 & 0+0 \\ 0+0 & 1+0 \end{bmatrix}$$

and $$B^2 = \begin{bmatrix} 0 & -i \\ i & 0 \end{bmatrix} \times \begin{bmatrix} 0 & -i \\ i & 0 \end{bmatrix} = \begin{bmatrix} 0-i^2 & 0+0 \\ 0+0 & -i^2+0 \end{bmatrix}$$

$$= \begin{bmatrix} -(-1) & 0 \\ 0 & -(-1) \end{bmatrix} = \begin{bmatrix} 1 & 0 \\ 0 & 1 \end{bmatrix}$$

$\therefore$ $$A^2 + B^2 = \begin{bmatrix} 1 & 0 \\ 0 & 1 \end{bmatrix} + \begin{bmatrix} 1 & 0 \\ 0 & 1 \end{bmatrix} = \begin{bmatrix} 2 & 0 \\ 0 & 2 \end{bmatrix} \qquad \text{...(ii)}$$

From (i) and (ii), we have

$(A + B)^2 = A^2 + B^2$.

Example 6(b): *If* $I = \begin{bmatrix} 1 & 0 \\ 0 & 1 \end{bmatrix}$

and $E = \begin{bmatrix} 0 & 1 \\ 0 & 0 \end{bmatrix}$ *prove that*

$(aI + bE)^3 = a^3I + 3a^2\, bE.$

Solution: We have

$$(aI + bE) = a\begin{bmatrix} 1 & 0 \\ 0 & 1 \end{bmatrix} + b\begin{bmatrix} 0 & 1 \\ 0 & 0 \end{bmatrix}$$

$$= \begin{bmatrix} a & 0 \\ 0 & a \end{bmatrix} + \begin{bmatrix} 0 & b \\ 0 & 0 \end{bmatrix} = \begin{bmatrix} a & b \\ 0 & a \end{bmatrix}.$$

Now,

$$(aI + bE)^2 = \begin{bmatrix} a & b \\ 0 & a \end{bmatrix} \times \begin{bmatrix} a & b \\ 0 & a \end{bmatrix}$$

$$= \begin{bmatrix} a^2+0 & ab+ab \\ 0+0 & 0+a^2 \end{bmatrix} = \begin{bmatrix} a^2 & 2ab \\ 0 & a^2 \end{bmatrix}.$$

$$(aI+bE)^3 = \begin{bmatrix} a & b \\ 0 & a \end{bmatrix} \times \begin{bmatrix} a^2 & 2ab \\ 0 & a^2 \end{bmatrix}$$

$$= \begin{bmatrix} a^3+0 & 2a^2b+a^2b \\ 0+0 & 0+a^3 \end{bmatrix}$$

$$= \begin{bmatrix} a^3 & 3a^2b \\ 0 & a^3 \end{bmatrix} \qquad \text{...(i)}$$

Now,

$$a^3I + 3a^2 bE = a^3\begin{bmatrix} 1 & 0 \\ 0 & 1 \end{bmatrix} + 3a^2b\begin{bmatrix} 0 & 1 \\ 0 & 0 \end{bmatrix}$$

$$= \begin{bmatrix} a^3 & 0 \\ 0 & a^3 \end{bmatrix} + \begin{bmatrix} 0 & 3a^2b \\ 0 & 0 \end{bmatrix}$$

$$= \begin{bmatrix} a^3 & 3a^2b \\ 0 & a^3 \end{bmatrix} \qquad \text{...(iii)}$$

From (i) and (ii), we have

$(aI + bE)^3 = a^3I + 3a^2 bE.$

Exampe 6(c): *If a matrix* $A = \begin{bmatrix} 3 & -4 \\ 1 & -1 \end{bmatrix}$, *prove that*

$$A^k = \begin{bmatrix} 1+2k & -4k \\ k & 1-2k \end{bmatrix}.$$

Solution: We shall prove that result by the method of mathematical induction. We can write

$$A = \begin{bmatrix} 3 & -4 \\ 1 & -1 \end{bmatrix} = \begin{bmatrix} 1+2\times1 & -4\times1 \\ 1 & 1-2\times1 \end{bmatrix}$$

$\Rightarrow$ the result is true for $k = 1$.

$$A^2 = A.A = \begin{bmatrix} 3 & -4 \\ 1 & -1 \end{bmatrix}\begin{bmatrix} 3 & -4 \\ 1 & -1 \end{bmatrix}$$

$$= \begin{bmatrix} 9-4 & -12+4 \\ 3-1 & -4+1 \end{bmatrix} = \begin{bmatrix} 5 & -8 \\ 2 & -3 \end{bmatrix}$$

$$= \begin{bmatrix} 1+2\times 2 & -4\times 2 \\ 2 & 1-2\times 2 \end{bmatrix}.$$

This shows that the result is true for k = 2.

Let us assume that the result is true for k = n.

$$\therefore \qquad A^n = \begin{bmatrix} 1+2\times n & -4\times n \\ n & 1-2\times n \end{bmatrix}$$

Consider $\quad A^{n+1} = A^n.A = \begin{bmatrix} 1+2n & -4n \\ n & 1-2n \end{bmatrix} \begin{bmatrix} 3 & -4 \\ 1 & -1 \end{bmatrix}$

$$= \begin{bmatrix} 1+2(n+1) & -4(n+1) \\ n+1 & 1-2(n+1) \end{bmatrix}$$

This shows that result is true for k = n + 1, if it is true for k = n. Hence, the result is true for all positive integers.

Example 6(c): *Show that*

$$\begin{vmatrix} a-b-c & 2a & 2a \\ 2b & b-c-a & 2b \\ 2c & 2c & c-a-b \end{vmatrix} = (a+b+c)^3$$

Solution:

L.H.S. $\begin{vmatrix} a+b+c & c+b+c & a+b+c \\ 2b & b-c-a & 2b \\ 2c & 2c & c-a-b \end{vmatrix}$ $C_1 \to C_1 + C_2 + C_3$

$$= (a+b+c)\begin{vmatrix} 1 & 1 & 1 \\ 2b & b-c-a & 2b \\ 2c & 2c & c-a-b \end{vmatrix}$$

$= (a+b+c)\begin{vmatrix} 1 & 0 & 0 \\ 2b & -b-c-a & 0 \\ 2c & c+a+b & -c-a-b \end{vmatrix}$ $\begin{matrix} C_2 \to C_2 - C_3 \\ C_3 \to C_3 - C_1 \end{matrix}$

$= (a+b+c)^3 \begin{vmatrix} 1 & 0 & 0 \\ 2b & -1 & 0 \\ 2c & 1 & -1 \end{vmatrix}$ taking common (a+b+c) from C_2 and C_3

$= (a + b + c)^3 [1(1 - 0)] = (a + b + c)^3.$

Example 7: *Show that* $\begin{vmatrix} 0 & ab^2 & ac^2 \\ a^2b & 0 & bc^2 \\ a^2c & b^2c & 0 \end{vmatrix} = 2^3b^3c^3.$

Solution: Taking a^2, b^2 and c^2 as common from C_1, C_2 and C_3 we get

$$\text{L.H.S.} = a^2b^2c^2 \begin{vmatrix} 0 & a & a \\ b & 0 & b \\ c & c & 0 \end{vmatrix}$$

$$= a^3b^3c^3 \begin{vmatrix} 0 & 1 & 1 \\ 1 & 0 & 1 \\ 1 & 1 & 0 \end{vmatrix}$$

Taking common a, b and c from R_1, R_2 and R_3

$= a^3b^3c^3 [- 1(0 - 1) + 1 (1 - 0)]$

$= a^3b^3c^3 (1 + 1) = 2a^3b^3c^3.$

Example 8: *Show that* $\begin{vmatrix} 1+a^2-b^2 & 2ab & -2b \\ 2ab & 1-a^2+b^2 & 2a \\ 2b & -2a & 1-a^2-b^2 \end{vmatrix}$

$= (1 + a^2 + b^2)^3.$

Solution:

Consider $C_1 \rightarrow C_1 - bC_3$ and $C_2 + aC_3$, we get

$$\text{L.H.S.} = \begin{vmatrix} 1+a^2+b^2 & 0 & -2b \\ 0 & 1+a^2+b^2 & 2a \\ b(1+a^2+b^2) & -a(1+a^2+b^2) & 1-a^2-b^2 \end{vmatrix}$$

$$= (1 + a^2 + b^2)^2 \begin{vmatrix} 1 & 0 & -2b \\ 0 & 1 & 2a \\ b & -a & 1-a^2-b^2 \end{vmatrix}$$

i.e. taking common $1 + a^2 + b^2$ from C_1 and C_2

$= (1 + a^2 + b^2)^2 [1(1 - a^2 - b^2 + 2a^2) - 2b(0 - b)]$

$= (1 + a^2 + b^2)^2 [(1 + a^2 - b^2 + 2b^2)]$

$= (1 + a^2 + b^2)^3$.

Example 9: *Show that* $\begin{vmatrix} 1+a & b & c \\ a & 1+b & c \\ a & b & 1+c \end{vmatrix} = 1+a+b+c$

Solution: Consider $C_1 \to C_1 + C_2 + C_3$, we get

$$\text{L.H.S.} = \begin{vmatrix} 1+a+b+c & b & c \\ 1+a+b+c & 1+b & c \\ 1+a+b+c & b & 1+c \end{vmatrix}$$

Taking common $1 + a + b + c$ from C_1, we get

$$= (1 + a + b + c)\begin{vmatrix} 1 & b & c \\ 1 & 1+b & c \\ 1 & b & 1+c \end{vmatrix}$$

$$= (1 + a + b + c)\begin{vmatrix} 1 & b & c \\ 0 & 1 & 0 \\ 0 & 0 & 1 \end{vmatrix} \begin{matrix} R_2 \to R_2 - R_1 \\ R_3 \to R_3 - R_1 \end{matrix}$$

$= (1 + a + b + c) . [1(1 - a)]$ (expanding along C_1)

$= 1 + a + b + c$.

Example 10: *Show that* $\begin{vmatrix} -a^2 & ab & ac \\ ab & -b^2 & bc \\ ac & bc & -c^2 \end{vmatrix} = 4a^2b^2c^2$.

Solution: Taking a, b and c common from C_1, C_2 and C_3 we get

$$\text{L.H.S.} = abc\begin{vmatrix} -a & a & a \\ b & -b & b \\ c & c & -c \end{vmatrix}$$

Again taking a, b and c common from R_1, R_2 and R_3 we get

$$= a^2b^2c^2\begin{vmatrix} -1 & 1 & 1 \\ 1 & -1 & 1 \\ 1 & 1 & -1 \end{vmatrix}$$

$$= a^2b^2c^2\begin{vmatrix} -1 & 1 & 1 \\ 0 & 0 & 2 \\ 0 & 2 & 0 \end{vmatrix} \begin{matrix} R_2 \to R_2 + R_1 \\ R_3 \to R_3 + R_1 \end{matrix}$$

$= a^2b^2c^2[-1(0-4)]$ (expanding along C_1)

$= 4a^2b^2c^2$.

Example 11:

Show that $\begin{vmatrix} 1+a & 1 & 1 \\ 1 & 1+b & 1 \\ 1 & 1 & 1+c \end{vmatrix} = abc\left(1+\frac{1}{a}+\frac{1}{b}+\frac{1}{c}\right)$.

Solution: Consider $R_2 \to R_2 - R_1$, $R_3 \to R_3 - R_1$

$$\text{L.H.S.} = \begin{vmatrix} 1+a & 1 & 1 \\ -a & b & 0 \\ -a & 0 & c \end{vmatrix}$$

$= (1 + a)(bc - 0) - 1(-ac - 0) + 1(0 + ab)$

$= bc + abc + ac + ab$

$= ab + bc + bc + abc$

$= abc\left(1+\frac{1}{a}+\frac{1}{b}+\frac{1}{c}\right)$.

Example 12(a): *Show that* $\begin{vmatrix} 1 & b+c & b^2+c^2 \\ 1 & c+a & c^2+a^2 \\ 1 & a+b & a^2+b^2 \end{vmatrix} = (a-b)(b-c)(c-a)$.

Solution: Consider $R_2 \to R_2 - R_1$, $R_3 \to R_3 - R_1$

$$\text{L.H.S.} = \begin{vmatrix} 1 & b+c & b^2+c^2 \\ 0 & a-b & a^2-b^2 \\ 0 & a-c & a^2-c^2 \end{vmatrix}$$

$$= (a-b)(a-c)\begin{vmatrix} 1 & b+c & b^2+c^2 \\ 0 & 1 & a+b \\ 0 & 1 & a+c \end{vmatrix}$$

$= (a - b)(a - c)[1(a + c - a - b)]$

$= (a - b)(a - c)(c - b)$

$= (a - b)(b - c)(c - a)$.

Example 12(b): *If x, y and z are all different and*

$$A = \begin{vmatrix} x & x^2 & 1+x^3 \\ y & y^2 & 1+y^3 \\ z & z^2 & 1+z^3 \end{vmatrix} = 0$$

then show that 1 + xyz = 0.

Solution: Consider $A = \begin{vmatrix} x & x^2 & 1+x^2 \\ y & y^2 & 1+y^3 \\ z & z^2 & 1+z^3 \end{vmatrix}$

$$= \begin{vmatrix} x & x^2 & 1 \\ y & y^2 & 1 \\ z & z^2 & 1 \end{vmatrix} + \begin{vmatrix} x & x^2 & x^3 \\ y & y^2 & y^3 \\ z & z^2 & z^3 \end{vmatrix}$$

$$= \begin{vmatrix} x & x^2 & 1 \\ y & y^2 & 1 \\ z & z^2 & 1 \end{vmatrix} + xyz \begin{vmatrix} 1 & x & x^2 \\ 1 & y & y^2 \\ 1 & z & z^2 \end{vmatrix}$$

Consider $C_1 \leftrightarrow C_3$ and then $C_2 \leftrightarrow C_3$ in the first determinant, we get

$$A = (-1)^2 xyz \begin{vmatrix} 1 & x & x^2 \\ 1 & y & y^2 \\ 1 & z & z^2 \end{vmatrix} + xyz \begin{vmatrix} 1 & x & x^2 \\ 1 & y & y^2 \\ 1 & z & z^2 \end{vmatrix}$$

$$= (1 + xyz) \begin{vmatrix} 1 & x & x^2 \\ 1 & y & y^2 \\ 1 & z & z^2 \end{vmatrix}$$

$= (1 + xyz)(x - y)(y - z)(z - x)$

Now given that A = 0

$\Rightarrow \quad (1 + xyz)(x - y)(y - z)(z - x) = 0$

But $(x - y) \neq 0$, $(y - z) \neq 0$

and $(z - x) \neq 0$

because x, y and z are all different

$\therefore \quad A = 0 \Rightarrow (1 + xyz) = 0.$

Example 12(c): *Solve* $\begin{vmatrix} 3x-8 & 3 & 3 \\ 3 & 3x-8 & 3 \\ 3 & 3 & 3x-8 \end{vmatrix} = 0$.

Solution: Consider $R_1 \to R_1 + R_2 + R_3$ we get

$$\begin{vmatrix} 3x-2 & 3x-2 & 3x-2 \\ 3 & 3x-8 & 3 \\ 3 & 3 & 3x-8 \end{vmatrix} = 0$$

$$\Rightarrow \quad (3x-2)\begin{vmatrix} 1 & 1 & 1 \\ 3 & 3x-8 & 3 \\ 3 & 3 & 3x-8 \end{vmatrix} = 0$$

Consider $C_2 \to C_2 - C_1$ and $C_3 \to C_3 - C_1$ we

$$\Rightarrow \quad (3x-2)\begin{vmatrix} 1 & 0 & 0 \\ 3 & 3x-11 & 0 \\ 3 & 0 & 3x-11 \end{vmatrix} = 0$$

$\Rightarrow \ (3x - 2)\ [1(3x - 11)\ (3x - 11)] = 0$

$\Rightarrow (3x - 2)\ (3x - 11)\ (3x - 11) = 0$

$\Rightarrow \ x = \frac{2}{3}, \frac{11}{3}$ and $\frac{11}{3}$.

Example 13: *Solve* $\begin{vmatrix} 1 & -2 & x+3 \\ 1 & x-2 & 3 \\ x+1 & -2 & 3 \end{vmatrix} = 0$.

Solution: Consider $C_1 \to C_1 + C_2 + C_3$ we get

$$\begin{vmatrix} x+2 & -2 & x+3 \\ x+2 & x-2 & 3 \\ x+2 & -2 & 3 \end{vmatrix} = 0$$

$$\Rightarrow \ (x+2)\begin{vmatrix} 1 & -2 & x+3 \\ 1 & x-2 & 3 \\ 1 & -2 & 3 \end{vmatrix} = 0$$

Consider $R_1 \to R_2 - R_1$

and $R_3 \to R_3 - R_1$ we get

$$\Rightarrow (x+2)\begin{vmatrix} 1 & -2 & x+3 \\ 0 & x & -x \\ 0 & 0 & -x \end{vmatrix} = 0$$

$\Rightarrow (x + 2)\ [1(-x^2 - 0)] = 0$

$\Rightarrow (x + 2)(-x^2) = 0$

$\Rightarrow x = 0, -2$

Example 14: *Show that*

$$\begin{vmatrix} (b+c)^2 & a^2 & a^2 \\ b^2 & (c+a)^2 & b^2 \\ c^2 & c^2 & (a+b)^2 \end{vmatrix} = 2abc(a+b+c)^2$$

Solution: Consider $C_1 \to C_1 - C_3$ and $\to C_2 - C_3$

$$\text{L.H.S.} = \begin{vmatrix} (b+c)^2 - a^2 & 0 & a^2 \\ 0 & (c+a)^2 - b^2 & b^2 \\ c^2 - (a+b)^2 & c^2 - (a+b)^2 & (a+b)^2 \end{vmatrix}$$

$$= \begin{vmatrix} (b+c+a)(b+c-a) & 0 & a^2 \\ 0 & (c+a+b)(c+a-b) & b^2 \\ (c+a+b)(c-a-b) & (c-a-b)(c+a+b) & (a+b)^2 \end{vmatrix}$$

$$= (a+b+c)^2\begin{vmatrix} (b+c-a) & 0 & a^2 \\ 0 & (c+a-b) & b^2 \\ (c-a-b) & (c-a-b) & (a+b)^2 \end{vmatrix}$$

Consider $C_1 \to C_1 + \frac{1}{a}C_3,\ C_2 \to C_2 + \frac{1}{b}C_3$

$$= \begin{vmatrix} (b+c) & a^2/b & a^2 \\ b^2/a & (c+a) & b^2 \\ b+c+b^2/a & c+a+a^2/b & (a+b)^2 \end{vmatrix}$$

Consider $R_3 \to R_3 - (R_1 + R_2)$

$$= (a + b + c)^2 \begin{vmatrix} (b+c) & a^2/b & a^2 \\ b^2/a & (c+a) & b^2 \\ 0 & 0 & 2ab \end{vmatrix}$$

Expanding by R_3, we get

$$= (a + b + c)^2 \left\{ 2ab\left[(b+c)(c+a) - \frac{a^2}{b}.\frac{b^2}{a} \right] \right\}$$

$$= (a + b + c)^2 \{2ab(bc + c^2 + ab + ac - ab)\}$$

$$= (a + b + c)^2.2ab(bc + ac + c^2)$$

$$= 2abc(a + b + c)^3.$$

Example 15: *Solve the following simultaneous equations : $3x + y = 19,\ 3x - y = 23.$*

Solution: Here $\Delta = \begin{vmatrix} 3 & 1 \\ 3 & -1 \end{vmatrix} = -6 \neq 0.$

By Cramer's Rule,

$$x = \frac{\Delta_x}{\Delta} = \frac{\begin{vmatrix} 19 & 1 \\ 23 & -1 \end{vmatrix}}{\begin{vmatrix} 3 & 1 \\ 3 & -1 \end{vmatrix}}$$

$$= \frac{-19-23}{-3-3} = \frac{-42}{-6} = 7$$

and $$y = \frac{\Delta_y}{\Delta} = \frac{\begin{vmatrix} 3 & 19 \\ 3 & 23 \end{vmatrix}}{\begin{vmatrix} 3 & 1 \\ 3 & -1 \end{vmatrix}}$$

$$= \frac{69-57}{-3-3} = \frac{12}{-6} = -2.$$

Example 16(a): *Using determinants, solve the simultaneous equations*

$$x + 2y + 3z = 6$$

$$2x + 4y + z = 7$$

$$3x + 2y + 9z = 14.$$

Solution: By Cramer's rule, we have

$$\frac{x}{\begin{vmatrix} 6 & 2 & 3 \\ 7 & 4 & 1 \\ 14 & 2 & 9 \end{vmatrix}} = \frac{y}{\begin{vmatrix} 1 & 6 & 3 \\ 2 & 7 & 1 \\ 3 & 14 & 9 \end{vmatrix}} = \frac{z}{\begin{vmatrix} 1 & 2 & 6 \\ 2 & 4 & 7 \\ 3 & 2 & 14 \end{vmatrix}} = \frac{1}{\begin{vmatrix} 1 & 2 & 3 \\ 2 & 4 & 1 \\ 3 & 2 & 9 \end{vmatrix}}$$

$$\Rightarrow \quad \frac{x}{-20} = \frac{y}{-20} = \frac{z}{-20} = \frac{1}{-20}$$

$\therefore \quad x = y = z = 1.$

Example 16(b): *Find A^{-1} for* $A = \begin{bmatrix} 1 & 0 & 2 \\ 2 & 1 & 0 \\ 3 & 2 & 1 \end{bmatrix}$.

Solution: $A^{-1} = \dfrac{\text{adj } A}{|A|}$

The adjoint of A, as calculated in example 1 of the preceding section, is as under :

$$\text{adj } A = \begin{bmatrix} 1 & 4 & -2 \\ -2 & -5 & 4 \\ 1 & -2 & 1 \end{bmatrix}.$$

$$|A| = \begin{vmatrix} 1 & 0 & 2 \\ 2 & 1 & 0 \\ 3 & 2 & 1 \end{vmatrix} = 1(1) + 2(1)$$, expanding by the first row

$= 3.$

$$A^{-1} = \frac{1}{3}\begin{bmatrix} 1 & 4 & -2 \\ -2 & -5 & 4 \\ 1 & -2 & 1 \end{bmatrix} = \begin{bmatrix} \frac{1}{3} & \frac{4}{3} & -\frac{2}{3} \\ -\frac{2}{3} & -\frac{5}{3} & \frac{4}{3} \\ \frac{1}{3} & -\frac{2}{3} & \frac{1}{3} \end{bmatrix}$$

Note : The answer can be verified from the fact that

$A^{-1}A = I$, as shown below.

$$A^{-1}A = \begin{bmatrix} \frac{1}{3} & \frac{4}{3} & -\frac{2}{3} \\ -\frac{2}{3} & -\frac{5}{3} & \frac{4}{3} \\ \frac{1}{3} & -\frac{2}{3} & \frac{1}{3} \end{bmatrix} \begin{bmatrix} 1 & 0 & 2 \\ 2 & 1 & 0 \\ 3 & 2 & 1 \end{bmatrix}$$

$$= \begin{bmatrix} \frac{1}{3}+\frac{8}{3}-2 & \frac{4}{3}-\frac{4}{3} & \frac{2}{3}-\frac{2}{3} \\ -\frac{2}{3}-\frac{10}{3}+4 & -\frac{5}{3}+\frac{8}{3} & -\frac{4}{3}+\frac{4}{3} \\ \frac{1}{3}-\frac{4}{3}+1 & -\frac{2}{3}+\frac{2}{3} & \frac{2}{3}+\frac{1}{3} \end{bmatrix} = \begin{bmatrix} 1 & 0 & 0 \\ 0 & 1 & 0 \\ 0 & 0 & 1 \end{bmatrix} = I$$

Example 17: *Find the A^{-1} through augmented matrix for*

$$A = \begin{bmatrix} 1 & 2 & 1 \\ 2 & 3 & 2 \\ 3 & 2 & 2 \end{bmatrix}.$$

Solution: We shall write the augmented matrix [A/I] and perform the elementary row operations so as to convert A into a unit matrix. This is given below :

$$\left[\begin{array}{ccc|ccc} 1 & 2 & 1 & 1 & 0 & 0 \\ 2 & 3 & 2 & 0 & 1 & 0 \\ 3 & 2 & 2 & 0 & 0 & 1 \end{array}\right] \xrightarrow[\substack{R_2^N=R_2-2R_1 \\ R_3^N=R_3-3R_1}]{} \left[\begin{array}{ccc|ccc} 1 & 2 & 1 & 1 & 0 & 0 \\ 0 & -1 & 0 & -2 & 1 & 0 \\ 0 & -4 & -1 & -3 & 0 & 1 \end{array}\right] \text{(Step 1)}$$

$$\xrightarrow[\substack{R_2^N=-R_2 \\ R_3^N=-R_3}]{} \left[\begin{array}{ccc|ccc} 1 & 2 & 1 & 1 & 0 & 0 \\ 0 & 1 & 0 & 2 & -1 & 0 \\ 0 & 4 & 1 & 3 & 0 & -1 \end{array}\right] \text{(Step 2)}$$

$$\xrightarrow[\substack{R_2^N=R_1-2R_2 \\ R_3^N=R_3-4R_2}]{} \left[\begin{array}{ccc|ccc} 1 & 0 & 1 & -1 & 2 & 0 \\ 0 & 1 & 0 & 2 & -1 & 0 \\ 0 & 0 & 1 & -5 & 4 & -1 \end{array}\right] \text{(Step 3)}$$

$$\xrightarrow[R_1^N=R_1-R_3]{} \left[\begin{array}{ccc|ccc} 1 & 0 & 0 & 2 & -2 & 1 \\ 0 & 1 & 0 & 2 & -1 & 0 \\ 0 & 0 & 1 & -5 & 4 & -1 \end{array}\right] \text{(Step 4)}$$

$$\therefore \quad A^{-1} = \begin{bmatrix} 2 & -2 & 1 \\ 2 & -1 & 0 \\ -5 & 4 & -1 \end{bmatrix}.$$

(The reader may verify the answer from the fact that $AA^{-1} = 1$).

Notes:

1. The symbol → stands for 'is equivalent to'. The row operations performed in each step are given below the symbol →.

2. More than one row operation may be performed in one step.
3. The element used for reducing the other element to zero by an elementary row operation is called the *pivot element* or *key element.* Thus, the element at the intersection of the first row and first column in step 1, the element 1 at the intersection of the second row and second column in step 3 and the element 1 at the intersection of the third row and third column in step 4 are the pivot elements in the respective steps.

Example 18: *Calculate the inverse of the matrix*

$$A = \begin{vmatrix} a & b \\ c & d \end{vmatrix}.$$

Solution: Here $|A| = \begin{bmatrix} a & b \\ c & d \end{bmatrix} = ad - bc$.

Now, $|A| = 0$, if $ad - bc = 0$

Let us assume that $ad - bc \neq 0$ so that A^{-1} exists.

But $A^{-1} = \dfrac{\text{adj } A}{|A|}$.

Now, we have

$A_{11} = d$, $A_{12} = -c$,

$A_{21} = -b$ and $A_{22} = a$.

$$\therefore \quad \text{adj } A = \begin{bmatrix} d & -b \\ -c & a \end{bmatrix}.$$

and $A^{-1} = \dfrac{1}{(ad - bc)} \begin{vmatrix} d & -b \\ -c & a \end{vmatrix}$.

Example 19: *Let* $A = \begin{bmatrix} 2 & -3 & 1 \\ 4 & 2 & 3 \end{bmatrix}$

and $B = \begin{bmatrix} 3 & -2 & 4 \\ 1 & 3 & -5 \end{bmatrix}$.

Show that $(A + B)' = A' + B'$.

Solution: $A + B = \begin{bmatrix} 2 & -3 & 1 \\ 4 & 2 & 3 \end{bmatrix} + \begin{bmatrix} 3 & -2 & 4 \\ 1 & 3 & -5 \end{bmatrix}$

$$= \begin{bmatrix} 5 & -5 & 5 \\ 5 & 5 & -2 \end{bmatrix}$$

$$\therefore \quad (A + B)' = \begin{bmatrix} 5 & 5 \\ -5 & 5 \\ 5 & -2 \end{bmatrix}.$$

Again, $$A' = \begin{bmatrix} 2 & 4 \\ -3 & 2 \\ 1 & 3 \end{bmatrix}$$

and $$B' = \begin{bmatrix} 3 & 1 \\ -2 & 3 \\ 4 & -5 \end{bmatrix}$$

$$\therefore \quad A' + B' = \begin{bmatrix} 5 & 5 \\ -5 & 5 \\ 5 & -2 \end{bmatrix}.$$

Hence, $(A + B)' = A' + B'$.

Example 20: *If* $A = \begin{bmatrix} 2 & 4 & -1 \\ -1 & 0 & 2 \end{bmatrix}$

and $B = \begin{bmatrix} 3 & 4 & 5 \\ -1 & 2 & 7 \\ 2 & 1 & 0 \end{bmatrix}$.

Compute $(AB)'$ *and* $B'A'$. *Hence verify that* $(AB)' = B'A'$.

Solution: Here A is the matrix of order 2×3 and B is of order 3×3. Hence,

$$AB = \begin{bmatrix} 2 & 4 & -1 \\ -1 & 0 & 2 \end{bmatrix} \begin{bmatrix} 3 & 4 & 5 \\ -1 & 2 & 7 \\ 2 & 1 & 0 \end{bmatrix}$$

$$= \begin{bmatrix} 0 & 15 & 38 \\ 1 & -2 & -5 \end{bmatrix}.$$

$$\therefore \quad (AB)' = \begin{bmatrix} 0 & 1 \\ 15 & -2 \\ 38 & -5 \end{bmatrix}$$

Now, $$B' = \begin{bmatrix} 3 & -1 & 2 \\ 4 & 2 & 1 \\ 5 & 7 & 0 \end{bmatrix}$$

and $$A' = \begin{bmatrix} 2 & -1 \\ 4 & 0 \\ -1 & 2 \end{bmatrix}.$$

$$\therefore \quad B'A' = \begin{bmatrix} 3 & -1 & 2 \\ 4 & 2 & 1 \\ 5 & 7 & 0 \end{bmatrix} \begin{bmatrix} 2 & -1 \\ 4 & 0 \\ -1 & 2 \end{bmatrix}$$

$$= \begin{bmatrix} 0 & 1 \\ 15 & -2 \\ 38 & -5 \end{bmatrix}.$$

Clearly, $(AB)' = B'A' = \begin{bmatrix} 0 & 1 \\ 15 & -2 \\ 38 & -5 \end{bmatrix}$.

Example 21: *Show that all positive integral powers of a hermitian matrix are hermitian.*

Solution: Let A be an n-square hermitian matrix, then $A^* = A$.

Now $A^p = (A\ A\ A\ \ldots\ p \text{ times})$, where p is a positive integer.

$$\therefore \quad (A^p)^* = (A\ A\ A\ \ldots p \text{ times})^*$$
$$= A^*\ A^*\ A^*\ \ldots p \text{ times}$$
$$= A\ A\ A\ \ldots p \text{ times}$$
$$= A^p$$

Hence A^p is hermitian.

Example 22:

Find the value of $\begin{vmatrix} 3 & 2 & 1 \\ 4 & 1 & -7 \\ 0 & 3 & 4 \end{vmatrix}$.

Solution: $\begin{vmatrix} 3 & 2 & 1 \\ 4 & 1 & -7 \\ 0 & 3 & 4 \end{vmatrix} = 3\begin{vmatrix} 1 & -7 \\ 3 & 4 \end{vmatrix} - 4\begin{vmatrix} 2 & 1 \\ 3 & 4 \end{vmatrix} + 0\begin{vmatrix} 2 & 1 \\ 1 & -7 \end{vmatrix}$

$= 3(4 + 21) - 4(8 - 3) + 0 = 55.$

Example 23: *Prove that* $\begin{vmatrix} 1 & 1 & 1 \\ a & b & c \\ a^2 & b^2 & c^2 \end{vmatrix} = (a - b)\ (b - c)\ (c - a).$

Solution:

$$\begin{vmatrix} 1 & 1 & 1 \\ a & b & c \\ a^2 & b^2 & c^2 \end{vmatrix} = \begin{vmatrix} 0 & 0 & 1 \\ a-b & b-c & c \\ a^2-b^2 & b^2-c^2 & c^2 \end{vmatrix},$$

where $C_1^N = C_1 - C_2,$

$C_2^N = C_2 - C_3$

$$= (a - b)\ (b - c) \begin{vmatrix} 0 & 0 & 1 \\ 1 & 1 & c \\ a+b & b+c & c^2 \end{vmatrix}$$

$$= (a - b)\ (b - c) \begin{vmatrix} 1 & 1 \\ a+b & b+c \end{vmatrix}$$

$= (a - b)\ (b - c)\ (b + c - a - b)$

$= (a - b)\ (b - c)\ (c - a).$

Note : C_i^N stands for new ith column and C_j stands for old jth column. Similar notations may be used to denote the new and old rows, viz. R_i^N and R_j.

Example 24: *Prove that*

$$\begin{vmatrix} -a^2 & ab & ac \\ ba & -b^2 & bc \\ ac & bc & -c^2 \end{vmatrix} = 4a^2b^2c^2$$

Solution: L.H.S. = abc $\begin{vmatrix} -a & b & c \\ a & -b & c \\ a & b & -c \end{vmatrix}$,

on taking out a, b and c common from R_1, R_2 and R_3 respectively.

$$= a^2b^2c^2 \begin{vmatrix} -1 & 1 & 1 \\ 1 & -1 & 1 \\ 1 & 1 & -1 \end{vmatrix},$$

on taking out a, b and c common from C_1,C_2 and C_3 respectively.

$$= a^2b^2c^2 \begin{vmatrix} 0 & 0 & 2 \\ 1 & -1 & 1 \\ 1 & 1 & -1 \end{vmatrix}, \text{ applying } R_1^N = R_1 + R_2$$

$= a^2b^2c^2 \,.\, 2(1 + 1) = 4a^2b^2c^2.$

Example 25: *Show that* $\begin{vmatrix} a & b & c \\ a-b & b-c & c-a \\ b+c & c+a & a+b \end{vmatrix}$

$= a^3 + b^3 + c^3 - 3abc.$

Solution:

$$\begin{vmatrix} a & b & c \\ a-b & b-c & c-a \\ b+c & c+a & a+b \end{vmatrix} = \begin{vmatrix} a+b+c & b & c \\ 0 & b-c & (c-a) \\ 2(a+b+c) & c+a & a+b \end{vmatrix},$$

operating $C_1^N = C_1 + C_2 + C_3$

$$= (a + b + c) \begin{vmatrix} 1 & b & c \\ 0 & c+a & c-a \\ 2 & c+a & a+b \end{vmatrix}, \text{ taking } (a + b + c) \text{ common from } C_1$$

$$= (a + b + c) \begin{vmatrix} 1 & b & c \\ 0 & b-c & c-a \\ 2 & c+a & a+b \end{vmatrix}, \text{ operating } R_3^N = R_3 - 2R_1$$

$$= (a + b + c) \begin{vmatrix} b-c & c-a \\ c+a-2b & a+b-2c \end{vmatrix}$$

$= (a + b + c) \{(b - c)(a + b - 2c) - (c - a)(c + a - 2b)\}$

$= a^3 + b^3 + c^3 - 3abc.$

Example 26: If $A = \begin{bmatrix} 2 & 3 & 5 \\ 3 & -6 & 2 \end{bmatrix}$,

find $-3A$.

Solution: $-3A = \begin{bmatrix} -3\times 2 & -3\times 3 & -3\times 5 \\ -3\times 3 & -3\times -6 & -3\times 2 \end{bmatrix}$

$$= \begin{bmatrix} -6 & -9 & -15 \\ -9 & 18 & -6 \end{bmatrix}.$$

Example 27: *Find a matrix A such that*

$$5A = \begin{bmatrix} 5 & 10 & 12 \\ 3 & 15 & 5 \\ 1 & 3 & 5 \end{bmatrix}.$$

Solution:

$$A = \begin{bmatrix} 5.\frac{1}{5} & 10.\frac{1}{5} & 12.\frac{1}{5} \\ 3.\frac{1}{5} & 15.\frac{1}{5} & 5.\frac{1}{5} \\ 1.\frac{1}{5} & 3.\frac{1}{5} & 5.\frac{1}{5} \end{bmatrix}$$

$$= \begin{bmatrix} 1 & 2 & \frac{12}{5} \\ \frac{3}{5} & 3 & 1\ 1 \\ \frac{1}{5} & \frac{3}{5} & 1 \end{bmatrix}.$$

Example 28: *Read the elements a_{24}, a_{41}, a_{13}, a_{23}, a_{31}, a_{22} and the corresponding 'b' elements in the following matrices :*

$$A = \begin{bmatrix} 7 & -4 & 3 & 2 \\ 2 & 0 & 3 & 5 \\ 1 & 3 & -5 & 9 \\ 3 & -6 & -1 & -4 \end{bmatrix}$$

$$B = \begin{bmatrix} 3 & 0 & 3 & 2 \\ 1 & 1 & 5 & 9 \\ 2 & 4 & 6 & 7 \\ -3 & -5 & 9 & 8 \end{bmatrix}.$$

Solution: (i) In matrix A, a_{24} indicates the element which appears in the second row and fourth column.

$\therefore \quad a_{24} = 5.$

Again, a_{41} indicates the element which appears in the fourth row and first column.

$\therefore \quad a_{41} = 3.$

Similarly, $a_{13} = 3,$

$a_{23} = 3,$

$a_{31} = 1$

and $\quad a_{22} = 0.$

(ii) In the same manner,

$b_{24} = 9,\ b_{41} = -3,$

$b_{13} = 3,$

$b_{23} = 5,\ b_{31} = 2$

and $b_{22} = 1.$

Example 29: *If A is hermitian (skew-hermitian), show that B^*AB is hermitian (skew-hermitian).*

Solution: If A is hermitian then

$$A^* = A$$

Now,
$$(B^* AB)^* = (AB)^* (B^*)^*$$
$$= B^* A^* B \qquad \text{(By reversal law)}$$
$$= B^* AB.$$

Hence $B^* AB$ is also hermitian.

IInd Part : When A is skew-hermitian we have $A = -A$. Then

$$(B^* AB)^* = (AB)^* (B^*)^*$$
$$= B^* A^* B = B^* (-A) B$$
$$= -(B^* AB)$$

Hence $B^* AB$ is also skew–hermitian.

Example 30: *Find $A \vee B$ of Boolean matrices A and B, where*

$$A = \begin{bmatrix} 1 & 1 \\ 0 & 1 \end{bmatrix}, B = \begin{bmatrix} 0 & 1 \\ 0 & 1 \end{bmatrix}.$$

Solution: $A \vee B = \begin{bmatrix} 1 \vee 0 & 1 \vee 1 \\ 0 \vee 0 & 1 \vee 1 \end{bmatrix} = \begin{bmatrix} 1 & 1 \\ 0 & 1 \end{bmatrix}.$

Example 31: *Find the value of the determinants*

$\begin{vmatrix} 3a & 2b \\ 2a & b \end{vmatrix}$ *and* $\begin{vmatrix} 5 & 7 \\ 3 & 8 \end{vmatrix}$.

Solution:

(i) $\begin{vmatrix} 3a & 2b \\ 2a & b \end{vmatrix} = 3ab - 4ab = -ab.$

(ii) $\begin{vmatrix} 5 & 7 \\ 3 & 8 \end{vmatrix} = 5.8 - 7.3 = 40 - 21 = 19.$

Example 32: *If* $A = \begin{bmatrix} 1 & 5 & 6 \\ -6 & 7 & 0 \end{bmatrix}$

and $B = \begin{bmatrix} 1 & -5 & 7 \\ 8 & -7 & 7 \end{bmatrix}$, *find A + B and A – B.*

Solution: Here

$$A + B = \begin{bmatrix} 1 & 5 & 6 \\ -6 & 7 & 0 \end{bmatrix} + \begin{bmatrix} 1 & -5 & 7 \\ 8 & -7 & 7 \end{bmatrix}$$

$$= \begin{bmatrix} 1+1 & 5-5 & 6+7 \\ -6+8 & 7-7 & 0+7 \end{bmatrix}$$

$$= \begin{bmatrix} 2 & 0 & 13 \\ 2 & 0 & 7 \end{bmatrix}$$

and $$A - B = \begin{bmatrix} 1 & 5 & 6 \\ -6 & 7 & 0 \end{bmatrix} - \begin{bmatrix} 1 & -5 & 7 \\ 8 & -7 & 7 \end{bmatrix}$$

$$= \begin{bmatrix} 1-1 & 5-(5) & 6-7 \\ -6-8 & 7-(-7) & 0-7 \end{bmatrix}$$

$$= \begin{bmatrix} 0 & 10 & -1 \\ -14 & 14 & -7 \end{bmatrix}.$$

Example 33: *Find the value of 3A – B + 5C, when*

$$A = \begin{bmatrix} -1 & 2 & -1 \\ 0 & -3 & -1 \\ 1 & 4 & 0 \end{bmatrix},$$

$$B = \begin{bmatrix} 1 & 3 & 5 \\ 2 & 4 & 6 \\ 3 & 5 & 7 \end{bmatrix},$$

$$C = \begin{bmatrix} 1 & 2 & 1 \\ 0 & 3 & 5 \\ 1 & 1 & 0 \end{bmatrix}.$$

Solution: 3A – B + 5C

$$3A - B + 5C = 3\begin{bmatrix} -1 & 2 & -1 \\ 0 & -3 & -1 \\ 1 & 4 & 0 \end{bmatrix} - \begin{bmatrix} 1 & 3 & 5 \\ 2 & 4 & 6 \\ 3 & 5 & 7 \end{bmatrix} + 5\begin{bmatrix} 1 & 2 & 1 \\ 0 & 3 & 5 \\ 1 & 1 & 0 \end{bmatrix}$$

$$= \begin{bmatrix} -3-1+5 & 6-3+10 & -3-5+5 \\ 0-2+0 & -9-4+15 & -3-6+25 \\ 3-3+5 & 12-5+5 & 0-7+0 \end{bmatrix}$$

$$= \begin{bmatrix} 1 & 13 & -3 \\ -2 & 2 & 16 \\ 5 & 12 & -7 \end{bmatrix}.$$

Example 34: *Show that*

$$\begin{vmatrix} y+z & x & y \\ z+x & z & x \\ x+y & y & z \end{vmatrix} = (x + y + z)\ (x - z)^2.$$

Solution:
$$\begin{vmatrix} y+z & x & y \\ z+x & z & x \\ x+y & y & z \end{vmatrix} = \begin{vmatrix} 2(x+y+z) & x+y+z & x+y+z \\ z+x & z & x \\ x+y & y & z \end{vmatrix},$$

operating $R_1^N = R_1 + R_2 + R_3$

$$= (x + y + z)\begin{vmatrix} 2 & 1 & 1 \\ z+x & z & x \\ x+y & y & z \end{vmatrix}, \text{ taking } (x + y + z) \text{ common from } R_1$$

$$= (x + y + z)\begin{vmatrix} 0 & 0 & 1 \\ x-z & z-x & x \\ x-y & y-z & z \end{vmatrix},$$

operating $C_1^N = C_1 - 2C_2$ and $C_2^N = C_2 - C_3$

$$= (x + y + z) \begin{vmatrix} x-z & z-x \\ x-y & y-z \end{vmatrix}$$

$$= (x + y + z)(x - z) \begin{vmatrix} 1 & -1 \\ x-y & y-z \end{vmatrix}$$, taking $(x - z)$ common from R_1

$$= (x + y + z)(x - z)(y - z + x - y)$$

$$= (x + y + z)(x - z)^2.$$

Example 35: *Show that the equations*

$$x + y + z = 6$$

$$x + 2y + 3z = 14$$

$$x + 4y + 9z = 36$$

are consistent and solve them.

Solution: The given system is equivalent to a single matrix equation

$$\begin{bmatrix} 1 & 1 & 1 \\ 1 & 2 & 3 \\ 1 & 4 & 9 \end{bmatrix} \begin{bmatrix} x \\ y \\ z \end{bmatrix} = \begin{bmatrix} 6 \\ 14 \\ 36 \end{bmatrix}$$

By $R_2 \rightarrow R_2 - R_1$, $R_3 \rightarrow R_3 - R_1$

$$\begin{bmatrix} 1 & 1 & 1 \\ 0 & 1 & 2 \\ 0 & 3 & 8 \end{bmatrix} \begin{bmatrix} x \\ y \\ z \end{bmatrix} = \begin{bmatrix} 6 \\ 8 \\ 30 \end{bmatrix}$$

By $R_3 \rightarrow R_3 - 3R_2$

$$\begin{bmatrix} 1 & 1 & 1 \\ 0 & 1 & 2 \\ 0 & 0 & 2 \end{bmatrix} \begin{bmatrix} x \\ y \\ z \end{bmatrix} = \begin{bmatrix} 6 \\ 8 \\ 6 \end{bmatrix}$$

Thus, the system of equivalent system is

$$x + y + z = 6$$

$$y + 2z = 8$$

$$2z = 6$$

$\therefore \quad x = 1, y = 2, z = 3$

Example 36: *Investigate for what values of λ and μ, be the eq[illegible]tions*

$x + y + z = 6$
$x + 2y + 3z = 10$
$x + 2y + \lambda z = \mu$

have (i) no solution (ii) unique solution (iii) an infinity of solutions.

Solution: We have

$$A = \begin{bmatrix} 1 & 1 & 1 \\ 1 & 2 & 3 \\ 1 & 2 & \lambda \end{bmatrix}, C = \begin{bmatrix} 1 & 1 & 1 & : & 6 \\ 1 & 2 & 3 & : & 10 \\ 1 & 2 & \lambda & : & \mu \end{bmatrix}$$

By applying $R_2 \to R_2 - R_1$, $R_3 \to R_3 - R_1$, on augmented matrix C, we get

$$C \sim \begin{bmatrix} 1 & 1 & 1 & : & 6 \\ 0 & 1 & 2 & : & 4 \\ 0 & 1 & \lambda - 1 & : & \mu - 6 \end{bmatrix}$$

By applying $R_3 \to R_3 - R_2$,

$$C \sim \begin{bmatrix} 1 & 1 & 8 & : & 6 \\ 0 & 1 & 2 & : & 4 \\ 0 & 0 & \lambda - 3 & : & \mu - 10 \end{bmatrix}$$

Now, we have

(i) For no solution, we have rank(A) ≠ rank(C). Hence if $\lambda = 3$ and $\mu \neq 10$, then rank(A) = 2 and rank(B) = 3 which satisfies the above condition. Thus, for no solution the values of λ and μ are given by $\lambda = 3$, $\mu \neq 10$.

(ii) For unique solution, we have $|A| \neq 0$; hence rank(A) = rank(B) = 3 = number of variables, which is possible only if $\lambda \neq 3$, whatever may be the value of μ. Thus there is a unique solution when $\lambda \neq 3$ for all values of μ.

(iii) For an infinity of solutions, we have rank(A) = rank(B) < 3. Now we have if $\lambda = 3$ and $\mu = 10$, then rank(A) = rank(B) = 2 < number of variables. Thus, for values $\lambda = 3$ and $\mu = 10$ the equations are consistent and there is an infinity of solutions.

Example 37: *Show that the following system of equations is inconsistent.*

$x_1 - 2x_2 + x_3 - x_4 + 1 = 0$

$$3x_1 - 2x_3 + x_4 + 4 = 0$$
$$5x_1 - 4x_2 + x_4 + 3 = 0$$

Solution: We have

$$A = \begin{bmatrix} 1 & -2 & 1 & -1 \\ 3 & 0 & -2 & 3 \\ 5 & -4 & 0 & 1 \end{bmatrix}$$

and augmented matrix

$$C = \begin{bmatrix} 1 & -2 & 1 & -1 & : & -1 \\ 3 & 0 & -2 & 3 & : & -4 \\ 5 & -4 & 0 & 1 & : & -3 \end{bmatrix}$$

Applying $R_2 \to R_2 - 3R_1$, $R_3 \to R_3 - 5R_1$,

$$C \sim \begin{bmatrix} 1 & -2 & 1 & -1 & : & -1 \\ 0 & 6 & -5 & 6 & : & -1 \\ 0 & 6 & -5 & 6 & : & 2 \end{bmatrix}$$

By $R_3 \to R_3 - R_2$

$$C \sim \begin{bmatrix} 1 & -2 & 1 & -1 & : & -1 \\ 0 & 6 & -5 & 6 & : & -1 \\ 0 & 0 & 0 & 0 & : & 3 \end{bmatrix}$$

Clearly rand(A) < rank(C), i.e., the condition rank(A) ≠ rank(C) is satisfied, so the equations are inconsistent and have no solution.

Example 38(a): *Solve completely the following system of equations.*

$$2w + 3x - y - z = 0$$
$$4w - 6x - 2y + 2z = 0$$
$$-6w + 12x + 3y - 4z = 0$$

Solution: We have

$$A = \begin{bmatrix} 2 & 3 & -1 & -1 \\ 4 & -6 & -2 & 2 \\ -6 & 12 & 3 & -4 \end{bmatrix}$$

Applying $R_2 \to R_2 - 2R_1$, $R_3 \to R_3 + 3R_1$,

$$A \sim \begin{bmatrix} 2 & 3 & -1 & -1 \\ 0 & -12 & 0 & 4 \\ 0 & 21 & 0 & -7 \end{bmatrix}$$

By $R_2 \to \left(-\frac{1}{4}\right)R_2, R_3 \to \left(\frac{1}{7}\right)R_3,$

$$A \sim \begin{bmatrix} 2 & 3 & -1 & -1 \\ 0 & 3 & 0 & -1 \\ 0 & 3 & 0 & -1 \end{bmatrix}$$

By $R_3 \to R_3 - R_2$

$$A \sim \begin{bmatrix} 2 & 3 & -1 & -1 \\ 0 & 3 & 0 & -1 \\ 0 & 0 & 0 & 0 \end{bmatrix} \qquad ...(i)$$

$\therefore$ rank(A) = 2 < n (n = 4, number of variables) .

Hence the equations are consistent and have an infinite number of solutions. Such solutions can be obtained on giving arbitrary values to two variables. From (i) an equivalent system of equation is

$$2w + 3x - y - z = 0$$

$$3x - z = 0$$

On taking $z = k_1$, $y = k_2$, the above equations give

$x = \frac{1}{3}k_1$, $y \neq k_2$, $z = k_1$, $w = \frac{1}{2}k_2$.

Example 38(b) : *Solve the following system of equations*

$$x_1 - x_2 + x_3 = 0$$

$$x_1 + 2x_2 - x_3 = 0$$

$$2x_1 + x_2 + 3x_3 = 0.$$

Solution: We have

$$A = \begin{bmatrix} 1 & -1 & 1 \\ 1 & 2 & -1 \\ 2 & 1 & 3 \end{bmatrix}$$

By applying $R_2 \to R_2 - R_1$ and $R_3 \to R_3 - 2R_1$

$$A \sim \begin{bmatrix} 1 & -1 & 1 \\ 0 & 3 & -2 \\ 0 & 3 & 1 \end{bmatrix}$$

By $R_3 \to R_3 - R_2$

$$A \sim \begin{bmatrix} 1 & -1 & 1 \\ 0 & 3 & -2 \\ 0 & 0 & 3 \end{bmatrix}$$

By $R_2 \to \left(\frac{1}{3}\right)R_2,\ R_3 \to \left(\frac{1}{3}\right)R_3$,

$$A \sim \begin{bmatrix} 1 & -1 & 1 \\ 0 & 1 & -2/3 \\ 0 & 0 & 1 \end{bmatrix}$$

$\therefore$ rank(A) = 3 = number of unknowns.

Hence, the given equations have only trivial solution

$x_1 = x_2 = x_3 = 0.$

Example 39: *Prove that*

$$\begin{vmatrix} b+c & c+a & a+b \\ q+r & r+p & p+q \\ y+z & z+x & x+y \end{vmatrix} = 2\begin{vmatrix} a & b & c \\ p & q & r \\ x & y & z \end{vmatrix}.$$

Solution: Applying property (v) to 1st column, we have

$$\text{L.H.S.} = \begin{vmatrix} b & c+a & a+b \\ q & r+p & p+q \\ y & z+x & x+y \end{vmatrix} + \begin{vmatrix} c & c+a & a+b \\ r & r+p & p+q \\ z & z+x & x+y \end{vmatrix}$$

Again applying the same property to 2nd column, we get

$$\text{L.H.S.} = \begin{vmatrix} b & c & a+b \\ q & r & p+q \\ y & z & x+y \end{vmatrix} + \begin{vmatrix} b & a & a+b \\ q & p & p+q \\ y & x & x+y \end{vmatrix} + \begin{vmatrix} c & c & a+b \\ r & r & p+q \\ z & z & x+y \end{vmatrix} + \begin{vmatrix} c & a & a+b \\ r & p & p+q \\ z & x & x+y \end{vmatrix}$$

In the third determinant C_1 and C_2 are identical; hence, its value is zero. Applying property (v) to the third columns of the remaining determinants, we get

L.H.S. =

$$\begin{vmatrix} b & c & a \\ q & r & p \\ y & z & x \end{vmatrix} + \begin{vmatrix} b & c & b \\ q & r & q \\ y & z & y \end{vmatrix} + \begin{vmatrix} b & a & a \\ q & p & p \\ y & x & x \end{vmatrix} + \begin{vmatrix} b & a & b \\ q & p & q \\ y & x & y \end{vmatrix} + \begin{vmatrix} c & a & a \\ r & p & p \\ z & x & x \end{vmatrix} + \begin{vmatrix} c & a & b \\ r & p & q \\ z & x & y \end{vmatrix}$$

$$= \begin{vmatrix} b & c & a \\ q & r & p \\ y & z & x \end{vmatrix} + \begin{vmatrix} c & a & b \\ r & p & q \\ z & x & y \end{vmatrix},$$

as the remaining four determinants are zero due to identical columns.

$$\begin{vmatrix} a & b & c \\ p & q & r \\ x & y & z \end{vmatrix} + \begin{vmatrix} a & b & c \\ p & q & r \\ x & y & z \end{vmatrix}$$, by interchaning the columns twice

$$= 2\begin{vmatrix} a & b & c \\ p & q & r \\ x & y & z \end{vmatrix}.$$

Example 40: *Solve the following system of equations :*

$$3x + y - 4z = 0$$

$$2x + 5y + 6z = 13$$

$$-x + 3y + 8z = 10$$

Solution : The matrix form of the above system is

$$\begin{bmatrix} 3 & 1 & -4 \\ 2 & 5 & 6 \\ -1 & 3 & 8 \end{bmatrix} \begin{bmatrix} x \\ y \\ z \end{bmatrix} = \begin{bmatrix} 0 \\ 13 \\ 10 \end{bmatrix}$$

We shall apply row operations to the augmented matrix

$$\left[\begin{array}{ccc|c} 3 & 1 & -4 & 0 \\ 2 & 5 & 6 & 13 \\ -1 & 3 & 8 & 10 \end{array}\right]$$

Now,
$$\left[\begin{array}{ccc|c} 3 & 1 & -4 & 0 \\ 2 & 5 & 6 & 13 \\ -1 & 3 & 2 & 10 \end{array}\right] \xrightarrow{R_1^N = \frac{1}{3}R_1} \left[\begin{array}{ccc|c} 1 & \frac{1}{3} & -\frac{4}{3} & 3 \\ 2 & 5 & 6 & 13 \\ -1 & 3 & 8 & 10 \end{array}\right]$$

$$\xrightarrow[R_3^N = R_3 + R_1]{R_1^N = R_2 - 2R_1} \left[\begin{array}{ccc|c} 1 & \frac{1}{13} & -\frac{4}{3} & 0 \\ 0 & \frac{13}{3} & \frac{26}{3} & 13 \\ 0 & \frac{10}{3} & \frac{20}{3} & 10 \end{array}\right]$$

$$\xrightarrow[\substack{R_2^N=\frac{3}{13}R_2 \\ R_3^N=\frac{3}{10}R_3}]{} \left[\begin{array}{ccc|c} 1 & \frac{1}{3} & -\frac{4}{3} & 0 \\ 0 & 1 & 2 & 3 \\ 0 & 1 & 2 & 3 \end{array}\right]$$

$$\xrightarrow[R_3^N=R_3-R_2]{} \left[\begin{array}{ccc|c} 1 & \frac{1}{3} & -\frac{4}{3} & 0 \\ 0 & 1 & 2 & 3 \\ 0 & 0 & 0 & 0 \end{array}\right]$$

Hence, we get

$$x+\frac{1}{3}y-z=0;\ y+2z=3.$$

Let $z = k$

$\therefore\quad y + 2k = 3 \Rightarrow y = 3 - 2k$

$\therefore\quad x+\frac{1}{3}(3-2k)-\frac{4}{3} \Rightarrow 2k-1$

Hence, the system has the infinite number of solutions of the form $x = 2k - 1$, $y = 3 - 2k$, $z = k$, where k is any number.

$$\left[\begin{array}{ccc} 1 & -3 & 4 \\ 3 & -8 & 11 \\ 2 & -5 & 7 \end{array}\right] \left[\begin{array}{c} 3 \\ 13 \\ 6 \end{array}\right] \xrightarrow[\substack{R_2^N=R_2-3R_1 \\ R_3^N=R_3-2R_1}]{} \left[\begin{array}{ccc} 1 & -3 & 4 \\ 0 & 1 & 1 \\ 0 & 1 & -1 \end{array}\right] \left[\begin{array}{c} 3 \\ 4 \\ -0 \end{array}\right]$$

$$\xrightarrow[R_3^N=R_3-R_2]{} \left[\begin{array}{ccc} 1 & -3 & 4 \\ 0 & 1 & 1 \\ -1 & 0 & 0 \end{array}\right] \left[\begin{array}{c} 3 \\ 4 \\ -4 \end{array}\right]$$

Hence, we get

$x - 3y + 4z = 3$

$y - z = 4$

$oz = -4$

Since $oz = -4$ is absurd, the system has no solution.

5

NUMBER THEORY

INTRODUCTION

These numbers are used to learn counting. Therefore they are also called *counting numbers.* While studying the natural numbers, we observe that there is no natural number x, satisfying the equation $x + n = n \ \forall \ n \in \mathbf{N}$. This necessiated the introduction of the symbol '0' called 'zero' with the property, $0 + n = n \forall \ n \in \mathbf{N}$. This symbol, when adjoined with the set of natural numbers, forms a new set, $n\mathbf{W} = \{0, 1, 2, 3, \ldots\}$, called the set of *whole numbers.* From our very childhood we are all quite familiar with the set **N** of *natural numbers.* Moreover, we have seen that for any two natural numbers m and n, $(m - n)$ is defined only when $m > n$. Thus while $5 - 4$ is defined, $4 - 5$ is not defined in the context of natural numbers.

Thus, the set **W** was extended to form a new set **Z** of *integers* such that :

(i) $\mathbf{W} \in \mathbf{Z}$

(ii) $x - y$ is defined $\forall \ x, y \in \mathbf{Z}$ and

(iii) Addition, multiplication and order relations on **Z** are so defined that they are the respective extensions on **N**.

Actually speaking, we introduce here some sort of negative counting numbers. We have $4 - 3 = 1$, we write $3 - 4 = -1$ (called minus one). Thus we have

$$\mathbf{Z} = \{\ldots, -3, -2, -1, 0, 1, 2, 3, \ldots)$$

The sets $\mathbf{Z}^+ = \{1, 2, 3, \ldots\}$ and $\mathbf{Z}^- = \{-1, -2, -3, \ldots\}$ are known as the sets of *positive integers* and of *negative integers* respectively.

Thus, $\quad \mathbf{Z} = \mathbf{Z}^+ \cup \{0\} \cup \mathbf{Z}^-$

Here, we will study some basic properties of integers as they are now used in the study of problems associated with the transmissions, coding and manipulation of numerical data.

BASIC PROPERTIES

The simple rules concerning addition and multiplication of these integers are given below :

(a) Properties of Addition of Z

(i) Addition of integers is commulative, *i.e.*,

$x + y = y + x \ \forall \ x, y \in \mathbf{Z}$.

(ii) The addition of integers is associative, *i.e.*,

$(x + y) + z = x + (y + z) \ \forall \ x, y, z \in \mathbf{Z}$.

(iii) 0 is additive identity in the set of integers, *i.e.*,

$x + 0 = 0 + x = x \ \forall \ x \in \mathbf{Z}$.

(iv) For each integer x, the integer –x is the additive inverse, *i.e.*,

$x + (-x) = (-x) + x = 0 \ \forall \ x \in \mathbf{Z}$.

(v) Cancellation laws hold for addition in integers, *i.e.*,

$x + z = y + z$

$\Rightarrow \quad x = y \ \forall \ x, y, z \in \mathbf{Z}$. (Right cancellation law)

and $\quad z + x = z + y$

$\Rightarrow \quad x = y \ \forall \ x, y, z \in \mathbf{Z}$. (Left cancellation law)

(b) Properties of Subtraction in Integers

For all $x, y, z \in \mathbf{Z}$;

(i) $(x + z) - (y + z) = x + y$

(ii) $x - (y - z) \neq (x - y) - z$

(iii) $(-x) + (-y) = -(x + y)$

(iv) $(x - y) + (y - z) = x - z$

(c) Properties of Multiplication of Integers

(i) If $x, y \in Z \Rightarrow x y \in \mathbf{Z}$

(ii) $xy = yx \ \forall \ x, y \in \mathbf{Z}$

(iii) $(xy)z = x(yz) \ \forall \ x, y, z \in \mathbf{Z}$

(iv) $x(y + z) = xy + xz \ \forall \ x, y, z \in \mathbf{Z}$

and $(x + y)z = xz + yz \ \forall \ x, y, z \in \mathbf{Z}$

(v) The integer 1 is the multiplicative identity

i.e., $1 \, . \, x = x \, . \, 1 = x \ \forall \ x \in \mathbf{Z}$

(vi) $xz = yz, z \neq 0 \Rightarrow x = y$ (Right concellation law), and $zx = zy, z \neq 0 \Rightarrow x = y$ (Left concellation law).

(vii) For all integers x, y and z

$x(y - z) = xy - xz$

$(-x)\, y = x\,(-y) = -(xy)$

$(-x)\,(-y) = xy.$

ABSOLUTE VALUE OF AN INTEGER

The absolute value or modulus of an integer a denoted by $|a|$ is defined as follows :

$$|a| = \begin{cases} a & \text{if } a \geq 0 \\ -a & \text{if } a < 0 \end{cases}$$

Thus, $|5| = 5$ and $|-5| = -(-5) = 5.$

Properties of Absolute Value

(i) $|a| \geq 0$.

Let a be any integer. Then one of the following three possibilities must held :

(i) $a = 0$ (ii) $a > 0$ (iii) $a < 0$.

Case I. When $a = 0$, then $|a| = |0| = 0$.

Case II. When $a > 0$, then $|a| = a > 0$.

Case III. When $a < 0$, then Let $a = -b$ where $b > 0$.

Then $|a| = |-b| = -(-b) = b > 0.$

$\therefore$ $|a| \geq 0 \ \forall = a > \mathbf{Z}.$

(ii) $|a| = 0 \Leftrightarrow a = 0$.

If $a = 0$, then by definition, $|a| = |0| = 0$. On the other hand, let $\neq 0$ and if possible, let $a \neq 0$.

Then either $a > 0$ or $a < 0$

Now, if $a > 0$ then $|a| = a > 0,$

and if $a < 0$ then $|a| = -a > 0.$

So, $a \neq 0 \Rightarrow |a| > 0$, contradicting the hypothesis that $|a| = 0$.

$\therefore$ $|a| = 0 \Rightarrow a = 0$

Hence, $|a| = 0 \Leftrightarrow a = 0$

(iii) $|a| \geq a$ and $|a| \geq -a$.

For any integer a, we have one of the following three possibilities:

(i) $a = 0$ (ii) $a > 0$ and (iii) $a < 0$.

Case I. When $a = 0$, we have $-a = -0 = 0$.

So, in this case, $|a| = |-a| = a$.

Case II. When $a > 0$, then $-a < 0$

So, in this case, $|a| = a$ and $|-a| = -(-a) = a$.

$\therefore \; |a| = |-a| = a$.

Case III. When $a < 0$, then $-a > 0$

In this case, $|a| = -a$ and $|-a| = -a$

$\therefore \quad |a| = |-a| = -a$.

(iv) $|ab| = |a|\,|b|$

Case I. $a = 0$ and $b = 0$.

In this case, $ab = 0$

$\therefore \quad |a| = 0, |b| = 0$ and $|ab| = 0$.

So, $\quad |ab| = |a|.|b|$

Case II. $a > 0$ and $b > 0 \Rightarrow ab > 0$

So, in this case, we have;

$|a| = a, |b| = b$ and $|b| = ab$.

$\therefore \quad |ab| = ab = |a|.|b|$.

Case III. $a > 0$ and $b < 0 \Rightarrow ab < 0$

So in this case, we have;

$|a| = a, |b| = -b$ and $|ab| = -(ab)$.

$|ab| = -(ab) = a(-b) = |a|.|b|$.

Case IV. $a < 0$ and $b < 0 \Rightarrow ab < 0$

So in this case, we have;

$|a| = -a, |b| = b$ and $|ab| = -(ab)$.

$\therefore \quad |ab| = -(ab) = (-a).b = |a|.|b|$.

Case V. $a < 0$ and $b < 0 \Rightarrow ab < 0$

So in this case, we have;

$|a| = -a, |b| = -b$ and $|ab| = ab$.

$\therefore \quad |ab| = ab = (-a)(-b) = |a|.|b|$.

Hence in all the cases we have

$|ab| = |a|.|b|$.

(v) $|\mathbf{a + b}| \le |\mathbf{a}| + |\mathbf{b}|$.

Case I. $a + b \ge 0 \Rightarrow |a + b| = a + b \le |a| + |b|$ [$\because a \le |a|$ and $b \le |b|$]

Case II. $a + b < 0 \Rightarrow |a + b| = -(a + b) = (-a) + (-b) \le |a| + |b|$

[$\because -a \le |a|$ and $-b \le |b|$]

(vi) $|\mathbf{a - b}| \ge |\mathbf{a}| - |\mathbf{b}|$.

We know that

$$|a| = |a - b + b| \le |a - b| + |b|$$

$\therefore$ $|a| - |b| \le |a - b|$

or $|a - b| \ge |a| - |b|$.

(vii) $|\mathbf{a - b}| + |\mathbf{b - c}| \ge |\mathbf{a - c}|$.

$$|a - c| = |a - b + b - c| \le |a - b| + |b - c|$$

$\therefore$ $|a - b| + |b - c| \ge |a - c|$

(viii) $|\mathbf{a}| + |\mathbf{b}| \ge |\mathbf{a - b}|$.

$$|a - b| = |a + (-b)| \le |a| + |-b| = |a| + |b|$$

$\therefore$ $|a| + |b| \ge |a - b|$

(ix) $\mathbf{a|b}$ **and** $\mathbf{b \ne 0 \Rightarrow |a| \le |b|}$.

Let $a|b$ and $b \ne 0$

$\Rightarrow$ $\exists$ a non-zero integer c s.t. $b = ac$ [$\because b \ne 0 \Rightarrow c \ne 0$]

$\Rightarrow$ $|b| = |a|.|c|$

But $c \ne 0 \Rightarrow |c| \ge 1$

$\Rightarrow$ $|a|\ |c| \ge |a|.1 = |a|$

$\Rightarrow$ $|a| \le |a|.|c| = |ac|$

$\Rightarrow$ $|a| \le |b|$ [$\because ac = b \Rightarrow |ac| = |b|$]

(x) $\mathbf{a|b}$ **and** $\mathbf{b|a \Rightarrow a = \pm b}$.

Since $a|b$ and $b|a$, we have $a \ne 0$ and $b \ne 0$.

Now $a|b$ and $b \ne 0$ $\Rightarrow |a| \le |b|$

and $b|a$ and $b \ne 0$ $\Rightarrow |b| \le |a|$

$\Rightarrow |a| = |b|$

$\Rightarrow a = \pm b$.

RELATIVELY PRIME INTEGERS

Two integer a and b are said to be relatively prime if their greatest common divisor is 1, i.e., if (a, b) = 1.

For example,

(i) 4, –9 are relatively prime integers since (4, –9) = 1.

(ii) 8, 14 are not relatively prime integers since (8, 14) = 2.

Theorem:

If a and b are relatively prime integers, we can find integers m and n such that ma + nb = 1.

Proof:

Since a and b are relatively prime, therefore (a, b) = 1. So by Euclidean algorithm there exists integers m and n such that

$$1 = ma + nb$$

ORDER RELATION IN THE SET OF INTEGERS

For any two integers x and y we define

$$x > y \Leftrightarrow x - y \text{ is positive}$$

$$x < y \Leftrightarrow x - y \text{ is negative}$$

Some Results on Order Relation on Z

(i) $x > y \Leftrightarrow y < x$

(ii) For any integer x

x is positive $\Leftrightarrow x > 0$

x is negative $\Leftrightarrow x < 0$

(iii) $x > y \Rightarrow x + z > y + z \ \forall\ x, y, z \in \mathbf{Z}$

(iv) $x > y$ and $z > 0 \Rightarrow xz > yz \ \forall\ x, y, z \in \mathbf{Z}$

(v) $x > y$ and $y > z \Rightarrow x > z$.

DIVISIBILITY IN INTEGERS

A non-zero integer a is said to be a divisor or a factor of an integer b if there exists an integer c, such that b = ac, and we write a|b'. Also if a is a divisor of b, then b is called an integer multiple of a.

For example,

(i) 2|8 since $8 = 2 \times 4$

(ii) –4|16 since 16 = (–4), (–4)

(iii) $a|0$ for all $a \in \mathbf{Z}$ and $a \neq 0$, since $0 = a.0$.

Proper and Improper Divisors

We have $a.1 = (-a).(-1) = a$ for every $a \in \mathbf{Z}$.

Therefore for every integer a, ± 1 and $\pm a$ are divisors of a. These are called *improper divisors* of a. If a has any divisors other than these, then they are called *proper divisors* of a.

Primes : *A non-zero integer p is called a prime if it is neither 1 nor −1 and if its only divisors are 1, −1, p, −p.*

For example,

(i) The integers 2 and −11 are primes, while

$6 = 2.3$ and $-36 = 3(-12)$ are not primes.

(ii) The first 10 positive primes are

2, 3, 5, 7, 11, 13, 17, 19, 23, 29.

It is obvious that −p is a prime iff p is a prime.

Composite Integer : *If an integer a can be written as $a = bc$, where b and c are integers such that $|b| > 1$ and $|c| > 1$, then a is called a composite integer.*

For Example, $6 = 2.3$ where $|2| > 1$ and $|3| > 1$. Therefore 6 is a composite integer.

Every integer $a \neq 0, \pm 1$ is either a prime or a composite.

Associates : *Two non-zero integers a and b are known as associates if we have both $a|b$ and $b|a$.*

For any integer a, a and −a are associates.

CONGRUENCE OF INTEGERS

Relation of "congruence modulo m" in the set of integers.

Let m be any fixed positive integer, i.e., $m > 0$. Then an integer a is said to be congruent to another integer b modulo m if $m|(a-b)$, i.e., if m is a divisor of $a - b$.

Symbolically, we write

$$a \equiv b \pmod{m}.$$

It will be read as "a is congruent to b modulo m".

Thus, $a \equiv b \pmod{m}$ if $a - b = km$ for some integer k.

For example,

$$89 \equiv 25 \pmod{4} \text{ since } 89 - 25 = 64 \text{ and } 4|64.$$

$$13 \equiv 3 \pmod 5 \text{ since } 13 - 3 = 10 \text{ and } 5|10.$$

$$153 \equiv -7 \pmod 8 \text{ since } 153 - (-7) = 160 \text{ and } 8|160.$$

But $24 \not\equiv 3 \pmod 5$ since $24 - 3 = 21$ and 5 is not a divisor of 21.

Some Properties of Congruences

Theorem 1:

If $a \equiv b(\text{mod } m)$, $c \equiv (\text{mod } m)$ $a + c \equiv b + d(\text{mod } m)$, $a - c \equiv b - d(\text{mod } m)$, $ac \equiv bd(\text{mod } m)$.

Proof:

We have $a \equiv b(\text{mod } m)$

$\Rightarrow$ $m|(a - b)$

and $c \equiv d(\text{mod } m)$

$\Rightarrow$ $m|(c - d)$

Now, $m|(a - b)$ and $m|(c - d)$

$\Rightarrow$ $m|\{(a - b) + (c - d)\}$

$\Rightarrow$ $m|\{(a + c) - (b + d)\}$

$\Rightarrow$ $a + c \equiv b + d(\text{mod } m)$.

Similarly, $m|(a - b)$ and $m|(c - d)$

$\Rightarrow$ $m|\{(a - b) - (c - d)\}$

$\Rightarrow$ $m|\{(a - c) - (b - d)\}$

$\Rightarrow$ $a - c \equiv b - d(\text{mod } m)$.

Finally, $m|(a - b)$ and $m|(c - d)$

$\Rightarrow$ $m|\{(a - b) + b(c - d)\}$

$\Rightarrow$ $m|(ac - bd)$

$\Rightarrow$ $ac \equiv bd(\text{mod } m)$.

Theorem 2:

Let d be the GCD of c and m i.e., $(c, m) = d$ and let $m = m_1 d$. Then prove that $ca \equiv cb(\text{mod } m) \Rightarrow a \equiv b(\text{mod } m_1)$. Also prove the converse, i.e., prove that if $a \equiv b(\text{mod } m)$, then $ca \equiv cb(\text{mod } m)$.

Proof:

We have $(c, m) = d$ and $m = m_1 d$. Let $c = c_1 d$. Since d is the greatest common divisor of c and m, therefore the greatest common divisor of c_1 and m_1 must be 1, *i.e.*, $(c_1, m_1) = 1$.

Note that c_1 and m_1 are the integers obtained on dividing c and m respectively by their GCD d.

Now, $ca \equiv cb \pmod{m}$

$\Rightarrow \quad m|(ca - cb)$

$\Rightarrow \quad m|c(a - b)$

$\Rightarrow \quad m_1d|c_1d(a - b)$ $\quad [\because\ m = m_1d \text{ and } c = c_1d\ ]$

$\Rightarrow \quad m_1|c_1(a - b)$ $\quad [\because\ d \neq 1]$

$\Rightarrow \quad m_1|(a - b)$ $\quad$ [m_1 and c_1 are relatively prime]

$\Rightarrow \quad a \equiv b \pmod{m_1}$.

Converse : We have $a \equiv b \pmod{m_1}$.

$\Rightarrow \quad m_1|(a - b)$

$\Rightarrow \quad m_1|c_1(a - b)$ $\quad [\because\ d \neq 1]$

$\Rightarrow \quad m_1d|c_1d(a - b)$

$\Rightarrow \quad m|c(a - b)$

$\Rightarrow \quad m|(ca - cb)$

$\Rightarrow \quad ca \equiv cb \pmod{m}$.

Theorem 2(a):

If $ca \equiv cb \pmod{m}$ and $(c, m) = 1$, then $a \equiv b \pmod{m}$.

Proof:

It is given that $(c, m) = 1$, *i.e.*, c and m are relatively prime.

We have $\quad ca \equiv cb \pmod{m}$

$\Rightarrow \quad m|(ca - cb)$

$\Rightarrow \quad m|c(a - b)$

Now, $\quad m|(a - b)$ $\quad [\because\ (c, m) = 1]$

$\Rightarrow \quad a \equiv b \pmod{m}$.

Theorem 2(b):

The relation "congruence modulo m" is an equivalence relation in the set of integers.

Proof:

Let **Z** be the set of integers. If m be any fixed positive integer, then we say that $a \equiv b \pmod{m}$ if $m|(a - b)$. We shall prove that this defines an equivalence relation in the set **Z**.

Reflexivity : Let a be any integer. Then $a - a = 0$, and $m|0$. Thus, $a \equiv a \pmod m$ $\forall$ $a \in \mathbf{Z}$. Therefore the realtion is reflexive.

Symmetry : Let $a, b \in I$ be such that $a \equiv b \pmod m$.

Then we have

$$\begin{aligned} m|(a - b) &\Rightarrow m|(-1)(a - b) \\ &\Rightarrow m|(b - a) \\ &\Rightarrow b \equiv a \pmod m \end{aligned}$$

Thus, $a \equiv b \pmod m \Rightarrow b \equiv a \pmod m$. Therefore the relation is symmetric.

Transitivity : Let $a, b, c \in \mathbf{Z}$ be such that $a \equiv b \pmod m$, $b \equiv c \pmod m$. Then we have

$$\begin{aligned} & m|(a - b) \text{ and } m|(b - c) \\ &\Rightarrow m|(a - b) + (b - c) \\ &\Rightarrow m|(a - c) \\ &\Rightarrow a \equiv c \pmod m. \end{aligned}$$

Thus, $a \equiv b \pmod m$ and $b \equiv c \pmod m$

$\Rightarrow a \equiv c \pmod m$. Therefore the relation is transitive.

Hence, this is an equivalence relation.

Theorem 3:

If a and b are two integers, then $a \equiv b \pmod m$ if an only if a and b have the same remainder when divided by m.

Proof:

Suppose a and b have the remainder r_1 and r_2 respectively when divided by m. Then for some integers q_1 and q_2, we have

$$a = q_1 m + r_1,\ 0 \le r_1 < m$$

$$\text{and} \qquad b = q_2 m + r_2,\ 0 \le r_2 < m.$$

Now suppose that $a \equiv b \pmod m$. Then to prove that

$$r_1 = r_2.$$

We have $\quad a - b = m(q_1 - q_2) + (r_1 - r_2)$

$\therefore \quad r_1 - r_2 = (a - b) + m(q_2 - q_1)$.

Now $a \equiv b \pmod m \Rightarrow m|(a - b)$. Also $m|m(q_2 - q_1)$

$\therefore \quad m|\{(a - b) + m(q_2 - q_1)\}$

$\Rightarrow \quad m|(r_1 - r_2)$

$\Rightarrow \quad r_1 - r_2 = 0 \qquad [\because 0 \le (r_1 - r_2) < m]$

$\Rightarrow \quad r_1 - r_2.$

Conversely : Suppose that $r_1 - r_2$. Then to prove that $a \equiv b(\text{mod } m)$.

We have $\quad a - b = m(q_1 - q_2) + r_1 - r_2$

$= m(q_1 - q_2)$, if $r_1 = r_2$.

$\therefore \quad m|a(a - b)$

$\Rightarrow a \equiv b(\text{mod } m)$.

Theorem 3(a):

If a is any integer, then $a \equiv r(\text{mod } m)$ where r is the remainder obtained by dividing a by m.

Proof:

Suppose r is the remainder obtained by dividing a by m. Then for some integer q, we have

$$a = mq + r$$

$$\Rightarrow \quad a - r = mq$$

$$\Rightarrow \quad m|(a - r)$$

$$\Rightarrow \quad a \equiv r(\text{mod } m).$$

Theorem 3(b):

If $a \equiv b(\text{mod } m)$, then $mn + a \equiv b(\text{mod } m)$ for some $n \in \mathbf{Z}$.

Coversely if $mn + a \equiv b(\text{mod } m)$ for some $n \in \mathbf{Z}$, then $a \equiv b(\text{mod } m)$.

Proof:

Suppose $a \equiv b(\text{mod } m)$. Then $m|(a - b)$.

But $\quad m|(mn) \ \forall\ n \in \mathbf{Z}$. Therefore

$m|\{(mn) + (a - b)\} \ \forall\ n \in \mathbf{Z}$

$\Rightarrow \quad m|\{(mn + a) - b)\} \ \forall\ n \in \mathbf{Z}$

$\Rightarrow \quad mn + a \equiv b(\text{mod } m)$ for all $n \in \mathbf{Z}$.

Conversely suppose that $mn + a \equiv b(\text{mod } m)$ for some integer n. Then

$m|\{(mn + a) - b\}$

But $\quad m|\{(mn)$

$\therefore \quad m|\{(mn + a) - b) - mn\} \Rightarrow m|(a - b)$

$\Rightarrow \quad a \equiv b\ (\text{mod } m)$.

Theorem 4:

If $a \equiv b(\text{mod } m)$, then, for all $x \in \mathbf{Z}$, $a + x \equiv b + x(\text{mod } m)$ and $ax \equiv bx(\text{mod } m)$.

Proof:

We have $a \equiv b(\text{mod m})$

$\Rightarrow$ $m|(a - b)$

$\Rightarrow$ $m|\{(a + x) - (b + x)\}\ \forall\ x \in \mathbf{Z}$

$\Rightarrow$ $a + x \equiv b + x(\text{mod m})\ \forall\ x \in \mathbf{Z}$

Similarly, $a \equiv b(\text{mod m})$

$\Rightarrow$ $m|(a - b)$

$\Rightarrow$ $m|x(a - b)$ for all $x \in \mathbf{Z}$

$\Rightarrow$ $m|(xa - xb)$ for all $x \in \mathbf{Z}$

$\Rightarrow$ $xa \equiv xb(\text{mod m})$ for all $x \in \mathbf{Z}$.

Residue Classes or Congruence Classes

*We know that if m is a fixed positive integer, then "congruence modulo m" is an equivalence relation in the set of integers. consequently it will partition **Z** into equivalence classes. These equivalence classes are called residue classes modulo m or congruence classes modulo m.*

We shall denote the set of all residue classes of integer modulo m by $\mathbf{I}_m$. If $a \in \mathbf{Z}$, then the residue class a or $[a] \in \mathbf{I}_m$ is given by

$$[a] = \{x : x \in \mathbf{Z} \text{ and } x \equiv a \ (\text{mod m})\}.$$

Similarly if $b \in Z$, then the residue class $[b] \in \mathbf{I}_m$ is given by

$$[b] = \{y : y \in \mathbf{Z} \text{ and } y \equiv b \ (\text{mod m})\}.$$

i.e. $m|(y - b)$.

We know that two equivalence classes are either disjoint or identical. Therefore if $[a] \in \mathbf{I}_m$ and $[b] \in \mathbf{I}_m$, then either $[a] = [b]$ or $[a] \cap [b] = \phi$.

Also $[a] = [b]$ if and only if $a \equiv b$ (mod m) *i.e.*, if an only if $m|(a - b)$. Thus $[a] = [a + m] = [a + 2m]$ and so on. Similarly $[1] = [1 + m] = [1 + 2m]$ ans so on. Also $[0] = [m] = [2m] = [-m]$ and so on.

The residue classes modulo 4, *i.e.*, the elements of the set $\mathbf{I}_4$ are

$[0] = \{..., -16, -12, -8, -4, 0, 4, 8, 12, 16, ...\}$

$[1] = \{..., -15, -11, -7, -3, 1, 5, 9, 13, 17, ...\}$

$[2] = \{..., -14, -10, -6, -2, 2, 6, 10, 14, 18, ...\}$

$[3] = \{..., -13, -9, -5, -1, 3, 7, 11, 15, 19, ...\}$

Obviously $[0] = [4] = [8]$ and so on.

Similarly $[1] = [5] = [9] = [13]$ and so on.

The basic properties of the residue classes modulo m are :

(i) If a and b are elements of the same residue class [s], then $a \equiv b \pmod{m}$.

(ii) If [s] and [t] are two distinct residue classes with $a \in [s]$ and $b \in [t]$, then $a \equiv b \pmod{m}$.

Theorem 5:

The set I_m of all residue classes of integers modulo m contains exactly m distinct elements.

Proof:

We clain that $\mathbf{I}_m = \{[0], [1], [2], ..., [m-1]\}$.

First we shall show that m residue classes [0], [1], ... [m − 1] are all distinct.

Let $0 \le i < m$, $0 \le j < m$ and $j > i$.

Then $[i] = [j]$

$\Rightarrow \quad i \equiv j \pmod{m} \Rightarrow i - j$ is divisible by m

$\Rightarrow \quad j - i$ is divisible by m.

But according to our assumption j − i is a positive integer less than m. So it can not be divisible by m. Therefore $[i] \neq [j]$ and thus [0], [1], ..., [m − 1] are all distinct.

Now we shall show that if a is any integer, then the residue class [a] is equal to one of the residue classes [0], [1], ..., [m − 1].

By division algorithm, we have

$a = km + r$, were $k, r \in \mathbf{Z}$ and $0 \le r < m$

$\Rightarrow \quad a - r = km$

$\Rightarrow \quad a - r$ is divisible by m

$\Rightarrow \quad a \equiv r \pmod{m}$

$\Rightarrow \quad [a] = [r]$

Since $0 \le r \le m - 1$, therefore the residue class $[a] = [r]$ is one of the residue classes [0], [1], ..., [m − 1].

Hence the set $\mathbf{I}_m$ has m distinct elements.

Note: The residue class [0] is called the *zero residue class.* We have [a] = [0] if and only if m|a. The set of integers mod m will have m – 1 distinct non-zero residue clasess.

UNIQUE FACTORIZATION THEOREM OR THE FUNDAMENTAL THEOREM OF ARITHMETIC

Unit : An associate of integer 1 is called a unit, *i.e.*, units are 1 and –1.

Theorem:

Every integer a(|a| > 1) can be expressed as a unit times a product of positive primes. This representation is unique except for the order of the prime factors, i.e.,

Proof:

$$a = p_1.p_2 \ldots . p_n, \text{ where } p_1, p_2 \ldots, p_n \text{ are primes.}$$

If a is prime, then it can be expressed as unit times the product of positive primes. Now, if a is composite, *i.e.*, neither prime nor a unit, let

$$|a| = |m|.|n|$$

where |m|, |n| are positive integers < |a|.

Assuming that the theorem is true for positive integers less than |a|, then by induction hypothesis, we have

$$|m| = p_1.p_2 \ldots . p_r,$$

$$|n| = q_1.q_2 \ldots . q_s,$$

Where $p_1, p_2 \ldots . p_r, q_1, q_2 \ldots . q_s$, are positive integers.

$$|a| = |m|, |n|$$

$$= p_1.p_2 \ldots . p_r.q_1.q_2 \ldots . q_s.$$

Hence, $a = k\, p_1 p_2 \ldots . p_r.q_1.q_2 \ldots . q_s$

where $k = 1$ or -1.

Hence the theorem is also true for a and therefore true for all integers by induction method.

Uniqueness : Let a second representation of a be

$$a = p'_1, p'_2 \ldots, p'_m, \text{ where } a > 1.$$

Then we have

$$p'_1.p'_2 \ldots . p'_r.q_1.q_2 \ldots \quad [illegible] \quad p'_1, p'_2 \ldots p'_m$$

or $p'_1\, p'_2 \ldots . p'_m = p_1\, p_2 \cdot$ [illegible] $_r = q_1\, q_2 \ldots q_s$

Then p'_1 must divide one of the primes on the right hand side, say p_1.

Hence, $p'_1 = p_1$

Therefore, $p'_2 \ldots p'_m = p_2 \ldots p_r q_1 q_2 \ldots q_s$

After repeating the argument a sufficient number of times we find that

$$m = s + r$$

Which gives a unique factorization of $|a|$ and hence of a except for the order of prime factors.

LOWEST COMMON MULTIPLE

A positive integer l is said to be the Lowest Common Multiple (LCM) of integers a and b iff.

(i) $a|l$ and $b|l$

(ii) if $a|m$ and $b|m$ then $l|m$.

and we denote it by [a, b]

Some Important Results on L.C.M. and G.C.D.

Theorem 1:

The lowest common multiple of two integers is unique.

Proof:

Let l_1, l_2 be the lowest common multiple of integers a and b, then

l_1 is L.C.M. of a and b and l_2 is a multiple of a and b $\Rightarrow l_1|l_2$.

Again, l_2 is L.C.M. of a and b

and l_1 is a multiple of a and b

$\Rightarrow l_2|l_1$.

Now, $l_1|l_2$ and $l_2|l_1$

$\Rightarrow l_1 = l_2$, since l_1 and l_2 are both positive.

Theorem 2:

The product of two positive integers is equal to the product of their lowest common multiple and greatest common divisor.

Proof:

Let a and b be any two positive integers. Let their greatest common divisor be d and lowest common multiple be l.

Let $a = pd$ and $b = qd$ ...(i)

Then $ab = d[pqd]$ ...(ii)

We claim that $(p, q) = 1$, for

$(p, q) \neq 1$

$\Rightarrow$ $\exists$ some $t \in \mathbf{N}$ such that $t|p$ and $t|q$

$\Rightarrow$ $p = th$ and $q = tk$ for some $h, k \in \mathbf{N}$

$\Rightarrow$ $a = thd$ and $b = tkd$

$\Rightarrow$ $a = t(hd)$ and $b = k(td)$

$\Rightarrow$ $td > d$ is a common factor of a and b,

and the same contradicts the fact that d is the greatest common divisor of a and b.

$\therefore$ $(p, q) = 1.$

Now we show that (pqd) is the lowest common multiple of a and b.

Let m be any common multiple of a and b.

Then $m = ya = zb$ for some $y, z \in \mathbf{N}$ and therefore

$m = ypd = zqd$ ...(iii)

Now $(p, q) = 1$

$\Rightarrow$ $\exists$ r and s such that $1 = rp + sq$

$\Rightarrow$ $m = rmp + sqm$

$\Rightarrow$ $m = rp(zqd) + sq(ypd)$ [Using (iii)

$\Rightarrow$ $m = pqd(rz + sy)$

$\Rightarrow$ $(pqd)|m$

Thus, pqd divides every common multiple of a and b.

So, $l = pqd$

This an substitution in (ii) gives $ab = dl$.

Algebra of Residue Classes

Addition of Residue Classes

If $[a], [b] \in \mathbf{I}_m$, then we define

$[a] + [b] = [a + b]$

Here '+' on the L.H.S. stands for addition of residue classes and '+' on the R.H.S. stands for addition of integers.

Since $a, b \in \mathbf{Z} \Rightarrow a + b \in \mathbf{Z}$, therefore $[a + b]$ is also a residue class, *i.e.*, $[a + b] \in \mathbf{I}_m$. Now we know that $[a] = [a + m] = [a + 2m]$, and so on.

Thus a residue class can be represented in several ways. Therefore we must show that addition of residue classes is well defined, *i.e.*, it is independent of the representation of any residue class. For this we are to show that if [a] = [c] and [b] = [d] then [a] + [b] = [c] + [d].

We have $[a] = [c] \Rightarrow a - c$ is divisible by m

Also $[b] = [d] \Rightarrow b - d$ is divisible by m.

Now $m|(a - c)$ and $m|(b - d)$

$$\Rightarrow m|\{(a - c) + (b - d)\}$$
$$\Rightarrow m|\{(a + b) - (c + d)\}$$
$$\Rightarrow a + b \equiv c + d \pmod{m}$$
$$\Rightarrow [a + b] = [c + d]$$
$$\Rightarrow [a] + [b] = [c] + [d]$$

Thus [a] = [c] and [b] = [d]

$$\Rightarrow [a] + [b] = [c] + [d].$$

Hence addition of residue classes is well defined.

Multiplication of Residue Classes

If [a], [b] $\in \boldsymbol{I_m}$ *then we define [a] [b] = [a b]*

Since a, b, $\in \mathbf{Z} \Rightarrow ab \in \mathbf{Z}$, therefore [ab] is also a residue class, *i.e.*, $[ab] \in \mathbf{I_m}$. But we must show that our multiplication of residue classes is *well defined*. For this we are to show that if [a] = [c] and [b] = [d], then [a] [b] = [c] [d].

We have $[a] = [c] \Rightarrow a \equiv c \pmod{m}$

$$\Rightarrow a - c \text{ is divisible by m}$$
$$\Rightarrow b(a - c) \text{ is divisible by m.}$$

Also $[b] = [d] \Rightarrow b - d$ is divisible by m

$$\Rightarrow c(b - d) \text{ is divisible by m.}$$

$\therefore$ [a] = [c] and [b] = [d]

$$\Rightarrow \{b(a - c) + c\,(b - d)\} \text{ is divisible by m}$$
$$\Rightarrow ab - cd \text{ is divisible by m}$$
$$\Rightarrow ab \equiv cd \pmod{m}$$
$$\Rightarrow [ab] = [cd]$$
$$\Rightarrow [a]\,[b] = [c]\,[d]$$

Hence multiplication of residue classes is well defined.

LINEAR CONGRUENCES

Consider the congruence

$$ax \equiv b \pmod{m} \qquad ...(1)$$

in which a, b, m are fixed integers with $m > 0$ and x is an unknown integer. This equation is called a *linear congruence.*

But a solution of equation (1) we shall mean an integer $x = x_1$ such that $ax_1 \equiv b \pmod{m}$ *i.e.*, $m|(ax_1 - b)$.

For example, 3 is a solution of the linear congruence $6x \equiv 2 \pmod{4}$ because $6.3 \equiv 2 \pmod{4}$. [$6.3 - 2 = 18 - 2 = 16$ and $4|16$].

Properties of Linear Congruences

Theorem 1:

If x_1 is a solution of $ax \equiv b \pmod{m}$, then any other integer $x_2 \equiv x_1 \pmod{m}$ is also a solution.

Proof:

Since x_1 is a solution of $ax \equiv b \pmod{m}$, therefore

$$ax_1 \equiv b \pmod{m}$$

Now if $x_2 \equiv x_1 \pmod{m}$, then

$$ax_2 \equiv ax_1 \pmod{m}$$

Since the relation 'congruent modulo m' is transitive, therefore

$$ax_2 \equiv ax_1 \pmod{m} \text{ and } ax_1 \equiv b \pmod{m}$$

$$\Rightarrow \quad ax_2 \equiv b \pmod{m}$$

$$\therefore \quad x_2 \text{ is a solution of } ax \equiv b \pmod{m}$$

Note: We know that if s is an element of the residue class $[x_1]$ modulo m, then $s \equiv x_1 \pmod{m}$. Therefore if x_1 is a solution of $ax \equiv b \pmod{m}$, then each element of $[x_1] \in \mathbf{I}_m$ will be a solution of $ax \equiv b \pmod{m}$. For this reason if x_1 is a solution of $ax \equiv b \pmod{m}$, then the congruence class $[x_1] \in \mathbf{I}_m$ is called a *congruence class of solutions of $ax \equiv b \pmod{m}$.*

For Example : 3 is a solution of $6x \equiv 2 \pmod{4}$. Each element of the residue class $[3] \in \mathbf{I}_4$ will be a solution of $6x \equiv 2 \pmod{4}$. Note that if $[3] \in \mathbf{I}_4$,

Then

$$[3] = \{..., -13, -9, -5, -1, 3, 7, 11, 15, 19, ...\}$$

The least positive integer belonging to [3] is 3.

Incongruent Solutions : *Suppose x_1 and x_2 are two solutions of the congruence $ax \equiv b \pmod{m}$. If $x_1 \not\equiv x_2 \pmod{m}$, then x_1 and x_2 are called incongruent solutions of $ax \equiv b \pmod{m}$.*

For example consider the congruence $6x \equiv 2 \pmod{4}$. We see that 1 and 3 are its solutions. Since $1 \not\equiv 3 \pmod{4}$, therefore 1 and 3 are incongruent solution of $6x \equiv 2 \pmod{4}$. On the other have 5 is also a solution of $6x \equiv 2 \pmod{4}$. But $5 \equiv 1 \pmod{4}$. Therefore 5 and 1 are congruent solutions of this linear congruence.

Existence of Solutions of $ax \equiv b \pmod{m}$

Theorem 2:

The congruence $ax \equiv b \pmod{m}$ has a solution if and only if the greatest common divisor of a and m, i.e., (a, m) divides b.

Proof:

Let $d = (a, m)$

Suppose $ax \equiv b \pmod{m}$ has a solution $x = x_1$. Then

$$ax_1 \equiv b \pmod{m}$$

$$\Rightarrow \quad m \mid (ax_1 - b)$$

$$\Rightarrow \quad ax_1 - b = mk \text{ for some integer } k$$

$$\Rightarrow \quad b = ax_1 - mk.$$

Now $d|a$ and $d|m$. Let $a = a_1d$

and $m = m_1d$

where a_1 and m_1 are some integers. Then

$$b = a_1dx_1 - m_1dk\ m = d\,(a_1x_1 - m_1k)$$

$\therefore$ $d|b$. This shows that if a solution exists,

then it is necessary that $d|b$.

Converse : Suppose that $d|b$. Then $b = b_1d$ where b_1 is some integer. Sin $d = (a, m)$, therefore by Equlidean algorithm there exist integers u and v such that

$$d = ua + vm$$

$$\Rightarrow \quad db_1 = uab_1 + vmb_1$$

$$\Rightarrow \quad b = a\,(ub_1) + (vb_1)\,m \qquad (\because db_1 = b)$$

$$\Rightarrow \quad a\,(ub_1) - b = -(vb_1)\,m$$

$$\Rightarrow \quad m|\{a\,(ub_1) - b\}$$

$\Rightarrow \quad a\,(ub_1) \equiv b \pmod{m}$

$\Rightarrow \quad x = ub_1$ is a solution of $ax \equiv b \pmod{m}$.

Thus we have shown that if $d|b$, then it is sufficient to say that $ax \equiv b \pmod{m}$ has a solution.

Examples:

(i) Consider the congruence $222x \equiv 12 \pmod{18}$. We have $(222, 18) = 6$ and $6|12$. Therefore this congruence must posses a solution.

(ii) Consider the congruence $207\,x \equiv 6 \pmod{18}$. We have $(207, 18) = 9$ and 9 is not a divisor of 6. Therefore this congruence has no solution.

Theorem 3:

Let $d = (a, m)$ divides b and let $a = a_1, d, b = b_1 d$, $m = m_1 d$. Then show that x_1 is a solution of the congruence $ax \equiv b$ (mod m) if and only if x_1 is a solution of $a_1x \equiv b_1 \pmod{m_1}$.

Proof:

Suppose x_1 is a solution of $ax \equiv (b \bmod m)$.

Then $\quad ax_1 \equiv b \pmod{m}$

$\Rightarrow \quad a_1dx_1 \equiv b_1d \pmod{m_1\, d}$

$\Rightarrow \quad a_1x_1 \equiv b_1 \pmod{m_1} \qquad [(d, \text{mid}) = d]$

$\Rightarrow \quad x_1$ is a solution of $a_1 \equiv b_1 \pmod{m_1}$

Converse : Suppose that x_1 is a solution of $a_1x \equiv b_1 \pmod{m_1}$. Then

$a_1\, x_1 \equiv b_1 \pmod{m_1}$

$\Rightarrow \quad da_1x_1 \equiv db_1 \pmod{d\, m_1}$

$\Rightarrow \quad ax_1 \equiv b \pmod{m}$

$\Rightarrow \quad x_1$ is a solution of $ax \equiv b \pmod{m}$

Theorem 4:

If $(a, m) = 1$, then the congruence $ax \equiv b$ (mod m) has a unique congruent solution modulo m.

Proof:

Since $(a, m) = 1$, therefore there exist integers u and v such that

$1 = ua + vm$

$\Rightarrow \quad b = bua + bvm$

$\Rightarrow \quad a\,(bu) - b = -(bv)\,m$

$\Rightarrow \quad m|\{a\,(bu) - b\}$

$\Rightarrow \quad a\,(bu) \equiv b \pmod m$

$\Rightarrow \quad x = bu$ is a solution of $ax \equiv b \pmod m$

This shows the existence of solution.

Now to show that $ax \equiv b \pmod m$ has a unique incongruent solution. Let x_1 and x_2 be its solution. Then

$$ax_1 \equiv b \pmod m \text{ and } ax_2 \equiv b \pmod m$$

$\Rightarrow \quad ax_1 \equiv b \pmod m$ and $b = ax_2 \pmod m$

$\Rightarrow \quad ax_1 \equiv ax_2 \pmod m$

$\Rightarrow \quad m|(ax_1 - ax_2)$

$\Rightarrow \quad m|a\,(x_1 - x_2)$

$\Rightarrow \quad m|(x_1 - x_2)$ $\qquad (\because (a, m) = 1)$

$\Rightarrow \quad x_1 \equiv x_2 \pmod m.$

Hence if $ax \equiv b \pmod m$ has two solutions, they are congruent to each other modulo m.

Therefore this congruence has a unique incongruent solution modulo m.

Number of Incongruent Solutions

Theorem: *If $d = (a, m)$ divides b, then the congruence $ax \equiv b \pmod m$ has exactly d incongruent solutions which can be expressed in the form $x_o + r_m$ for $r = 0, 1, 2, \ldots, d - 1$, where x_o is an arbitrary solution and $m = d\,m_1$.*

Let $b = b_1 d$, $a = a_1 d$, $m = m_1 d$, where b_1, a_1, m_1 are some integers. Since d is the greatest common divisor of a and m, therefore $(a_1\ m_1) = 1$.

Since $d|b$, therefore $ax \equiv b \pmod m$ possesses a solution. Let x_0 be an arbitrary solution of this congruence. Let x_1 be any other solution of this congruence. We know that $x = y$ is solution of $ax \equiv b \pmod m$ if and only if y is a solution of $a_1 x \equiv b_1 \pmod{m_1}$. Therefore x_o and x_1 are also solutions of $a_1 x \equiv b_1 \pmod{m_1}$. But $a_1 x \equiv b_1 \pmod{m_1}$ has a unique incongruent solution modulo $m_1$because $(a_1, m_1) = 1$. Therefore

$x_1 \equiv x_o \pmod m$

$\Rightarrow \quad m_1|(x_1 - x_0)$

$\Rightarrow \quad x_1 - x_o = rm_1$ for some integer r.

$\Rightarrow \quad x_1 = x_o + rx_1.$

Hence every solution x_1 of the congruence $ax \equiv b \pmod m$ can be expressed in the form $x_1 = x_o + rm_1$ for some integer r.

Further for every integer r, we have $x_0 + rm_1 \equiv x_0 \pmod{m_1}$. Therefore for every integer r, $x_0 + rm_1$ is a solution of $a_1x \equiv b_1 \pmod{m}$and so also of $ax \equiv b \pmod{m}$. Hence all the solutions of $ax \equiv b \pmod{m}$ are found among the set of integers $x_0 + rm_1$. Let us consider the following d integers in this set.

$$x_0, x_0 + m_1, x_0 + 2m_1, \ldots, x_0 + (d-1)\, m_1.$$

Now no two of these d integers are congruent to each other modulo m. For if $o \le i < d$ and $o \le j < d$, then

$$x_0 + im_1 \equiv x_0 + jm_1 \pmod{m}$$

$$\Rightarrow \quad x|\{(x_0 + jm_1) - (x_0 + jm_1)\}$$

$$\Rightarrow \quad m_1d|(i-j)\, m_1 \qquad (\because\ m = m_1d)$$

$$\Rightarrow \quad d|i - j = 0$$

$$\Rightarrow \quad i - j = 0 \qquad (\because\ 0 \le i - j < d)$$

$$\Rightarrow \quad i = j$$

$$\Rightarrow \quad x_0 + im_1 = x_0 + jm_1.$$

Hence any two of these d integers are incongruent (mod m).

Further if r is any integer, then we shall show that $x_0 + rm_1$ is congruent to one of the d integers given above.

Applying division algorithm for the integers r and d, we get

$$r = ds + q,\ 0 \le q < d.$$

$$\begin{aligned} \text{Then } x_0 + rm_1 &= x_0 + (ds + q)\, m_1 \\ &= x_0\, dsm_1 + qm_1 \\ &= (x_0 + qm_1) + dsm_1 \end{aligned}$$

$$\begin{aligned} \text{Now } (x_0 + rm_1) - (x_0 + qm_1) &= (x_0 + qm_1) + dsm_1 - (x_0 + qm_1) \\ &= dsm_1 = sm. \end{aligned}$$

$$\therefore \quad m|\{(x_0 + rm_1) - (x_0 + qm_1)\}$$

$$\Rightarrow \quad x_0 + rm_1 \equiv x_0 + qm_1 \pmod{m}.$$

Since $o \le q < d$, therefore $x_0 + qm_1$ is one of the above d integers.

Hence $ax \equiv b \pmod{m}$ has exactly d incongruent solutions modulo m.

Note: If we are to find the least positive incongruent solutions modulo m of $ax \equiv b \pmod{m}$, then we should first find the least positive integer, say x_0, satisfying $a_1x \equiv b_1 \pmod{m_1}$ where $d = (a, m)$, $m = m_1d$, $b = b_1d$, $a = a_1d$. Then $x_0, x_0 + m_1, x_0 + 2m_1, \ldots, x_0 + (d-1)\, m_1$ will give us d least positive incongruent solutions modulo m of $ax \equiv b \pmod{m}$.

DIVISION ALGORITHM

If a is any integer and b is a non-zero integer, then there exist unique integers q and r such that.

$$a = bq + r, \text{ where } 0 \le r < |b|$$

Proof: Let S = $\{a - bx : x \in \mathbf{Z}\}$

Then S is non-empty, since a can be written as

$$a = a - b.0 \text{ and } 0 \in \mathbf{Z} \text{ and so at least } a \in S.$$

Also, we claim that S surely contains non-negative integers, for, $b \neq 0 \Rightarrow$ either $b < 0$ or $b > 0$.

Case I. $b > 0$

$\Rightarrow$ $b \ge 1$

$\Rightarrow$ $b.(-|a|) \le -|a| \le a$

$\Rightarrow$ $a - b.(-|a|) \ge 0$

and $a - b(-a|) \in S$, since $-|a| \in \mathbf{Z}$.

So [$a - b.(-|a|)$ is at least one non-negative integer in S.

Case II. $b < 0$

$\Rightarrow$ $b \le -1$

$\Rightarrow$ $b.|a| \le -|a| \le a$

$\Rightarrow$ $a - b.|a| \ge 0$

and $a - b.|a| \in S$, since $|a| \in \mathbf{Z}$.

So $a - b.|a|$ is at least one non-negative integer in S.

Thus in both the cases, S always contains non-negative integers.

Now every subset of the set of all non-negative integers has a least element, so there exists a smallest non-negative integer r is S.

Let $r = a - bq$ where $q \in \mathbf{Z}$.

Since r is non-negative, so $0 \le r$.

Now, it remains to show that $r < |b|$.

First we assert that $(r - |b|) \in S$, whether $b > 0$ or $b < 0$.

Case I. $b > 0$

$\Rightarrow$ $|b| = b$

$\Rightarrow$ $r - (|b|) = r - b = a - bq - b$

$$= a - b(q + 1) \in S \quad [\because (q + 1) \in \mathbf{Z}]$$

Case II. $b < 0$

$\Rightarrow$ $|b| = -b$

$\Rightarrow$ $r - (|b|) = r + b = a - bq + b$

$= a - b(q - 1) \in S \quad [\because (q - 1) \in \mathbf{Z}]$

Thus, in each case $(r - |b| \in S$.

Now, $b \neq 0 \Rightarrow r - |b| < r$.

But $r - |b| \in S$ and r is the least non-negative integer in S and so, it follows that

$r - |b| < 0$ or $r < |b|$

$\therefore$ $0 \leq r < |b|$

Also $r = a - bq$

$\Rightarrow$ $a = br + r$.

Uniqueness of q and r : Let, if possible there be another pair of integers q' and r' such that

$a = bq' + r'$,

where, $0 \leq r' < |b|$.

$$\left.\begin{array}{ll}\text{Then} & a = bq + r\\ \text{and} & a = bq' + r\end{array}\right\} \Rightarrow b(q - q') = (r' - r)$$

$\Rightarrow$ $b(q - q') = (r' - r)$

$\Rightarrow$ $b|(r' - r)$

But $0 \leq r \leq |b|, 0 \leq r' < |b|$

$\Rightarrow$ $0 \leq (r' - r) < |b|$

Now, $b|(r' - r)$ and $0 \leq (r' - r) < |b|$

$\Rightarrow$ $r' - r = 0$

$\Rightarrow$ $r = r'$

Now putting $r' = r$ in $bq + r = bq' + r'$ we obtain $q = q'$

Hence q and r are unique.

Remark: In division algorithm theorem, the integers a, b, q and r are known as dividend, divisor, quotient and remainder respectively.

Thus, *Dividend = (Divisor × Quotient) + Remainder*

Examples:

(i) Suppose $a = 16$, $b = 5$, then we can write

$16 = 5.3 + 1$, where $0 \leq 1 < |5|$

(ii) Suppose a = 17, b = –3, then we can write

$$17 = (-3), (-5) + 2 \text{ where } 0 \le 2 < |-3|$$

(iii) Suppose a = –24, b = 7, then we can write

$$24 = (7), (-4) + 4 \text{ where } 0 \le 4 < |7|.$$

GREATEST COMMON DIVISOR

A greatest common divisor (GCD) of two integers a and b is a positive integer d such that

(i) $d|a$ and $d|b$, and

(ii) if, for an integer c, $c|a$ and $c|b$, then $c|d$.

We shall use the notation (a, b) for the greatest common divisor of two integers a and b. The greates common divisor is sometimes also called the *highest common factor* (HCF).

For example,

(i) ±1, ±2, ±3, ±4, ±5, ±12, are common divisors or 24 and 60

(ii) 12 is the greatest common divisor of 24 and 60.

Since the H.C.F. of two integers is a positive integer by definition, so

$$(a, b) = (a, -b) = (-a, b) = (-a, -b) = (|a|, |b|)$$

EXISTENCE AND UNIQUENESS OF GREATEST COMMON DIVISOR (EUCLIDEAN ALGORITHM)

Theorem: *Every pair of integers a and b, not both zero, has a unique greatest common divisor (a, b) which can be expressed is the form (a, b) = ma + nb for some integers m and n.*

Uniqueness of GCD

First we shall prove that if the greatest common divisor of a and b exists, then it is unique. If possible let d_1 and d_2 be two greatest common divisors of a and b. Then by definition of greatest common divisor, we have

$$d_1|d_2 \text{ and } d_2|d_1$$

$$\Rightarrow \quad d_1 \text{ and } d_2 \text{ are associates}$$

$$\Rightarrow \quad d_2 = \pm d_1$$

Since d_2 is positive, therefore we must have $d_2 = d_1$. Thus, greatest common divisor is unique, if it exists.

Now, we shall prove the existence of greatest common divisor. Consider the set S = {sa + tb; s, t ∈ **Z**}. Since one of a or b is not zero, say a ≠ 0, therefore by taking s = 1, t = 0 we see that a ∈ S. Therefore, there are non-zero integers in S. If $x = sa + tb$ is in S. then $-x = (-s)\,a + (-t)$ is also in S. Therefore S contains positive integers. Let d be the smallest positive integer belonging to S. Since $d \in S$, therefore d has the form $d = ma + nb$, where m, n are some integers. We claim that $d = (a, b)$ *i.e.*, d is the greatest common divisor of a and b.

To fulfil our claim we shall first prove that if $x = sa + tb$ is any integer belonging to S. then d is a divisor of x. Now, by division algorithm, we have

$$x = dq + r \text{ where } 0 \le r < d.$$

$$\Rightarrow \quad sa + tb = (ma + nb)q + r \quad [\because\ x = sa+tb \text{ and } d = ma+nb]$$

$$\Rightarrow \quad r = (s - mq) + (t - nq)b$$

$$\Rightarrow \quad r \in S \text{ since } s - mq \text{ and } t - nq \text{ are integers.}$$

Since $0 \le r < d$ and d is the smallest positive integer belonging to S, therefore we must have $r = 0$. Then we get $x = dq$. Therefore d is a divisor of $x\ \forall\ x \in S$.

Now, we can write $a = 1a + 0b$ where $1, 0 \in \mathbf{Z}$.

Therefore $a \in S$.

Similarly we can write $b = 0a + 1b$.

Therefore $b \in S$. hence $d|a$ and $d|b$.

Now suppose that $c|a$ and $c|b$. Then $c|(ma + nb)$ *i.e.*, $c|d$.

Therefore d is the greatest common divisor of a and b, *i.e.*, $d = (a, b)$. Also we have shown that

$$d = ma + nb \text{ for some } m, n \in \mathbf{Z}.$$

SOLVED EXAMPLES

Example 1: *Find (26, 118) and express it in the form 26m + 118n.*

Solution: By repeatedly applying the process of division algorithm, we get

$$118 = 26.4 + 14 \qquad ...(1)$$

$$26 = (14).1 + 12 \qquad ...(2)$$

$$14 = (12).1 + 2 \qquad ...(3)$$

$$12 = (2).6 + 0 \qquad ...(4)$$

Hence $\quad 2 = (26, 118)$.

Now, from equation (3), we get

$$2 = 14 - 12.1 = 14 - 12 \qquad ...(5)$$

From equation (2), we get

$$12 = 26 - 14.1 = 26 - 14$$

Putting this value of 12 in (5), we get

$$2 = 14 - (26 - 14) = 2(14) - 26 \quad ...(6)$$

From equation (1), we get 14 = 118 – (26).4. Putting this value of 14 in (6), we get

$$2 = [118 - (26).4] - 26$$
$$2 = (118) - 9(26).$$

Hence, (26, 118) = 2 and if 2 = 26m + 118 n, then m = –9, n = 2.

Example 2: *Find (427, 616) and express it in the form 427m + 616n.*

Solution: By repeated application of division algorithm, we get

$$616 = (427).1 + 189, \quad ...(1)$$
$$427 = (189).2 + 49, \quad ...(2)$$
$$189 = (49).3 + 42, \quad ...(3)$$
$$49 = (42).1 + 7, \quad ...(4)$$
$$42 = (7).6 + 0 \quad ...(4)$$

Hence $\quad (427, 676) = 7.$

Now, from equation (4), we get

$$7 = 49 - (42).1$$
$$= 49 - [189 - (49).3].1 \quad \text{[by eqn. (3)}$$
$$= (49).4 - 189$$
$$= [427 - (189).2].4 - 189 \quad \text{[by eqn. (2)}$$
$$= (427).4 - (189).9$$
$$= (427).4 - (616 - (427).1]9 \quad \text{[by eqn. (1)}$$
$$= (427).13 + (616).(9).$$

Example 3(a): *If (a, b) = (b, c) = 1, prove that (ab, c) = 1.*

Solution: Let $\quad$ (ab, c) = d, where d > 1

Then $\quad d|ab, d|c$

$\therefore \quad d = mab + nc, m, n \in Z \quad ...(-1)$

Now, $\quad$ (a, c) = 1 and $d|c \Rightarrow$ d is not a divisor of a.

$\quad = d|b$ [from (1)] $\quad ...(2)$

But $\quad$ (b, c) = 1 and $d|c$

$\Rightarrow \quad$ d is not a divisor of b $\quad ...(3)$

Thus from (2) and (3) there is a contradiction.

Hence $(ab, c) = 1$.

Example 3(b): *Find the least positive congruent solution of:*

(a) $235x \equiv 54 \pmod 7$

(b) $13x \equiv 9 \pmod{25}$

(c) $259x \equiv 5 \pmod{11}$

Solution: (a) We have $(235, 7) = 1$. Therefore the congruence

$$235x \equiv 54 \pmod 7 \quad ...(1)$$

has a single incongruent solutin.

We have

$$231x \equiv 49 \pmod 7 \quad ...(2)$$

[Note that $235 = 231 + 4$ where $7|231$ and $0 \le 4 < 7$]

From (1) and (2), we get

$$235x - 231x \equiv (54 - 49) \pmod 7$$

or $\quad 4x \equiv 5 \pmod 7 \quad ...(3)$

But $\quad 5 \equiv 12 \pmod 7 \quad ...(4)$

[Note that 12 is the least positive integer divisible by 4 and also congruent to 5 modulo 7.]

From (3) and (4), we get

$4x \equiv 12 \pmod 7$ (by transitivity of congruence relation]

$\Rightarrow \quad 4x \equiv 4.3 \pmod 7$

$\Rightarrow \quad x \equiv 3 \pmod 7 \qquad (\because (4, 7) = 1)$

Now, $x = 3$ is a solution of this congruence. Each element of the residue class $\{3\} \in \mathbf{I}_7$ will be a solution of this congruence. We see that 3 is the least positive integer in the residue class

$$\{3\} \in \mathbf{I}_7$$

Hence 3 is the required solution.

(b) We have $(13, 25) = 1$. Therefore the congruence $13x \equiv 9 \pmod{25}$ has a single incongruent solutin. Here the modulus 25 is large hence the GCD process enables us to find the solution as follows:

Since $(13, 25) = 1$, therefore we can find integers m and n such that

$$1 = 13m + 25n$$

We have $\quad 25 = 13.1 + 12$

$$13 = 12.1 + 1$$

Now, $1 = 13 - 12.1 = 13 - (25 - 13.1) . 1$

$= 13.2 + 25 (-1)$

$\therefore$ $9 = 13.18 + 25 (-9).$

Now $13x \equiv 9 \pmod{25}$ is equivalent to

$13x \equiv 13.18 + 25 (-9) \pmod{25}$ ...(1)

But $O \equiv 25 (-9) \pmod{25}$ ...(2)

Subtracting (2) from (1), we get

$13x \equiv 13.18 \pmod{25}$

Showing that $x = 18$ is a solution.

Obviously, 18 is the least positive integer in the residue class $[18] \in \mathbf{I}_{25}$. Hence $x = 18$ is the required solution.

(c) We have $(259, 11) = 1$. Therefore the congruence

$259x \equiv 5 \pmod{11}$ ...(1)

has a single incongruent solution.

We have $259 = 23.11 + 6$

or $259 = 253 + 6$

Now, $253x \equiv O \pmod{11}$ ...(2)

From (1) and (2), we get

$259x - 253x \equiv 5 - 0 \pmod{11}$

$\Rightarrow$ $5x \equiv 5 \pmod{11}$ ...(3)

Now, $5 \equiv 60 \pmod{11}$ ...(4)

[Note that 60 the least positive integer divisible by 6 and also congruent to 5 modulo 11].

From (3) and (4), we get

$6x \equiv 60 \pmod{11}$

$\Rightarrow$ $6x \equiv 6.10 \pmod{11}$

$\Rightarrow$ $x \equiv 10 \pmod{11}$ $(\because (6, 11) = 1)$

$\Rightarrow$ $x \equiv 10$ is a solution.

Obviously 10 is the least positive integer in the residue class $[10] \in \mathbf{I}_{11}$. Hence $x = 10$ is the required solution.

Example 3(c): *Find the least possible incongruent solution of :*

(a) $35x \equiv 14 \pmod{21}$

(b) $x + 50 \equiv 39 \pmod{7}$.

Solution: (a) We have $(35, 21) = 7$ and $7|14$.

Therefore $35x \equiv 14 \pmod{21}$ has 7 incongruent solutions $\pmod{21}$.

Now, $35x \equiv 14 \pmod{21}$ is equivalent to

$$7.5\, x \equiv 7.2 \pmod{7.3}$$

$$\Rightarrow \quad 5x \equiv 2 \pmod 3$$

$$\Rightarrow \quad 2x \equiv 2 \pmod 3 \qquad (\because 3x = 0 \pmod 3)$$

$$\Rightarrow \quad x \equiv 1 \pmod 3 \qquad (\because (2, 3) = 1)$$

Showing that $x = 1$ is a solution of $5x \equiv 2 \pmod 3$.

Now 1 is the least positive integer satisfying $5x \equiv 2 \pmod 3$ since 1 is the least positive integer in the residue class $[1] \in \mathbf{I}_3$. Therefore the 7 required solutions of $35x \equiv 14 \pmod{21}$ are

$$1,\ 1 + 3,\ 1 + 2.3,\ 1 + 3.3,\ 1 + 4.3,\ 1 + 5.3,\ 1 + 6.3$$

i.e. $\quad 1, 4, 7, 10, 13, 16, 19$

(b) The given congruence is

$$x + 50 \equiv 39 \pmod 7$$

We have $\quad 50 \equiv 1 \pmod 7$

Therefore the given congruence is equivalent to

$$x \equiv 38 \pmod 7$$

$$\Rightarrow \quad x \equiv 3 \pmod 7$$

Now, $(7, 1) = 1$. Therefore the congruence $x \equiv 3 \pmod 7$ has a single incongruent solution. We see that $x = 3$ is a solution. Obviously 3 is the least positive integer in the residue class

$$[3] \in \mathbf{I}_7$$

Example 4: *If $(a, b) = 1$, $a|c$ and $b|c$ prove that $ab|c$.*

Solution: Since $\quad (a, b) = 1$

$\therefore \quad 1 = ma + nb, \quad m, n \in \mathbf{Z}$

$\therefore \quad c = cma + cnb$

Also, $\quad a|c \Rightarrow c = ax, \quad x \in \mathbf{Z}$

and $\quad b|c \Rightarrow c = by, \quad y \in \mathbf{Z}$

$\therefore \quad c = cma + cnb$

$\quad = byma + axnb$

$\quad = ab\,(my + nx)$

i.e., $\quad ab|c$.

Example 5: *Show if p, b, p, > 0 ∈* ***Z*** *then* $(a + b)^p \equiv a^p + b^p \pmod{p}$.

Solution: By the binomial theorem,

$$(a + b)^p = a^p + pa^{p-1}\, b + \frac{p\,(p-1)}{21}\, a^{p-2}\, b^2 + \ldots + pa\, b^{p-1} + b^p$$

$$\Rightarrow \quad (a + b)^p = (a^p + b^p) + p\left[a^{b-1}\, b + \frac{p-1)}{21}\, a^{p-1}\, b^2 + \ldots + ab^{p-1}\right]$$

$$\Rightarrow \quad p|\{a + b)^p - (a^p + b^p)\}$$

$$\Rightarrow \quad (a + b)^p \equiv (a^p + b^p) \pmod{p}.$$

Example 6(a): *Find the least positive integers to which the integers 107, 429 and 107 × 429 are congruent modulo 9.*

Solution: Since $107 = 11 \times 9 + 8$ we have

$$107 = 8 \pmod{9}.$$

Also $\quad 429 = 9 \times 47 + 6 \qquad (\therefore 429 = 6 \pmod{9})$

and therefore, $\quad 107 \times 429 \equiv 8 \times 6 \pmod{9}$

But $\quad 48 = 8 \times 5 + 3$

$\therefore \quad 107 \times 429 \equiv 3 \pmod{9}.$

Example 6(b): *Show that* $122.133.155 = 1 \pmod{11}$

Solution: Since $122 = 11.11 + 1 \qquad \therefore 122 = 1 \pmod{11}$

$133 = 11.12 + 1 \qquad \therefore 133 = 1 \pmod{11}$

$155 = 11.14 + 1 \qquad \therefore 155 = 1 \pmod{11}$

$$\therefore 122.133.155 \equiv 1.1.1 \pmod{11}$$

$$\equiv 1 \pmod{11}.$$

Example 6(c): *Show that the congruence* $x + 50 \equiv 39 \pmod{7}$ *possesses a solution.*

Solution: Since $50 = 7.7 + 1 \qquad \therefore 50 \equiv 1 \pmod{7}$

Again, since $\quad 39 = 7.5 + 4 \qquad \therefore 39 \equiv 4 \pmod{7}$

$\therefore x + 50 \equiv 39 \pmod{7} \qquad \Rightarrow x + 1 \equiv 4 \pmod{7}$

$\Rightarrow x \equiv 3 \pmod{7}$

Example 7: *show that* $15x \equiv 12 \pmod 5$ *does not possesses a solution.*

Solution: Since greatest comman divisor of 15 and 5 is 5 and 12 is not divisible by 5; hence it does not possess a solution.

Example 8: *Find the incongruent solution of* $3x + 2 \equiv 0 \pmod 7$

Solution: Since $0 \equiv 7 \pmod 7$, but 7 – 2is not divisible by 3, hence we write,

$$0 \equiv 14 \pmod 7 \text{ so that}$$

$$3x + 2 \equiv 0 \pmod 7 \Rightarrow 3x + 2 \equiv 14 \pmod 7$$

$$\Rightarrow 3x \equiv 12 \pmod 7$$

$$\Rightarrow x \equiv 4 \pmod 7.$$

Example 9: *If* $a|b$, *then* $a|(bm)\ \forall\ m \in \mathbf{Z}$.

Solution: We have $a|b \Rightarrow b = ak$ for some $k \in \mathbf{Z}$. Now $bm = (ak)m = a(km)$, where $km \in \mathbf{Z}$. Therefore $a|(bm)$.

Example 10(a): *If* $a|b$ *and* $a|c$, *then* $a|(bx + cy)\ \forall\ x, y \in \mathbf{Z}$.

Solution: We have $a|b \Rightarrow b = as$ for some $s \in \mathbf{Z}$.

Also, $a|c \Rightarrow c = at$ for some $t \in \mathbf{Z}$.

Now, $bx + cy = (as)x + (at)y = a(sx + ty)$

where, $sx + ty \in \mathbf{Z}$.

$\therefore$ $a|(bx + cy)$

Example 10(b): *If* $a|b$, *and* $b \neq 0$, then $|b| \geq |a|$.

Solution: We have $a|b \Rightarrow b = ac$ for some $c \in Z$. Since $b \neq 0$, therefore $c \neq 0$ and consequently $|c| \geq 1$.

Now, $b = ac \Rightarrow |b| = |ac|$

$\Rightarrow |b| = |a|.|c|$

Further, $|c| \geq 1 \Rightarrow |a|.|c| \geq |a|$

$\Rightarrow |b| \geq |a|$

Example 11: *If* $a|b$ *and* $b|a$, *then* $b = a$ *or* $b = -a$, *i.e., the only associates of a are* $\pm a$.

Solution: Since $a|b$ and $b|a$, therefore neither $a = 0$ nor $b = 0$.

Now, $a|b \Rightarrow b = ac$ for some $c \in \mathbf{Z}$.

Also, $b|a \Rightarrow a = bd$ for some $c \in \mathbf{Z}$.

Now, $a.b = (bd)(ac) = (ab)(cd)$

Since $ab \neq 0$, therefore by cancellation law, we get

$$1 = cd$$

$\Rightarrow$ either $c = 1, d = 1$ or $c = -1, d = -1$.

$\Rightarrow$ either $b = a$, or $b = -a$.

Example 12:** The number of positive primes is infinite* ***(Euclid's Theorem).

Solution: Suppose there are only a finite number of positive primes, say n, and they are $p_1, p_2, p_3, \ldots, p_n$ arranged in order of magnitude.

Now form the product $a = p_1.p_2.p_3 \ldots p_n$ and consider the integer a +1. As no one of the p's is a divisor of a + 1, we conclude that either a + 1 is a prime $> p_n$ or has a prime $> p_n$ as factor. But this controdicts our assumption that p_n is the greatest prime.

Hence, the number of positive primes is infinite.

EXERCISES

1. $91 \equiv 19 \pmod 9$.
2. $741 \equiv 1 \pmod{10}$.
3. $7.6.5.4 \equiv 0 \pmod 6$.
4. $104.431 \equiv 9 \pmod{11}$.
5. Show that the congruence $35x \equiv 14 \pmod{21}$ has seven incongruent solutions (mod 21).
6. Find the incongruent solution of
   (a) $235x \equiv 54 \pmod 7$
   (b) $51x \equiv 32 \pmod 7$
   (c) $3x \equiv 2 \pmod 7$
7. Show that $363x \equiv 99 \pmod{22}$ possesses a solution.
8. Show that $25x \equiv 12 \pmod{10}$ does not possess a solution.
9. Solve the equation $18x \equiv 15 \pmod{31}$.
10. Show that x, y, z, u are integers:
    (a) $(-x)(-y) = xy$,
    (b) $-(x + y) = (-x) + (-y)$
    (c) $(x - y)(z - u) = (x.z + y.u) - (x.u + y.z)$

11. Find the g.c.d. of 595 and 252 and express it in the form of 595 m + 252n in two ways.
12. Find (489, 167) and express it in the form 489m + 167n.
13. If (a, b) = 1 and if b|ac, prove that b|c.
14. If (a, b) = d,

    $a = a_1d$, $b = b_1d$,

    prove that $(a_1, b_1) = 1$.
15. Find the least positive congrent solution of $11x \equiv 2 \pmod{317}$.
16. Find the least positive incongruent solution of:

    (a) $52x \equiv 28 \pmod{20}$

    (b) $222x \equiv 12 \pmod{18}$.
17. Show that the congruence $a + 58 \equiv 53 \pmod 9$ possesses a solution and find it.
18. $23.215 \equiv 3 \pmod 7$.
19. $7 + 5 + 3 + 1 \equiv 2 \pmod 7$.